REPORT of the OTTAWA-CARLETON REVIEW COMMISSION

Henry B. Mayo,
M.A., D.Phil., D.Litt., F.R.S.C.

Commissioner

October, 1976

For copies of this Report, enquiries should be addressed to (a) the Ministry of Treasury, Economics and Intergovernmental Affairs (TEIGA), Eastern Ontario Region, 244 Rideau Street, Ottawa, Canada, K1N 5Y3; *or* (b) directly to the same Ministry, Local Government Organization Branch, Frost Building North, Queen's Park, Toronto, Canada, M7A 1Y7; *or* (c) Ontario Government Bookstore, 880 Bay Street, Toronto, Canada, M7A 1N8.

Ottawa-Carleton in Review: A Basic Information Booklet, August, 1975, may also be obtained from the above source(s). This Report and the Information Booklet, are available in both English and French.

ISBN 0-7709-0000-3

Contents

	Page
Letter of Transmittal	ix
Preface	xi

Chapter 1. A Municipality Not Like the Others 1
　　　　　　Like the Others? Yes!
　　　　　　Like the Others? No!

Chapter 2. Introduction to the Ottawa-Carleton Region 4
　　　　　　The Area
　　　　　　Demographic Characteristics
　　　　　　Historical Overview
　　　　　　Municipal Organization — an Outline
　　　　　　Area (Local) Municipalities
　　　　　　Population Projections

Chapter 3. The Economic Base of Ottawa-Carleton 17
　　　　　　The Federal Impact
　　　　　　Non-Government Employment
　　　　　　The Primary Sector
　　　　　　The Secondary Sector
　　　　　　Incentives
　　　　　　The Construction Industry
　　　　　　The Tertiary Sector
　　　　　　Retailing
　　　　　　Convention Business and Tourism
　　　　　　Quaternary Industry
　　　　　　Location of Employment

Chapter 4. Planning in Ottawa-Carleton 32
　　　　　　Introductory
　　　　　　The Official Plan
　　　　　　The "Satellites"
　　　　　　Public Land-Banking
　　　　　　The Greenbelt
　　　　　　Citizen Participation

Chapter 5.	Roads and Public Transport	46

                          Introductory
                          Transport and Land Use
                          Transport Management
                          Roadways
                          Public Transit
                          Rapid Transit
                          Transit Administration
                          Transit Financing
                          Other Transportation

Chapter 6.	Housing	57

                          Projected Housing Demand in the RMOC
                          Supply of Housing: Past, Present and Future
                          The Affordability Problem
                          Land Costs
                          Zoning
                          Housing Programmes in the RMOC
                          Public Housing
                          Housing for the Elderly
                          Summary

Chapter 7.	Municipal Finance	73

                          Introductory
                          Assessment
                          Revenue — Local Taxation
                          Revenue — Grants and Subsidies
                          Revenue — Payments-in-Lieu of Taxes (1) Federal
                          Revenue — Payments-in-Lieu of Taxes (2) Provincial
                          Revenue — Payments-in-Lieu of Taxes (2) Provincial
                                        and Municipal
                          Expenditure
                          Long Term Debt
                          Summary

Chapter 8.	Municipal Boundaries	96

                          Introductory
                          One Tier or Two?
                          External Boundaries
                          Internal Boundaries
                          A Few Other Points

Chapter 9.   Elections and Sundry Matters 110
             Regional Council:
                 (a) Representation
                 (b) Method of Election
                 (c) The Chairman
                 (d) Committees
             Area Municipalities
                 (a) Representation on Councils
                 (b) Heads of Councils
                 (c) Committees
             Elections
             Sundry Matters
             Intergovernmental Relations
             Labour Relations

Chapter 10. Education in Ottawa-Carleton 124
             Introductory
             The Existing School Boards
             School Financing
             No School Boards at all?
             A Regional School Board
             A Board on Linguistic Lines
             The Public School Boards
             Term of Office
             Composition of Boards
             Teaching Material and Training of Teachers
             Instruction in a Second Language
             French Immersion
             Exchange of Teachers; and Monitors
             Concluding Remarks

Chapter 11. Language of Services 143
             Introductory
             Present Trends
             Who is Responsible?
             Some Remedies
             A Council for Bilingualism
             Conclusion

Chapter 12. Recreation, Parks and Libraries 154
             Introductory
             Federal Recreation Activities
             Other Actors in the Recreation Field
             Libraries

v

Chapter 13.   Social Services 164
             Introductory
             (1) General Welfare Assistance (RMOC)
             (2) Family Benefits (Provincial Direct Assistance)
             (3) Supplementary Aid and Special Assistance
             (4) Low Income Supplement Experiment (L.I.S.E.)
             (5) Other Services:
                 (a) Day Care
                 (b) Homemakers and Nurses' Services
                 (c) Children's Aid Society
                 (d) "Senior Citizens" (i.e., the elderly)
                 (e) Homes for the Aged
                 (f) Information Services
                 (g) "Multi-Service" Centres
                 (h) Volunteers

Chapter 14.   Health Services 179
             Hospitals
             District Health Council
             Public Health Unit

Chapter 15.   Police and Fire Services 183
             Costs of Policing
             Policing "Needs"
             Amalgamated Support Services and Cost Benefits
             Fire Services
             Evaluation
             Amalgamation?

Chapter 16.   Environmental Services 198
             Introductory
             Water Supply
             Sewerage
             Hydro (Electricity)
             Garbage
             Pollution Control
             Conservation Authorities

vi

Chapter 17.	The Capital Question 209
			Introductory
			What is the Capital?
			The Fullerton Report (a) General
			The Fullerton Report (b) Form of Government
			Who Speaks for the Federal Government?
			Who Speaks for the Municipalities?
			The Capital as Microcosm and/or Symbol
			The Regional Municipality

Chapter 18.	Summary of Recommendations and Suggestions 223

Appendix A	Briefs Heard at Public Meetings 235

Appendix B	Other Meetings Held or Attended.............................. 237

Appendix C	Some Private Briefs, Letters, etc. 239

Letter of Transmittal

Ottawa-Carleton Review Commission
October 1976

The Honourable Darcy McKeough
Treasurer of Ontario
Queen's Park,
Toronto, Ontario

Dear Mr. Minister,

It is my pleasure to submit to you this Report of the Ottawa-Carleton Review Commission. My hope is that it may be useful to the Province, the Regional Municipality, the area municipalities in the Region, and other organizations and interested citizens. If anything in the Report is of some application to municipalities elsewhere in the Province, so much the better.

The Report is the result of some two years work, mostly part-time. It has been a fascinating and demanding task, and I appreciate the opportunity of doing it.

Yours faithfully,

HB Mayo

H. B. Mayo,
Commissioner

Preface

This Commission was established by the Ontario Ministry of Treasury, Economics and Intergovernmental Affairs in late July, 1974, although work did not get fully underway until the autumn of that year, when the Review Prospectus was approved.

The mandate given to the Commission was wide-ranging: "to examine, evaluate, and make recommendations on the structure, organization and operations of local government" in the Ottawa-Carleton area, with particular reference to:
* social and economic conditions and growth
* resources and services requirements of the municipalities
* regional and local boundaries
* the division of functions among all governments concerned, including the provincial government
* the organization of municipal councils and their committee systems- and policy-making
* the system of representation on municipal councils
* municipal revenues and expenditures
* the unique relationship between the federal and municipal governments, and the impact of any action present or expected concerning the National Capital Region
* and finally, a nice "Catch 22" clause, "any other matter which the study commissioner considers relevant. . ."

The system of municipal government in this area was reorganized when the Regional Municipality of Ottawa-Carleton began operation on January 1, 1969. Ottawa-Carleton was the first of a series of regional governments set up in Ontario over the last few years.

It is provincial policy to review these re-organized municipal systems after they had been in operation a number of years. Thus Metropolitan Toronto, established in 1954, was reviewed by H. Carl Goldenberg (now Senator) in 1965, and is under review again by the Honourable John Robarts. Similarly, the Niagara Regional Municipality (1970) is being examined by William Archer, Q.C.

The independence of these Reviews is a point worth stressing. Review Commissioners are neither provincial nor municipal employees, although it is the Province which commissions them on contract. Commissioners are entirely free from provincial or any other instruction. Their research, the conduct of their inquiry, their findings and recommendations, are carried out without direction from Queen's Park, and I for one should like to pay tribute to the Ontario Government for the way they have left me alone to do my work. No scholar could ask for more (not even from the Canada Council) especially when, as I suspect, parts of this Report may not please all Provincial Ministries.

In carrying out the Review a variety of methods was used:

(1) An extensive advertising programme, in daily and weekly newspapers, was carried out to elicit opinions from all and sundry. Interviews took place on radio and T.V. Letters were written to all mayors, reeves, wardens, within and near the Region's boundaries; and to some 150 private organizations. A number of public speeches were given. It is hard to estimate the effects of this publicity campaign. (The campaign had been preceded by a press conference at Regional Council, held by the Honourable Donald Irvine; and by a lively, bilingual exhibit put on by the Ministry of Treasury, Economics, and Intergovernmental Affairs (TEIGA) at the Central Canada Exhibition in Ottawa, 1974.)

(2) A large number of researchers participated in various aspects of the project, some for a short time, others for longer. They conducted many interviews, searched the literature, and we had endless discussions on points that arose.

(3) Municipal politicians have provided extensive information on numerous topics. Some expressed very strong views, while others had equally strong but quite conflicting views. Municipal and provincial staff too (the latter in provincial offices within the Region and in Toronto) gave us freely of their time and information; and so did federal officials when requested. Among the staff of TEIGA in Toronto, a warm vote of thanks goes to Gardner Church and his colleagues.

(4) A Liaison Advisory Committee was set up, which included the heads of the larger municipalities, plus one representative from the eastern (outer) area, and one from the western (outer) area. The Committee meetings certainly helped in defining and discussing issues to be studied.

(5) In August of 1975, the Commission issued *Ottawa-Carleton in Review: A Basic Information Booklet* which presented many of the facts and figures concerning the structure and operation of municipal government in Ottawa-Carleton. It also raised provocative questions about possible changes in the current system. The Booklet had a wide distribution throughout the Region, in both English and French. Before that, in the Spring of 1975, a heavy volume of municipal statistics had been compiled, and given a smaller circulation to interested persons.

(6) Public meetings were advertised and held, and a day-long conference was held at Algonquin College, in co-operation with the College. The value of such meetings, although they give people a chance to let off steam, is lessened to some extent because the discussion tends to lack focus: too many issues are raised to do justice to any of them.

(7) Some 66 public briefs were presented at a series of open hearings from November 1975 to April 1976, where I took the opportunity to question and to discuss in detail issues raised by the briefs. These sessions and briefs were among the most useful of the whole enterprise. In holding these meetings, we travelled from one end of the Region to the other (and sometimes outside it).

(8) Many people preferred to send or bring in a brief or letter and discuss matters privately. We deferred to their wishes and held many of these private discussions. This procedure was justified, I think, especially in the case of employees whose views were not always those of their employers.

(9) Some people thought that preliminary recommendations should be publicized and that a second (or even third) round of public hearings should be held, before the writing of the final Report. This manner of proceeding was never contemplated, either by the Province or myself. I know it is done with county restructuring studies (which are financed by municipalities and Province combined), but it is not done or required in the reviews of regional governments.

Another way of putting this is to say that the "politicking" or public debate will take place after the Report is distributed in the Region and elsewhere. My role is strictly advisory, which is as it should be. No government or anyone else is obliged to follow the advice. Our much maligned but indispensable politicians, both provincial and local, are the people who will negotiate on any or all of the recommendations in the Report. In doing so they will of course, as they nearly always do, listen to the interested public. But in the end, the politicians make the decisions, and that too is as it should be.

Besides thanking in general terms all those groups of people mentioned above who helped with their "input" into the Report, I should like to thank specifically the following: Robert Fox, who worked for a year as research assistant, and Natalie Myhal who succeeded him. They also attended many public hearings with me. Other researchers whom I thank are Bella Duclos, Kathy McMullen, Louis Sola, Guy Morin, Joe Rizzotto, Chernoh Sesay, Ray Grenier, Barry Malmsten and Peter Haggeraats. Some were from the University of Ottawa and from Carleton University. Among those who typed various drafts of this Report, Mrs. Mary Bourassa was outstanding and deserves special thanks. Peter Katznelson was our helpful cartographer.

But two, among all, must be given unstinted credit and thanks. Mrs. Andrée Duhme was quite remarkably efficient, in both languages, as she played her several roles, among them secretary and office manager. She is, I think, the best secretary one could hope to find.

The other is Clinton Archibald, whose enormous help made him virtually a co-commissioner, at public meetings and in other ways. He gave me constantly a "feel" for the plight of the Franco-Ontarians in the Region (although not one himself); translated a lot, and supervised the rest, of this Report.

As to the Report itself a few points:

(a) the writing style in this Report is partly in the third person, impersonal, but to avoid a stilted effect, I have often used the editorial "we". (The first person singular sounded a trifle egotistic).

(b) the cut-off date for our information is August, 1976. Events since then may have overtaken some of the Report. There will unquestionably also be some errors, despite checking and re-checking. I take consolation from the fact that no one is infallible, not even the young, and certainly not professors.

(c) I have used initials frequently, as with RMOC to denote the Regional Municipality of Ottawa-Carleton. Sometimes the acronym means Regional Council, sometimes the geographical area. This should cause no confusion since common usage is similar, as when one says "city" meaning either the Council or the territory.

(d) The recommendations are put together, as considered judgments, from many sources, including most of a lifetime spent studying local and other governments. Naturally I am not an expert on all the topics mentioned. So the recommendations will probably please a few, and displease many. That is a good thing, because it is likely to lead to controversy and public debate, and when the dust settles, perhaps even to an improved local government system. I am a firm believer in municipal government, though not in all the rhetoric about it.

HB Mayo

H. B. Mayo
Commissioner

RMOC and ADJACENT MUNICIPALITIES

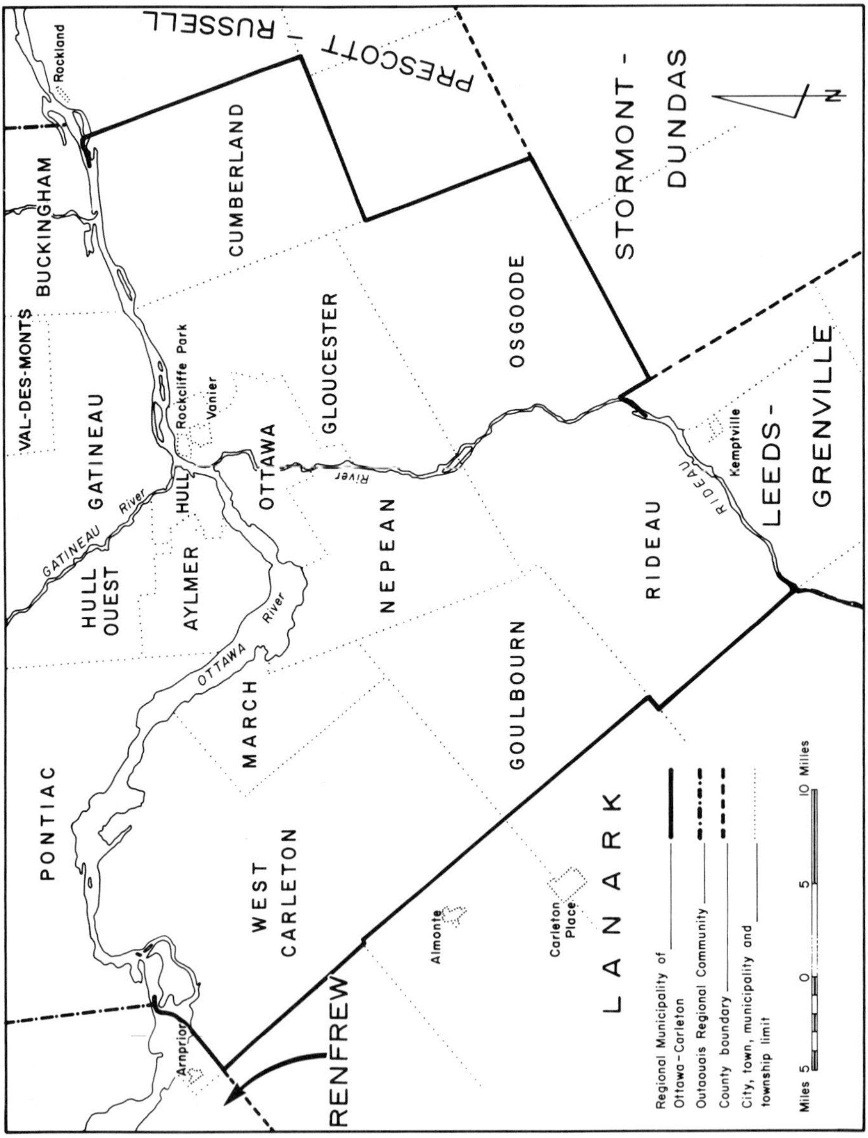

CHAPTER 1

A Municipality Not like the Others

"There is no theory of local government . . . In fact, the subject is a very base one, if we measure it by academic standards; it has seldom been treated with elegance and precision, and if you scan the textbooks of political thought you will find no accounts, or very shoddy accounts, of theories about local government." [1]

A Municipality Like the Others ? Yes!

The structure of local government in Ontario has been greatly altered and improved in the last two decades. Virtually all the large reforms have been initiated by the provincial government. There is a simple reason for this: municipalities capable of radically reforming themselves are as rare as snow in summer.

The favourite rhetoric is to praise local government, and to call for more autonomy, while at the same time demanding more money from senior governments to support the alleged autonomy. Speakers at municipal conferences often give the impression that they are ambassadors from sovereign states, like a meeting of the U.N. Assembly.

The first of these large local reforms in Ontario was the setting up of Metropolitan Toronto in 1953. The chief architect of this momentous step was the late Lorne Cumming, who by this measure immortalized himself. Ten years later Metro Toronto was studied and revised again. Now, a decade later still, it is being studied by another Royal Commission (The Robarts Commission).

The dozen or so Regional Governments (as distinct from Metro Toronto) did not start until 1968. In that year the Regional Municipality of Ottawa-Carleton (hereafter referred to as the RMOC) was established by the Ontario Legislature, and began operation on 1 January 1969. Apart from Metro Toronto, it is thus the oldest of the regional municipalities. Altogether more than 60% of the Ontario population now lives in these organized regional (or district) municipalities — counting Metro Toronto.

The general principle of a regional municipality is easy to understand. It is what is known as a "two-tier" system of local government for any given area. That is to say, the upper tier — or regional municipality — is given certain functions of local government; while the constituent units — the lower tier, or the "area municipalities" — are left with other functions.

The guiding principle as to which functions should be upper tier, and which lower tier, is easy to state, but difficult to put into practice. Endless debate has taken place on this matter, and very likely will go on for generations yet unborn. This is characteristic of general principles: they are not self-interpreting, and do not determine the outcome of particular cases. This fact was well known to St. Thomas Aquinas, and is known today (or should be known) to every judge, lawyer, politician and citizen. The guiding principle is this: matters of purely local concern should be left to the lower tier, and matters of region-wide concern should be

---

[1] W. J. M. Mackenzie, *Theories of Local Government*, L.S.E. 1961, p. 5

handled by the upper tier. The difficulty is glaringly obvious: how does one decide what is purely local, and what is of regional importance? Alas, there is no touchstone by which this can be decided. It is a matter of political or "prudential" judgment, exercised upon a number of conflicting criteria. Canadians, of all people, ought to understand this, because they live in a federal state, with its century-old tradition of federal-provincial "politicking." "Finality is not the language of politics" (Disraeli).

In some slight respect these regional governments resemble the counties and townships of Ontario, which (for all practical purposes) were established in 1849. The main point of resemblance is that the counties are also two-tier. But counties have so few functions, however, that they are weak indeed when compared with the regional municipalities. (If a county is "re-structured," as with Oxford County, 1975, it then becomes, in effect, a regional municipality.)

The counties differ from regional municipalities in that cities, and sometimes towns, were allowed to "separate" from county jurisdiction. As a result, maps of counties tend to look like blankets with large holes — the cities and separated towns — burned out. There are only a few such "separated" towns left in Ontario, and these may well become integrated into their "restructured" counties.

The people of Ontario who lived in counties — e.g., in Carleton County surrounding Ottawa — find it fairly easy to understand the two-tier system of local government. It is what they have always lived under, in spite of weak county councils (upper tier). For people in the separated cities and towns it comes less natural for them to understand and to live with a two-tier system, especially when the upper tier is strong. Formerly, these cities and towns, being single tier, were "monarchs of all they surveyed."

In all of the dozen or so regional municipalities we find many of the same problems, whether they are dealt with at the upper or lower tier. To mention a few: planning, transport, housing, growth (or no growth), water supply, social welfare, and above all finance. Indeed these problems are usually met within all municipalities, whether regional or not. To them we may add more recent concerns, such as those over the environment and of citizen participation. These problems, which are nearly universal, are also found in the RMOC. Here they are often greatly complicated, because of the unique features of the Region.

Like the Others? No!

The *first* of the unique features is that the RMOC contains the seat of government (or capital) of Canada, i.e., the City of Ottawa. As it is put in S.16 of the BNA Act, 1867: "Until the Queen otherwise directs, the Seat of Government of Canada shall be Ottawa."

This close relation between the RMOC and the capital city gives rise to federal-provincial-municipal problems of a peculiar and intimate sort, and on a daily basis. For instance, the municipalities of the region — in particular the RMOC and the City of Ottawa — must deal much more with the federal government than other municipalities in Ontario do. This is on top of the ordinary provincial-municipal relation.

The federal government is not of course a monolithic body, and so the federal-municipal relations involve a considerable number of federal departments, agencies and crown corporations.

Of these, the National Capital Commission (the NCC) is the most visible, because of its parks and driveways, its huge land holdings, its planning, etc. But there is also the CMHC, so closely related to the NCC in planning, and urban development. There is also the

Department of Public Works, with its powers of expropriation and building for the federal government. Then again there is the Department of Finance, especially its Municipal Finance Division. And the Departments of Agriculture and Defence with their large holdings, and Parks Canada with the Rideau Canal, and several more federal points of contact (and sometimes friction) with the municipalities. All of these points are treated at greater length in later chapters.

The *second* of the unique features is that the federal government is the chief employer in the Region. This is important enough to merit special discussion, influencing as it does income levels, growth and housing, the demographic composition, attempts at diversifying the economic base, etc.

Thirdly, the federal government, through the Department of Finance, is the largest single taxpayer. To be more exact, the "taxes," so-called, are "grants-in-lieu of taxes." From this arise questions of the property assessment on which payments are made, of adequacy of the payments, and of their distribution to the municipalities in the Region.

Fourthly, the RMOC is at the very centre of the federal bilingualism policy, with all that it entails. It affects not only the question of government employment, but also that of municipal policy, to say nothing of language teaching in the schools, and the provision of service in both English and French by police, courts, hospitals; and all municipal departments.

Finally, no other regional municipality adjoins another province — in this case the Province of Quebec. This in turn raises questions of public transit policy, of bridges, of relations with Quebec and the Outaouais Regional Community, as well as with the federal government.

It is difficult enough to review and evaluate any complex regional municipality in Ontario. But when to the usual problems are added those five unique features of the RMOC, mentioned above, the task is formidable indeed. The surprise should be, not that it is done well, but to find that it can be done at all.

We can sympathize with Judge Learned Hand when he wrote, from long experience:

> "The simplest problems which come up from day to day seem to me quite unanswerable as soon as I try to get below the surface. Each side, when I hear it, seems to me right till I hear the other. I have neither the time nor the ability to learn the facts, or to estimate their importance if I knew them; I am disposed to accept the decision of those charged with the responsibility of dealing with them."[2]

---

[2] Learned Hand, *The Spirit of Liberty*, New York, 1952 and 1959, p. 72.

CHAPTER 2

Introduction to the Ottawa-Carleton Region
or
Is There Any Other Place You'd Rather Be?

". . . the gay, cosmopolitan milieu of Ottawa, the Paris of the Quebec-Ontario border (at least between Arnprior and Montebello).[1]

The Area

The Regional Municipality of Ottawa-Carleton (RMOC) is located at the confluence of the Rideau and the Ottawa Rivers. The Province of Quebec is directly to the north across the Ottawa River. To the south the Region is only 50 miles from the United States border at the St. Lawrence River. Altogether the RMOC encompasses an area of 1,100 square miles, and over one-half of the population of Canada lies within about a 300-mile radius.

The climate is described officially as "a fairly typical temperate, continental climate" with a mean yearly temperature of six degrees Celsius (42 Fahrenheit), and an average precipitation of 85.04 centimetres (33.48 inches). These statistics do little to convey the realities of the Ottawa valley seasons — the sweltering summer, the glorious fall and the incredible winters that have earned Ottawa the title of "the coldest national capital in the world."

Demographic Characteristics

Ottawa-Carleton in 1971 had a population of some 472,000, or 2% of the population of Canada, and 6% of Ontario. Between 1961 and 1971, the population increased by 31.7%. The greatest percentage increase between 1961 and 1971 and to 1975 occurred in March Township. The population of the City of Vanier actually declined by 8.5% during this same period. The suburban share of population has increased sharply — especially in Nepean and Gloucester Townships, while the City of Ottawa's share of the total has decreased from 74.8% in 1961 to 64.1% in 1971, and even less in 1975 (See Table 2-1). The City of Ottawa, with about 3/5 of the population, is still by far the dominant area municipality, and this in turn raises problems of representation, taxation, etc., for the RMOC itself.

---

[1] George Bain, *I've Been Around*, Toronto 1964, p. vii. (Bain was writing before the National Arts Centre was put up, and before much of the downtown area was rebuilt). I should like to pay a tribute to George Bain, whose Parliamentary reporting for the Globe and Mail was so knowledgeable and refreshing.

Table 2–1

Population in the RMOC and Area Municipalities, 1961-1975

Municipality	Census Population 1961	Census Population 1971	Assessed Population 1975	% of RMOC Population 1975
Ottawa	268,206	302,341	302,124	59.6
Vanier	24,555	22,477	20,146	4.0
Rockcliffe Park	2,084	2,135	2,229	.4
Cumberland	5,478	9,295	11,458	2.3
Gloucester	18,301	37,145	53,322	10.5
Goulbourn	4,869	9,455	12,489	2.5
March	968	5,825	6,910	1.4
Nepean	19,751	64,605	74,000	14.6
Osgoode	5,786	7,775	8,286	1.6
Rideau	3,649	4,895	7,860	1.6
West Carleton	4,763	6,005	7,782	1.5
RMOC	358,410	471,930	506,606	100.0

Source: Statistics Canada, Census of Canada, 1961, 1971, and Financial Reports of RMOC and area municipalities, 1975.
Caution: The Census figure is not quite the same as that for the "Assessed Population." The latter is obtained every year. The few amalgamations that took place in 1973 do not seriously affect municipalities, other than Rideau Township.

Contrary to popular opinion, females do not dramatically outnumber males in the RMOC. In 1971, for every 100 females in the Region, there were 96 males. Children and people of old age were under-represented in the RMOC as compared to the national average, with a compensating higher proportion aged 20-64.

In 1971, 56.1% of the population of Ottawa-Carleton was of British Isles descent and 24.9% was of French descent. The next highest "ethnic" groups were Germans and Italians. The all-Canada distribution was 44.6% British, 28.7% French and 26.7% "other." Table 2–2 shows the ethnic origin of the populations of the area municipalities. As can be seen, the four municipalities with the greatest proportion of people of French descent are Vanier, Cumberland, Gloucester and Ottawa. Some 85% of the RMOC population was born in Canada, about the same as in the nation as a whole, and more than in Ontario which has 78% native born.

Descent is one thing, but language spoken at home is quite different and probably of more importance for schools, official language policy, etc. Of the population, 77.6% spoke English at home, as compared to 67.0% in Canada and 85.1% in Ontario. Some 17.4% spoke French in the home, as compared to 25% nationally and 4.6% in all Ontario. A language other than English or French was spoken at home by 4.9% of the population, with the national percentage being just under 7.3%, and in the province being 10.3%.

Two things are clear from these figures. One is that the RMOC is less cosmopolitan than the province and country as a whole, whether judged by descent or by language spoken at home. The other is that the RMOC has a much higher French speaking proportion (17.4%) than the province at large (4.6%).

Table 2–2

Ethnicity in the RMOC, 1971

Municipality	% British Isles Descent	% French Descent	% "Other" Descent
Ottawa	55.2	24.9	19.9
Vanier	22.0	68.6	9.4
Rockcliffe Park	73.6	13.8	12.6
Cumberland	38.7	49.6	11.7
Gloucester	49.3	36.6	14.1
Goulbourn	75.2	8.7	16.1
March	77.5	4.6	17.9
Nepean	67.8	10.1	22.1
Osgoode	71.2	12.4	16.4
Rideau	77.3	9.0	13.7
West Carleton	83.6	6.1	10.3
RMOC	56.1	24.9	19.0

Source: Statistics Canada, Census of Canada, 1971.

As for official language (a measure of bilingualism), whereas only 9.3% in Ontario were bilingual, the proportion was about 27% in the RMOC — a figure mostly (but not entirely) accounted for by the bilingualism of the French speaking population.

The religious affiliations of most citizens in the Region are close to the national pattern. In 1971, Catholics represented 47.5% of the population, while Protestants in all their variety accounted for 43.3%. The proportion of Jews in the Region represented 1.3% of the population. Other religions accounted for 2.8% of the total, while the proportion of the population of the RMOC with no religious affiliation was 5.1% — highest in March Township at 13.1% and lowest in Vanier at 2%. In the Province, 34.1% of the population reported that they were Catholics, 58.3% were Protestants, and 1.6% were Jewish. The proportion of the population of Ontario with no religious affiliation was 5.1%.

The population of Ottawa-Carleton is on the average more educated than that of the country or the province as a whole. Even so, it brings out the fact that those who go on for advanced education are barely more than 20% of the population, and those who get a degree only 11%. We are obviously not a highly educated people in any "formal" sense. Many fascinating, but probably not provable, conclusions may be drawn from this fact. (Let those who will, do so.) Of the population 15 years of age or over, the educational attainments were as follows in 1971:

Table 2–3

Formal Education of RMOC Population

(15 years of age and over)

Highest Grade Attained	*% of RMOC Population*
Less than Grade 9	19.0
Less than Grade 12	50.4
Finished Grade 12 or 13	29.3
Some university	9.2
One or more university degrees	11.0

Source: Statistics Canada, Census of Canada, 1971.

Historical Overview

There are a number of general histories of Ottawa, and of parts of the Region — including the Ottawa and Rideau Rivers. So it is not necessary here to attempt any large historical review.[2] The Indians were here first. Then came the usual pattern — explorers first, next trappers and traders who sought furs, and missionaries who sought souls; then settlers (at first on the Quebec side) who came for the timber and to homestead around 1800.

The word Ottawa comes from an Indian name for the river. Some say that the Indian word for Ottawa, *adawe*, means "to trade."[3] Today, this is something of a misnomer. Employees in trade — both wholesale and retail — account for only 13.8% of the labour force of the RMOC. Manufacturing employment accounts for 6.4%, while the category which encompasses federal government employment, "Other Service," is in the highest position with 59.6% of the labour force.[4] The RMOC — whether we look at the City of Ottawa or the former Carleton County around it — is heavily dependent on public service employment.

Ottawa and Hull were established and grew as a result of their trading and timbering functions. Three rivers meet in the area — the Ottawa, the Rideau and, on the Quebec side, the Gatineau. The area was originally forested, with a good deal of swampy flat land especially on the Ontario side, which was relatively easy to clear for farming. The Chaudiere Falls and other lesser falls served as convenient sources of power, encouraging sawmills and industrial growth, and trade with Britain in squared timber.

The building of the famous Rideau Canal, 1826-32, largely accounts for the growth of the new settlement, which was at that time called Bytown. Colonel By got little thanks for his work in building the Canal, and died unhonoured a few years later in England. The Rideau Canal and River, going through the RMOC, are today a delight to residents and tourists alike.

In 1855, Bytown (population about 10,000) was incorporated as a city and renamed Ottawa.[5] Two years later, the city was chosen as the compromise capital of the Province of

---

[2] Perhaps the best history is Wilfrid Eggleston, *The Queen's Choice*, Ottawa, 1961.

[3] Sheila Bennett, *Ottawa*, Willowdale, Garner/Hounslow, 1973, p. 4.

[4] RMOC, *Official Plan*, 1974, p.2-33.

[5] One theory has it that the Ottawa (English for the Outaouais tribe of the Algonquins) "had the peculiar custom of wearing large ear-rings which stretched the ears to exaggerated proportions, the lobes actually reaching the shoulder. They are described in some references as the tribe with the big ears." Hence, *Ottawa, City of the Big Ears*, by Robert Haig, Ottawa, n.d., p. 26.

Canada, i.e., the union (in 1840) of the two previously separate colonies of Lower Canada (Quebec) and Upper Canada (Ontario). Those who disliked it, chiefly in Montreal and Toronto, sneered at it as "The Westminster in the Wilderness."[6] Goldwin Smith is supposed to have called it "A sub-arctic lumber-village converted by royal mandate into a political cockpit."

When chosen as the capital of the new Confederation, in 1867, Ottawa had acquired a few dignified (Gothic) public buildings, the three main buildings on Parliament Hill. The population was some 18,000. Other public buildings followed. Railways connected the city with points in Canada and the United States. Ottawa was the site for a time of the largest sawmills and papermills in Canada. Small industries serving the local market also sprang up. By the end of the nineteenth century, the banks of the Rideau Canal were cluttered with warehouses, lumber yards and factories based mainly upon local wood and farm supplies. The demand for public transit increased as the population grew. In 1891, the Ottawa Electric Street Railway Company began its electric tram service, and soon replaced the horse-drawn tram cars, to serve a population of 45,000.

One writer says that at the turn of the 20th century "Ottawa was torn between the role of a great industrial and commercial centre and that of the stately national capital," — a somewhat dubious opinion.[7] Mackenzie King's opinion of Ottawa in 1900 was that "of a provincial town, not interesting but tiresome. Ottawa is not a pretty place, save about the Parliament Buildings."

From about that time the federal government became concerned with the appearance of the capital. In 1899, the Ottawa Improvement Commission (OIC) was created with a federal grant of $60,000 annually. In 1915, the Holt Commission recommended that a Federal District be created. In a previous plebiscite (1906), 45% of voters had approved the proposal that Ottawa should become a national district. A similar debate flares up sporadically today over the question of a Federal District, usually without much knowledge of what such a District would or could entail.

The federal government continued its involvement in the beautifying of the capital. The Federal District Commission (FDC) replaced the OIC in 1927, its chief contribution perhaps being the expropriations and demolitions to create what is now Confederation Square (sometimes called Confusion Square).

Shortly after World War II ended, an area of 900 square miles on both sides of the Ottawa River was designated the National Capital District. Jacques Gréber, a French planner, had been asked by Mackenzie King in the late 1930's to advise on planning for the National Capital District. King was a weird man in some ways. One cannot help wondering whether he thought of himself as a European monarch, say Louis Napoleon with his Baron Haussmann laying out the boulevards of Paris and the Bois de Boulogne, with Gréber playing the role of Haussmann.

The main proposals of the Gréber Report (1950) which were implemented by the National Capital Commission (NCC) — established in 1958 — and by its predecessor, the FDC, involved the removal of railway lines from the inner city, open space and the construction of new parkways, the relocation of government buildings away from the city

---

[6] Hull was incorporated as a city and renamed from Wrightstown to Hull in 1875. Hull and its predecessor began as mainly English-speaking and Protestant. By 1870 it was about half English-speaking and half of French descent.

[7] Thomas L. Nagy, *Ottawa in Maps*, Ottawa, Public Archives Canada, 1974, p. 38.

core, the enlargement of Gatineau Park, and the acquisition of large land holdings as a Greenbelt.

The Greenbelt, a ring of open land encircling the city, and taking in parts of the suburban townships, was designed as a barrier to urban expansion by the City. The Greenbelt was purchased and/or expropriated because it was the only way to control land use. Small self-contained satellite towns beyond the Greenbelt were to be constructed to house the spillover population and provide employment. Gréber had not foreseen the great surge in population growth in the years after the war. The Greenbelt has proven to be ineffective, because it is so narrow, in containing urban development. Growth has merely jumped the Greenbelt, has not been under City control, and Carleton County (like most if not all counties) had no overall planning for itself and none jointly with the City.

Municipal Organization — an outline

The Regional Municipality of Ottawa-Carleton (RMOC) was set up by the Province of Ontario to begin operation on January 1, 1969 — the first of the regional municipalities (excluding Metro Toronto). The major responsibilities of the Region are: water supply and distribution, sewage collection and treatment, the design and maintenance of regional roads, overall planning, debt financing, and the provision of social services. In 1972, the Region acquired the responsibility for the Ottawa-Carleton Regional Transit Commission (OC Transpo). Public transit had formerly been a function of the City of Ottawa.

The council of the RMOC is composed of members of the local councils in the Region. The City of Ottawa sends all 11 aldermen, plus the four controllers and its Mayor, to the Regional Council for a total of 16; Nepean Township is represented on Regional Council by three members; the City of Vanier and Gloucester Township each have two. The remaining seven municipalities are represented at Regional Council by the head of the local council, for a total of 14 (See Table 2–4).

The chairman of the RMOC serves as the head of Council and its "chief executive officer". He is elected by the Regional Council itself, and may come from within the Council or outside it. For his first term of office he was appointed by the Province, the usual practice followed in setting up regional municipalities.

If a member of an area council is elected Chairman, he must then resign his local seat. The local seat is then filled by the local council by appointment as outlined in *The Municipal Act*, S. 44, as follows: if the vacancy occurs in the office of a councillor or alderman, any person qualified to hold office may be appointed to fill the vacancy created by the election of the Chairman of the Regional Municipality. If the Chairman previously held the office of mayor, reeve, deputy reeve or controller, the vacancy must be filled from within the local council.

Regional Council has an executive committee, composed of eight members and the Chairman of the Council. Not more than half of the members of the Executive Committee may come from the council of the City of Ottawa. The Executive Committee possesses the same powers as a board of control. Recommendations of the executive committee have priority at council meetings. A two-thirds majority vote of Regional Council is required to approve expenditures that have not previously been approved by the Executive Committee.

Regional Council has five permanent Committees. These are: a Planning Committee, a Transportation Committee, a Social Services Comiittee, a Homes for the Aged Committee of Management, and a Land Division Committee. Committee members are recommended by the Chairman to the Executive Committee. These appointments must then be approved by Council. Ad hoc committees are set up to report on specific matters. There are also many special committees, boards and commissions made up in whole or in part of Regional councillors (e.g., the Board of Health).

Table 2-4

Population and Representation for RMOC and Area Municipalities 1975

Municipality	1975 Population	% of RMOC Population	Composition of Council	Method of Election
Ottawa, c.	302,124	59.6	Mayor*	At large
			4 Controllers*	At large
			11 Aldermen*	By ward (11)
Vanier, c.	20,146	4.0	Mayor*	At large
			8 Councillors (1)*	By ward (4)
Rockcliffe Park, vl.	2,229	.4	Reeve*	At large
			4 Councillors	At large
Cumberland, twp.	11,458	2.3	Reeve*	At large
Gloucester, twp.	53,322	10.5	Reeve*	At large
			Deputy Reeve*	At large
			3 Councillors	At large
Goulbourn, twp.	12,489	2.5	Mayor*	At large
			8 Councillors	By ward (4)
March, twp.	6,910	1.4	Reeve*	At large
			4 Councillors	At large
Nepean, twp.	74,000	14.6	Reeve*	At large
			Deputy Reeve*	At large
			5 Councillors (1)*	At large
Osgoode, twp.	8,286	1.6	Reeve*	At large
			4 Councillors	At large
Rideau, twp.	7,860	1.6	Mayor*	At large
			6 Councillors	By ward (3)
West Carleton, twp.	7,782	1.5	Mayor*	At large
			6 Councillors	By ward (3)
RMOC	506,606	100.0	Chairman	Indirect

Source: Municipal Financial Reports, 1975.
* Indicates representative sits on Regional Council.
(1) Indicates one of the councillors sits on Regional Council.

The heads of all departments report to the Chairman of the RMOC. At a weekly meeting of department heads the agenda for the Executive Committee is prepared. Most departments are headed by "commissioners." The departments are: Planning, Social Services, Homes for the Aged, Works, Finance, Legal Department, and Transportation.

Total Local Reps.	Population per Local Rep.	No. of RMOC Reps.	% of RMOC Reps.	Population per RMOC Rep.
16	18,883	16	53.0	18,883
9	2,238	2	6.7	10,073
5	446	1	3.3	2,229
5	2,292	1	3.3	11,458
5	10,664	2	6.7	26,661
9	1,388	1	3.3	12,489
5	1,382	1	3.3	6,910
7	10,571	3	10.0	24,667
5	1,657	1	3.3	8,286
7	1,123	1	3.3	7,860
7	1,112	1	3.3	7,782
		31	100.0	16,342

The representation of lower-tier municipalities on the Regional Council is not proportional to the population. (See Table 2-4.) The City of Ottawa and the Townships of Gloucester and Nepean are under-represented on Regional Council. All of the remaining municipalities are over-represented, taking the average for the Region of one regional councillor for 16,342 people. The extremes are shown by comparing Rockcliffe Park Village and Gloucester Township. The Reeve of the Village of Rockcliffe Park represents a municipality of 2,229 persons, while each of the two councillors from Gloucester Township represents 26,661 people. This is obviously absurd, if one believes in the principle of representation by population. The Regional Council is as undemocratic as the U.S. Senate in its composition.

Area (Local) Municipalities

The Regional Municipality is made up of eleven "area" or local municipalities. Before January 1, 1974, there were 16 local municipalities in the Region. In 1973 the numbers were reduced. The Township of West Carleton was created by the amalgamation of the former townships of Fitzroy, Huntley and Torbolton. Rideau Township was created from the former townships of Marlborough and North Gower, with annexation of small parts of Gloucester, Nepean and Osgoode Townships in the Manotick area. The present Goulbourn Township was formed by the amalgamation of the Villages of Richmond and Stittsville with the former Goulbourn Township.

The City of Ottawa is the only municipality in the RMOC to have a council-board of control system. This political structure exists as a result of provincial legislation which, until 1962, required every municipality with over 100,000 population to have a board of control. This system can now be altered by a two-thirds vote of council and with the approval of the Ontario Municipal Board (OMB).

The mayor and four controllers of the City are elected at large. The Board of Control is responsible for the preparation of the budget, acting upon the advice of the Department of Finance. The Board of Control is also responsible for the nomination of senior administrative personnel. Its recommendations have priority at Council meetings, and may be carried by a simple majority of Council, except for spending, for which a two-thirds vote is required. One alderman is elected from each of the eleven wards in the City of Ottawa. The two major committees of council are Community Development and Physical Environment, both made up of aldermen. These two standing committees correspond to two major operating departments, and are responsible for the formulation of policy and the recommendation of budgetary priorities to the Board of Control, with the advice of their respective commissioners. The Policy and Procedures Committee is made up of five aldermen plus one controller. Many other committees, commissions and boards exist: the Community Centres Board, the Liaison Committee (City of Ottawa and School Boards), the Central Canada Exhibition Association, the Civic Hospital Board of Trustees, the Committee of Adjustment, the Day Care Advisory Committee, the Design Review Committee, and the Housing Advisory Committee — to mention only a few. Some of these bodies are made up of people outside the City Council, nominated by Board of Control. City staff is organized into seven departments: Community Services, Physical Environment, Finance, Personnel Services, Executive Services, Legal, Fire, plus the Lansdowne Park administration. A committee of department heads, under the chairmanship of the mayor, co-ordinates the work of the departments and reports to the Board of Control.

The other ten municipalities which make up the RMOC do not have boards of control. Each has a council made up of a mayor or reeve elected at large, and several councillors elected at large or by ward. The Village of Rockcliffe Park and the Townships of Cumberland, Gloucester, March, Nepean and Osgoode elect their councillors at large. The question of election at large or by wards is examined later on. (See Chapter 9.)

Population Projections

Nothing is more uncertain than predicting the future, something which is proven so often by the weather office. Estimates of future population levels vary with the methods and assumptions employed by researchers. During the 1930's demographers were predicting stationary populations in Western nations; and Jacques Gréber, in his Plan, was still partially influenced by the slow growth trends of those years. He estimated that the population of the National Capital Region would be 500,000 by 1980. This threshold was reached by 1966. The expansion of federal government activities, the post-World War II baby boom and immigration led to a rapid rate of population growth.

Several studies have been undertaken projecting population growth in the Ottawa-Carleton area. Three territorial areas have been studied: the Regional Municipality of Ottawa-Carleton (RMOC), the Ottawa-Hull Census Metropolitan Area (CMA), and the National Capital Region (NCR). These three areas, unfortunately, have different boundaries, and so the figures are not easily and exactly reconciled. The RMOC is the smallest of these three areas. (See Figure 2-1 in this chapter.)

The *first* area is that of the RMOC with its eleven municipalities: the City of Ottawa, the City of Vanier, the Village of Rockcliffe Park, which are all urban; the rapidly growing suburban Townships of Nepean and Gloucester; and an outer ring of so-called "rural" Townships — Cumberland, Goulbourn, March, Osgoode, Rideau and West Carleton.

The *second* area is the Ottawa-Hull CMA which takes in areas on both sides of the Ottawa River, i.e., in Ontario and Quebec. Its limits follow municipal boundaries — but not all of them. In Ontario, the CMA includes the City of Ottawa, the City of Vanier, the Village of Rockcliffe Park and the Townships of Cumberland, Gloucester, Goulbourn, March and Nepean. But it leaves out Rideau, Osgoode and West Carleton.

The *third* area is the National Capital Region (NCR) which also extends over both sides of the Ottawa River. The NCR does not follow municipal boundaries, although it is not greatly different on the Ontario side. It extends slightly further than the RMOC in the west, to include Almonte, and parts of the Townships of Pakenham, Ramsay and Beckwith — all in Lanark County. In the south, the NCR excludes a part of Rideau and of Osgoode Townships. In the east, the NCR encompasses a portion of Russell Township (not in the RMOC), but excludes part of Cumberland Township which is entirely in the RMOC.

A reasonable comparison of the populations of the three areas is possible, however. In 1971, 453,280 people lived in the Ontario portion of the Ottawa-Hull CMA, while the NCR (Ontario side) held 477,643 people.[8] The population of the RMOC in 1971 was 471,930.

The studies on population and employment growth completed during the 1960's used the boundaries of the NCR as their limits. These studies were: the Larry Smith Report

---

[8] This figure is derived by taking 76% of the NCR population total of 628,477 as suggested in Douglas Fullerton, *The Capital of Canada, How Should It be Governed?*, Ottawa, 1974. On p. 23 of the Fullerton Report, however, it is claimed that the total NCR (Ontario) population in 1971 was 471,930 — which is the same population as given by Statistics Canada for the RMOC.

Fig. 2.1
RMOC with NCR, CMA and GREENBELT

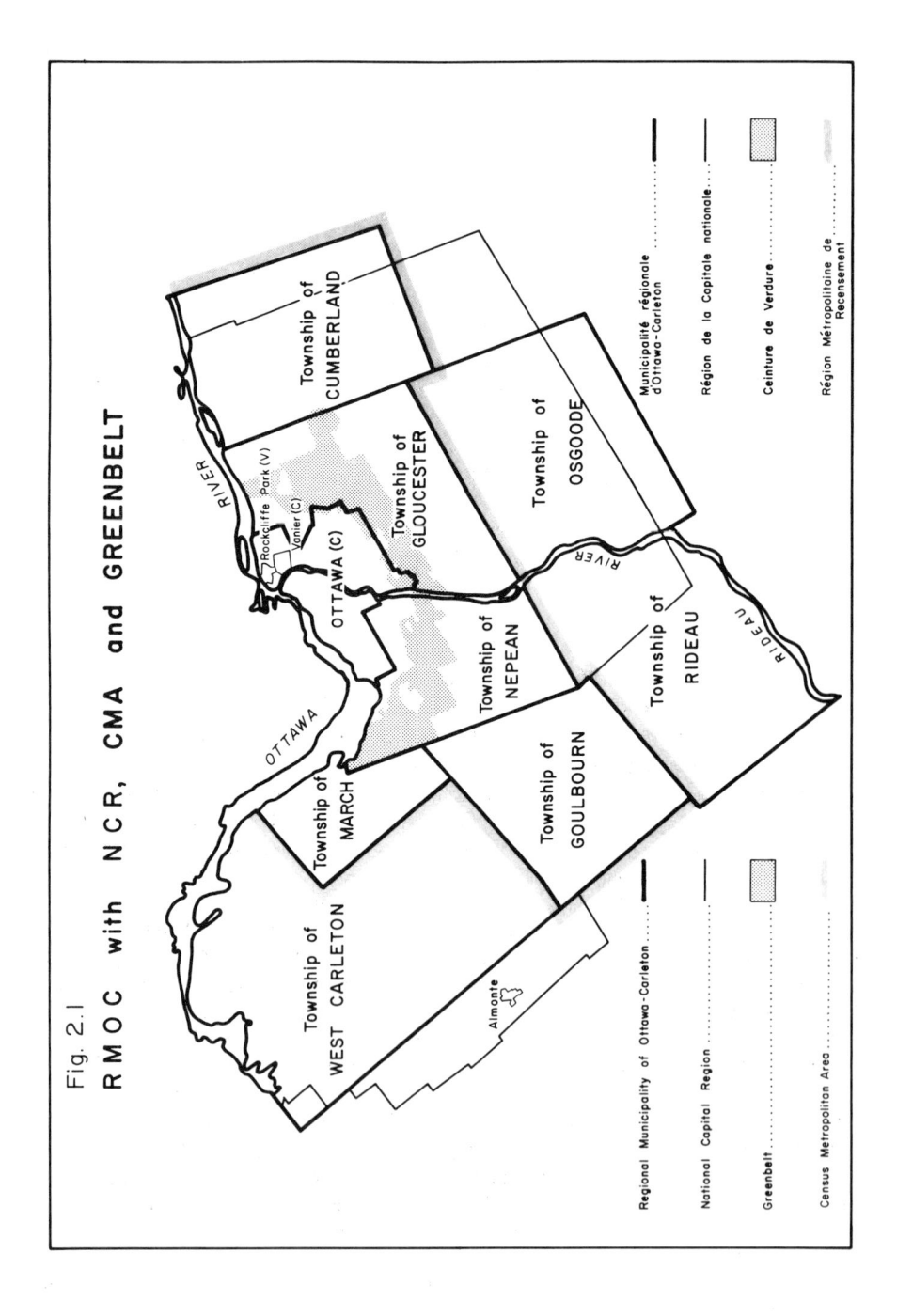

(1963), the Hammer Report (1969), the NCC Report (1969), and the Hospital Report (1970). Another study, — the MacLaren-Richards Report (1970) — based its projections on the NCC Report, and forecast that the National Capital Region was expected to reach 1,000,000 by the year 2030.

Population projections have been developed by the RMOC for use in the Official Plan. If population continues to increase each decade by the same percentage rate as it increased between 1961 and 1971, the population will reach one million by the year 1998. If the population increases by the same numerical amount in each decade as it did between 1961 and 1971, the one million figure will not be attained until the year 2015. These estimates are needed to facilitate planning. The RMOC Official Plan, as adopted, does not imply that the population levels they mention are optimal or desired. In any case, who knows what is "optimal"? Hence, the figures will be changed if conditions warrant.

"Between the years 1966 and 1973, the population of the Ottawa-Hull metropolitan area increased at an average rate of 2.3% per year."[9] Federal employment in the NCR grew at a rate of 3.9% per year between 1951 and 1971. This rate is expected to decrease slightly in the future. The NCC's concept plan, *Tomorrow's Capital* (1974), finds it desirable that the annual federal employment growth rate of the NCR decrease to about 3% per year over the next few decades.[10] At that rate (3%), the growth in total population will also slow down, if one assumes a constant federal to non-federal employment ratio. On the other hand, to expect a slower growth of government employment is a triumph of faith over reason. (It may be, of course, that growth could slow down in the RMOC, but increase on the Quebec side of the NCR, as government offices are shifted to Hull.)

According to recent provincial statements, past estimates of population growth in the Province as a whole have been too high. The Design for Development Report, *Ontario's Future: Trends and Options*, (1976), predicts a population of 11,650,000 for the Province by the year 2001. Previously, Ontario's population had been expected to reach 13,300,000.[11] The trend towards urbanization is expected to continue, as all the signs indicate. In 1971, 6.2 million people lived in urban areas. By the year 2001, 10 million out of 11.7 million population expected in Ontario will live in urban areas. (An "urban area" is defined by the Census as all settlements of 1,000 or more people, and suburbs adjacent to settlements of over 5,000, provided that the suburban density is at least 1,000 per square mile. This definition covers some villages, towns, and small cities, and so may mislead the ordinary citizen, who often thinks of "urban" as big).

Larger urban areas are probably of more significance, since these contain the majority of the people, and are growing faster. For instance, the proportion of people in the six major Census Metropolitan Areas in southern Ontario is expected to be 80% of the population of southern Ontario by 2001, from the present 60%. The overall density of southern Ontario is approaching 170 people per square mile.[12]

The RMOC has been planning for a population of one million by approximately the year 2000. City of Ottawa planners use a population figure of 900,000 for their planning

---

[9] National Capital Commission, *Tomorrow's Capital*, Ottawa, 1974, p. 10.

[10] *Ibid.*, p. 10.

[11] Ontario, Ministry of Treasury, Economics & Intergovernmental Affairs (TEIGA), *Ontario's Changing Population*, Vol.2, 1976, p. 16.

[12] Ontario, TEIGA, *Ontario's Future: Trends and Options*, 1976, pp. 4, 11.

purposes, while the NCC's concept plan, *Tomorrow's Capital*, plans for a population of 925,000 in the Ontario portion of the National Capital Region. In March 1976, the Province issued a new study which predicts that the population of Ottawa-Carleton will reach only 811,000 by the year 2000.[13] This lower provincial estimate throws doubt on the future number planned by the RMOC. Perhaps some of the "satellites" — e.g., that to the south — may not be needed, or at any rate may not be as large as planned.

At present the growth rate does seem to be slowing down. The 1975 assessed population of the RMOC was 506,606. The average annual growth rate over the last three years was 2.7%. Ottawa-Carleton now accounts for 6% of Ontario's population, but by the year 2000, it is expected to account for approximately 8% of the provincial total.

Because the Region is so dependent on federal employment, population projections must make assumptions (which may be shaky) about federal policy. For instance, the federal policy seems to be one of moving some offices to other parts of Canada through its programme of regional development. Whether this will make much difference in the RMOC (or indeed in the NCR) is doubtful.

Then there is the Province of Ontario which also appears to have a population policy (and an economic plan). It has said that it wishes to achieve an "optimum distribution of people, urban places, and economic activities."[14] The trouble with this high ideal (or rhetoric) too is: what is meant by "optimal"? And what would be the costs and benefits of redistribution, and can it be done at all? To answer these questions is as hard as finding out "what song the sirens sang" to Ulysses and his crew.

The proportion of the population in the Central Ontario Lakeshore Urban Complex Planning Region (COLUC), of which Toronto is the heart, has increased from 36% of Ontario's total in 1951 to 43% in 1971. The Province wishes to redirect growth to other areas to increase their development, and so relieve the serious pressures on land, housing and servicing costs in the COLUC Region. New centres of development will not be created (although two new towns are planned); instead, existing centres will be enlarged after consultation with municipalities involved. It is not going to be easy to carry out these plans.

Some of the methods proposed for reducing provincial economic disparities are: building upon the existing human and resource base of "regions"; clustering industrial growth; making available financial and managerial assistance for the development of entrepreneurial talent; assisting new industries if they are deemed beneficial to the locality.

Eastern Ontario has been designated in the provincial plan as one of the economic "regions" in need of more economic activity. Within Eastern Ontario, Ottawa has been chosen as the focus of one of the six sub-systems of urban places which will be aided by the Province in becoming "regional" service centres. The province wishes to capitalize on the existing impetus of growth in Ottawa in order to divert growth from more populated areas of the Province. We endorse this intention to direct growth from the crowded areas of south western Ontario. Only time will tell the outcome.

---

[13] Ontario, TEIGA, *Ontario's Changing Population*, 1976, Vol. 2, p. 144.

[14] Ontario, TEIGA, *Ontario's Future: Trends and Options*, 1976, p. 2.

CHAPTER 3

The Economic Base of Ottawa-Carleton
or
Don't Let Anybody Take the Feds Away

"Ottawa-Carleton, oh luckiest of Regions,
That swarms with civil servants in their legions.
This is our economic base, which can't go wrong
Because — Himself has said — 'The land is strong'."

The Federal Impact

The presence of the federal government accounts largely both for the stability and prosperity of the Region's labour force. Strikes, lay-offs and factory closings seldom affect the economic vitality of Ottawa-Carleton. As for income, the Ottawa-Hull CMA had the highest average income of the 22 CMA's in Canada in 1973, and every year is among the top few. As for "occupational status" — a measurement of the skills of the labour force — it has been rated in first position.[1] In 1971, Ottawa-Hull had the second lowest unemployment rate, only 4.4% of the labour force.

The federal civil service in the National Capital Region has increased greatly in the last 30 years, a fact which should surprise no one. In 1951, there were 30,069 federal employees in the NCR and in 1961 there were 46,095. By 1974, the number of federal employees in the NCR was probably about 100,000.[2]

This expansion led to a construction boom in central Ottawa and in the suburbs. The downtown core became revitalized — or at any rate, rebuilt — as office buildings were put up for government use and support services. Ottawa-Hull housing starts have also been increasing at a faster rate than in any other major cities in Canada. By the time the RMOC population reaches one million, the *Official Plan* predicts that there will be 450,000 jobs in the RMOC. Of these, 109,000 are likely to be federal government jobs.[3]

The dependence on a "single industry" is shown by the current "freeze" on government employment. The number of people employed in public administration in the last quarter of 1975 was lower than the number employed in the last quarter of 1974. Various projects announced for federal buildings and properties were cancelled as a part of federal

---

[1] Canada, Ministry of State for Urban Affairs, *Urban Indicators*, Ottawa, Information Canada, 1976, pp. 45, 49, 53. (Information Canada is now defunct, with none to mourn its passing. There can hardly have been a more inept and inefficient operation.)

[2] Estimate by Douglas Fullerton, *The Capital of Canada, How Should It Be Governed?*, Ottawa, Information Canada, 1974, p. 144. The fact that this is an estimate only, and cannot be made exact, shows how hard it is for the federal government — perhaps any large government — to keep track of how many people it employs.

[3] RMOC, *Official Plan*, 1974, p. 2-33.

economy measures. Consequently, employment in the construction trades has also fallen recently.[4]

Again, there are the decentralization policies of the federal government. Part of the Royal Canadian Mint, and of the Departments of National Revenue and of Supplies and Services have moved from from Ottawa-Hull. Further, other federal departments have set up regional offices across Canada.

This macro-scale decentralization trend has not affected the employment levels in the RMOC to the extent that micro-scale decentralization to the Outaouais Regional Community (ORC) is likely to do. Several government departments have already moved to Hull. These include Environment Canada, Labour Canada, and Consumer and Corporate Affairs. By the time the RMOC population reaches one million, 36,000 federal jobs are expected in the ORC — 25% of the total.[5] The mayor of Ottawa has warned that Ottawa could become a "ghost town" because of a sharp rise in vacant office space predicted for the future in the City of Ottawa core. (A politician, as Edmund Burke said, is permitted a certain amount of hyperbole.)

Apart from the effect on employment, the location of federal buildings has a great effect also on residential, commercial and transportation patterns in the Region. Jacques Gréber had recommended the decentralization of federal buildings to such areas as Tunncy's Pasture, Confederation Heights and Booth Street. This has been done and has by and large been a success from the point of view of public transit.

Spokesmen for Goulbourn and Nepean Townships have expressed a desire for federal buildings to be located in their municipalities. We support such proposals in principle, and suggest that the federal government consider decentralizing some of its buildings to selected points in the RMOC outside of the City of Ottawa: the buildings to be clustered in several nodes to facilitate public transit, and reduce traffic by automobiles.

The suggestion above follows the RMOC *Official Plan* in its stress on public transit and "the need to create activity centres as foci for newly developing areas."[6] The *Official Plan* calls for 100,000 workers (22.2% of total Ottawa-Carleton employment) to be located in the "Central Area" when the total population of the Region reaches one million (about the year 2000).[7] In 1971, 68,000 people (34.3% of all workers) were employed in the "Central Area."

Non-Government Employment

Approximately one-third of the employment of Ottawa-Carleton is directly provided by the federal government. This is the main part of the economic base of the RMOC. Other jobs exist in firms which provide services and materials for the federal government which thus, directly or indirectly, accounts for most of the employment in the Region. It is very difficult, indeed almost impossible, to calculate exactly the extent of the indirect employment.

---

[4] Canada, Department of Manpower and Immigration, *Ontario Region*, Vol. 9, No. 1, 1976, pp. 9, 10.

[5] RMOC, *Official Plan*, 1974, p.2-33.

[6] RMOC, *Official Plan*, 1974, p. 2-35.

[7] The "Central Area" is defined by the RMOC *Official Plan* as "the area which is bounded by Bronson, Gloucester, Laurier, east of the Canal, King Edward, St. Patrick, and the Ottawa River." (A slightly unclear description of the "Central Area.")

A sample survey conducted by a member of our staff (Natalie Myhal) found that 70% of the firms in the Ottawa-Carleton sold over two-thirds of their products within the Ottawa area. One may assume that a substantial proportion of these purchases was made by the federal government and its many agencies.

The RMOC, like every city in a market or mixed economy, needs the private sector to provide the goods and services used by people in everyday life. In 1971, there were 198,400 people employed in various occupations in the RMOC. This number of jobs existed when the population of the RMOC was 455,000.

In 1971, the "participation rate" for Ottawa-Carleton was 63.7 per cent. (The "participation rate" is defined as the percentage the labour force forms of the population 15 years and over.) Table 3-1, taken from the RMOC *Official Plan* shows the numerical distribution of jobs among different employment categories in 1971, and when the population of the Region is expected to be one million.

The *Official Plan* predicts that non-federal employment will increase more rapidly than federal employment. Policies of the Province of Ontario support this trend, since Ottawa-Carleton was identified as one of the five major growth centres in Ontario. A recent provincial report states that Ottawa-Carleton "is not considered as requiring economic stimulation, but would greatly benefit from diversification."[8] The same opinion was also expressed by March Township in its brief to this Commission, and it seems a reasonable view.

Table 3-1

Employment in the RMOC 1961, 1971 and at the threshold population of one million

Employment Groups	1961	1971	Estimate One Million
Total	138,031	198,400	450,000
Primary	3,486	3,000	2,000
Manufacturing	11,616	13,500	25,000
Construction	9,088	13,000	25,000
Transportation, Utilities & Communication	9,703	13,200	30,000
Trade	18,693	27,400	65,000
Finance, Insurance & Real Estate	6,774	10,000	30,000
Other Service (including federal)	78,701	118,300	273,000

Source: RMOC, *Official Plan*, 1974, p. 2-33

Although various levels of government can perhaps accelerate or slow down growth, the trend to diversification is already occurring. As the size of a city increases, more and more industries achieve their minimum threshold of production. The market is

---

[8] Ontario, TEIGA, *Ontario's Future: Trends and Options*, 1976, p. 45.

self-reinforcing as firms sell to each other (take in one another's washing). Apart from anything else, this diversification is bound to make the Region a more interesting place to live. A city composed almost wholly of civil servants is not something to contemplate with equanimity.

Between 1962 and 1968, for every one federal job created, 3.12 non-federal jobs came into being.[9] By the time the population of Ottawa-Carleton reaches one million, the percentage of federal jobs will decline to approximately 24% of the total. This cannot of course be a firm prediction. On the one hand, there is the tendency of government to grow, by a kind of Parkinson's Law. Counteracting this, there are federal policies to establish Departments and agencies elsewhere — in Quebec and throughout the country.

The Primary Sector of the Economy

Workers in the primary sector are employed in agriculture, mining, fishing, trapping and forestry. Historically, primary sector employment has been declining in all industrial or post-industrial countries, while manufacturing and tertiary employment has risen. In 1974, 4.9% of the labour force in Ontario was engaged in primary occupations. In the RMOC, primary employment makes up a smaller proportion of the labour force, being only some 1.5%. Nearly all of this is farming.

The RMOC has experienced the same trends in the agricultural sector as the rest of Canada and the Province of Ontario. In Ontario, between the years of 1951 and 1971, agricultural employment declined from 200,000 to 130,000. In Ottawa-Carleton too the number of farms has been declining, while the number of farmers reporting off-farm work increased. The number of rural residents however has remained fairly stable and even increased: rural non-farm residents have replaced rural farm dwellers. This trend is especially pronounced around Toronto, Ottawa and Windsor.[11]

Future urban uses will not apparently take up a large percentage of the agricultural land in Ontario. The Province estimates that an extra 400 to 580 square miles will be needed to house and serve the population of Ontario when it reaches 12 million. This urban growth is estimated to take only 2$^{1}/_{2}$% of Ontario's agricultural land.

The Ministry of Agriculture and Food is developing policy recommendations for the preservation of agricultural land. For instance, municipalities will be compensated for higher servicing costs which may be incurred as development shifts to land not suitable for farming. A land use policy should be firm at the provincial level, especially for agricultural land, in order to strengthen land use controls at the municipal level.

A different question is encountered when one considers the potential profit farmers will lose by not being permitted to sell their farmland for urban development. Around the proposed Pickering Airport site, farmland was selling for five times its value as farmland, a fairly typical figure.

The Ontario Federation of Agriculture has come out strongly in favour of compensating farmers for having their land frozen in agricultural use. It is hard to agree with this principle of compensation. According to basic common law principles, people are not compensated for legitimate regulation. Urban homeowners are not compensated for being limited in their actions by residential zoning. A homeowner cannot open a commercial establishment, or

---

[9] RMOC, Planning Department, *Technical Report No. 3*, 1974.

[11] Ontario, TEIGA, *Ontario's Future: Trends and Options*, op. cit., p. 11.

build a high-rise in a low-density residential area. And there is no compensation either for "down-zoning," which is a clear loss to a property owner. As Ontario's Minister of Agriculture and Food has said, "Where would you draw the line in paying compensation to anyone in Ontario whose property drops in value?"[12]

Some people lose, some gain, whether by market forces or by government decisions such as zoning. That is the way the cookie crumbles. We do not think that the public, nor any political party in this province, is willing to siphon off the gains made by some, or compensate for losses incurred by other, brought about by zoning.

Other methods of helping farmers can be adopted. In 1975, farmers received 9.5% more for their products than in 1974. However, their expenses rose by a greater amount, so that their net incomes were 2.7% less in 1975 than the precious year.[13] For this reason, an income stabilization programme for farmers may be necessary. The Ontario Institute of Agrologists said that "The best means of combatting the loss of good land was a prosperous farming community whose members wouldn't need to sell land for security."[14]

The Ontario Federation of Agriculture proposes an Ontario Farm Income Protection Act to provide additional income to farmers when prices are low; a reasonable proposal, which could build on the present policies of the federal government (such as ARDA) and of the Province (such as the recent proposal for exemption of farm land from property tax).

The agricultural sector will probably continue to become increasingly mechanized and in need of large capital capital outlays; and farms to be a larger size in order to use modern machinery profitably. This will presumably make farming more profitable, but will reduce the number of farmers.

The Secondary Sector

The Region is included in the Windsor-Quebec "corridor" — sometimes called Canada's "Main Street" — in which 70% of Canada's manufacturing employment is located. The "corridor" has attracted industry in accordance with the old Biblical phrase of "to him that hath shall be given." The economy of Ottawa-Carleton however is not known for its strength in the manufacturing sector.[15] For a Region of more than one-half million population, Ottawa-Carleton has remarkably few industries. However, many firms which do operate from a plant in Ottawa-Carleton find their location advantageous.

In 1972, there were 297 manufacturing establishments in Ottawa-Carleton, with some 13,532 employees. Of these, 7,306 men and women were production and related workers, while 6,226 people were administrative, office, and other non-manufacturing employees.[16]

The proportion of people working in manufacturing establishments was only 6.4% of the total labour force of Ottawa-Carleton in 1971. Ottawa-Carleton's proportion is the second lowest of Ontario's 55 "regions" as listed by the Census in 1971. For comparison purposes, one may look at the percentage of manufacturing employment in other Ontario

---

[12] William Newman, "Dispelling Some Myths," *An Address to the Canadian Daily Newspaper Publishers Association*, April 21, 1976, p. 20.

[13] *Ibid.*, p. 28.

[14] *Ottawa Citizen*, January 26, 1976.

[15] M. Yeates, *Main Street*, Toronto, Macmillan, 1975, p. 26.

[16] Ontario, TEIGA, *Ontario Statistics*, Vol. 2, Toronto, 1975, pp. 659, 661.

counties and metropolitan regions: Toronto — 24.4%; Wentworth — 35.0%; Waterloo — 38.0%.[17] In Ontario, in 1974, 27% of the labour force was employed in the manufacturing sector.

In 1972, the distribution of manufacturing plants and employment by municipality was as follows:

Table 3-2

Distribution of Manufacturing Establishments and Employees, 1971

Municipality	Number of Establishments	Number of Employees
City of Ottawa	184	8,628
Nepean	50	2,774
Gloucester	24	640
Vanier	15	163
Others	24	1,327
Total RMOC	297	13,532

Source: Statistics Canada, Cat. No. 31- 209, pp. 120-125

Note: Comparable data were not available for the other municipalities in the RMOC. However, in 1973, there were nine plants in March Township, employing 1,201 workers. (Ontario, Ministry of Industry and Tourism, *Industrial Survey*, 1973.)

Employment in the manufacturing industries of Ottawa-Carleton is growing very slowly. Between 1961-66, employment in Ontario industries grew by 28.4% while in Carleton County the growth rate was only 10.6%.[18]

Until recently, only one hundred to two hundred acres of industrial land were developed yearly. This amount of new land entering the market indicates fairly slow industrial growth. Montreal and Toronto are still the two dominating industrial centres in Eastern Canada. Ottawa-Carleton is on the second level of the urban industrial hierarchy in the Montreal-centred region.[19]

To study the future growth of its industries, we must look at the Region's position in the inter-urban hierarchy and at its own population projections. As D. Michael Ray has pointed out, Eastern Ontario is in the "economic shadow" of south-western Ontario with respect to the location of American-owned branch plants in Canada.[20] The Eastern Ontario market is small. Manufacturing companies presumably choose their plant locations carefully. Most plants need to be in areas with highly developed infrastructures. Industries located in south-western Ontario benefit from a highly developed transportation network, a large skilled labour pool, and proximity to firms producing their component parts and buying their

---

[17] *Globe and Mail, Report on Business,* January 5, 1976.

[18] RMOC, Planning Department, *Technical Paper No. 2*, p. 5.

[19] Jay Siegel and Monty Woodyard, "Urban growth and the urban hierarchy," in Larry S. Bourne, et al., eds., *Urban Futures for Central Canada: perspectives on forecasting the urban growth and form*, Toronto, University of Toronto Press, 1974, p. 104.

[20] D. Michael Ray, "Urban Growth and The Concept of Functional Region," in N. H. Lithwick and Gilles Paquet, *Urban Studies: A Canadian Perspective*, Toronto, Methuen, 1968, pp. 40-91.

highly-specialized products. Frequent personal contact is important for these firms. Heavy industries are not found in Ottawa-Carleton as the Region has comparatively poor transportation facilities, no port, almost no natural resources.

Locating near raw material sources is no longer important to most manufacturing firms as the nature of industrial production has changed to the use of highly specialized, light inputs costing approximately the same in many areas. Market-orientation is now one of the most important factors in plant location.

A survey by Natalie Myhal of the Commission staff found that of the 62 manufacturing industries in the sample group, only five firms (8%) noted that they considered choosing locations other than in the Ottawa region for their plants. Seventy per cent of firms interviewed sold over two-thirds of their products in the Ottawa area. It must be concluded that the manufacturing industries of the Region were set up primarily to serve the local market (both public and private).

Industrial firms not only provide employment opportunities and necessary goods to local residents, but also enlarge the tax base, and give citizens more personal choice of occupation; they also attract new residents, convention visitors, retail stores, service industries, and other manufacturing firms. Another example of the harmful effects of a dominant single employer in the Region was the student job shortage in the summer of 1976 when federal employment was frozen. In other cities, summer jobs for students are available in private industry, but in Ottawa-Carleton, few jobs can be provided by the small industrial base.

Several submissions were received from municipalities and organizations which argued that industrial growth should be encouraged in the Region. We agree with the proposal for a moderate rate of growth. The emphasis is on "moderate," because it will throw less strain upon municipal finance and services than would a rapid growth.

An interesting point was made by the Commercial and Industrial Development Corporation of Ottawa-Carleton (CIDC) in its submission to the National Capital Commission and the Joint Parliamentary Committee on the National Capital Region (1976). The CIDC brief states that: "a Capital which depends upon the public service for the majority of its employment does not symbolize Canada as a nation, and does not reflect the ingenuity of the Canadian people."[21] In the future, Ottawa should develop into a capital-city with a diversity of life-styles and opportunities (and good restaurants). Ottawa originated as a non-government town. The RMOC must not confine itself to being only a government Region.

If the provincial policies for Eastern Ontario (mentioned earlier) contribute to the diversification of the Region, Ottawa-Carleton may have more than the 25,000 manufacturing workers at the Regional threshold population of one million as outlined in the *Official Plan*.

Manufacturing employment is likely to increase because of the particular "mix" of industries in Ottawa-Carleton. Medium and high technology firms have experienced the greatest growth trends in the recent past. Industries which benefit from contacts with universities, libraries and other centres of knowledge will very likely continue to locate in Ottawa-Carleton. Future growth in these research-oriented and light manufacturing fields (computers, electronics, etc.) should be substantial, while more traditional manufacturing stabilizes in employment. Incentives and government policies should therefore encourage light manufacturing and research-oriented firms to locate in the Region.

---

[21] CIDC, *A Brief on the National Capital Region*, February 1976, p. 5.

Industrial facilities and industrial land can presumably be expanded. The "snowball effect" of existing firms attracting new activities may very well ensure that private-sector employment will increase moderately in the future, aided by the CIDC — a non-profit organization which promotes industrial growth.

The largest number of employees in Ottawa-Carleton manufacturing plants are in the Standard Industrial Classification Categories of Electrical Products, Paper and Allied, Printing and Publishing, and Food and Beverage Industries. (See Table 3-3.) According to our classification of firms listed by the CIDC, the four major SIC classes employ 63.3% of the manufacturing labour force. The labour force for the industries located in the RMOC is drawn from the whole metropolitan area of Ottawa-Hull.

The following comments illustrate the importance of manufacturing industries to the Ottawa-Carleton economy. In 1972, the total wages paid to production and related workers in Ottawa-Carleton amounted to $53.7 million. The total paid to administrative, office and other "non-production" workers employed in the manufacturing plants of the Region was $58.8 million. The cost of materials, supplies and goods for resale was $173.9 million. The value of shipments and other revenue amounted to $346.1 million, while the value added in Ottawa-Carleton plants was $174.9 million.[22] Manufacturing firms also provide employment for local construction and service industries.

As can be seen on Table 3-3, Ottawa-Carleton firms may be found in 18 out of 20 SIC groups. Fewer than 5% of the manufacturing labour force is employed 13 out of 20 classes. The manufacturing structure of Ottawa-Carleton appears viable and diversified, in spite of the small proportion (6.4%) of the labour force which it employs.

The task of attracting industries to an area is a difficult one. Sarnia advertises its chemical industries; Oakville emphasizes its central location between Toronto and Hamilton; Cornwall stresses its transportation facilities and port. Thunder Bay points out that it is a port at the centre of a continent. The two industrial development corporations in the National Capital Region (in Ontario and Quebec) promote their areas by stressing that the federal government is located in the area. In Ottawa-Carleton, the task of industrial promotion is performed by the Commercial and Industrial Development Corporation. Its promotional literature stresses all the facilities of government, such as national research bodies and scientific libraries that are at hand for the use of firms in the area.

The CIDC was formed in 1962 to co-ordinate efforts of attracting new businesses to Greater Ottawa (City of Ottawa, the City of Vanier, the Townships of Nepean, Gloucester and March). Its programme preceded the formation of the RMOC by seven years. The founding businessmen and politicians realized that the question of the location of industries was a Regional concern. This is certainly a wise policy, inhibiting as it does a wasteful competition for industry among the area municipalities.

The CIDC brief to the Joint Parliamentary Committee on the National Capital Region criticized the NCC's publication, *Tomorrow's Capital: An Invitation to Dialogue*. The brief went on to say:

> "As a result of this presentation, the CIDC was concerned that the NCC has completely ignored the commercial and industrial requirement of the area as well as the people in the Region who depend for their livelihood on the well-being of the private sector."[23]

---

[22] Ontario, TEIGA, *Ontario Statistics*, Vol. 2, op. cit., pp. 659-661.

[23] CIDC, *Brief On The National Capital Region*, February, 1976, p. 1.

Table 3-3

The Industrial Structure of Ottawa-Carleton, 1973

	Number of Firms	Number of Employees	Per Cent of employees as proportion of Total Manufacturing Labour Force
1. Food & Beverage Industries	35	1,954	11.5
2. Tobacco Products Industries	—	—	0
3. Rubber & Plastics Products Industries	3	20	.1
4. Leather Industries	1	169	1.0
5. Textile Industries	9	110	.6
6. Knitting Mills	—	—	0
7. Clothing Industries	8	245	1.4
8. Wood Industries	7	550	3.2
9. Furniture & Fixture Industries	25	162	1.0
10. Paper & Allied Industries	6	2,824	16.6
11. Printing, Publishing & Allied Industries	47	2,753	16.2
12. Primary Metal Industries	8	199	1.2
13. Metal Fabricating Industries	37	1,232	7.3
14. Machinery Industries	8	399	2.4
15. Transportation Equipment Industries	7	229	1.3
16. Electrical Product Industries	19	3,277	19.3
17. Non-Metallic Mineral Products Industries	21	1,255	7.4
18. Petroleum & Coal Products Industries	3	106	.6
19. Chemical & Chemical Products Industries	18	1,120	6.6
20. Miscellaneous Manufacturing Industries	31	370	2.2
Total	293	16,974	100.0

Note: Firms as listed by the CIDC, and classified by Commission staff.

It went on to say that the NCC and the federal government own 40% of the industrial land within the Greenbelt. The NCC will only lease, not sell, land to industry. Few firms wish to invest large amounts of capital in plant and equipment on leased land. For this reason, some firms decide not to locate in Ottawa-Carleton. The NCC also withholds land from development, thus raising prices on remaining privately-owned land.[24] These are serious charges against the NCC, and we are not satisfied that they are wholly valid, although we agree that the concept of the Greenbelt should be revised. (See Chapter 4).

The CIDC has made similar charges against the RMOC. It argued that the long process of drafting and approving the *Official Plan* of the RMOC created difficulties for industries wishing to locate in the area. Again, the validity of this charge may be called in question.

There are both municipal and privately owned industrial parks. The City of Ottawa, Gloucester Township, Nepean Township and March Township have provided industrial parks which have almost complete occupancy or are completely sold out. Two fully serviced industrial parks recently opened in the east end of Ottawa. An industrial park of 110 acres in Goulbourn Township is scheduled for completion in 1976 and a 400-acre industrial park will soon open in March Township. These industrial parks will make possible employment opportunities (and taxes) for the large population growths expected. Industrial development is also planned for the Southern growth area.

There are fourteen industrial parks in the RMOC. The Planning Department of the RMOC pointed out that there were 10,250 acres of land designated for industrial uses in Draft and Approved Official Plans of area municipalities.[25] The RMOC *Official Plan* shows 7,000 acres of land zoned for industry on its Schedule "B". In 1971, 1,800 acres of land in the RMOC were actually used by industries for their operations.[26]

Other land may be zoned for industry in the Southeast, Southwest and South Gloucester by amendment to the *Official Plan*. This will become necessary if a new city is created in the southern part of the Region. The proposed ratio of industrial land to population in growth areas is 270 acres for every 25,000 people.[27] We recommend that plans for new urban centres provide employment opportunities in light manufacturing and research fields. In this way, new centres will not become merely dormitory towns.

We have hinted earlier that we expect manufacturing employment to reach more that the number planned for in the *Official Plan*. Even so, sufficient land appears to be available for industrial uses. There will be no long-term shortage of industrial land in the RMOC. The problem — if there is a problem — is one of the short term. We recommend to the RMOC and the area municipalities that they ensure that industrial land is serviced and made available as quickly as possible.

Incentives

Although natural market forces will attract many firms to the Ottawa-Carleton Region, federal and provincial incentives can perhaps increase this number.

The Ontario Business Incentives Programme gives Eastern Ontario an advantage over southwestern and central Ontario in attracting industry. Under this programme the Province provides long-term, low and no-interest loans up to one million dollars to manufacturing, service, and tourist industries. The programme in the RMOC is administered by the Eastern Ontario Development Corporation. We recommend to the Province of Ontario that it continue its valuable programme of assistance to local industry through the Eastern Ontario

---

[24] *Ibid.*, p. 8.

[25] RMOC Planning Department, *Industrial Land*, undated, p. 2.

[26] RMOC, *Official Plan*, op. cit., p. 2-42.

[27] RMOC Planning Department, *Industrial Land*, Technical Report No. 10, n.d., p. 19.

Development Corporation. Any means that can shift growth away from the Toronto centred megalopolis is surely welcome.

Other programmes in operation are loans to small businesses, loans for pollution-control equipment, and for venture capital. Industries locating in the Region also have access to financing provided by the Export Development Corporation, and to many Research and Development programmes of the federal government.

The Construction Industry

The construction sector, a part of the secondary industries, builds for residential, industrial, commercial and institutional purposes. In 1971, 13,000 employees worked in the construction sector. In the recent past, this sector has not changed substantially in its techniques or in building materials used. In the future however we may expect that as labour costs increase, more housing will be produced in factories; and as fuel costs rise so will the quality of insulation, and perhaps new forms of housing, incorporating, say, solar heating. Output in the construction industry is expected to double in Ontario by the year 2001 without a significant increase in employment.[28]

The Tertiary Sector

Tertiary jobs are concentrated in urban areas. They include jobs in transportation, utilities, wholesale and retail trade, finance, insurance, real estate, public administration and defence and service industries. In Ontario the service industry employs the greatest number of people as shown in the Table below:

Table 3-4

Labour Force by Industry, Ontario 1966-1974 (000's)

	1966	1969	1974
All Industries	2,719	3,032	3,671
Primary	194	189	178
Manufacturing	845	889	990
Construction	184	198	246
Transportation & Other Utilities	198	228	266
Trade	422	484	606
Service (including finance)	866	1,030	1,367
Never worked	8	14	17

Source: Ontario, TEIGA, Ontario Statistics, Vol. 2, Table 10.9

During the twentieth century, the greatest increase in employment in Canada has occurred in the tertiary sector. This indeed is a characteristic of all industrialized countries. The pattern in Ontario is similar to that of Canada as a whole; however, Ontario statistics show a slightly greater concentration in service and manufacturing industries as the Province

---

[28] John N. H. Britton and Gerald M. Barber, ''Forecasting the regional economy of Ontario,'' in Larry S. Bourne et al., eds., *Urban Futures for Central Canada: Perspectives on forecasting urban form and growth*, Toronto, University of Toronto Press, 1974, p. 172.

becomes more urbanized. In 1951, about 45 per cent of the labour force in Ontario was engaged in providing services. In 1971, the proportion of the labour force in service groups had risen to 57%.[29] In Canada, the greatest recent increases occurred in the service occupations, and, in the future, these will provide most of the new jobs. By the year 2001, 74% of employment is expected to be in the tertiary sector.[30] The Ontario projections are not radically different.

In 1961, the proportion of Eastern Ontario's labour force employed in the service sector was almost double that of any other of the ten economic "regions" in Ontario.[31] In Ottawa-Carleton the proportion of workers employed in the tertiary sector is higher than in the Province of Ontario as a whole for the simple reason that federal government employment is counted in this category.

The tertiary sector is likely to grow quickly in Ottawa-Carleton as in other Regions because of several factors. As incomes rise, the demand for services becomes greater. People make use of restaurants, entertainment and other services to a greater extent. A large part of discretionary income is spent on personal services and luxury goods. The tertiary sector is labour-intensive, in which productivity gains are low.

The following table illustrates the number of workers employed in the tertiary sector in the RMOC in 1971 and the number expected at the threshold population of one million.

Table 3-5
Employment in the Tertiary Sector, RMOC

	1971	Threshold
Transportation, Utilities & Communications	13,200	30,000
Trade	27,400	65,000
Finance, Insurance & Real Estate	10,000	30,000
Other Service (including government)	118,300	273,000

Source: RMOC, *Official Plan*, p. 2-34.

By the time the Region reaches a population of one million, it is estimated that the tertiary sector will provide approximately 88% of all jobs.

Retailing

In 1972, there were 599 shopping centres in Canada accounting for $5.5 billion in annual sales. Since the 1950's, many downtown department stores have opened stores in the suburbs of the RMOC to be near the middle and higher income groups which have moved there. The personal disposable income of residents in the area is 27% above the national average. The Region's economy is stable, and in such an environment retail stores prosper. In 1974, retail sales had grown to $1,147.1 million in Ottawa-Carleton, an increase of 16.8% in one year.[32]

---

[29] Ontario, TEIGA, *Ontario's Future: Trends and Options*, op. cit., p. 13.
[30] Britton and Barber, op. cit., p. 164.
[31] *Ibid.*, p. 169.
[32] CIDC, *Enterprise Ottawa-Carleton,* April 1975.

Ottawa-Carleton has become one of North America's most dynamic retail centres (though not necessarily the best). The square footage of department stores in Ottawa-Carleton is one of the highest in Canada at 4.48 square feet per capita as compared to 4.16 square feet per capita in Vancouver, 3.06 square feet per capita in Toronto and 2.63 square feet per capita in Montreal. Forty-one department stores serve the region.[33]

Planners have recently been concentrating more heavily on the downtown cores of cities. The Rideau Centre Plan is intended to revitalize the Rideau Street area of the City of Ottawa (east of the Canal). It is a joint project; the NCC and the Department of Public Works are the leaders, with other participants being the City of Ottawa, the Regional Municipality, the Rideau Centre Corporation (which represents the business and property owners); and private citizens, who became represented in the planning stage later by the Rideau Centre Public Advisory Committee.

The NCC is planning to develop the Rideau Street area in Ottawa in the next few years. Some federal office space is planned for the area in addition to commercial and hotel development. The area is to employ 15,000 to 20,000 people in federal jobs by the year 2000. This will reduce the pressure on transportation systems in the area south of Wellington Street. We agree with this proposed city development by the NCC, since commercial functions as well as federal employment should both be found in the core area. There is room however for the NCC to engage in more consultation in the planning process, and perhaps also for more housing in the plan.

Convention Business and Tourism

In 1975, Ottawa had the third highest number of conventions in Canada after Montreal and Toronto. That year about 290 conventions were held in Ottawa. The City of Hull meanwhile is planning a convention centre with 60,000 to 80,000 square feet for exhibits and meetings and banquet facilities for 2,500 to 3,500 people.[34] Ottawa businessmen are worried that Ottawa will not be able to compete with the specially designed centre in Hull.

We believe however that Ottawa will benefit from the conventions which are held in Hull. The Civic Centre located in Ottawa will be able to continue to provide adequate facilities for most large conventions. The cost of building a new centre in Ottawa has been estimated at $10 million by the past president of Canada's Capital Visitors and Convention Bureau. We are doubtful that the Region can afford this amount of money on a new convention centre at this time. We believe other priorities have a higher rank in these times of restraint. And we all know that part of "Murphy's Law" which says "everything will cost more than you think." (Perhaps this should now be re-named Mr. Drapeau's Law.)

In 1975, tourism was a $120-million industry in Ottawa-Carleton.[35] There have been many reports that tourists have difficulty in finding tourist information. Accordingly we recommend that more tourist information centres be established especially at all main entry points into the Region — on highways, and at the airport, train and bus terminals, and that information offices in the centre be better sign-posted.

---

[33] CIDC, *Enterprise Ottawa-Carleton,* July 1975.

[34] *Ottawa Citizen*, May 26, 1976.

[35] *Ibid.*

Quarternary Industry

Quarternary industry thrives in Ottawa-Carleton because the Region is the site of the federal government, two universities and Algonquin community college with its many campuses. Small firms benefit from management services provided sometimes by students in business courses. The head offices of many national organizations locate in Ottawa-Carleton to be in close proximity to federal departments and Parliament.

Canadians are traditionally somewhat suspicious of "lobbying." They regard it as the Victorians regarded sex — something necessary but not quite nice, and certainly not to be enjoyed by ladies. Yet "lobbying" — which can take many forms — is among the chief reasons why national organizations set up headquarters in Ottawa-Carleton. And they are perfectly right in doing so. If we knew of a way of encouraging more to do so, we would recommend it. But we don't, so we won't. (There is, however, a case for the federal registration of lobbyists in the Region.)

Government departments buy computer services from many firms in the Region. Canada ranks among the world leaders in air photography, remote sensing and mapping. Survey aircraft firms clustered around the Ottawa International Airport are said to carry out 40% of the air survey work performed in countries outside the communist parts of the world.[36] These firms obtain contracts from the United Nations, CIDA and directly from foreign countries. The major increase in employment in the future of Ontario will probably be in business, financial, social and government services.

Location of Employment

At the threshold population of one million, the employment in the non-federal sector is expected to be 341,000. The location of these jobs is of prime importance to the structure of the RMOC. The distribution proposed by the RMOC is as follows (Table 3-6):

Table 3-6
Employment Distribution in the RMOC

	1971 Number	%	Threshold Number	%
Greater Central Area	92,000	46.5	147,000	32.7
Elsewhere within the Greenbelt	99,000	50.0	211,000	46.9
Urban "Communities" outside the Greenbelt	<1,000		83,000	18.4
Rural	7,000	3.5	9,000	2.0
TOTAL	198,000	100.0	450,000	100.0

Source: RMOC, *Official Plan*, 1974, p. 2-37.

The NCC and the RMOC differ in their proposals as to the distribution of jobs between the central core which is in the City of Ottawa, and the suburban and rural portion of the RMOC. The NCC's *Tomorrow's Capital* proposes that the Ottawa-Hull area be of a compact

---

[36] CIDC, *Enterprise Ottawa-Carleton*, June 1975, p. 1.

form. On the Ontario side, the NCC wants a strong, "balanced" core spread over both sides of the Rideau Canal. It believes the area south of Wellington Street has been overbuilt. The west central area of the City of Ottawa is well developed with the Sparks Street Mall, new hotels, office buildings and federal employment. The NCC wishes to maintain a balance between the three major nodes of the Ottawa-Hull core — Rideau Street, the area south of Wellington Street, and the Hull Island (bounded by the Gatineau and Ottawa rivers, and Brewery Creek.)

The RMOC *Official Plan* endorses also the importance of a strong shopping area in the central core. Regional Council realizes that the proportion of total retail sales made in the shops in the centre of the city is declining.

Finally, the difference between the NCC plan and that of the RMOC is, in effect, one of timing, degree, and geographic emphasis. At the moment, the RMOC Plan is going ahead faster, as we think it should, with the Carlsbad Springs area in lower priority.

CHAPTER 4

Planning in Ottawa-Carleton
or
Can't I do what I like with my own?

"The best laid schemes o'mice and men.
Gang aft a-gley."
Robert Burns.

Planning is somewhat different from other municipal functions, in that it delivers no services that people can see, such as roads or parks or social welfare. Among some sections of the public, planning appears still as merely restrictive. They say, can't I do what I like with my own property? The answer, of course, is "no," or we should have chaos. Would you like a pig farm next door? Or haphazard and more costly growth? Or pollution of land, water and air? Is there no public good which must sometimes over-rule private interests?

Like so much on the municipal scene, planning was initiated by Father (the Province). The need for municipal planning was timidly recognized in early statutes, but for good and all, in The Planning Act of 1946, with its amendments. A huge backlog of projects — for roads, water supply, sewage disposal, housing, etc., — had accumulated from the war and depression years, and all of it required planning. The Planning Act is now being reviewed by a special provincial committee. The Act has served well in its day, but "New occasions teach new duties; Time makes ancient good uncouth."

By a judicious use of the carrot — in the form of field workers and grants — the Province has cajoled and persuaded municipalities to take on the planning function. The stick can be wielded too, by such means as withholding provincial approval for severances, sub-divisions, etc. The result is that planning now has municipal support, and is widely accepted. Evidence of this is the larger planning staffs, and larger expenditure on planning. (See Table 4-1) (In ensuring municipal acceptance of planning, urban renewal, and city design, one should also salute the efforts of the Community Planning Association of Canada, largely initiated by men such as Humphrey Carver, who worked tirelessly under the aegis of CMHC and The National Housing Act.)[1]

The Planning Act deals with the creation of planning areas and boards; with official plans and the methods of carrying them out, such as land acquisition, subdivision control, zoning by-laws, maintenance and occupancy by-laws, demolition control, and urban renewal legislation. Plan-making is mandatory for the RMOC and its constituent area municipalities.

---

[1] See, for example, the pleasant and urbane account in Humphrey Carver's *Compassionate Landscape*, University of Toronto Press, 1975.

Table 4-1

Planning Expenditures, RMOC and Area Municipalities, 1974-1975

Municipality	Population 1974	Population 1975	Expenditure on Planning & Zoning ($) 1974	Expenditure on Planning & Zoning ($) 1975	Per Capita Expenditure ($) 1974	Per Capita Expenditure ($) 1975
RMOC	489,879	506,606	838,506	1,155,683	1.71	2.28
Ottawa	295,530	302,124	932,259	1,439,188	3.15	4.76
Vanier	20,523	20,146	66,646	129,137	3.25	6.41
Rockcliffe Park	2,166	2,229	1,799	5,184	0.83	2.02
Cumberland	11,384	11,458	3,855	36,125	0.34	3.15
Gloucester	48,489	53,322	356,289	460,095	7.35	8.63
Goulbourn	10,775	12,489	23,030	45,192	2.14	3.62
March	6,537	6,910	28,092	42,189	4.30	6.10
Nepean	71,482	74,000	153,311	247,389	2.14	3.34
Osgoode	8,230	8,286	21,063	49,743	2.56	6.00
Rideau	7,307	7,860	20,420	7,790	2.79	0.99
West Carleton	7,393	7,782	—	18,101	—	2.33
Total Region			2,445,270	3,635,816	4.99	7.18

Source: Financial Reports, 1974 and 1975, for RMOC and area municipalities

One may state the objectives of planning in broad terms. Expressed in this way, they "cover the waterfront." In the jargon of planners, planning ensures ". . . development that takes place in the planning area should meet needs arising from population, social, economic and technological trends in a manner that protects cultural, visual and ecological qualities of the environment."[2]

This mouthful of general aims must be spelled out in more specific terms, and that is what official plans do, with the zoning by-laws that accompany them.

The Official Plan

An official plan is defined as:

. . . a programme and policy, or any part thereof, covering a planning area or any part thereof, designed to secure the health, safety, convenience or welfare of the inhabitants of the area, and consisting of the texts and maps, describing such programme and policy, approved by the Minister (of Housing) from time to time as provided in this Act.[3]

No by-law may be passed and no municipal work carried out if it conflicts with an official plan.

---

[2] RMOC, *Official Plan*, 1974, p. 1-1.
[3] *The Planning Act*, S. 12.

As provided in The Ottawa-Carleton Act, the Regional Council is the planning board for the Region. It began the planning process early, publishing the first Proposals in mid-1972, the Draft Plan in the following year, and the Official Plan was finally passed by Council in October, 1974. There was a large amount of consultation and public participation, which filled many volumes with comments and reaction. In most of the local municipalities the Council is the Planning Board (in the City of Ottawa it is the Board of Control), and a few have the older type of Planning Board (some councillors plus some citizens not on Council). Any local official plans within the RMOC, and existing restricted area by-laws, must be amended to conform with the Regional Official Plan once it has received provincial approval.

Before gaining full legal status, an official plan must be approved by the Ministry of Housing, the Ministry of Treasury, Economics and Intergovernmental Affairs (TEIGA), and many other provincial ministries and agencies who have an interest in selected parts of the plan. Provincial approval of official plans is required to ensure that developments at the Regional and local levels conform to provincial policies.

If an objection to any part of the Plan (by municipalities or interested residents) is lodged with the Minister of Housing he can refer the matter to the Ontario Municipal Board (OMB) for a public hearing and a decision.[4] The only appeal beyond the OMB is to the provincial cabinet. Without the OMB and provincial policy on planning, it is likely that many Ontario municipalities would be in a sorry mess.

Several area municipalities (Ottawa, Vanier, Goulbourn, March, Osgoode) have their official plans already approved by the Ministry; others are partly approved (Gloucester, West Carleton); Nepean's is awaiting approval; and two others are drafted and/or are in preparation (Cumberland, Rideau).

The Province has already delegated some responsibilities for planning to Regional Council. This devolution is indeed one of the purposes in setting up the regional municipalities. The RMOC now has planning control in that it may: (1) approve plans of subdivision (delegated June 1975); (2) comment to the OMB on restricted area by-laws passed by the local municipalities (delegated September 1974); and (3) monitor severances granted by its own Land Division Committee and Committees of Adjustment, and Committees of Adjustment in any area municipality (delegated August 1974). After the Regional Official Plan has been approved by the Province, the RMOC will have the authority to approve the official plans and amendments of the area municipalities.

Because at present an official plan and amendments must be approved by many branches of the provincial government, and usually the OMB is also involved, long delays may, and do, occur. In these times of inflation and rising land costs, such delays are particularly unfortunate, by adding so much to the costs of the development.

Full approval, especially that from the Province, may take two or three years or more. The RMOC Official Plan (1974), now at the OMB stage, is a case in point. Surely, the development approval process can be arranged to take a shorter time. Montaigne remarked that his mother had carried him for a period of eleven months. This may not be true (it could only have been heresay evidence). But the gestation period — up to more than three years — is too long before the official plan of a municipality is finally delivered. This is even longer than the gestation period for elephants. If full citizen participation is allowed in plan-making

---

[4] The OMB has other duties too, the chief being the approval of municipal borrowing.

— which is now common, with numerous public hearings on draft plans — this too adds to the delay.

The population of the Region is growing at approximately 12,000 persons per year according to the Official Plan. To accommodate future population a policy of "satellite city" development has been adopted by Regional Council. Population distribution within the RMOC at the threshold population of one million people is planned as follows (in approximate figures): 630,000 persons within the inner limit of the Greenbelt (not all in the City of Ottawa); 285,000 persons in three "satellite cities"; and 100,000 persons in present "rural" areas, in villages and on large country lots. The so-called "satellites" are so close to the City of Ottawa, however, that they may more correctly be called "suburbs."

A policy of developing three, more or less self-contained, urban centres in the RMOC outside the Greenbelt is seen as fulfilling several objectives. *First*, a reduced volume of commuting to points within the Greenbelt should occur. *Second*, the existing Greenbelt, which provides public open space for the residents of the Region, will be preserved. *Third*, "satellite city" development provides the opportunity to plan them well. For instance, integrated housing types and a variety of dwelling densities (generally thought desirable) can be carried out. *Fourth*, urban sprawl can be to some extent avoided, thus reducing the costs of future urban growth while at the same time keeping damage to the natural environment to a minimum.

Through zoning by-laws, industries can be encouraged to locate in designated areas outside the Greenbelt. The extension of sewage and water systems, and public transit, required to serve the satellite cities can be phased carefully to match future growth. The federal government, by means of employment decentralization in the Region, can also play a part in the achievement of the planning objectives.

The Regional Council, of course, recognizes these factors and the Official Plan takes notice of them. General guidelines are set out for the co-ordination of a variety of facilities, including future public transit and roads, schools, health centres, libraries, parks and social services. The preservation of historical and environmental values is also borne in mind. For example, the Official Plan for the RMOC has designated "river corridors" along the Rideau and Ottawa Rivers, in which development will be strictly limited. (This is rather late in the day; much of the Rideau is built up and resembles a highway strip development). Other ecologically sensitive areas, such as part of Mer Bleue in Gloucester Township, are protected through zoning by-laws which designate these for nature study, wildlife, and recreation. (Part of Mer Blue is in the Greenbelt, owned by the NCC).

Within the broad confines of the Regional Plan, much latitude exists for the area municipalities to determine the nature of their growth. This includes such matters as housing mix, residential density, dedication to public use of some land in new developments by builder-developers (to a minimum of 5% of the land area), and the amount of the levies imposed by area municipalities on lots for building.

The "Satellites"

Three locations have been chosen to accommodate future urban growth in the RMOC. (1) The existing Kanata–Glen Cairn–Bridlewood development is expected to house approximately 100,000 people by the year 2000. This area is referred to as the "Western Urban Community" in the Official Plan. It straddles the boundaries of three Townships — March, Nepean and Goulbourn.

(2) The Orleans-Queenswood area — the "Eastern Urban Community" — is projected to grow to approximately 35,000 people, although the total population may reach 50,000 people if suitable transportation is provided.

(3) The "South Urban Community" is expected to reach a total population of approximately 135,000 people. Of this total, 100,000 people will be located in South Nepean, including Barrhaven, with the remainder to be in South Gloucester.[5] The Rideau River divides this southerly development.

Much controversy has arisen over the location of these satellite cities. This is particularly the case with regard to the "South Urban Community". Several points have arisen in the controversy: (a) The NCC has developed a conflicting plan wherein a compact satellite city is planned for the south-east, near Carlsbad Springs, rather than to the south. (b) The capability of the NCC proposed site to support buildings, is in doubt. This is because of soil conditions in the south-east, on the building potential of which the experts disagree. (c) Environmental considerations for the protection of prime agricultural land and the Rideau and Jock Rivers have come to the fore. (d) The federal NCC, and the provincial government through the Ontario Housing Corporation (OHC), have "land-banked" a total of 9,000 acres of land in the Carlsbad Springs area. Of this total, 4,000 acres are owned by the NCC and 5,000 acres by the OHC.

The NCC feels that growth in the south-east on low quality land would help preserve Class 1 and 2 farmland in south Nepean and south Gloucester. The boundaries of the "South Urban Community" however coincide almost exactly with the boundaries of Class 1 and 2 soils.

The distribution of soil types in Nepean and Gloucester Townships as found in the RMOC Official Plan, differs slightly from that shown on our map.[6] (See Figure 4-1). In making the RMOC Official Plan, the only soil data was several decades old. The Soil Research Institute of Agriculture Canada conducted a new soil survey during 1974-75.[7] The detail of study is much finer and more precise than previous surveys. The results show that a "southern satellite city" will consume several thousand acres of prime agricultural land.

This raises several problems. The Region has little agriculture. (See Chapter 3). There is considerable variation in land quality throughout the Region, and some of it is good for farming. In Nepean Township south of the Greenbelt, Class 1 and 2 land forms 61% of the land area. In Gloucester south of the Greenbelt, only 29% of the land area is made up of Class 1 and 2 soils. (See Figure 4-2). Regional Council has stated that the protection of agricultural resources forms one of its policy objectives.[8]

In light of the newer soil surveys, it is possible that the RMOC may like to modify its plan regarding the "South Urban Community." At present, the "satellites" to the west and east are designated for immediate development. This is also the case for Barrhaven in south Nepean which is projected to grow to approximately 65,000 people.[9] The remainder of the "South Urban Community" is not expected to begin developing until 1980.

If the RMOC reaches a population of only 811,000 people rather than one million, the

---

[5] RMOC, *Official Plan*, p. 2-11.

[6] See also RMOC, op. cit., Map 28.

[7] Interview with Dr. Julian Dumanski, Soil Research Institute, June 1976.

[8] RMOC, op. cit., p. 5-3.

[9] Nepean, *Official Plan*, 1975, p. 14.

37

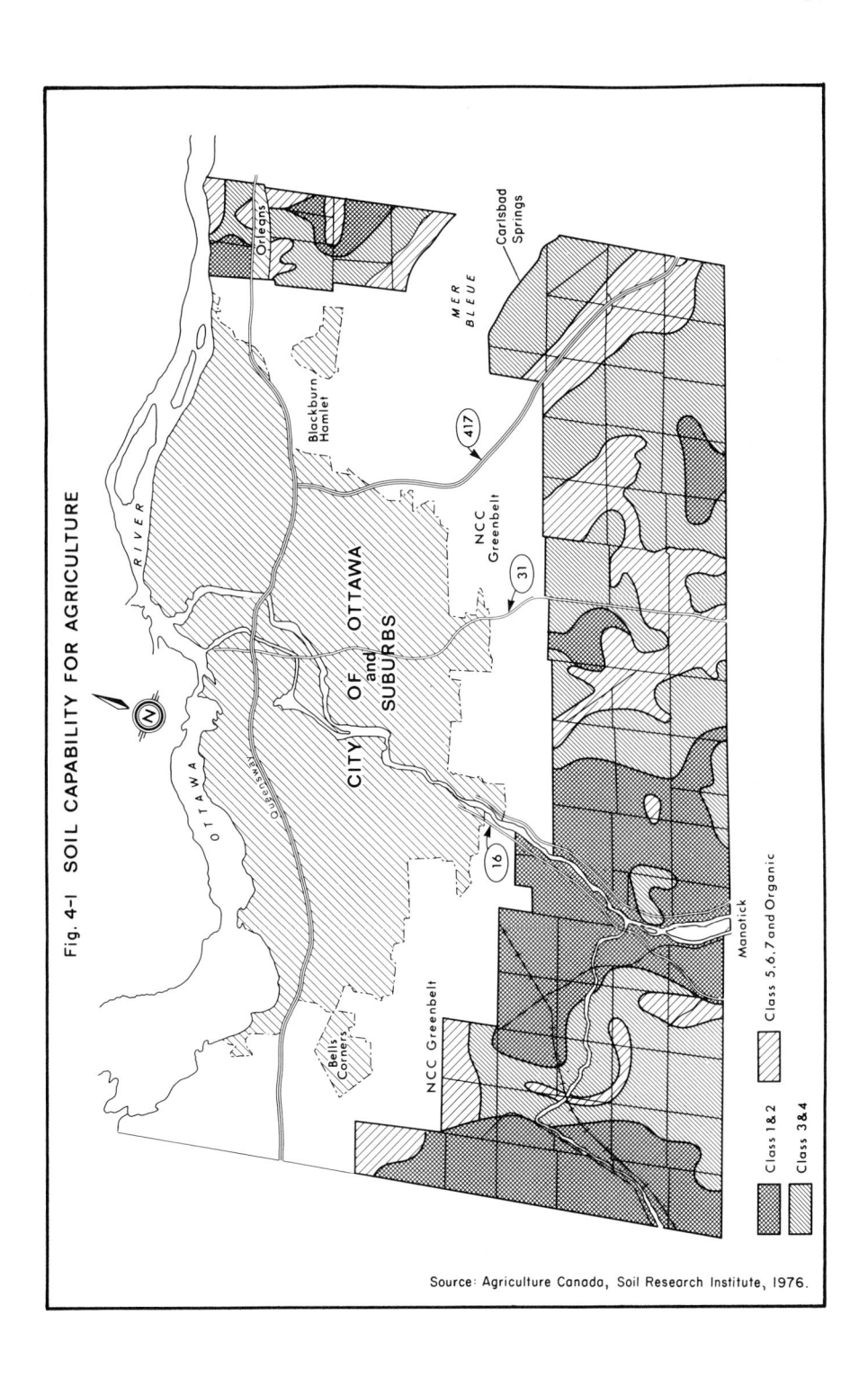

Fig. 4-1 SOIL CAPABILITY FOR AGRICULTURE

Class 1 & 2
Class 3 & 4
Class 5, 6, 7 and Organic

Source: Agriculture Canada, Soil Research Institute, 1976.

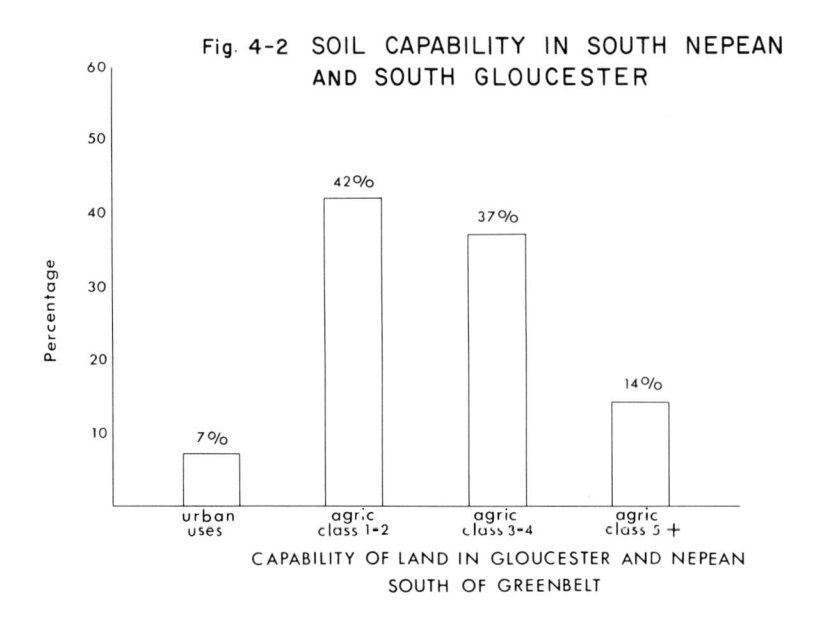

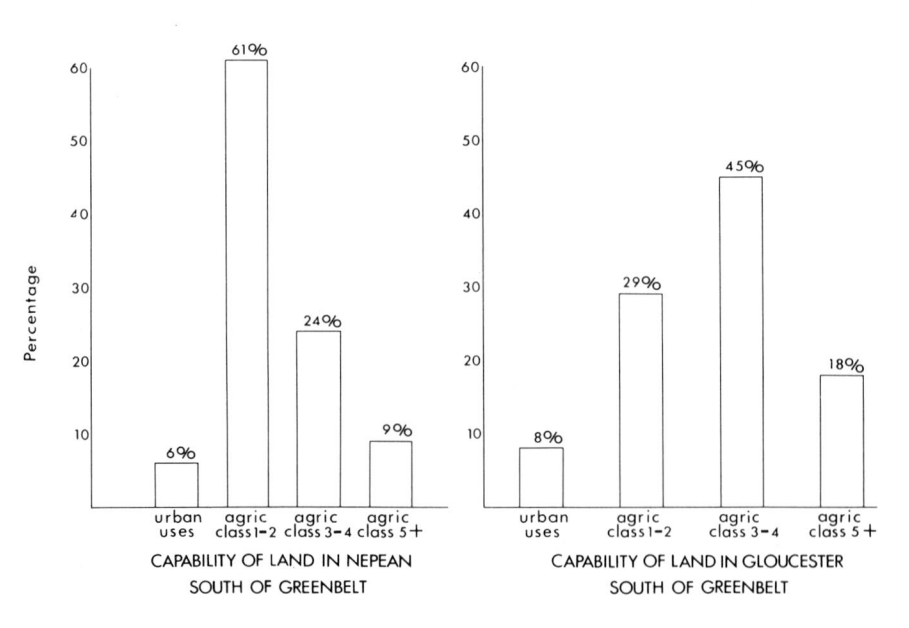

Fig. 4-2 SOIL CAPABILITY IN SOUTH NEPEAN AND SOUTH GLOUCESTER

CAPABILITY OF LAND IN GLOUCESTER AND NEPEAN SOUTH OF GREENBELT

- urban uses: 7%
- agric class 1-2: 42%
- agric class 3-4: 37%
- agric class 5+: 14%

CAPABILITY OF LAND IN NEPEAN SOUTH OF GREENBELT

- urban uses: 6%
- agric class 1-2: 61%
- agric class 3-4: 24%
- agric class 5+: 9%

CAPABILITY OF LAND IN GLOUCESTER SOUTH OF GREENBELT

- urban uses: 8%
- agric class 1-2: 29%
- agric class 3-4: 45%
- agric class 5+: 18%

Source: Agriculture Canada, Soil Research Institute, 1976.

remainder of the "South Urban Community" will not be needed by the year 2000. There is thus something of a case for protecting parts of Nepean and Gloucester as farm land. On the other hand, who could afford to farm such expensive land as that in south Nepean and Gloucester? And the utility lines and roads are easily laid to it. The land in question could, of course, be "down zoned" to agriculture. There is no legal or moral right, so far as we can see, to guarantee a profit to large developers or speculators. But there would be a lot of political pressure against such "down zoning," and the screams of anguish would be long and loud. To paraphrase Machiavelli slightly, men will forgive more easily the death of their father than the loss of their property.

Some concern has been expressed that the southern "satellites" could cause harm to the Rideau and Jock Rivers. The RMOC Official Plan recognizes the sensitivity to pollution of these river corridors, and so does the Nepean Plan. Only the following activities will be allowed on those parts of the river banks that remain undeveloped: farming, excluding farm housing; open air recreation; forestry; and those activities that will assist in conserving or managing water supplies, wildlife or other natural characteristics. These restrictions are aimed also at retaining the shorelines for public use.[10] No waste will be released into the Rideau or Jock Rivers, and only treated waste will be released into the Ottawa River.

The area in south Gloucester to be included in the "South Urban Community" is not far from the Ottawa International Airport. Some noise problems could result from this. The plan for the new "community should be flexible enough, to permit the future development of airport-related uses such as warehouses, hotels and other commercial facilities in the vicinity of the airport". The development of such uses will be subject to the "Compatible Land Use Table" prepared by the Canadian Air Transport Administration.[11]

The major criticism of the Carlsbad Springs site has been that the soil-types in the area will present structural problems in the construction phase and in later years. The area is made up primarily of Leda clay, which is high in water-content. (Some of the existing built-up area of the RMOC is already on this clay, but this took place before the dangers and/or disadvantages of the Leda clay were fully realized).

A consulting firm hired by the NCC and the OHC concluded that the Carlsbad Springs area could accommodate a range of structures normally required for the size of the urban area proposed, providing that these are located in the parts of the site capable of carrying the corresponding structure loads.[12] For some of these structures, foundation sizes would have to be wider or larger than those normally required. Construction costs will increase accordingly. Other protective measures will be needed, for example, retention ponds for storm water flow, to prevent erosion. There would be the risk of repeating in this Region the awful disaster that struck St. Jean de Vianney in Quebec in 1971.

Special controls and design methods will also be required to minimize "dewatering" of the clays to prevent the settling of buildings, with its accompanying damage. Extra sanitary and storm sewer services, foundation waterproofing, special road construction, piles for buildings, procedures for disposal of excavated Leda clay and extra pumping stations will also be required.

A similar report was prepared for the Council of the Township of Gloucester by J. L.

---

[10] RMOC, op. cit., and the Nepean *Official Plan*, 1975.

[11] RMOC, *South Urban Community Background Report*, June 1976, p. 35.

[12] DeLeuw Cather, *Final report — Preliminary Engineering Investigation Summary*, March 1975, p. 6.

Richards and Associates Limited (1976) which took into account finances as well as geology. They concluded that the ". . . additional costs of development for South East City as compared to a "normal" site, together with trunk service costs, will lie in the range of $200,000,000 to $300,000,000".[13] The characteristics of a "normal" site were not defined, but it is presumably one with no major soil complications for construction, etc.

These two reports, in spite of some apparent disagreement, do indicate that a site with less sensitive soils would be more economical in terms of construction costs. The southern "satellite," for example, presents fewer problems, and so does the growth to the west.

With regard to land costs, the land-banking near Carlsbad Springs is already done. This land was bought partly on the open market and partly by expropriation, before the present inflated prices. In south Nepean and south Gloucester, the bulk of the land is owned by private developers, which may mean that the final cost of homes and commercial and industrial sites will be higher than if the governments were selling or leasing their sites on a non-profit basis. At any rate, such is the theory, but if put into practice, problems arise. (See below.)

This Region is unique in that two planning bodies — the RMOC and the NCC — are active in the Region. Senior levels of government cannot be controlled by municipalities. In this case, the NCC and the Ontario Housing Corporation (with CMHC help) undertook a land-bank scheme. It is possible perhaps to look upon the conflict between the two Plans, as one of timing and emphasis, thus reconciling the irreconcilable.

Public Land-Banking

The basic idea of public land-banking is that land can be bought more cheaply in advance, by governments, before prices have been inflated by proposed urbanization (say by an Official Plan, or by zoning). Three advantages are associated with such a programme.

First, land costs are lower, whether the land is bought on the market or expropriated. The carrying charges associated with holding land are also lower for public bodies since they can borrow money at lower rates of interest.[14]

Second, public land-banking makes planning easier since governments can actually control the location, design, sequence and speed of development. Examples of government involvement in urban growth exist in this Region.

The LeBreton Flats area in Ottawa has been held idle by the NCC since 1962 when it was expropriated. In the first phase it is being planned by a team representing the NCC, the CMHC, the RMOC, the City of Ottawa, the Department of Public Works, and citizens' groups. The project is intended as an example of intergovernment and citizen co-operation (after some pressure by municipalities and citizens). The population of the area is expected to reach 8,850.[15] Phase IV, Site Improvements and Construction, is scheduled to take place in 1977-78.

The LeBreton Flats project forms a portion of the National Capital Core Area Plan, prepared by the NCC in 1971. One of the general goals identified in the plan is ". . . to create

---

[13] J. L. Richards & Associates Limited, *A Preliminary Assessment of Special Development Costs for the Proposed 'South East City' Development*, May 1976, p. 9.

[14] Bureau of Municipal Research, "Land-Banking: Investment in the Future", *Civic Affairs*, Toronto, 1973, No. 1.

[15] NCC and CMHC, *LeBreton Flats: Phase 1, Pre-Planning*, 1976.

in the heart of the National Capital an urban environment of exemplary quality — a model for urban development in Canada."[16] Medium-to high density dwellings, with commercial and recreational facilities are planned. The future population of LeBreton Flats is to represent a cross-section of socio-economic groups in a variety of housing types.

Progress has been slow (15 years!) and several disputes have yet to be resolved. Although agreement has been reached (recently) on the need for public housing and citizen participation, further studies are required regarding the social mix and the amount of commercial building. The major planning issue seems to be transportation in the area. (This is discussed again in Chapter 5.)

The development of LeBreton Flats has been divided into four phases, of which the "Pre-Planning" stage with citizens and municipalities is completed. The stage (or stages) concerned with the actual housing design, transit and other infrastructures is still to come. Whether the project for LeBreton Flats can be a "model" development for other cities is doubtful. Other cities do not have the NCC, and the CMHC is not so near.

Another "model" development, located in Nepean Township at Baseline Road and Woodroffe Avenue, is being planned and financed by CMHC. The area, to house 12,000 to 14,000 people, will contain a mixture of housing types (rental, ownership, co-operative). Commercial, entertainment and cultural facilities will be located at the centre of the development. The project is an attempt to demonstrate to developers methods of reducing housing costs, something which it is hardly credible that the CMHC has not done before throughout its long history. William Teron of CMHC, in a briefing to Regional Council, said that the cheapest home will cost $35,000.[17] This figure represents the lowest possible housing cost that can be achieved today. Delays in completing the project, however, will mean that this figure will rise as costs continue to react to inflation and intense demand. It is expected that the houses will be marketed by 1982.

An additional development, the "eastern community," will be a medium-density area bounded by Conroy, Hawthorne, Hunt Club and Johnston Roads. The total population is expected to reach 30,000 people. This is a project dear to the heart of the Mayor of Ottawa. (When built, therefore, the development might appropriately be called "Greenberg"). According to the newspapers (which are probably wrong) it is supposed to be built largely from the experience gained in building the city of Tapiola, in Finland.

A *third* advantage associated with public land-banking is that profits from land, rather than accruing to private developers, can be made to accrue to the public. Increasingly, land gains its value from the decisions of government. Decisions to direct growth to particular areas, to build roads and highways and to install utilities cause the value of some sites to increase. If these sites are held privately, then the increase in their value represents "socially created profits" to the owner.

If the aim of government is to restrain increases in housing prices, then the publicly-owned lots could be sold on a non-profit basis. As illustrated by the Home Ownership Made Easy (HOME) programme, such a scheme is very difficult to administer fairly. Unless controls are enforced on the resale value of these subsidized homes, windfall profits accrue to the initial home owners, rather than to the public. An alternative is to allow purchase of the house only, while retaining the lot under public ownership and leasing it. The

---

[16] NCC and CMHC, *LeBreton Flats: Progress Report, No. 1*, December 1974, p. 7.

[17] *Ottawa Citizen*, May 13, 1976.

price of the lease could be adjusted upward as the houses are sold from time to time. The benefits of public land-banking can then be extended to several families over a period of many years, set by the government which owns the land.

Careful screening of applicants is needed, to prevent wealthy persons from taking advantage of programmes intended to help lower income families to buy their own home. For example, under the provincial First Home Buyer Grant (1975 only), many charges have been laid, and much money lost through fraud.[18] The Plan itself was no doubt well intentioned (to encourage home buying and housing construction); but the legislation seems to have been hastily drafted, and the method of checking and monitoring not fully worked out.

We consider that a public land-banking scheme operated by the RMOC could be useful in achieving certain desirable goals, especially the provision of public housing for needy households in the Region. We recommend that the RMOC have the power to "land-bank."

A detailed plan could be made for a land-banked area. To avoid subsidizing the wealthy, some lots could be sold to them at full market value. Low-cost integrated housing could be provided for poorer people by the retention of some lots in public ownership (with safeguards). The scheme could be administered by the Ontario Housing Corporation and the Ottawa Housing Authority, and could be co-ordinated possibly by a Regional Housing Committee. (But see Chapter 6 for better recommendations on housing.)

Two financial benefits could result from the operation of a land-bank programme on an ability-to-pay basis. The profit from the sale of the majority of the lots at market price, could help to support the subsidizing of public housing tenants, and also to allow further purchases to replenish the land-bank. We therefore commend such a programme to the attention of the RMOC. (See Figure 4-3 for land ownership in the Region.)

The Greenbelt

The Gréber plan for the National Capital Region (1950), recommended that a belt of land approximately two and one-half miles wide be established around the existing built-up area. The inner limit of the Greenbelt was determined by the area designated for the provision of economic municipal services.[19] Some call the Greenbelt a "necklace," which is rather odd, since it is only half a necklace. Others call it a "chastity girdle" around the City of Ottawa, but it is not a very efficient one.

Several years elapsed before the Greenbelt actually came into existence. Much of the delay was caused by the unwillingness of Gloucester and Nepean Townships to designate land within their boundaries as Greenbelt. Developers and private owners also opposed the plan. Finally, in 1958, the federal government, through the NCC, decided to acquire all those parts of the Greenbelt not already in public ownership. The land was bought, and expropriated where necessary.

Several purposes were to be served by the Greenbelt: further urban sprawl was to be avoided; agricultural land was to be protected; the open area itself was to provide sites for future government buildings, other public institutions, and recreation facilities such as parks

---

[18] *Globe and Mail*, July 22, 1976. This was the scheme (from April to December, 1975) by which first-time home owners were eligible for a grant of $1,000, and people being what they are (greedy), well-to-do persons cheerfully took the $1,000. This was not illegal, but it certainly was immoral and against the spirit of the Plan.

[19] National Capital Commission, *Urban Greenbelts*, pamphlet, n.d.

Fig. 4-3 LAND OWNERSHIP

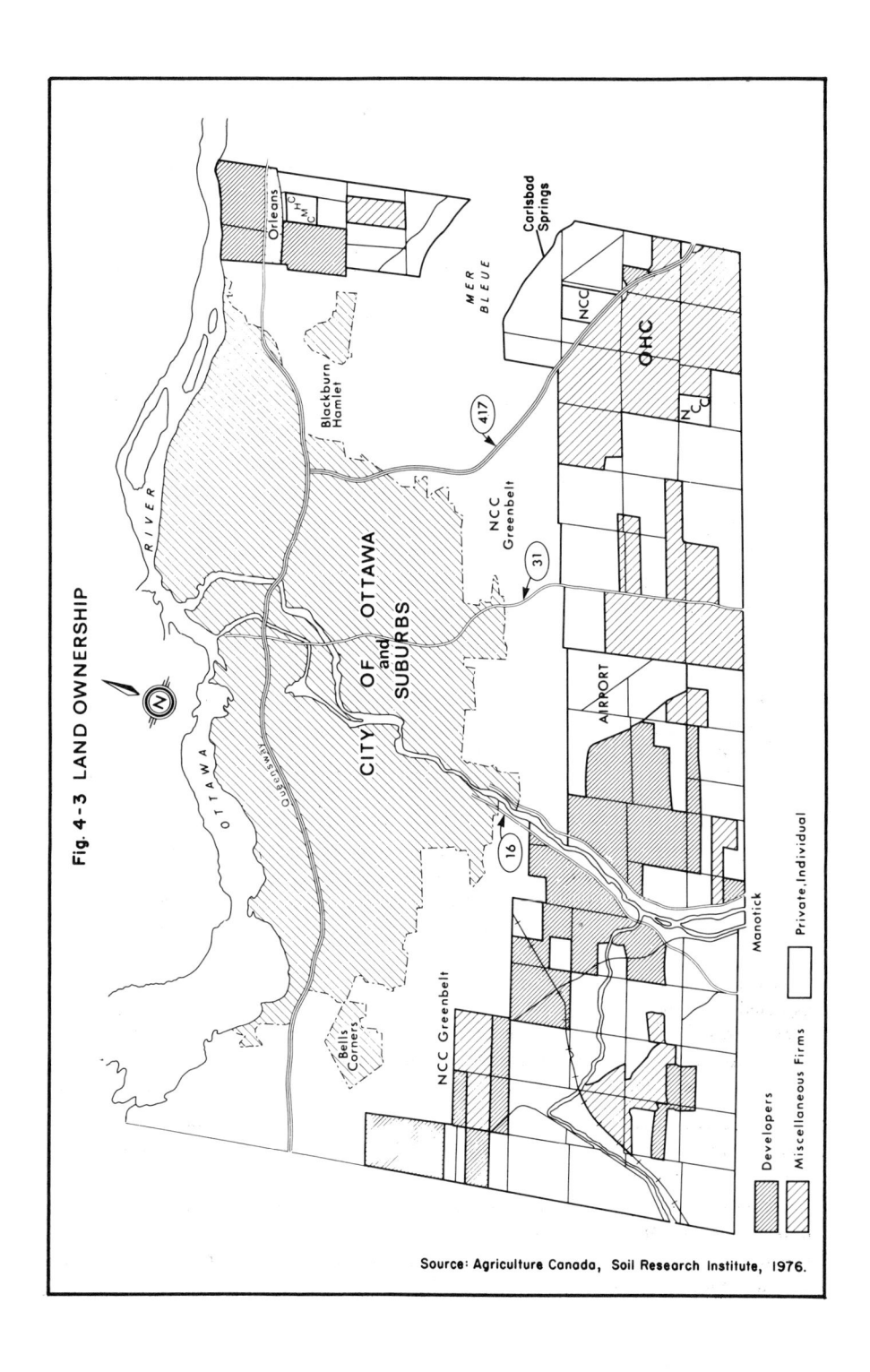

Source: Agriculture Canada, Soil Research Institute, 1976.

and golf courses. Finally, it was "... to place a practical limit on the growth of the capital by confining intensive building development to an area which could be provided with municipal services at a reasonable cost."[20]

In retrospect, one can see that the Greenbelt planners possessed a rather short-range vision. The population of the Region has surged ahead much faster than envisaged twenty-six years ago. As the City of Ottawa filled up, the bulk of new growth leap-frogged the Greenbelt and is still doing so. Urban sprawl and highway ribbon development cannot be controlled by this belt of federal land. So far as we can find out, nowhere in the world has urbanization been successfully confined.

The time has come to reconsider Greenbelt uses.[21] Since its purpose of confining urbanization has failed, we suggest the belt should now take the form of "green wedges" or "green corridors" between the "satellite cities." Much of it still for recreational use, yes, but some of it for more urban uses. The wedge (or corridor) is especially important in the case of the "Western Urban Community" and the "South Urban Community." It is conceivable that in a few years both of these urban areas could expand and meet in central Nepean, especially with the building of the Outer Ring Road.

Several benefits would result from the creation of a "green corridor" in south-west Nepean. *First*, it could prevent the growing together of the southern and western satellite cities. *Second*, access to open space would be improved for residents in the outlying municipalities beyond the Greenbelt. *Third*, several thousand acres of Class 1 and Class 2 farmland in south-west Nepean could be preserved. (See also Chapter 12).

Citizen Participation

Planning is not always seen as a co-operative effort, and antagonism sometimes develops between planners, politicians and citizens' groups.

A large number of citizens' organizations exist in the Region, many of them representing local neighbourhoods. Some of these groups are becoming highly organized and are having an effective voice in planning and related matters.

For example, the Glebe Community Association has been very active (and successful) in modifying the road system in the Glebe. In order to reduce the volume of through-traffic, several streets have been made one-way or have been closed to through-traffic. The Citizens' Committee of Sandy Hill was established to provide local input into planning. Its activities "... make it clear that participation is not a one-shot affair but rather an arduous, time- and effort-consuming process."[22]

Many citizens' groups are also involved in the planning of new urban growth in dispersed areas throughout the Region. The encouragement of citizen participation in planning was part of the process leading to the adoption of the RMOC Official Plan. It also became part of the LeBreton Flats planning by the NCC, and to a lesser extent of the Rideau Centre Scheme. The Woodroffe Association Advisory Council represents the future

---

[20] *Ibid.*, p. 10. Farms in the Greenbelt are leased. One is a PMU farm (Pregnant Mare Urine), the product of which is used in The Pill.

[21] Greenbelts recently established around Edmonton and Calgary are also coming in for severe criticism. *Globe and Mail*, 20 August, 1976.

[22] Stinson, A., (ed.), *Citizen Action: An Annotated Bibliography of Canadian Case Studies*, Ottawa: Community Planning Association of Canada, 1975.

residents of the development at Baseline Road and Woodroffe Avenue, while residents from the surrounding areas are represented by the Neighbours' Advisory Council.

Some citizens' groups are not based on neighbourhoods or territory. Their cohesion is based instead on a common interest over a wide area. A few major examples are the Citizens' Advisory Committee to the Regional Department of Social Services, the Social Planning Council of Ottawa-Carleton, and the Ottawa Tenants Council for Public Housing. The resource centre and "umbrella" body which brings many different groups together is the Federation of Citizens' Association, which has been active in stimulating and creating mechanisms for citizen participation, and is housed in an NCC building downtown.

Regional Council provides minutes which record decisions of all meetings. Possibly voting records of all Council members should be publicized more, as should the voting records of the local Councils.

We recommend that Regional Council formalize citizen participation in decision-making, as it has done with the admirable Social Services Advisory Committee, and that similar advisory committees be set up to work with other Departments. (More specific recommendations are made later on this point.)

CHAPTER 5

Roads and Public Transport
or
Are Legs becoming Obsolete?

"Many components of a city are highly desirable, but only two are absolutely essential. One is people, the other is transportation . . . Without transportation the people would be unable to build shelter or feed themselves . . . urban men would choke on some of their own waste products and find themselves buried in others." [1]

Introductory

"Transportation services" in Ottawa-Carleton consist of the construction and maintenance of the roadway system and related works, and the provision of public transit. Arterial roadways are the responsibility of the RMOC and local roads are under the area municipalities. Certain main highways (e.g., the Queensway, Highway 417) are provincial, and there is also a federal component — the parkways and driveways of the NCC. Public Transit, which is presently a bus system, is the responsibility of the RMOC and is operated by a special purpose body, the Ottawa-Carleton Regional Transit Commission (OC Transpo).

The importance of transport is reflected in the expenditures of the RMOC and area municipalities. Spending on transport amounts to 16% of all municipal expenditures within the Region (in 1969 the proportion was 13%). (See Table 5-1). For some of the outlying municipalities the figures are more striking, with more being spent on transport — nearly all on roads — than on any other single item, except for education.

Table 5-1 shows a decline in transport expenditures as a per cent of total municipal expenditures for all area municipalities except Nepean (which was a low percentage anyway). The absolute amounts have all increased for the area municipalities, but not so much as the dramatic increase in the expenditures of the RMOC itself, which spends on Regional roads and also on OC Transpo.

Transport and Land Use

Over one-half of the land in the downtown core of Ottawa is allegedly devoted to roads and parking lots. However, this large road network is barely able to deal with the number of cars at rush hour, although by comparison with larger cities rush hour traffic is not so bad. If employment levels in the core increase, as expected, by 47% at the end of the century,[2] the situation can only worsen.

There is a limit beyond which the present roads cannot be widened; therefore most of the

---

[1] Roger Starr, *Urban Choices: The City and Its Critics*, Penguin, 1967, p. 185.

[2] RMOC, *Official Plan*, p. 3-8.

Table 5-1

Expenditures on "Transportation Services,"[1] RMOC and Area Municipalities, 1969-1975

Municipality	1969 ($000's)	As a % of Total Municipal Expenditures	1975 ($000's)	As a % of Total Municipal Expenditures	Transport Expenditure Per Capita 1975
RMOC	5,828	22	28,852[2]	39	$57
Ottawa	8,567	10	12,528	8	41
Vanier	409	13	669	8	33
Rockcliffe Park	112	14	117	8	52
Cumberland	215	26	621	23	54
Gloucester	510	11	1,670	10	31
Goulbourn	184	16	363	12	29
March	127	14	252	10	37
Nepean	583	5	2,006	7	27
Osgoode	198	24	356	19	43
Rideau	158	23	412	20	52
West Carleton	419	40	656	30	84
Total Region	17,310	13	48,502	16	96

Source: Financial Reports, RMOC and area municipalities, 1969-1975.

Notes: [1] "Transportation Services" include roadways, transit, traffic control and street lighting.

[2] Included in this figure is the 1975 OC Transpo deficit of $12.6 million. The deficit is covered by a Regional transit levy upon area municipalities, plus a generous provincial grant.

increase in commuters will have to be absorbed by the public transit system. The Regional Plan cautions, though, that even with improved public transit and roads, the transport system as a whole may fail to cope with the expected congestion.[3]

Congestion in the downtown core, then, may well strangle the very vitality that the Regional Plan and the City of Ottawa are trying to promote, unless something is done. One suggestion to avoid the "strangle" is to ban automobiles from the downtown area. This seems a harsh step. Moreover, the Science Council of Canada warns that this drastic action would have serious effects upon the social and economic functioning of the City.[4]

Rather than banning cars from the downtown area, traffic can be manipulated by rearranging the land uses that represent the traffic destinations. This approach therefore advocates the decentralization of employment. If the employment is widely scattered throughout the whole Region, however, it will play havoc with the transport system, by making public transit less direct and more costly, thereby increasing automobile usage.

---

[3] RMOC, *Official Plan*, p. 3-8.

[4] Science Council of Canada, *Cities for Tomorrow*, 1971, p. 34. (Caution: The Science Council's dicta are not always to be relied upon when they are outside of the natural scientist's expertise.)

Employment *centres*, on the other hand, in the proposed new built-up areas (e.g., in the West) will allow commuter densities high enough to discourage the use of the automobile while allowing the transit system to operate more efficiently.

We therefore endorse the Official Plan in this respect, which is that decentralized employment centres be created in the "satellites." (See also Chapter 4, Planning)

Transport Management

The Murray Jones Report, which reviewed local government in this Region in 1965, stated that, "Continuous co-ordination of roads, public transport, traffic engineering and public parking will be required for an efficient total transportation system."[5]

At present, the Regional Transportation Department is oriented chiefly toward roadways and traffic control, while public transit is handled by OC Transpo, a semi-independent body. Parking, which is largely privately run, is separate from both of these. It does not seem sensible to have transport policy fragmented among these different components of the system.

Accordingly, we recommend that the Regional Muncipality, through its Transport Department, be responsible for the planning, co-ordination and policy-making for all roads, public transit, rapid transit, parking lots and traffic control facilities of the transport system. (In a sense, this merely strengthens much of what the Department already does.)

The Department should deal with the short and long-range planning required for transport facilities, and — subject to RMOC Council approval — should establish pricing policies and regulations for public transit and parking. Such pricing could perhaps shift more users to public transit.

We are not necessarily advocating that the RMOC should own and operate parking lots, although this may be advisable at the terminals of express bus routes. Nor are we saying that the area municipalities should own and operate parking lots, although they may wish to do so.[6] Nor are we abolishing the distinction between Regional and local roads.

In order to create a transport system which is not only efficient but also socially acceptable, we further recommend that the Transport Department have an advisory committee, along the lines of the Social Services Advisory Committee. The Traffic Advisory Committee should be composed of one or two staff members, several citizen traffic "experts" and several "ordinary" citizens. Such participation would perhaps help to ensure better transport decisions, and ensure that they are carried out with as little citizen conflict as possible. It would report to, and work with, the Standing Committee and with the Transport Commissioner and Department.

Roadways

The private automobile is the primary means of transport for most of the Region's residents. In 1974 there were 186,000 motor vehicles registered in the Ottawa-Carleton Region, about one for every three residents. Judging by recent trends, the automobile is going to continue to be important in the Region for commuting, shopping and recreational

---

[5] Murray Jones, *Ottawa, Eastview and Carleton County Local Government Review*, 1965, p. 9.

[6] A minor suggestion: it would be helpful if a company, such as City Parking Limited, could be deprived of its present name which causes much confusion and annoyance, especially to visitors who believe it is a City-owned enterprise.

purposes.

Present automobile usage represents 80% to 85% of all journeys. This may possibly decline in the future, owing to the rising cost of gasoline, public concern for the protection of the environment, and the increasing public willingness to subsidize public transit. The National Capital Commission, however, feels that automobile usage will not drop below 60% for the following reasons: car ownership is expected to remain high; an urban road system will continue to be required for property access, movement of goods and bus transit, and this will tend to perpetuate car travel; certain types of trips are better handled by automobile; and a percentage of the population will continue to be "auto captive."[7] "Auto captive" refers to people who must rely on their automobiles because they are not served by public transit or because they require their car for their job. It has been calculated that 15% to 18% of the Region's labour force falls into this category.[8]

The RMOC assumes responsibilty for the upkeep and maintenance, including "winter control," of those roads which make up the Regional road system. It has jurisdiction over access to Regional roads, land within 150 feet of a Regional road, and certain other matters (some of which concern roads within the jurisdiction of the area municipalities). The construction and maintenance of all sidewalks is solely the responsibility of the area municipalities.

Table 5-2 summarizes the expenditures by the RMOC and area municipalities for roadways in 1969 and 1975. The total expenditures increased 164% during this period. Expenditures on roadways make up a large proportion of the total transport expenditures, especially in the case of the more rural municipalities. The breakdown of expenditures for roadways within each of the municipalities varies considerably from one year to the next, although maintenance is generally the largest single item, followed by "winter control" — a euphemism for salting, sanding, ploughing and disposal of snow.

The Province normally assumes 50% of the cost of road improvements but when a plan of construction and maintenance has been submitted to and approved by the Minister, the RMOC is eligible for subsidies from the Province to cover up to 80% of the expenditures. Area municipalities are also required to submit road improvement expenditures to the Minister for subsidy approval, although the maximum provincial subsidy to area municipalities for road improvement is 50%. Of the $30 million spent on roads in 1975, $8.4 million was recovered in direct provincial subsidies. Once again, we see how dependent municipalities are on the Province for money.

The road capacity required to meet the rush hour peaks is far in excess of the average capacity required by the system throughout the rest of the day. This peak pressure is mainly funnelled along the busiest 5% of the road system, where it results in traffic congestion. This congestion problem will not be solved with the construction of new roads, or the widening of existing roads without more effective traffic management to keep the traffic moving.

The Regional Transportation Department is currently developing a computerized traffic control system. This system, when implemented, should increase the traffic flow by 20% to 25%, thereby reducing some of the demand for more road space. Road bottlenecks, such as those that occur on Bank Street and around Confederation Square will, it is hoped, be eliminated or diminished with computerized traffic control.

---

[7] NCC, *Tomorrow's Capital*, 1974, p. 68.

[8] RMOC, Planning Department, *Travel Forecasts and Analysis*, 1973, p. 2-5.

Table 5-2
Roadway Expenditures, RMOC and Area Municipalities, 1969-1975

Municipality	1969 ($000's)	1975 ($000's)	% Increase 1969-1975	Expenditure Per Capita 1975
RMOC	4,488	13,536	202	$27
Ottawa	4,388	10,405	137	34
Vanier	243	366	51	18
Rockcliffe Park	60	93	55	42
Cumberland	190	549	189	48
Gloucester	533	1,471	176	28
Goulbourn	176	350	99	28
March	122	229	88	33
Nepean	442	1,691	283	23
Osgoode	189	346	83	42
Rideau	156	394	153	50
West Carleton	399	649	63	83
Total Region	11,386	30,079	164	59

Source: RMOC and area municipalities, Financial Reports, 1969-1975.

Other bottlenecks in the Region occur at the river crossings. In response to this, the RMOC has planned for two more bridges across the Ottawa River,[9] but this requires co-ordination with the Outaouais Region. A wider bridge is being built by the National Capital Commission at Hog's Back, across the Rideau Canal and River, and the RMOC plans to build a bridge further south across the Rideau River as part of the outer-ring road.

Public Transit

Although the private automobile is still the chief means of personal transport in the whole Region, 20% of the households in the Region did not own or lease an automobile in 1971.[10] The people in these households are known in the trade as "transit captive," since they must rely on public transit or taxis for their mobility. To this group must be added those in households with a car but who cannot drive about, because the wage earner drives the car to work. The young, the old and the physically handicapped — all those who for one reason or another cannot drive — must be counted as well. These people all rely on the public transit system.

Public transit now plays a much larger role in the Region than when it was run by the City of Ottawa. As a public service it can relieve automobile congestion, reduce the need for expressways and parking facilities, reduce air pollution and it could help save the downtown area from aesthetic damage. It could even, in some circumstances, reduce the journey time of

---

[9] RMOC, *Official Plan*, Schedule C.

[10] Statistics Canada, Census of Canada, Housing Characteristics, 93-787, 1971.

all travellers if nearly everyone was persuaded to travel to work by bus rather than by car.[11] This, however, is not likely to come about in this Region, because some people have to commute by car — there is no alternative from some areas, especially from the outlying municipalities. In effect therefore, this makes a case for slower growth, especially if it is scattered, in these municipalities.

Public transit by bus is not a panacea for all our transport problems. (There simply are no panaceas for urban problems.) It can help, however, to reduce the number, magnitude, and cost of road improvements. With respect to the high employment levels in the downtown core, public transit remains the most efficient and least costly method of reaching one's work, if one lives within reach of the transit lines.

Failure to increase public transit to accommodate the future increases in downtown employment will result in massive congestion problems. It will also have substantial disruptive effects on the existing residential neighbourhoods in the inner city. It is these neighbourhoods which will have to bear the ill effects of the increased automobile usage, the pollution, noise, increased on-street parking and through traffic.

At present, 57% of the persons entering the downtown area do so by use of public transit. The Transit Commission would like to increase this share to 80%. In order to reach this goal, OC Transpo has adopted a more aggressive approach to customer service and marketing. Routes have been added, improving service particularly to suburban residents. Established routes have been altered to increase speed and efficiency. Bus lanes on downtown streets during rush hours have helped to speed service, and the introduction of monthly bus passes, used by nearly one-third of all the passengers, has made public transit more attractive and economical to commuters. OC Transpo has also used innovations such as tele-transpo (dial-a-bus) for the convenience of passengers, to say nothing of the doubling of the number of buses, and the erection of some 250 bus passenger shelters (so necessary in this climate).

Co-operation by the federal government has also helped OC Transpo to increase its ridership. The cancellation of free parking for some civil servants led to a daily increase of 3,000 bus passengers.[12] The use of express bus lanes along the federal Ottawa River Parkway led to a 24% increase in ridership on those routes.[13] The introduction of flexible (or staggered) work hours by the federal civil service, a move initiated at the suggestion of OC Transpo, has resulted in more people using public transit over a longer period, thus improving both system efficiency and passenger comfort.

Despite all of these improvements, continued reliance on the present bus system to handle increases in the further future may be unwise. More and more buses, running on regular city streets, will encounter problems with, and add to, traffic congestion. This will in time decrease their efficiency and discourage riders.

---

[11] Webster, F. V., *A Theoretical Estimate of the Effect of London Car Commuters Transferring to Bus Travel*, Road Research Laboratory Report LR165, London, 1968.

[12] *Ottawa Journal*, May 8, 1975.

[13] *Ibid.*, April 3, 1975.

Regarding continuing reliance on the bus system, the words of A. D. Godley are à propos, in making a case for separate "busways."

> What is this that roareth thus?
> Can it be a Motor Bus?
> Yes, the smell and hideous hum
> Indicat Motorem Bum! . . .
> Whither shall thy victims flee?
> Spare us, spare us. Motor Be! . . .
> How shall wretches live like us
> Cincti Bis Motoribus?
> Domine, defende nos
> Contra hos Motores Bos!

Rapid Transit

The answer being promoted by most groups as an alternative to present bus travel is some form of rapid transit on a separate right of way. (This of course is in addition to the locating of employment centres outside of the downtown core.)

A variety of rapid transit systems has been suggested for the Ottawa-Carleton Region. The proposals vary from the commuter rail system of the Nepean-Lucerne Transportation Committee, to the busway system proposed in a study by DeLeuw Cather (1975), to the advanced technology system proposed by the Ontario Government (1974) — monorail magnetic levitation and all the rest.

One should perhaps not be too skeptical of advanced transport concepts. They may work, in spite of our doubts. After all, it has been demonstrated that the bumble-bee can't possibly fly: ". . . because the size, weight and shape of his body in relation to the total wing span make flight impossible. But the bumble-bee, being ignorant of these scientific facts . . . does fly — and makes a little honey too."

In order to be feasible, rapid transit systems require high population densities and high ridership levels. The Region's urban area has a low population density (6,800 persons per square mile),[14] and low transit ridership levels (80 rides per year per capita compared to 110 for Montreal and 130 for Toronto).[15] There is no city in North America with a population of less than 1.5 million that has a rapid transit system. Edmonton, however, with a population of only 500,000, has started the construction of a subway line with 70% provincial funding, but we shall have to wait to see if the system can operate successfully there without further heavy subsidies. The RMOC should watch this project, and evaluate its results with an eye to the possible application of rapid transit in this Region.

It has been calculated that a rapid transit system can be financially feasible in a city of one million people if existing and suitable rights of way exist.[16] The population in the Region is expected to reach this level by the end of the century; therefore, in order for a rapid transit system to be feasible at that time, we recommend that the RMOC take steps to preserve

---

[14] Reynolds, D. J., *Urban Canada: Problems and Prospects 3, The Urban Transport Problem*, CMHC, Ottawa, 1971, p. 61.

[15] *Ibid.*, p. 60 (Montreal and Toronto have subways, as every Canadian knows. Each also has a population of some 2½ million.)

[16] *Ibid.*, p. 42. (There are a lot of "ifs" in this estimate.)

existing, and to expand proposed, rapid transit corridors. (Again, this is not much more than endorsing present policy for separate rights of way for buses.)

Rapid transit is sometimes viewed as the solution to all our traffic problems. There is growing evidence, however, that rapid transit may be no more successful than highways in solving traffic congestion when conditions of high density land use are uncontrolled. In order to prevent such high density, strict land use controls will have to be enforced by the Region and by the area municipalities; and, given these, public rapid transit can assist in achieving the development goals of the Region. (See Chapter 4, Planning.)

Transit Administration

The Ottawa-Carleton Regional Transit Commission, known as "OCTranspo," is a statutory body that was established in 1972 through amendments to the RMOC Act. It took over management of the transit (bus) system from the Ottawa Transportation Commission. The Commission is responsible to the Regional Municipality for over-all financial affairs, and is presently composed of five members, each of whom is a member of Regional Council. The Commission is chaired by the Chairman of Regional Council and has as its other four members the heads of councils from the four area municipalities with the greatest urban population in the Region — Ottawa, Nepean, Gloucester and Vanier.

We recommend that the Ottawa-Carleton Transportation Commission be dissolved, and its powers be placed within the Regional Transport Department, where it would be more closely accountable to Regional Council, and hence to the public.[17] One of the chief principles guiding our whole Report is that *ad hockery* (through special purpose bodies) be abolished. We want to simplify government structures, and focus responsibility upon the elected Councils where it belongs in a representative democracy. The citizen can then better understand local government, have improved access to it, and know whom to hold accountable for decisions made.

The day-to-day transit operations should be left in the hands of the "OC Transpo" staff (headed by the Transport Commissioner), but other matters should all be subject to the approval of the same Regional Council which approves the Region's land use and development plan. The Transport Advisory Committee (recommended earlier in this Chapter) would also be able to have some "input" into transit decisions.

Transit Financing

OC Transpo capital expenditures, including the purchase or leasing of vehicles, are financed principally through the special assistance programme of the Province, which covers 75% of the approved capital costs. The remaining capital debt is financed on behalf of the OC Transpo through debentures issued by the RMOC.

Operating expenditures of the Commission are paid only partly by revenue from bus fares. Any deficit incurred by the Commission (a regular situation since 1970) is recovered on an annual basis from two sources, the Province of Ontario and a levy upon the municipalities within the Region which receive transit services. Provincial assistance to public transit covers approximately 50% of the Commission's operating deficit.

The apportionment of the Regional Transit levy (deficit) among Ottawa, Vanier, Rockcliffe Park, Nepean and Gloucester is based on the proportion of revenue miles and the

---

[17] A proposal to this effect was recently (1976) introduced in Regional Council, but was defeated.

equalized assessment for each area municipality. As of 1975, an amendment to the legislation enables the RMOC to levy the *projected* deficit of the Commission on those municipalities in the year in which they occur. In the past, the deficit was not levied until the following year. This change has resulted in the 1974 and 1975 deficits appearing together in the OC Transpo 1975 financial report (which is why the figures look so high for 1975).

The performance of OCTranspo is noted in Table 5-3. Between 1969 and 1975, the number of passengers carried by OC Transpo (and its predecessor, the OTC) increased by 52%. Despite this, the Commission has faced an increasing deficit each year. Rising costs, expansion of routes, better service, doubling the number of buses, etc., and a desire by provincial and local governments to stabilize passenger fares have all contributed to this situation.

Table 5-3

Public Transit (OC Transpo) in the RMOC, 1969-1975

	1969	1972	1975	% Increase/Decrease 69-72	72-75	69-75
Number of Passengers (000's)	35,642	37,957	54,260	6	43	52
Number of Buses	312	368	629	18	71	102
No. Passengers per Bus (000's)	113	103	86	—9	—17	—24
Revenue (Operating) Miles (000's)	8,437	9,137	19,883	8	118	136
No. of Passengers per Mile	4.2	4.2	2.7	0	—36	—36
Revenue (000's)	$7,946	$9,704	$14,737	22	52	85
Expenditures (000's)	$8,252	$11,460	$27,325	39	138	231
Deficit (000's)	$ 305	$ 1,756	$12,587	476	617	4,027
Deficit per Passenger (cents)	0.8	4.6	23.2	475	404	2,800
Deficit per Mile (cents)	3.6	19.2	63.3	433	230	1,658
Expenditure per Capita*	$26	$27	$60	4	122	131
Deficit per Capita*	$1	$4	$28	300	1,100	2,700

Source: Ottawa Transportation Commission (1969) and Ottawa-Carleton Regional Transit Commission, Financial Statements (1972, 1975).
* Based on the population of the urban transit area.

There were 113,000 passengers per bus in 1969, but only 86,000 passengers per bus in 1975. Where the buses used to carry an average of 4.2 people per mile, they now carry only 2.7 people per mile. These seeming productivity losses are largely the result of the great improvement in service, especia$y to the outlying suburban areas. Some new routes, while performing a useful function, have not yet established themselves as profitable. Public transit, giving good service, runs at a loss nearly everywhere, not merely in this Region.

Public transit is in fact becoming more and more like a social service, as it becomes apparent that public transit needs subsidizing. This should disturb only the few surviving "Manchester liberals", dinosaurs left over from a golden age of laissez-faire which, if it ever existed, is not likely to return. Since most people live in cities and towns, there is a strong case for federal and provincial aid to urban transit, just as there is for subsidized housing. The Province is already subsidizing urban transit. Can the federal government be far behind? Fortunately, there are signs that the federal government is already stepping into this field, with its five-year, $100 million programme, for commuter services; and its proposed talks with provincial governments. The sooner the federal government negotiates and expands its programme, the better.

Partly because of the greater financial aid from higher levels of government, roads generally receive a higher priority in cities than does public transit. This is borne out in the Region, where 67% of the total municipal transport expenditures are for roads and only 22% for public transit. If Regional Council is going to maintain its objective to "give precedence to rapid transit and/or commuter service over all other forms of road construction or road widenings"[18] it will have to re-evaluate its priorities in transport spending. It will also have to join other municipalities in pressing for more federal aid for public transit.

The comparing of public transit with social services (made above) is perhaps not the best. A better comparison is with police and fire services, which are provided out of general revenue, as essential city services.

Other Transportation

The main modes of transport in the Region are the private automobile and the bus, but there are one or two other modes of transport in the bloodstream of the Region.

The taxi industry offers a para-transit service. Its efficiency, and convenience to residents in the Region, are hampered by two problems: (a) Taxis are regulated by each area municipality and once out of their licensed territory they are not allowed to pick up passengers. This regulation results in a lot of empty runs for the taxis as they return to their home base. (b) At present there are several brokers and many dispatchers in the Region. This means that a telephone customer does not have access to all of the cabs in the Region, and may have to wait a long time for a taxi, while other taxis operating through another dispatcher sit idle. Central dispatching and Regional licensing would overcome both of these problems and benefit the taxi industry as well as taxi customers.

Therefore, we recommend, as our first choice, that the RMOC assume responsibility for licensing and control of all taxis in the Region, and that it assist in setting up a Regional dispatching system.

As a second choice, we recommend that the licensing be retained by area municipalities; but that some of the present regulations be flung out the window. That is, taxis should be allowed to "cruise" and be flagged down on the streets, and allowed also to carry and pick up passengers anywhere in the Region. The present system is absurdly inconvenient for the public, and less profitable for the taxis (except for the largest firm, which is getting close to a monopoly position).

---

[18] RMOC, *Official Plan*, p. 3-17.

Bicycling is increasing in significance, both for business and pleasure. The National Capital Commission estimated that their recreational bikepaths were used by 550,000 cyclists in 1974. The number of bicycles and bicycle racks appearing outside office buildings reflects the increasing use of the bicycle as a functional means of transport.

The inter-urban terminal facilities, such as the Ottawa International Airport, the Ottawa Railway Station and the associated freight yards, and the Walkley Railyards, are not under municipal jurisdiction. However, these areas are generators of movement to and from their terminals and as such they have an impact on the Region. Usually the Region must supply some transport facilities and services (i.e., roads and buses) to these areas, as well as ensuring that conflicting land uses do not arise, as could conceivably happen, with the "southern urban community" in Gloucester and the proposed expansion of the Ottawa Airport.

In order that conflicts do not arise, the RMOC should have an input at all stages, including the planning stage, with the operators of these inter-urban terminals. The object of this is to ensure co-ordination of traffic facilities. On a more human scale, these facilities act as a welcoming doorway and supply the first impressions of many visitors to the Region, and thus attain civic importance. This is all the more reason why the RMOC should be allowed to have some input into the planning of these inter-urban facilities. We recommend that the RMOC endeavour to set up an inter-urban transport committee composed of representatives from the RMOC, federal government and private transport organizations, to co-ordinate the inter-urban transport activities (Airport, Rail Stations, Railyards, Bus Lines).

Finally, when all is said and done, it may be that we shall never get rid of traffic problems in the cities of Canada. Rush hour congestion has always existed, whatever the transport technology, and came into existence well before the age of the motor car.

> "History and geography both tell us that no matter how people move in big cities, there is almost always an uncomfortable degree of congestion and frustration. Often it seems that the more affluent a nation becomes, and the more advanced its technology the less successful it is in coping with its traffic problems."[19]

City transport is one of the most studied of urban problems.[20] At the same time, it is one of the most intractable. Perhaps we may be forgiven for ending on this gloomy note (used in another context by Hilaire Belloc, but used here of the "transport problem").

> Physicians of the Utmost Fame
> Were called at once; but when they came
> They answered, as they took their Fees,
> 'There is no Cure for this Disease'.

---

[19] Wilfred Owen, *Transport: Key to the Future of Cities*, The Brookings Institution, Washington, 1969, p. 207.

[20] The economists have not been of great help on transport. Now that the subject is a branch of welfare economics, and is acknowledged to be "the pre-eminent example of an external cost industry", we may expect better analyses. But in the end the basic transport decisions are political. See, e.g., J.M. Thomson, *Modern Transport Economics*, Penguin, 1974, pp. 12, 92, 260.

Chapter 6

Housing
or
Home, Sweet Home, Where Has It Gone?

"There is no housing shortage. It's only a nasty rumour spread by people who can't find a place to live."

Projected Housing Demand in the RMOC

In order to estimate future housing demand, the first step is to estimate the future population. As noted in Chapter 2, one method gives the figure of one million people in the RMOC by 1998, the other gives the same population in 2025.[1]

In order to house one million people, an extra 222,770 dwelling units will be required, plus an additional 15,000 units to replace demolished stock.[2] The assumptions here are that the trend toward smaller families, and an increased number of single-person households will continue, leading to fewer persons per dwelling.

As average income increases, the demand for single-family housing of all kinds also increases. Fewer families are forced to share accommodation for financial reasons, and so more dwelling units will be required to house what Statistics Canada quaintly calls "undoubled" families. (Possibly they should also speak of "untrebled" or "unquadrupled" families?) At any rate, whatever the motivation of people, from 1969-71 the number of households in the RMOC increased by approximately 50%, while total population increased by only about 33%.

At present, the local involvement in housing comes at the area municipality level, although the RMOC, through its Official Plan, does have an indirect effect on housing.

Should more direct responsibility for housing be handled at the Regional level? Several arguments support this view.

First, serious inequities result from the fragmentation of housing responsibility among the area municipalities. Moderate and low income groups must find accommodation somewhere and, so far, Ottawa and Vanier are the only municipalities which make serious attempts to satisfy the demand for public housing.

Second, a more balanced socio-economic mix throughout the Region could be achieved. New housing of a variety of types and densities could be allocated among area municipalities on a proportional basis. In this way, large concentrations of low-income households in one area could be avoided, thus reducing the social and psychological ill-effects that are said to arise from such areas.

Third, on financial grounds, the placing of housing responsibilities under Regional authority can be seen as more equitable for the area municipalities themselves. Low-income groups require services the same as, if not more than, other households, but the amount they

---

[1] RMOC, *Official Plan*, 1974, p. 2-13.

[2] *Ibid*.

pay in property taxes is less. The financial consequences of this should be shared by the Region as a whole, not just the City of Ottawa which to some extent (through its public housing) bears the social costs of the other municipalities.

We therefore recommend that certain housing responsibilities be handled at the Regional level, as outlined in the remainder of this Chapter and summarized at the end.

Supply of Housing in the RMOC: Past, Present and Future

From 1961 to 1971, for every additional two persons, one dwelling unit was completed. Between 1972 and 1974, the ratio of completions to population rose to 1:1 1/4.[3] This could be regarded as improvement to the housing stock, and so of course could the repairs that were made at the same time.

In Ottawa, Rockcliffe Park and Vanier, on the basis of a three-year annual average, housing starts increased progressively from 1963 to 1974 (except for 1966-68). Although housing starts for these three inner areas showed a 48% increase during 1972-74 over 1969-71, performance for 1974 showed a 46% decrease compared with the previous year.

Housing starts in 1974 in Nepean and Gloucester also showed a decrease from those of 1973 (40%), and even when housing starts in the outer "rural" townships of March, Goulbourn and Cumberland are taken into account, this represents a net decline in the Ontario portion of the Census Metropolitan Area of 4,624 housing starts in 1974,[4] compared with the year before. The year 1975 was the worst year for housing starts since 1967, with a decrease of 40% compared to 1974.

In terms of starts by dwelling type, several significant trends can be discerned from the CMA data for 1962-74. Detached, semi-detached and duplexes have formed a decreasing proportion of annual housing starts, whereas row and apartment units have formed a progressively greater proportion. In 1962, 42% of housing starts were of the detached, semi-detached and duplex types, and 58% were row and apartment units.[5] By 1974, however, only 18% of housing starts in the Ontario portion of the CMA were of the former types, while row and apartment units made up 82%. Approximately 80% of the multiple-family units starts were in Ottawa, Rockcliffe Park and Vanier, both for the period 1963-65 and 1972-74, with a marked difference among the area municipalities in terms of housing mix and population density.

Housing completions for the Ontario portion of the CMA increased by 17% in 1974 compared to 1973, but unfortunately this rate of increase was not carried over into 1975 when completions declined 27%. Rental units registered the greatest decrease.

The number of housing completions, of course, depends largely on the number of housing starts in the previous year. Therefore, as the performance in starting dwelling units continues to decline, the picture with regard to housing completions will be accordingly bleak. Again, row and apartment units dominated in the number of completions, with Ottawa, Rockcliffe Park and Vanier gaining 79% of all row and apartment units completed in 1972-74 in the Ontario portion of the CMA.

The Regional Official Plan (1974) states as a desirable goal that a minimum of 27 1/2% of

---

[3] Paterson Planning and Research Limited, *Housing in Ottawa-Carleton, Technical Report*, May 1975, p. 35.

[4] *Ibid.*, p.39.

[5] *Ibid.*, p. 40.

Fig. 6-1 NUMBER OF DWELLING STARTS, BY TYPE,
ONTARIO PORTION OF OTTAWA-HULL C.M.A.

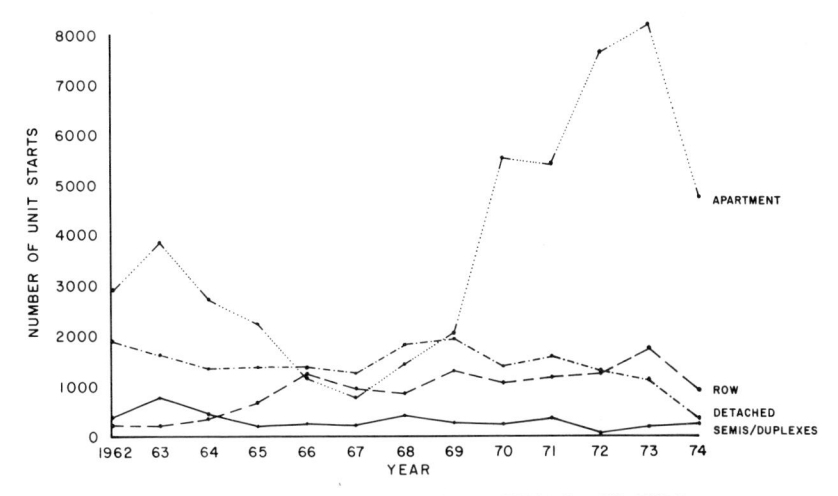

NUMBER OF DWELLING COMPLETIONS, BY TYPE,
ONTARIO PORTION OF OTTAWA-HULL C.M.A.

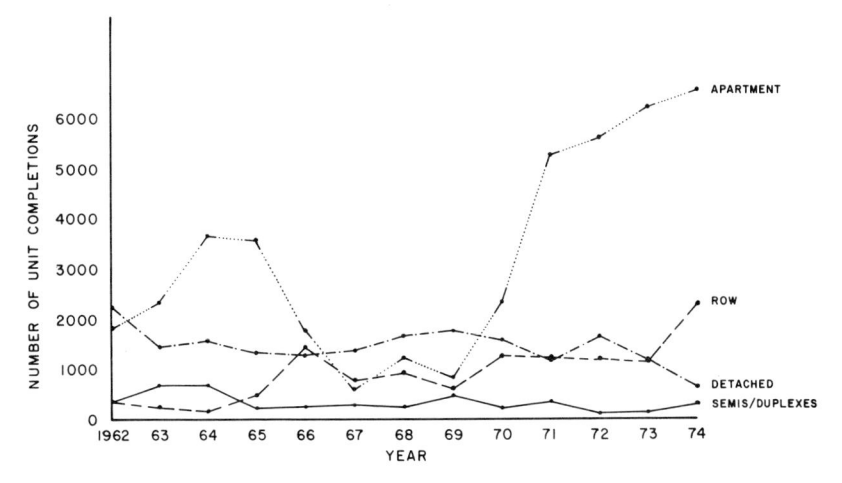

* C.M.A. boundaries as defined in 1961. These include the Cities of Ottawa and Vanier, the Village of Rockcliffe Park and the Townships of Nepean and Gloucester only. The 1971 C.M.A. is somewhat larger than the 1961 C.M.A., but the trends are the same in both areas. SOURCE: Paterson Planning and Research Limited. Housing in Ottawa-Carleton, Technical Report, May 1975, p. 40-41.

new housing units be of the ground-oriented, detached and semi-detached type. It also states that ". . . both existing residential districts and residential districts yet to be built should be developed into communities with a mixture of housing types . . .".[6] It thus appears that Regional Council would like to alter the existing trend toward fewer detached and semi-detached units in the immediate future. A considerable shift in the distribution of multiple-family structures is also implied, so that a larger proportion of row-houses and apartments are meant to be constructed in the townships (especially the suburbs) of the RMOC.

The Regional goal recognizes that present social attitudes favour detached and semi-detached houses. This preference for privacy, space and security is to a great extent the traditional North American attitude toward private property. However, in view of the present housing market, the goal of 27½% ground-oriented detached and semi-detached dwellings seems unrealistic, and overly directed toward satisfying the demand of the well-to-do.

We must concur with the Paterson Report (1976), and recommend that Regional Council relax this requirement and shift a larger portion of its estimates to multiple-family use, including those for rental, and even to the extent of permitting lower standards.

The Ontario Advisory Task Force on Housing Policy came to a similar conclusion, stating that:

> The type and kind of housing to be produced should move toward the provision of housing which more closely matches, not expectations, but needs. At current costs, *it is not possible* to house the people of Ontario in single-family houses at today's standards and expect a majority to be able to pay the full price. Other forms of housing, at different and more realistic development standards than currently demanded, will be needed.[7]

As the Canadian population becomes increasingly concentrated in a few large urban areas — notably Toronto, Montreal, Vancouver and Ottawa-Hull — urban densities and lifestyles will undergo significant changes. Most West European countries have already experienced and adjusted to these phenomena. Less public resistance was encountered in these countries because private ownership of land is less dominant. Historically, too, West European cities were more densely populated than those in North America, having been largely built in the pre-automobile age; while during most of the 20th century, the automobile did not become as ubiquitous as in North America; instead, public transit played a larger role. As a result of this and other factors low density suburban living has not become the idealized way of life that it has in Canada and the United States. It may be that with the national and global population trends of today, individual ownership of detached dwellings will ultimately cease to be the norm for most people, though not for all.

The Affordability Problem

Although average family incomes in the RMOC rose 36% from 1971 to 1974, house prices increased by 71%, while rents increased by 18%.[8] During the 1960's, however,

---

[6] RMOC, *op. cit.*, p. 249.

[7] Ontario Advisory Task Force on Housing Policy, *Report*, Queen's Printer, Toronto, 1973, p. 30.

[8] Paterson Planning and Research Limited, *Housing in Ottawa-Carleton, Final Report*, February, 1976, p. v.

increases in average income kept pace with increases in house prices. Thus, the affordability problem is relatively recent, beginning in earnest in 1970 and gathering momentum since.

A useful indicator of the affordability of housing is the shelter-cost-to-income ratio. The Economic Council of Canada considers that the acceptable expenditure on shelter should be not greater than 20% to 25% of gross annual income. In Ottawa from 1969 to 1972, the ratio increased from 14.9% to 16.0% for all families and unattached individuals.[9] These figures, like all averages, are misleading. According to the Ottawa Welfare Council, in 1975 low income groups spent 30% to 40% of their gross income on shelter; moderate income groups spent 25%; higher income groups spent 16%; and the really upper-crust spent only 10% to 14%.[10]

The facts may be put in a more striking way: In the Ontario portion of the CMA in 1971, expenditures on shelter were beyond the acceptable proportion of income for 32% of all households; and 12% were housed in inadequate shelter.[11] Of those people earning less than $6,500 per annum — the maximum then permitted for public housing tenants — 72% were paying more for shelter than they could afford and 15% were housed inadequately. This situation can only worsen as the supply of new housing rises slowly while the population increases faster.

Land Costs

The three fastest growing Metropolitan Areas in Ontario — Toronto, Ottawa and Kitchener — are growing at a rate of 15% to 20% every 5 years.[12] As population growth keeps on, so does the demand for well-located land. However, the supply of serviced land has failed to keep pace with the growth in demand, hence the large rise in land costs. In the RMOC, from 1971 to 1974, land costs for an average serviced lot increased 44%, from $7,439 to $13,061. In the City of Ottawa in 1974, lot costs ranged from $30,000 to $40,000.[13]

Both small landowners and large developer-builder companies have made large gains from these rising land costs. For example, when the Ontario Housing Corporation first began to purchase land in the Carlsbad Springs area, the price per acre was $700; however, later purchases reached more than $2,000 per acre as landowners became more aware of the value of their land for non-farm uses.[14]

In the area near Ottawa, very little land designated for development in the near future remains in the hands of small landowners. Instead, a few large companies have "banked" substantial acreages, and through their oligopolistic position are able to control effectively the timing of the release of this land and its sale price. In this way, artificial shortages are created. According to a study for CMHC, in 1973 eight developers in the Ottawa area owned 9,416 acres, which was enough land then to supply the local housing market for eight years at

---

[9] Paterson Planning and Research Limited, *Housing in Ottawa-Carleton, Technical Report*, May, 1975, p. 61.

[10] *Ottawa Journal*, May 20, 1975.

[11] The Paterson Report defines inadequacy on the basis of persons per room (crowding), families per dwelling (sharing), and state of repair of dwelling.

[12] Advisory Task Force on Housing Policy, *op. cit.*, p. 33.

[13] *Ottawa Journal*, December 15, 1975.

[14] *Ottawa Journal*, March 19, 1976.

current new-house densities and projected growth rates. Campeau Corporation alone owned 78.3% of this land area.[15]

The same study estimates that in 1972-73, "returns to scarcity" (sales revenue minus all development costs) can make up 60% of the price of a residential lot in Ottawa.[16] Since the cost of a serviced lot may amount to about 40% of the cost of a home, Draconian controls on land-holding costs, profits, etc., could theoretically reduce housing costs significantly. But no one has put forward a feasible way of doing this. Draco was not, after all, an elected politician, nor did he consult with citizen groups. It is surely too much to expect that this present Report should solve a problem that, like a spectre, haunts all North America. The only realistic solution we can see is more and more public housing, by one means or another. After all, since the first National Housing Act a generation ago, the government has intervened in the housing market, mainly to the benefit of middle and high income people.

Some people have suggested the direct control of land prices, say by the provincial government. But to what level should prices be held (or rolled back)? Should all lots or acreages be held to the same level, regardless of location? Such questions are enough to rule out both the political feasibility and the public acceptance of this method of reducing housing costs.

There may be more to be said for methods whereby the supply of serviced land is increased. For instance, pressure could be put on developers to release lots through a holding tax on development land. But administration of such a tax would be a nightmare, and it may work out that this would merely drive up prices for building lots as the tax was passed on to the buyer.

Alternatively, a very high capital gains tax could be imposed. However, this could be realized only after land appreciation is demonstrated by sales, and would probably not discourage land hoarding nor lower the sale price.

Under The Ontario Land Speculation Act (1974) a tax of 50% is already placed on the increase in value realized on the sale of certain designated land and buildings. This applies (a) to vacant land sales where no substantial improvements have been made or are about to be made; (b) to transactions in houses which are not the vendor's principal residence; and (c) at a reduced rate on transactions in apartment buildings owned for less than 10 years.

The restricted application of this Act has not, so far as we can judge, noticeably improved the housing market. Moreover, as a side effect, in the long run ". . . the Act may lead to an even larger proportion of the supply of housing being produced by a few large development firms."[17]

Some have suggested restricting the holdings of any one developer, or even the "nationalization" of potential building land. But what mouse will bell these cats?

England has had considerable experience with land control, particularly as regards the question of land values. Several schemes have been attempted from time to time whereby the development rights of land were nationalized, and a development charge or a "betterment levy" was imposed on land developers to collect some or all of the difference between the

---

[15] P. Spurr, *Land and Urban Development*, Toronto, James Lorimer and Company, 1976, p. 203.

[16] *Ibid.*, pp. 56-58.

[17] Canada, Ministry of State for Urban Affairs, *Human Settlement in Canada*, May 1976, p. 51.

existing-use value and the development value.[18] Complementary schemes of compensation for loss of development value resulting from planning restrictions were also attempted.

The concept behind the betterment levy schemes was that, in large measure, the increase in the value of land is generated by urbanization and "planning permission," and therefore the increase should accrue to the public, not the land owner or developer. The English schemes were beset with enormous difficulties despite several revisions. It is ample evidence of the highly political nature of planning and land control that these betterment and compensation schemes were alternately introduced by Labour governments and abolished by Conservative governments. As Cullingworth correctly states, "Planners may talk in technical terms, but the essential issues are political." The English experience, as well as that of other European countries, in handling problems associated with land development could well bear closer examination.[19]

Developers alone are not at fault for high land prices although they make easy targets. Delays in granting planning approval for subdivisions, etc., also add to land costs (as noted in Chapter 4); and if amendments are made, they too must wend their weary way through the same sequence of steps as the original proposal. The result is ". . . a sequence which is time-consuming, wasteful and ill-suited to promote either good provincial-municipal relations or public acceptance of the planning process".[20] Planning approvals, like the mills of God, grind slowly and they grind exceeding small.

Increasing the density of buildings on land is another method of reducing the cost of housing. The effect of increased densities is to reduce the land portion of the total unit cost, which in some cases now approaches half of the total. The recent trend toward row housing, garden homes and the like is an example of this alternative (high density but not high rise). A new grant programme of CMHC encourages this approach by awarding a grant of $1,000 per unit to municipalities which permit housing projects at densities of 10 units or more per acre. The "model community" being developed by CMHC on Woodroffe Avenue at Baseline will incorporate, amongst other features, high density housing (averaging 20 units per acre), but be designed in such a way as to reduce the negative side effects sometimes associated with high densities.

So far we have concentrated on the supply side of housing — making land available faster, and increasing housing density. But there may also be the possibility of reducing demand for housing. Yes, this is possible, provided cities and towns stop growing; or at least, provided that families stop "undoubling," as the Census puts it, and are willing to live in harmonious "togetherness," But do we really want to go back to the extended family with, say, three generations under the same roof? Surely not. About the only thing young people today can tolerate from their parents is a subsidy. And parents in their turn are only too glad to get rid of their troublesome offspring when (or before) they come of age.

Another faint possibility on the demand side is that we reduce our expectations, and perhaps live in communes. This would perhaps be easy to do if some modern cult came along that converted us all to a simple life, like that which Thoreau and Rousseau wrote about. But

---

[18] J. B. Cullingworth, *Town and Country Planning in Britain*, London: George Allen and Unwin Ltd., 1974, pp. 144-160.

[19] Beginning perhaps with Dalton Kehoe, et al (eds.), *Public Land Ownership: Frameworks for Evaluation*, Lexington Books, Toronto, 1976.

[20] Ontario Economic Council, *Subject to Approval*, Toronto, 1973, p. 53.

where are the modern prophets to preach this doctrine? Or rather, which of the gurus shall we follow?

Zoning

Zoning was devised as a means of maintaining the established character of localities and of preventing land uses detrimental to adjacent properties or to the wider area. When used for this purpose in a stable urban environment, zoning by-laws are reasonably effective. However, when frequent and rapid land use change is common, a cumbersome amendment procedure may bring costly delay. In recent years, zoning has been used as a development control device in fringe areas where growth and change are occurring rapidly. The "... rigidity and the absence of qualitative content"[21] make zoning by-laws ill-suited for this purpose.

Municipalities have tended more and more to charge developers lot fees, and to make developers provide service requirements for lots, whereas formerly servicing was a municipal function. According to Campeau Corporation, the cost to the developer of servicing raw land is $200 per foot frontage.[22] These costs are recouped by constructing bigger houses, with many amenities, at low densities for which high prices may be charged, and where zoning by-laws exclude other types of housing. Such exclusionary zoning by-laws reflect "... the primacy of suburban goals of homogeneity."[23] They are a disguised form of discrimination against low-income groups.

The Ontario Advisory Task Force on Housing Policy states with respect to zoning and standards that:

> Municipalities have generally established minimum development standards — relating to such factors as lot size and house size, lot setbacks, garages, etc. — which go far beyond what is required to meet health, safety and convenience needs. These unnecessarily high standards derive from a wide-spread desire to ensure the "quality" of development and to secure a suitable tax return. The imposition of such standards affects the cost of providing housing, and serves to exclude from many communities families of low and moderate income . . . The application of unnecessarily high development standards and exclusionary occupancy standards does not conform to all segments of the community and should not be permitted as a matter of provincial policy.[24]

In Montreal, the cost of a serviced lot is significantly lower than in Toronto, Vancouver and Ottawa. In Quebec, services are provided by the municipalities, not by the developer, and are paid for over several years by "local improvement taxes."[25] (The quality of services provided may also vary and thus account for part of the price difference.)

---

[21] Ontario Economic Council, *op. cit.*, p. 74.

[22] *Ottawa Journal*, December 15, 1975.

[23] L. B. Sagalyn and B. Sternlieb, *Zoning and Housing Costs*, New Jersey: Rutgers University Centre for Urban Policy Research, 1973, p. 15.

[24] Advisory Task Force on Housing Policy, *op. cit.*, p. 40.

[25] Canada, Ministry of State for Urban Affairs, *Human Settlement in Canada*, May, 1976.

The more affluent in Ottawa-Carleton have tended to live on the urban fringe while the less wealthy were relegated to older and/or poorer quality housing in the more densely built-up areas of the City. As housing prices continue to increase, however, more upper-income families are remaining in inner city areas, renovating older homes. Fewer older homes amenable to conversion to apartment units then become available, and consequently the lowest-income groups are squeezed out of the private housing market altogether.

Some area muncipalities in the RMOC have recognized the potential of integrated communities. In March Township, for instance, Kanata is planned on the principle of clusters of neighbourhoods. A range of housing types is found there, including detached, semi-detached, town houses and high-rise apartments.[26]

Mobile homes can also provide an acceptable alternate type of dwelling for some people. Regulations regarding standards of mobile homes could be made mandatory in building by-laws, at least up to the requirements of the Canadian Standards Association. We recommend (a) that the RMOC be given the power to prevent local zoning by-laws from vetoing mobile home parks and (b) that RMOC be able to designate areas within the Region for establishing mobile home parks.

Mortgage rates are also an important factor in the cost of housing. The increase of interest rates by the federal government (as a monetary tool to regulate the economy) has contributed to increased housing costs. This side effect has been somewhat softened by compensating adjustments of CMHC policy, for instance, increases in the mortgage loan ceilings under the National Housing Act.

Housing Programmes in the RMOC

It almost exceeds the wisdom of Solomon, let alone ordinary human beings, to find a way through the jungle of housing programmes and housing aid in the Region. Useful reference outlines are contained in *Housing Ontario*, January/February, 1976, and in the reports by Paterson Planning and Research Limited (1975, 1976), and in the RMOC Technical Reports.

In view of the complexities, we recommend that the RMOC maintain a well publicized housing information service for the Region. This would be a part of the RMOC role in housing that we recommended earlier.

The ancestors of the present federal role in housing were the National Housing Acts of the 1930's. These were not of much help in housing the poor. What, after all, could one expect of federal governments under R. B. Bennett and Mackenzie King? And the economists knew hardly any better than the politicians what to do.

Even the new Act of 1944 was primarily designed to stimulate the economy via the construction industry. Concern for housing, especially for the poor, was a kind of subsidiary aim of the CMHC set up shortly afterwards (1946). Mr. L. St. Laurent (not yet prime minister) had stated firmly in 1947, "No government of which I am a part will ever pass legislation for subsidized housing," but a little later, the government in fact did so. (In politics one should never say "never.")

Nor should we judge politicians harshly for inconsistency over time. After all, if they didn't change their minds and policies there would be no forward movement at all. And to

---

[26] Kanata, however, is not for the poor.

what point should we turn back the clock of history in order to be consistent? To Sir Mackenzie Bowell? To 1867? To the time when Indians and buffalo roamed the continent? To the garden of Eden? No: the governments of Canada and of Ontario are essentially pragmatic, and let us give thanks that they are so; and that they are not under the sway of dogmatic ideologies — especially those of human perfectibility and instant Utopias, whether these are derived from Karl Marx, B. F. Skinner, or the latest fashion in Oriental gurus.

The National Housing Act, through the CMHC mortgage programmes, has helped hundreds of thousands of people to buy houses. These have been chiefly for the middle class and well to do.

For those in need, i.e., the poor, several housing programmes now exist; federal, provincial, municipal, and sometimes all three in combination.[27] For instance:

(a) The federal Non-Profit Housing Assistance (1973). This provides loans at reduced interest rates to housing groups such as churches, charities, and municipal housing corporations for low rental housing for families with annual incomes of $8,000-$12,000. For provincial non-profit organizations, loans to a value of 95% of the appraised value are available, plus a 10% capital grant.

(b) Under the provincial Community Sponsored Housing Programme (1973) the province matches the 10% federal grant. The purpose of this is to reduce mortgage payments, thus lowering rents or housing charges for all units within the proposed housing project.

(c) The federal Cooperative Housing Assistance (1973) is also directed to families having annual income from $8,000-$12,000. CMHC provides a 100% mortgage, a $10,000 start-up grant and a 10% capital grant. Cooperative Housing (for ownership), through the elimination of a large down payment, allows low and moderate income families to break into the housing market.

(d) The federal Assisted Rental Housing (1975) is directed at developers and landlords rather than families. CMHC pays a subsidy of $600 maximum per unit annually, over a 5 to 15 year period, in order to allow the developer or landlord to meet the difference between non-profit rents and market rents.

(e) Several programmes are available also which provide aid to homeowners and municipalities for repairs to deteriorated housing. The federal-provincial Neighbourhood Improvement Programme (NIP), the federal Residential Rehabilitation Assistance Programme (RRAP) and the provincial Ontario Home Renewal Programme (OHRP) are aimed at low and moderate income groups, whereas federal Home Improvement Loans (1955) were designed primarily for middle and high income groups.

The effectiveness of some of these programmes is limited somewhat by lengthy delays, since the release of funds must be approved by agencies at all three levels of government (in addition to public participation). It is only common sense to rationalize and accelerate the application approval process.

---

[27] There are some two dozen or so federal, provincial and sometimes municipal housing programmes in Ontario (depending on how one counts them). See Ministry of Housing, *Housing Ontario*, Jan./Feb. 1976, Vol. 20, No. 1.

(f) The Assisted Home Ownership Programme, administered by CMHC, is designed to help householders acquire a home without spending more than 25% of their "adjusted" income on monthly mortgage payments. CMHC provides a 95% first mortgage, and will contribute toward monthly payments at an effective rate of interest of 8%. For lower income families, extra grants of up to $750 per year will be given. The home price ceiling in the Ottawa area is $38,000. In order to stimulate the supply of medium priced housing, the federal government has also a Municipal Incentive Programme. Under this, a $1,000 grant per unit to subsidize servicing costs is given to municipalities for moderately priced, medium density dwelling units.

(g) The provincial Home Ownership Made Easy (H.O.M.E.) Plan is to help middle income families to buy homes. When first initiated in 1967, the maximum family income permitted was $14,500 for a single wage-earner and $17,000 in the case of two wage-earners. Lower priced housing was made possible through the leasing of the lot from the Province for a 5-year period with an option to purchase.

To stimulate more public interest, the programme was later modified. In 1976, the maximum incomes permited were increased to $17,000 and $19,000 for one and two wage-earners respectively, and the 5-year waiting period before purchase of the lot was eliminated. As a result families purchasing homes are now selling them within a few months and realizing substantial profits. Considerable criticism has arisen over the H.O.M.E. Plan.

The Plan was never meant, and should not be meant, to give a free capital gain for those lucky enough to get a H.O.M.E. lot. We recommend that the H.O.M.E. Plan be revised to avoid giving free capital gains to the middle class.

(h) The purpose of the Ontario Housing Action Programme (O.H.A.P. 1974-1976) is to reduce the cost of homes through facilitating the servicing of land, and encouraging home construction in higher growth areas. Grants are made to municipalities for the provision of major services and for planning studies. The programme is aimed at providing lower-priced housing for families having incomes of $14,000 to $20,000 per annum.

Public Housing

During the present high housing prices, low-income groups have experienced the greatest hardships. This should come as news to no one. The poor always do get the short end of the stick: that is the meaning of being poor. Or as the old lines go:
"It's the rich that get the gravy,
It's the poor that get the blame.
It's the same the whole world over,
Ain't it all a bleeding shame?"

Home purchase is no longer a possibility for the poor; instead, they must depend on rental housing. However, recent trends in the rental market show that the rate of apartment construction has been decreasing, leading to an increase in rent levels. The influence of rent control has almost certainly been to discourage the construction of rental accommodation and to encourage the conversion of rental units to condominiums. So things are getting worse. (In Ottawa-Carleton, however, the RMOC can now prohibit the conversion of rental units to condominiums.) This power should be exercised.

From January 1971 to March 1975, the Ottawa rent index increased by 11.7%.[28] Part of this increase has been caused by a steadily rising demand for rental housing: in 1961, 51% of the dwellings in Ottawa were rented units, but, by 1971 this proportion had increased to 58%. In Vanier, in 1971, 75% of the dwellings were tenant occupied. By comparison, in the other area municipalities, the proportion of rentals ranged from 14% in Cumberland to 34.2% in Nepean.[29] From 1972-74, Ottawa, Rockcliffe Park and Vanier gained 79% of all row and apartment unit completions. Nevertheless, apartment vacancy rates in Ottawa have decreased significantly, from 7.7% in 1966 to 3.9% in 1974,[30] and, as of October 1975, the average apartment vacancy rate for Ottawa, Vanier, Gloucester and Nepean was 2.3% (according to a CMHC survey). Vacancy rates are below 2% for the total of rental housing according to other reports. The rental market here, as in many Canadian cities, is obviously pretty tight.

A number of federal and provincial programmes exist to provide aid to low-income families who are unable to keep shelter costs within 25% of their income. The rent-to-income housing programme is directed at families and "senior citizens" whose annual incomes are less than $8,000.[31] Frequent complaints relate to the density and scale of accommodation provided under this programme and to the lack of nearby facilities.

A characteristic of large-scale public housing is that it tends to group low-income families together, and they are perceived as different from other groups. The "ghettoization" of public housing tenants into separate developments, often in high-rise apartment buildings, is emotionally damaging since a certain amount of stigma is attached to the tenants. That is why we recommend the RMOC have the authority to locate public housing anywhere within the Region, and that no area municipality have a veto power.

In the RMOC, 9% of the households are headed by females; but 75% of households in public housing are headed by females.[32] Since one of the conditions for rent-to-income benefits is that a family have children, the concentration of these families into high-rise buildings often has undesirable social effects. A frequent complaint is that play areas and day care facilities are inadequate. After seeing some of the accommodations, one cannot help but sympathize with this complaint.

The provincial Rent Supplement programme is directed at low-income families on the Ontario Housing Corporation (OHC) waiting lists. To ensure integration with other housing, not more than 25% of the units in a single project may be taken by rent-supplement tenants. The landlord is paid the difference between rent-to-income payments and the normal market rent. The Community Integrated Housing Programme provides a similar service.

The provincial government also gives a capital grant of up to 10% to non-profit and co-operative housing groups, if 25% of the units are provided for rent-supplement. Tenants need not be selected from OHC waiting lists, and the housing is mainly for persons with

---

[28] Paterson Planning and Research Limited, *op. cit.*, p. 28. It is my belief that this figure of 11.7% grossly understates the rise in rents.

[29] *Ibid.*, p. 28.

[30] Ontario, *Ontario Statistics*, 1975, Vol. 1, Social Series, p. 360.

[31] "Senior citizen" is an annoying euphemism for "elderly", or the blunter "old folks". One expects any day now that the word "child" will be banished from the language in favour of "junior citizen".

[32] Ottawa Tenants Council for Public Housing, *op. cit.*

annual incomes of less than $8,000.[33] Additional projects include Low Rental Housing Assistance, Accelerated Family Rental Housing Programmes, and several others.

Briefs presented to this Commission by the Ottawa Tenants Council for Public Housing and the Social Planning Council of Ottawa-Carleton Housing Committee voiced several major complaints. The *first* relates to segregated versus integrated housing. This situation is being tackled by the federal and provincial governments and should improve with time, especially if the RMOC is given the power to plan the location of public housing projects, as we have recommended.

The *second* relates to the income/rent scales. The 25% of income maximum rent currently employed is an arbitrary figure devised in 1947.[34] On the Rent Scale in Ottawa-Carleton, rents theoretically vary between 17% and 25% of a tenant's income, depending on income and the number of dependents. But according to the Ottawa Housing Authority (OHA), in Ottawa 97% of all public housing tenants who are employed pay 25% of their income on rent. For those on welfare, 30% to 40% of the tenants' incomes go to shelter costs.[35]

The problem then becomes one of the amount of discretionary income, that is, the money that remains after rent payments and other necessary expenses. Because of inflation, this "extra" money has been shrinking, leaving public housing tenants with a very low standard of living. Obviously, we have not yet reached the promised land of a "just society".

We recommend that the Rent Scale used for public housing tenants be reviewed by the Ministry of Housing. We also recommend a relaxing of the Rent Scale for a limited period in some cases, so that as their income increases, public housing tenants may have the time to acquire enough capital to become independent of the rent-to-income programme. This would of course only be put into effect if there were no needier cases on the waiting list; and would require careful monitoring, preferably by the RMOC, which would act as a kind of referee or "ombudsman".

A *third* common criticism of public housing is that tenant participation is inadequate. We cannot agree, however, that the projects should be administered entirely by tenants. The fact is that tenants in any accommodation, public or private, cannot have their every demand satisfied. The channels of communication between public housing tenants and the management, however, can and should be improved. We recommend therefore that at least two elected tenant representatives be guaranteed a place on every board of directors for public housing, and so form a direct link between the tenants and the management. We also recommend that tenants, potential or actual, be brought in from the start, i.e., in the design and planning stages of all public housing.

Within the RMOC, a distinct imbalance exists in the distribution of public housing units. About 80% of the public housing in the Region is owned by the Ontario Housing Corporation (OHC); and of this, some 98% is located in the City of Ottawa and is administered by the Ottawa Housing Authority (OHA).

A definite demand for public housing units also exists outside Ottawa. As of June 1975, 165 applications for family and senior citizen accommodation were outstanding in the

---

[33] Paterson Planning and Research Limited, *op. cit.*, p. 110.

[34] Social Planning Council, *Brief*, February 23, 1976.

[35] Ottawa Tenants Council for Public Housing, *op. cit.*

townships of Nepean, Gloucester and March.[36] This may well be a misleadingly low figure. "Senior citizen" housing is also being built in Rideau, and is planned for Osgoode and West Carleton.

Table 6-1

Public Housing Units, Built and Under Construction in RMOC — 1975-76

Municipality	Managed by OHC or OHA Senior Citizens	Families	Managed by COHC[*1] Senior Citizens	Families	Total
Ottawa, c.	4,636[a] 129[2a]	3,382[c]	755[a]	818[c]	9,591 129[2]
Vanier, c.	96[a] 225[2a]	15[c]			111 225[2]
Gloucester	30[a] 12 (rent supplement)[a]				30 12
Goulbourn	—	19[a]			19
March	40[a]				40
Nepean	54[a]	15[d]			69
Rideau	16[2b]				16
RMOC Total (existing)	4,868	3,431	755	818	9,872
Total Proposed	370				370

Source:
a — The Council on Aging of Ottawa-Carleton, *First Annual Report to the Community*, March 1976; and letter from Area Manager, OHC, 31 Aug. 1976.
b — *Rideau Township Bulletin*, April 1976.
c — *Housing in Ottawa-Carleton, Technical Report*, May 1975.
d — Ottawa Citizen, March 24, 1976.
*1 — City of Ottawa Housing Company Limited.
2 — Proposed or being built.

Housing for the Elderly

A growing proportion of persons aged 65 years and over tend to live independent of family and institutional care. Because of low income after retirement, many of the elderly require housing assistance. In the Ottawa area, low-rent housing for the elderly is provided by the City of Ottawa Housing Company Limited, the Ontario Housing Corporation (OHC), and a co-operative housing group. Some 98% of the apartments so provided are located in the Cities of Ottawa and Vanier, with the small remainder being distributed among the Townships of March, Nepean and Gloucester. All but a few of the units are located in 20 high-rise apartment buildings.

We recommend that the elderly not be placed in high-rise apartments (unless they wish it), but rather that they be integrated into new or already established low-rise developments. A greater range of choice with regard to the location of elderly persons' units should be developed, so that "senior citizens" can remain in familiar surroundings, close to family and friends, especially in small "rural" settlements. In urban areas, "senior citizens" housing should be located close to convenient facilities, so as to allow those able to care for

---

[36] *Ottawa Citizen*, July 26, 1975.

themselves to purchase food and other household supplies. These units should be located where public transportation is easily accessible. (A British architect, who for 20 years designed many high-rise buildings, has now recanted his previous views and espouses low-rise for families and the elderly. Good for him. It is better to repent than to carry on with one's sins.)

Table 6-2

Housing for the Elderly in the City of Ottawa, By Type, 1976

	Bachelor	*Semi-Bachelor*	*One-Bedroom*	*Two-Bedroom*	*Total Units*
COHC	421	30	304		755
OHC	119		4,425	22	4,566
CO-OPERATIVE	18 shares		35 shares	51 shares	104

Source: The Council on Aging of Ottawa-Carleton, *First Annual Report*, 1976.

In the rent-to-income-housing programme, no two-bedroon apartment units are available. The OHC housing programme attempts to remedy this through its rent supplement programme. A need exists for a number of two-bedroom units on a rent-to-income basis because often, with failing health, elderly couples require two bedrooms.[37]

Experience has shown that in buildings where elderly alcoholics are housed, severe conflicts have arisen. These people undergo great suffering because, when their lease is terminated, they have no place to go. The Council on Aging recommends that it should work with Regional Health Services, Nursing Care Services and the Alcoholism and Drug Addiction Research Foundation, with a view to establishing a separate residence for elderly alcoholics. We support this proposal. We also recommend that social services provided to the elderly be expanded in scope. In particular, the successful "Meals on Wheels" programme should be expanded.

Summary

In view of the diverse and complex nature of this Chapter (a reflection of the complexity of the whole housing policy field), a summary of our recommendations concerning housing is warranted:

1. (a) A Regional Housing Department should be established, headed by a commissioner responsible to Regional Council, and assisted by a citizens' advisory committee and a standing committee.
   (b) The Regional Housing Department should take over responsibility for all public housing projects in the Region, i.e., those which are now handled by the Ottawa Housing Authority and by the City of Ottawa Housing Company Ltd., and by the Ontario Housing Corporation in other area municipalities. It is clear from this that we disagree with the Paterson recommendation that these duties be handled by an "independent" Regional Housing Authority. That is, we agree that public housing should be a Regional function, but not with the argument that it be administered by a special purpose body. Municipalities are governed, not managed. Public housing

---

[37] *Report to the Council on Aging from the Housing Committee, op. cit.*

decisions are essentially political, not technical, and politics in a democracy should be out in the open, not driven underground for *apparatchiki* to deal with.
- (c) Where a local board of directors is set up by the Housing Department to administer a particular public housing project, at least two members of the board should be tenants. And tenants should take part in the planning stages.
- (d) The Regional Housing Department should administer the assisted housing programmes of senior governments, such as rent supplement schemes (where the landlord is a private person or a company).
- (e) The Housing Department should maintain an information office to which all area municipalities, co-operative groups, and individuals may obtain information on all housing programmes.
2. For all triune housing programmes (some of which have been outlined in the text above), the RMOC should be the negotiating and administering level of municipal government rather than the area municipalities. (Some steps in this direction have already been taken in the Regional Muncipality of Waterloo.)
3. Regional Council should also be vested with powers to determine
   - (a) the location and distribution of public housing
   - (b) the location and distribution of mobile home parks
   - (c) the housing density and "mix" in all subdivisions. (We are not saying that all subdivisions should be alike.)
4. In order to reduce the initial cost of housing, municipal lot charges should be abolished and developers should be required to provide fewer services. The municipality should recover its development costs by local improvement taxes. This is a recommendation to the area municipalities. A preferred recommendation is that the Province forbid municipalities to levy lot fees, and amend its legislation accordingly.

CHAPTER 7

Municipal Finance
or
It's money makes the world go round

"In financial matters it is always essential to be realistic. As the available resources are always limited in one way or another, this is why it might well come about that objectives which are completely justified socially or economically cannot be attained, or that their achievement must be postponed." [1]

Municipal finance, in one form or another, is usually at the centre of municipal problems. This is only natural, since almost all decisions (or even decisions by default) have their financial aspects. There is nothing more political than a budget. At the personal level it is also true that hard choices have to be made. As Al Capp once said, "Whether you're rich or whether you're poor, it's nice to have lots of money".

And when money questions arise for a municipality, inevitably they bring up the further question of local taxation — the chief source of municipal revenue. And this in turn leads to the question of assessment of real property, since it is from the mill rate on property assessment that municipalities get most of their local revenue.

Assessment

In 1970, the Province of Ontario took over municipal assessment and established "regional" assessment offices throughout the province. Before then, the assessment function had been done by local municipal assessors — some good, some bad, some indifferent. (The trend to provincial assessment is found in several other provinces as well.)

The general purpose of the 1970 move was to standardize assessment practices, and so make assessments uniform and equitable throughout this fair Province. All taxable properties were to be reassessed at market value. Province-wide reassessment has been postponed however, and indications are that market value will not be in use until 1978. When completed it will replace the present systems which are at widely varying percentages of full market value. The present assessed values of properties are, in most municipalities, those which were taken over and "frozen" at their 1970 level. (Some of these assessed values go as far back as 1940). The intention is, according to the Provincial Treasurer, to phase in the new tax system over a period of up to five years to prevent abrupt taxation changes.

Under The Assessment Act, as amended, market value for all real property (except farm land) is defined as the dollar value that the property might be expected to realize if sold in the open market by a willing seller to a willing buyer. This value is generally established by averaging the sale prices of properties of the same class. Some difficulty arises where less

---

[1] Jean Lesage, cited from Scott and Oliver (eds.), *Quebec states her case*. MacMillan, Toronto, 1964, p. 20.

than five properties, of a given class, have been sold.

Farms, on the other hand, are assessed at their market value *for farming purposes only*. A recent Budget Paper[2] proposed to separate farm land from farm dwellings, with the latter to include only residences and a "reasonable amount" of land. Farm houses will then fall into the same category as any other residential property. The tax on farm land, however, will be remitted, i.e., paid by the Province as part of the provincial policy to encourage farming and to keep the land in farm production. This goes well beyond past policies to help farmers and food production, and is probably a far-sighted policy. It increases the amount of tax relief for the farmer-ratepayer, and at the same time the municipality does not lose revenue. (This rebating of the tax on farm land is very like the "de-rating" of agricultural land in Britain in 1929, which was also done in order to aid farming). Let us clearly recognize however that farming will be the only type of business which will pay no tax at all on its business property (farm land and outbuildings). Other businesses please note.

When "market value" assessment does come into full use, the assessed value of properties (except farms) will rise substantially. It is generally recognized that certain classes of property will show greater increases than others.

The market value (i.e., roughly the sale price) of residential properties has increased faster in recent years than that of commercial and industrial properties. To prevent an undue shifting of the tax burden onto residential properties, the proposed reforms to the property tax system, being examined by a provincial commission under the chairmanship of Willis Blair, include provisions for taxing residences on only 50% of their market value and commercial/industrial properties on 100%.

The Township of West Carleton requested introduction of market value assessment during 1975, ahead of the province-wide scheme. Reforming an ancient assessment scheme inevitably results in some property owners gaining and some losing, as they compare their new assessments with the old. Not unexpectedly, over 900 appeals were made from West Carleton property owners to the Assessment Review Court after new assessment notices were sent out in early November of 1975.[3] The introduction of the new market value scheme in one municipality of this Region, only two years before its province-wide application, was of doubtful wisdom.[4]

The more recent proposed scheme is of course not that used in West Carleton in 1975. The newer scheme is for 50% of full market value assessments on residences, not 100%.

Since assessment formerly varied a good deal from one municipality to another, the Province calculated "equalization factors", to make assessment rates approximately uniform among municipalities (See Table 7-1).

The equalization of assessment amongst municipalities is important for several reasons: the Regional and school board levies are apportioned on the basis of assessment; certain provincial grants are awarded on the same basis; and so are some inter-municipal cost-sharing agreements. Thus it is highly desirable that the municipalities' measure of wealth (their assessment) be calculated on the same basis for all municipalities. The new market value assessment will produce a more accurate inter-municipal measure of wealth, and so be more equitable.

---

[2] *Budget Paper E: Reform of Property Taxation in Ontario, 1976.*

[3] Committee of Concerned Ratepayers of the Township of West Carleton, *Brief*, Jan. 27, 1976, p. 6.

[4] A view supported in a study made by the Municipal Finance Branch of TEIGA, Sept. 1975.

Table 7-1
Equalization Factors in the RMOC, 1975

Municipality	Equalization Factor (%)	Municipality	Equalization Factor (%)
Ottawa	31.4	March	14.5
Vanier	29.85	Nepean	14.3
Rockcliffe Park	19.3	Osgoode	13.6
Cumberland	16.4	Rideau	15.9
Gloucester	18.5	West Carleton	15.6
Goulbourn	14.4		

Source: Municipal Financial Reports.

The new assessment, unlike the old, will also bring equity to properties *within* a given municipality. Newer properties, having been assessed later, tend to bear a larger portion of the municipal tax than properties frozen at their 1970 level. This inequity within municipalities has existed for several years.

Assessment is on three types of property: (a) residential and farm, (b) commercial and industrial and (c) exempt. The first two are taxable, the third is not, although on a portion of exempt assessment, payments in lieu of taxes are made (see later in this Chapter).

The distribution of commercial and industrial assessment is very uneven amongst the area municipalities. In Ottawa and Vanier commercial and industrial form 37% and 30% respectively of total taxable assessment. Nepean is next at 27%, and the rest fall well below this, with the five outlying municipalities having less than 10%.

It seems unjust to us that the tax revenues derived from commercial and industrial assessment (which includes at present both the property tax and the business tax) should go exclusively to the municipality in which the assessment is located. Many social costs arising from residential assessment, particularly for the very expensive education function, bear more heavily on the municipalities and dormitory suburbs which have a lower proportion of commercial and industrial assessment.

In terms of financial equity in bearing such social costs, a strong case can be made for pooling all commercial and industrial assessment in the Region and then apportioning it to the area municipalities, say on the basis of population. We recommend that this be done. (On the implications of this for school boards, see Chapter 10, Education).

If the commercial/industrial assessment base is thus spread throughout the Region, then the resource equalization grants received by the area municipalities will also have to be adjusted. These provincial grants are now paid to municipalities on the basis of their assessment deficiency. With pooling, the resource equalization grant should probably be turned over to the Region, and used to reduce Regional levy upon the area municipalities. We recommend that this be done, with the calculation of each grant being performed by the Province.

Revenue — Local Taxation

Assessment serves as the basis of the property tax, which is calculated by applying the mill rate to the assessed property value. The property tax has been and continues to be the largest source of local revenue in almost all Canadian municipalities. (A province such as Newfoundland is an exception to this rule, as it is with regard to time zones.)[5]

Indeed, the property tax is a major component of the total Canadian tax system, being the fourth largest tax source in the country, following personal and corporation income taxes, and sales taxes. It produced approximately $4 billion in 1974.[6] In Ottawa-Carleton over $164 million was raised through local taxation in 1975, which represents roughly $325 for every man, woman and child in the Region. The yield was divided amongst the Regional Municipality, the school boards, and the local municipalities in the following proportions: 22% for the RMOC, 43% for schools, 35% for local purposes.

These proportions are averages, and are different among the municipalities, as may be seen in Table 7-2. There will also probably be a shift towards a somewhat larger proportion being used by the school boards, because in 1976 there was a levelling off of provincial education grants combined with large salary increases for school board employees.

Table 7-2
Analysis of Local Taxation, 1975

Municipality	Local Municipal Purposes $000's	% of Total Tax	Regional Share $000's	% of Total Tax	School Boards Share $000's	% of Total Tax	Total $000's
Ottawa	34,403	31	28,195	26	47,981	43	110,578
Vanier	3,002	55	867	16	1,620	29	5,490
Rockcliffe Park	280	25	274	25	561	50	1,115
Cumberland	779	43	191	11	849	46	1,819
Gloucester	5,538	42	2,153	17	5,366	41	13,057
Goulbourn	568	27	322	16	1,189	57	2,079
March	506	25	490	25	998	50	1,993
Nepean	10,350	43	3,482	15	9,933	42	23,765
Osgoode	390	30	199	16	687	54	1,276
Rideau	328	22	248	17	899	61	1,476
West Carleton	551	36	220	14	764	50	1,535
Totals	56,695	35	36,641	22	70,847	43	164,183

Source: *Municipal Financial Reports*, 1975.

Possible reforms to the property tax system have received much attention in recent years. The property tax is said to have many faults. This complaint has been heard

---

[5] Municipal government came only recently to most Newfoundland outports, and near riots have taken place against the imposition of a property tax. *Royal Commission on Municipal Government in Newfoundland and Labrador*, St. John's, 1974. (This document, of exceptionally high calibre, makes fascinating reading for those who like that sort of thing).

[6] Canadian Tax Foundation, *Provincial and Municipal Finances*, 1975, p. 63.

throughout the lifetime of everyone now living, and in our opinion is likely to go on through the lifetime of our descendants, to the third and fourth generation. It serves to remind us that political problems are sometimes insoluble, or that if some are solved others will rise to take their place.

One often hears that the property tax is regressive, falling more heavily on the poor, and forming a higher proportion of their income. While this has been widely accepted, recent studies do not give full support to the notion. In fact, little can be conclusively said one way or another about the incidence of property taxation.[7] On the positive side, however, this is one of the few taxes on wealth that the wealthy cannot avoid, unlike the income tax which the rich can partially evade by many ingenious tax dodges. The fact that the regressiveness of this tax is not a settled matter however, has not prevented certain tax relief measures from being adopted. The Province offers property tax credits for farmers and "senior citizens", and has a general rebate system depending upon income and occupancy costs, thereby reducing the alleged regressiveness of the tax.

The property tax is often said to be insufficiently responsive to economic growth, and so necessitates more and more transfers from senior governments to finance the growing service requirements of municipalities. This is the major conclusion of the recent Tri-Level Task Force on Public Finance, chaired by the late Dr. John Deutsch.[8] The general argument is that with costly growth and better social services there is a widening gap between municipal resources and commitments.

This is a very broad question, and the municipal case for fiscal reform has some validity. Two elements are involved here: one, the reform of the property tax system itself; and two, alternatives to the property tax. Certainly, with infrequent reassessments, the tax base of municipalities has not been a growth base which rises automatically with incomes. The assessment base only grows as new properties and improvements are added. However, with market value assessment, and frequent periodic reassessment (as proposed by the Province) the property tax base will grow as a result of increasing market values (at least during times of inflation).

There is a more important way of increasing the property tax base — by the elimination of all tax exemptions. At present, properties owned by senior governments; and by educational, charitable and religious institutions are tax exempt, although payments-in-lieu of taxes are made on some of these properties. (See later in this Chapter.) These exemptions have the effect of narrowing the tax base, and result in an increased burden on the taxable property.

Any tax exemption is tantamount to a hidden subsidy on the exempt property. There is no getting around this stubborn fact, however nasty it may be. As Oscar Wilde put it, "The truth is never pure, and seldom simple." From the viewpoint of public accountability, it is preferable to remove every tax exempt status, of whatever kind, and have visible grants made instead, as a conscious decision in the regular budgetary process. The hidden subsidies could

---

[7] Richard M. Bird, "The incidence of the Property Tax: Old Wine in New Bottles", *Canadian Public Policy*, II Supplement, 1976. (The argument that the property tax is regressive assumes some or all of the following: (a) that wealthy misers may live in shacks, and so pay little property tax; (b) that people with low incomes live in costly housing and so pay high tax; (c) that poor people live in relatively over-assessed housing; (d) that expensive housing (of the wealthy) tends to be under-assessed, and hence under-taxed. Only (c) and (d) appear to have much validity.)

[8] *Report of the Tri-Level Task Force on Public Finance in Canada*, February, 1976.

then be seen, even if they are merely bookkeeping entries on both the revenue and expenditure sides of municipal financial reports, as they might well be for certain charities, churches, and the like.

Two final issues concerning administrative aspects of the property tax system deserve mention. *First,* the question of the most appropriate manner of collecting the school boards' tax levies has surfaced again recently. Certain municipal and school board spokesmen have suggested that the school boards should issue their own tax bills and collect their school taxes directly. This is a revival of an ancient debate, that was settled many years ago by the Province, when it decided to abolish the taxing power of school boards.

Under the present system, the school boards requisition upon the area municipalities, who in turn tax their ratepayers. In effect the municipalities act as tax collectors for the school boards. Some municipal officials have expressed discontent with this arrangement, fearing that their ratepayers will "blame" them for increases in the school portion of the tax levy.

Nevertheless, to have one tax collection agency is much more efficient than two, independent of each other, with each issuing tax bills and collecting taxes. It is also more convenient for the ratepayer. The concern of the municipalities that they may get "blamed" for the school levy can be met satisfactorily by itemizing and explanation on the single bill now sent out by the municipalities. Indeed many municipalities do this already on their tax notices, showing the relative proportions of the property tax being collected for school boards, the RMOC, and local municipal purposes. It would be a retrograde step, as well as an unnecessary expense and duplication to establish separate tax billings. We must assume that tax payers can read their tax bills, and are not invincibly stupid. We recommend no change in the present system.

A *second* administrative issue is how often property taxes should be collected. In the old days collection was of course only once a year — after the fall harvest, when farmers had cash to pay their taxes. Modern municipalities require a more regular cash flow to meet their vastly enlarged expenses. Therefore, to avoid temporary borrowings and the associated interest costs (which benefit only the banks) more frequent tax billing is required. Most municipalities in the Region now require quarterly payment, but a few bill less often. To avoid cash flow problems (and borrowing) we recommend that all municipalities institute at least quarterly tax billing. A further advantage of more frequent tax payment was stated by the Smith Committee, ". . . we have no doubt that regular, smaller instalments would do much to reduce the subjective burden of the tax and go far toward easing what must now be a serious payment problem for many families".[9]

One of the 1976 Ontario Budget proposals for property tax reform was to reduce drastically the extent of tax exempt properties. We completely support this policy, and go even further. We do not see any justification for continuing to exempt any property whatever from local taxation. We are encouraged in this view by the stand taken some years ago by one of the churches which went on record as not wishing to be indirectly subsidized by the state through the exemption of any of its church property. We therefore recommend that all local tax exemptions *of whatever kind* be eliminated, even if (as we have said earlier) counter-balancing municipal or provincial grants may be given on some classes of exempt property.

---

[9] *The Ontario Committee on Taxation*, Vol. II, 1967, p. 276.

A veritable hurricane of protest is bound to arise from such a drastic recommendation. "It is never easy to dislodge a privilege that has enjoyed long acceptance". Yet the Smith Committee, nine years ago, also recommended the gradual reduction of exemptions even for churches;[10] and the recent proposals by the Province went very far indeed towards eliminating exemptions.

Our recommendation then is for the abolition of exempt status for all private and all public property, whether the latter is owned by municipalities, school boards, special purpose bodies, or by the province and its many agencies.

We cannot *recommend* the same for all federal properties (it is not within our jurisdiction to do so) but we strongly *suggest* that the federal government make payments in lieu of full taxes on all its properties and those of all its numerous agencies.

Obviously, on this point as on many others in this Report, the recommendations (and suggestions) go beyond the boundaries of the RMOC, and affect the Province at large.

As for alternatives to the property tax, this is a search that has gone on for a long, long time. It has been crowned with no more success than the search for an easy north-west passage to Asia. Today the search has taken a slightly different turn. It is common in municipal circles now to talk of revenue sharing, i.e., allowing municipalities a share of major "ear-marked" taxes collected by federal and provincial governments, especially income and sales taxes.

In about ten states in the U.S.A., municipal income taxes are levied, while sales tax levies are also used locally. As Queen Victoria said, "We are not amused." As we say several times in this Report, there is no need to copy the bad habits of the U.S.A. Municipal income tax was long ago used in some Canadian cities but, happily, we are now free of them. Local sales taxes, too, were not unknown to Canada, having been levied in some cities in the Province of Quebec until 1964, when they were discontinued.

A new tax sharing scheme was started in Manitoba last year, whereby municipalities receive roughly 5% of the provincial personal income tax and 8% of the provincial corporation tax, the distribution to the municipalities being on a per capita basis. As one writer puts it, "This tax sharing arrangement is more like a grant scheme than the local income taxes levied in the United States, but it does provide for an automatic increase in money transferred to localities rather than depending on legislative changes in grant formulae."[11]

This kind of tax sharing, where the senior government is responsible for levying the shared tax would, of course, help municipalities to avoid the political consequences of tax increases. As Thomas Plunkett has pointed out, the existence of a new source of revenue would help act as a counter-balance to the excessive concern with effects on the property tax base often exhibited in municipal dexision-making.[12] But apart from something like the Manitoba scheme, we are not told what new sources of local revenue can be found. Municipalities have always sought the Holy Grail of a new tax source. But, alas, there may

---

[10] *Op. cit.*, p. 160.

[11] J. A. Johnson, "Municipal Tax Reform — Alternatives to the Real Property Tax", *Canadian Public Policy*, op. cit., p. 336. (The provincial legislature can of course change or abandon this tax sharing scheme as easily as it can change other provincial grant formulae that automatically increase grant money).

[12] T. J. Plunkett, "The Property Tax and Municipal Case for Fiscal Reform", *Canadian Public Policy*, op. cit., p. 320.

be no Holy Grail.

Naturally, an innovation of the kind just mentioned (for Manitoba) would be appropriate on a Province-wide basis only, and could not be applied to Ottawa-Carleton alone. Some think it unfortunate that the Province has not agreed to engage in further Tri-Level conferences to discuss "basic reforms" to the system of intergovernmental finance as it affects the municipalities. We are doubtful of this view, because we do not see any such "basic reform" that is either necessary or feasible. Provincial (and even federal) aid already finds its way to the municipalities in ever increasing amounts. And if we take a longer view, the functions transferred from local to senior governments have been numerous. It is curious too that this obsession with the property tax and possible alternatives, should surface now, when Canadians have never been more affluent or had more disposable income.

A study done by one of our staff found that the average property tax had not risen any faster than disposable income from 1969 to 1973 in the Census Metropolitan Area. ("Disposable income" figures were not available from Statistics Canada for later years.)

The figures for tax arrears (as a percentage of the total levy) have declined in the last decade, in all the area municipalities except one (and that was a very special case). There is a lot of grumbling, but not a tax "revolt". Those with memories of the 1930's will recall that properties were commonly sold for tax arrears, and the arrears made up a high proportion of the levy. It is perfectly true that property taxes are rising, but so is the price of nearly everything; and we expect more and better services for our property taxes, as indeed for all our taxes. There is no getting around the fact that if we have rising expectations we must be prepared to pay to have them satisfied.

Considerable local publicity has been given to figures purporting to show that residential property tax levels in Ottawa-Carleton (average residential tax per household) are the highest of 30 large municipalities in the Province. These calculations appear to have a very dubious base, and we have been unable to substantiate the figures.

The allegation that Ottawa-Carleton residential taxes were the highest was certainly not true in 1974, as the TEIGA provincial estimates plainly show. The nature of the data and the methodology involved make such comparative figures difficult to compile, and unreliable when they are compiled. But the topic may perhaps be worth more detailed examination, given time and money enough to do so, and making allowances for the imprecision of the probable results.

Revenue — Grants and Subsidies

The second most significant source of revenue for municipal governments is made up of the grants and subsidies received from senior governments, chiefly from the Province. The RMOC itself is heavily subsudized by the Province, with over half of its current revenue coming from grants. The lower tier municipalities are somewhat less subsidized on current account, although the proportions vary considerably from one municipality to another, as shown in Table 7-3.

The school boards receive a greater proportion of their revenues from the Province than the municipalities do. The Carleton Roman Catholic School Board, for example, received approximately 85% of its 1975 current revenues from the Province, although this percentage is admittedly the highest for the four boards in the Region. (See Chapter 10, Education).

Table 7-3
Current Revenues in the RMOC, 1969-1975

	General Taxation				Payments in Lieu of taxes				Grants and Subsidies				Other Sources				Totals	
	1969 $000's	%	1975 $000's	%	1969 $000's	%	1975 $000's	%	1969 $000's	%	1975 $000's	%	1969 $000's	%	1975 $000's	%	1969 $000's	1975 $000's
Ottawa	60,654	71	110,578	70	13,148	15	28,144	18	5,862	7	7,876	5	6,175	7	9,286	6	85,839	155,885
Vanier	2,298	77	5,490	70	6	.2	71	01	461	15	1,609	20	236	8	679	9	3,001	7,849
Rockcliffe Park	621	79	1,115	78	72	9	199	14	48	6	80	6	41	5	38	3	782	1,432
Cumberland	583	69	1,819	68	5	.6	12	0	208	25	460	17	50	6	397	15	846	2,689
Gloucester	3,388	70	13,057	75	651	14	1,134	7	554	12	2,278	13	228	5	906	5	4,821	17,364
Goulbourn	884	78	2,079	71	2	.2	7	0	206	18	509	17	43	4	340	12	135	2,936
March	653	68	1,993	75	142	15	254	10	133	14	187	7	35	4	221	8	962	2,655
Nepean	9,621	82	23,765	78	554	5	1,317	4	1,077	9	2,475	8	417	4	2,937	10	11,669	30,494
Osgoode	574	73	1,276	70	3	.4	3	0	193	24	334	18	22	3	199	11	792	1,812
Rideau	500	72	1,476	74	12	2	20	1	156	23	336	17	25	4	155	8	693	1,987
West Carleton	563	54	1,535	70	23	2	36	02	439	42	546	25	24	2	84	4	1,048	2,202
RMOC	10,082*	38	39,102*	47	—	—	—	—	15,156	57	42,294	51	1,212	5	2,298	3	26,450	83,694
Total	90,421	66	203,285	67	14,618	11	31,197	23	24,493	18	58,984	19	8,508	6	17,540	6	138,038	310,999

* Levies on area municipalities.

Source: Municipal Financial Reports 1969, 1975.

Grants to municipalities are paid under an assortment of statutes, and by means of a variety of formulae and subject to a multiplicity of conditions. The grant structure which municipalities face is exceedingly complicated, and well qualified local officials are necessary to make sure that a municipality gets all that it is entitled to. On finances and other matters, municipal relations with the Province are, in Stefan Dupré's words, "a pattern of hyper-fractionalized quasi-subordination".

Provincial grants may be divided into two categories, unconditional and conditional (or specific). Specific grants apply to many municipal services and are available for both current and capital purposes. Fire protection is one of the very few municipal services for which no grant at all is received.

The unconditional grants have been awarded in the last few years in response to municipal agitation that local "autonomy" was being seriously weakened with increases in the levels and variety of specific grants. The three main unconditional grants are the general support grant, the resource equalization grant, and the unconditional per capita grant.

The question of the extent to which provincial grants should be conditional or specific is a continuing debate. On the one hand, there is the municipal argument that only unconditional grants permit the municipalities to determine their own spending priorities; on the other side is the argument that the Province is ultimately responsible for the municipalities (seen, e.g., in the work of the Ontario Municipal Board) and the further point that only specific grants, with standards set by the Province, can ensure that certain services are provided equitably throughout the Province.

The whole argument seems like that of the irresistible force meeting the immovable object. But the force, i.e., the Province, is in fact stronger, and it can never give up all specific grants because of its province-wide, even national, responsibilities. Nevertheless, through negotiation and consultation (as in the Provincial-Municipal Liaison Committee), there has been a move towards more unconditional transfers, and perhaps even more "deconditionalization" of provincial money will come about.

Table 7-4 shows the amounts and the ratio of unconditional to conditional grants. While there is considerable variation, for the eleven area municipalities combined the amount of money received from the Province is nearly the same for both types of grants. For the Regional Municipality, a much higher proportion (88%) of provincial money is conditional, largely because of grants for Regional roads, social services, and OC Transpo.

A further issue with respect to provincial grants is their rate of growth. At the second National Tri-Level Conference at Edmonton, in 1973, an agreement was reached, widely referred to as the Edmonton Commitment. The main feature of the so-called Commitment was a promise by the provincial government that its transfer of money to municipalities would increase at the same rate as the Province's own revenues. While the exact meaning of this Commitment has been the subject of some dispute,[13] nonetheless the figures for the municipalities in Ottawa-Carleton appear to show that the Province has more than met its promise between 1973 and 1975. Table 7-5 illustrates the growth rate of current grants in the Region for this two-year period compared with the growth in provincial revenues.

At a less general and philosophic level, the most useful and practical changes that could be made to the system of provincial grants involve a simplification of the grant structure. The present system is of extreme administrative complexity. Perhaps the current Provincial

---

[13] M. J. Smither, "The Edmonton Commitment", *Municipal World*, January 1976, pp. 4-9.

Committee established to examine the grant system will make specific recommendations which can be of help in simplifying the system.

Table 7-4
Provincial Grants to RMOC and Area Municipalities, 1975

	(A) Unconditional ($000's)	(B) Conditional** ($000's)	Ratio of (A) to (B) (%)
Ottawa	7,240*	6,979	51:49
Vanier	1,504*	519	74:26
Rockcliffe Park	30	56	35:65
Cumberland	236*	443	35:65
Gloucester	2,041*	1,272	62:38
Goulbourn	328*	632	34:66
March	44	200	18:82
Nepean	2,197*	1,753	56:44
Osgoode	170	394	30:70
Rideau	149	536	22:78
West Carleton	164	727	18:82
Total Lower Tier	14,103	13,511	51:49
RMOC only	6,117*	48,144	11:89
GRAND TOTAL	20,220	61,655	25:75

Source: Municipal Financial Reports.
* The per capita police grant which is paid to the RMOC, then credited to the Regional levy of the four area municipalities with police forces, is included in the grants figure for the area municipalities, not in that of the RMOC.
** Includes Capital Grants.

Table 7—5
Provincial Grants and Subsidies, 1973-75
The Edmonton Commitment in Ottawa-Carleton
($000's)

	1973	1974	1975	1973-74 % Increase	1974-75 % Increase
Lower-Tier Total	10,272	13,383	16,701	30.3	24.8
RMOC	26,417	31,721	42,294	20.1	33.3
TOTAL	36,689	45,104	58,995	22.9	30.8

Provincial Revenue
% Increase

74/75 over 73/74	75/76 over 74/75
19.5	9.9

Source: Municipal Financial Reports, 1973–75; Ontario Budget, 1976.

Revenue — Payments-in-Lieu of Taxes (1) Federal

Table 7-6 sets forth, *inter alia*, the amount of payments made by the federal government and its agencies in lieu of taxes to the eleven area municipalities in the Region. The total amount of such payments is over $25 million, or about 11% of total current revenues received by all lower tier municipalities. This is a very high proportion compared with municipalities elsewhere in the Province. The bulk of these payments is made to the City of Ottawa — some $22.6 million or 14.5% of current City revenues. This is a result of the heavy concentration of federal properties in the City.

Table 7-6

Payments-in-Lieu of Taxes, 1975

Municipality	$000's Total Federal	Federal Payments as a % of Total Total Revenue	$000's Total Provincial and Municipal	Provincial/and Municipal Payments as a % of Total Revenue
Ottawa	$22,604	14.5	$5,561	3.6
Vanier	28	0.4	41	0.5
Rockcliffe Park	198	14.1	1	0.1
Cumberland	4	0.1	8	0.3
Gloucester	891	5.1	193	1.1
Goulbourn	5	0.2	3	0.1
March	252	9.5	2	0.1
Nepean	1,014	3.3	302	1.0
Osgoode	1	0.1	1	0.1
Rideau	2	0.1	18	0.9
West Carleton	14	0.6	22	1.0
Total	$25,013	11.0	$6,152	2.7

Source: Municipal Financial Reports, 1975.

Section 125 of the BNA Act specifically exempts the Crown from taxation. However, since 1952, federal payments-in-lieu of property taxes have been made under The Municipal Grants Act. In addition, an Order-in-Council of March 1967 instructed Crown agencies to pay "full grants-in-lieu of taxes" on their properties if they were not already doing so. Some points about these federal grants are worth noting:

First, the federal government does not make payments-in-lieu on all of its properties. Several categories of property are exempted by The Municipal Grants Act, including parks, museums, art galleries, historic sites or monuments, libraries, and "self-contained" defence establishments.

Second, the federal government and its agencies do not make payments-in-lieu of the municipal business tax except on a few properties such as the Bank of Canada, the CNR, Eldorado Nuclear, and a few other "profit-oriented" crown corporations. (It is surely ironic to say the CNR has anything to do with "profit".)

Third, the federal government makes "service deductions" from some of its payments. This is done because certain "municipal-type" services are provided by the government to some of its own properties, e.g., fire and police protection. These deductions have, however, been to a great extent removed in the last two years. Rightly so, in our opinion, since no private property by providing some of its own services can use these as an excuse for not paying all its municipal taxes.

Since the total amount of federal properties in the Region, particularly in Ottawa, is large, the exemptions and non-payments amount to a considerable revenue loss. The City estimated in 1973 that the total tax loss amounted to some $16 million annually, i.e., $16 million less than if the payments were equal to full taxation, including business tax.[14]

The federal government is perfectly within its legal rights to pay or not to pay as it deems appropriate. However, the federal government has advanced several arguments for non-payment or partial payment. For instance, the federal government has stated that the presence of their properties confers great benefits on the local municipalities. This is surely an illogical argument. Any private property owner, say of an office building that gives employment or is aesthetically pleasing, could argue thus, but would not thereby escape local taxes.

Regarding the non-payment of business taxes, the federal position is that most federal properties are not "businesses" in the normal sense of the word, i.e., not profit-oriented. It also argues that if these full payments were made, the City of Ottawa would benefit "unduly", and that many of the expenditures by the NCC compensate for them in any case. The federal rationale for not going all the way, once the principle of payments-in-lieu is accepted, is open to question. Let us take each of the points in turn:

(a) To say that most properties are not profit-making "businesses" is true enough but is beside the point. The intent of the business tax is to supplement the realty tax, especially on residences, because the realty tax alone is not sufficient to finance municipal services, and so the commercial and industrial portion of the assessment base should bear a heavier tax load than the residential portion. The municipal services, in turn, are part of the externalities (or social costs) which any employer and his property throws upon a municipality — for roads, schools, public transit and social services.

The business tax is levied at varying rates from 25% to 140% of assessed value, depending on the type of business. The highest rates are levied on those businesses which, though not a crime, are thought to be not quite respectable, such as distilleries and breweries. (Ottawa, alas, has no brewery now — the last having moved to Toronto a few years ago. O tempora, O mores!)

If the business tax were not levied, the realty tax would have to be increased. The effect of non-payment by the federal government of this tax is to shift a greater burden of taxation to other properties.

There is also the point that whenever the federal government (or any government) rents an office building which was formerly rented by a private tenant the business tax is lost to the municipality. This is because the business tax is levied on the occupant, not on the owner.

Still, the federal argument has some validity. It can be regarded as an "essentially contestable" proposition, and doubtless the debate over the non-payment of the business tax

---

[14] *A Submission of the City of Ottawa on the Federal Government Policy on Grants-In-Lieu of Municipal Taxation*, May, 1973. For 1976, the City estimates that the federal non-payments amounted to some $27 million, 1/3 on account of property tax, 2/3 on account of business tax.

on all commercial government property will go on for years to come. (In a sense the whole argument is about definitions and we are trapped by the categories: (a) residential/farm, and (b) commercial/industrial. Most federal properties are not (a), then they must be (b)).

(b) The point about the "undue" benefits that would accrue to the City of Ottawa if the federal exemptions and non-payments were discontinued has two elements.

First, if federal policy were changed, all municipalities throughout Canada would receive additional payments in proportion to the amount of federal properties contained within their boundaries. To that, one can only say, so what.

Second, however, this raises the broader question of who should benefit from the revenues arising from non-residential property. If the preceding argument relating to the sharing (or pooling) of commercial and industrial assessment is valid, then it is equally valid in the case of payments-in-lieu of exempt assessment. If the social costs that must be met by municipalities are to some extent incurred in the residential, suburban and outlying municipalities of the Region, then the revenues resulting from employment-generating properties in the City should be shared on a Regional basis.

(c) As for the NCC "compensating expenditures", this is a frail reed on which to rest. It destroys itself, so to speak, by reason of the fact that the NCC does make certain payments-in-lieu of taxes. In any case the NCC functions were never meant to "compensate" for grants in-lieu, but are in recognition of the special federal interest in beautifying the National Capital Region on both sides of the Ottawa River. It may be noted that the latter was the precise federal argument used of Ottawa when the Ottawa Improvement Commission was set up in 1899. Nothing was said about payments-in-lieu, or "compensation" — (the argument used recently in the Fullerton Report).

As mentioned already the provincial governments proposals for property tax reform call for elimination of tax exempt status of nearly all properties under provincial statutes. The Province has indicated its desire that the federal government harmonize policies in this matter with those of the Province. We support such consistency.

Revenue — Payments-in-lieu of taxes: (2) Provincial and Municipal

As with properties owned by the federal government, provincial and municipal properties are also legally exempt from property taxation. However, the Province and its agencies make payments-in-lieu on many of their properties, such as hospitals, parks, universities, Ontario Hydro properties, Liquor Control Board stores, Ontario Housing Corporation properties and others.

These payments are made under a variety of statutes and do not always bear any relationship to the value of the property concerned. For instance payments-in-lieu on universities and colleges are calculated on the number of students attending the institution. In addition, a few municipal special purpose bodies such as Hydro Commissions and the Regional waterworks make payments-in-lieu. Certain of the provincial payments-in-lieu, for instance those on behalf of the O.H.C. and universities earmark a portion of the money for the school boards and the Regional Government.

The total amount of provincial and municipal payments-in-lieu of property taxes in Ottawa-Carleton as shown in the preceding table, (table 7-6), was over $6 million in 1975 or slightly less than 3% of total current revenues. Although only about a quarter the total amount of federal payments-in-lieu, it represents nonetheless an important revenue source. As with the federal payments, there is considerable variation in the proportion going to the different area municipalities. The bulk, however — over $5½ million — goes to the City of Ottawa where most of the provincial properties in the RMOC are located.

As we have mentioned, the Province proposes to remove the tax exempt status of nearly all public property. The only remaining public exemptions will be "unpatented lands, highways, and public cemeteries". All government administrative facilities are to be subject to an additional assessment of 50% of market value for business taxes. This is exactly the same base for the business tax as that to be used for all private businesses, and the result will then be a uniform rate of 50% replacing the present variable rate of 25% to 140% depending on the type of business. And it will, moreover, be uniform throughout the province.

These proposals are fundamentally sound and progressive, and one hopes that the provincial government will implement them along with the other proposed reforms to the property tax system, and that the federal government will follow suit.

Expenditure

As the following summary (Table 7-7) indicates, local current spending has increased since 1969, when the RMOC and amalgamated school boards were formed, by a total of some 128%. The total amount spent by all local jurisdictions in Ottawa-Carleton came to over $400 million in 1975, or slightly less than $800 for every inhabitant of the Region. An additional $100 million was spent on capital expenditures during 1975.

Table 7-7
Current Expenditure Summary, Municipalities and School Boards, 1969-75

	(millions of dollars) 1969	1975	% Increase 1969-1975	% of Total 1969	1975
Total Lower Tier	48.6	117.6	142	28	29
RMOC	26.5	82.8	212	15	21
Total School Boards	101.3	201.0	98	57	50
Grand Total	$176.4	$401.5	128%	100	100

Source: Municipal Financial Reports
School Board Financial Statements.

Because the cost of the Regional Government has been a subject of considerable public controversy since the Region was established, this topic merits further examination. *First*, the school boards are the biggest spenders, between them accounting for as much money as all eleven area municipalities and the Regional Government combined. The rate of increase of education spending since 1969 however, has not been as great as municipal spending. This is in part because of spending "ceilings" imposed by the Ministry of Education, as well as the fact that the two Ottawa Boards have experienced a decline in the number of students. The rate of spending increase for the two Carleton Boards is more than double that for the Ottawa Boards, as the Carleton Boards have had to accommodate an increasing student population. (Education policies are dealt with in more detail in Chapter 10).

Second, looking at the seven year rate of increase in municipal spending one sees that the expenditures of the RMOC have increased more quickly than the aggregated lower tier. However, several of the area municipalities *individually* have experienced more rapid spending increases than the RMOC. In part the rapid increases in townships such as Nepean,

Gloucester, Rideau and Cumberland can be explained by population growth. If their expenditures are analysed on a per capita basis, which separates out the growth component, one can see their spending increases are not nearly as dramatic. (See Table 7-8.) In one case, however, that of Vanier, spending per capita has increased at a greater rate than total spending.

Before a closer look is taken at what lies behind these aggregated figures, we should try to keep municipal expenditure in perspective by comparing it with that of senior governments. Over the same period (1969-1975) federal budgetary expenditures increased by 142% (from $10.8 billion to $26.1 billion) and Ontario provincial budgetary expenditure has gone up 143% (from $3.6 billion to $8.7 billion).[15]

Table 7-8
Current Expenditures, Municipal and School Boards, 1969-1975*

Municipality	Total ($000's) 1969	1975	% Increase	Per Capita 1969	1975	% Increase
Ottawa	38,480	79,182	106	131	262	100
Vanier	1,804	5,359	197	76	266	250
Rockcliffe Park	317	558	76	141	250	77
Cumberland	346	1,570	354	46	137	198
Gloucester	2,019	9,423	367	72	177	146
Goulbourn	385	1,414	267	56	113	102
March	321	1,138	255	73	165	126
Nepean	3,757	16,047	327	66	217	229
Osgoode	325	928	186	46	112	143
Rideau	237	868	266	61	110	80
West Carleton	572	1,135	98	113	146	29
RMOC only	26,530	82,842	212	60	163	172

School Boards	Total (000's)		% Increase	Per Student		% Increase
Ottawa Bd. of Ed.	52,606	86,891	65	1,015	1,834	81
Ottawa Separate	18,984	31,610	67	618	1,342	117
Carleton Bd. of Ed.	23,493	63,236	169	845	1,679	99
Carleton Separate	6,203	19,265	211	620	1,245	101
Grand Total Municipal & Education	$176,375	$401,466	128%			

Source: Municipal Financial Reports, 1969, 1975.
School Board Financial Reports, 1969, 1975.
* To avoid double counting, current expenditures for lower tier municipalities are net figures, i.e. Total Current Expenditures less Regional and School levies.

---

[15] Public Accounts of Canada; Ontario Budget 1976.

Third, we can try to explain why the increased spending took place. Besides simple growth in the number of people to be served there are several other factors which account for the increases in municipal spending. In general terms these are: (a) inflation, (b) new or expanded services, and (c) upgraded or improved services.

In a recent comparative analysis of municipal spending over the period 1970-1975 throughout the Province conducted by the Ministry of TEIGA, inflation was cited as the single most important factor contributing to the higher costs of municipal government.[16] Indeed, inflation rates for the Regional Government areas exceeded those for the remainder of the Province (Metro Toronto and the County areas). The general rate of national inflation during the period under consideration, (1969-1975), as measured by the Consumer Price Index, was 47%. A contributing inflationary factor is that with reorganization and amalgamation of formerly separate municipalities, salaries and wages tend to increase to the level of the highest of the units being merged.

New or improved services have certainly played a large role in increasing municipal costs in Ottawa-Carleton. A look at RMOC expenditures (Table 7-9) reveals several important points. (It should be noted that expenditure comparisons between the former Carleton County (1968) and the RMOC would be extremely misleading for two reasons: (1) the RMOC now includes the cities of Ottawa and Vanier which were not part of Carleton County; and (2) the RMOC carries out several major responsibilities which were not handled at the upper-tier level in Carleton County, e.g., water, main sewerage, social services).

One of the costliest new services taken on by the RMOC (1971) was public transit. The Region took over the Ottawa Transit Commission and began to expand bus service beyond the City, adding new lines, buying new buses and building hundreds of bus shelters. Of the $37.3 million spent by the RMOC on "transportation services" in 1975, over $21 million went for public transit. (See also Chapter 5, Roads and Transport.) The citizens have wanted better public transit, and the RMOC has provided it. It is therefore foolish to blame the RMOC for this increase in spending. Or to blame the municipalities in general, for higher spending, when the public has demanded more and better services.

Table 7-9
RMOC Current Expenditures, by Service Category, 1969-75

	1969 $000's	1969 % of Total	1975 $000's	1975 % of Total	% Increase
General Government	2,501	9.4	6,449	7.8	158
Transportation	5,828	22.0	37,294	45.0	540
Environment	3,176	12.0	5,480	6.6	73
Health	3,256	12.3	5,999	7.2	84
Social & Family Services	10,699	40.3	24,956	30.1	133
Planning & Development	45	.2	1,967	2.4	4271
Other	1,024	3.9	697	.8	—32
TOTAL	$26,530	100%	$82,842	100%	212%

Source: RMOC Financial Statements 1969, 1975.

---

[16] Ontario Ministry of TEIGA, *Regional Government in Perspective: A Financial Review*, May, 1976.

Another RMOC service which has shown a large percentage increase is planning, although planning still represents a very small proportion of total RMOC expenditures. The lack of area-wide and systematic municipal planning was one of the major reasons for creation of Regional Governments. It follows that the RMOC had to acquire and expand a planning staff, and that the planning budget should grow since 1969. Expenditure on planning is to a large degree a long run investment and has to be weighed against the hidden costs which would result from lack of over-all planning, especially since such costs often do not appear until several years after development has occurred.

Social and family services, which make up the second largest category in the Regional budget, have also been expanded considerably in the last few years. Unless we are totally lacking in compassion, we can hardly object to these increases. (In any case, most of the money comes from senior governments, and is merely administered by the RMOC). Spending on day care alone, a relatively new service, rose from $228,000 in 1969 to over $3¼ million in 1975. For several other services the story is much the same. Since the Region began, the capacity of sewage treatment plants has been greatly expanded, new public health clinics opened, Regional roads reconstructed and upgraded, and so on. A further new service to be provided at the Regional level from 1976 is "solid waste disposal", i.e., the operation of what used to be called "garbage dumps".

Similarly for the area municipalities, expansion of services has contributed strongly to cost. In addition to the spending increases associated inevitably with growth in the suburbs, there are increases due to improved levels of service. The culture and recreation field (including "community development") is among the fastest growing. Planning at the local level has also shown a strong increase, although as at the Regional level, it takes only a small proportion of municipal budgets. Table 7-10 shows increases in spending by category for each of the area municipalities. These figures are summarized and aggregated in Table 7-11. Taking into account all the factors mentioned one finds it impossible to sustain a charge of extravagance or incompetence.

Capital expenditures, illustrated in Table 7-12, have shown an even greater rate of increase than current expenditures. These have been incurred to finance the expansion and upgrading of services. The increase in capital spending at the Regional level has been particularly marked. The largest Regional capital expenditures during 1975 were for the sanitary sewer system. Who, with any concern for the environment, can deny the case for this spending?

Capital spending in many area municipalities appears to have tapered off during the last year or two before restructuring, as well as in the year of restructuring (1969), perhaps in anticipation of the creation of the RMOC. This contributed to a backlog of capital projects to be financed in later years. In a general review of municipal spending across Ontario this factor was identified as being significant in contributing to increased capital spending by several Regional governments.[17] A similar factor identified by the Henderson Report — the running down of financial assets (reserves and surpluses) just prior to reorganization — does not appear to have been a factor in Ottawa-Carleton.[18]

One of the accusations often made against the two-tiered system of Regional government is that there is costly duplication of staff and services. Upon closer examination, however, the importance of this argument seems to be greatly exaggerated. A small amount

---

[17] *Report of the Special Program Review* (The Henderson Report), Ontario, November 1975, p. 196.
[18] Special study done by TEIGA for the Ottawa-Carleton Review Commission, 1976.

of duplication is inherent in any two-tier system. This is perhaps most evident in the area of "general government", which includes the costs of councils and the central administrative functions (clerks' department, treasurers' department and so on). In this regard it is the area municipalities, rather than the RMOC, which have increased more rapidly their spending on administration. Compare Tables 7-9 and 7-11 under the heading of "general government".

As to the other functions that are carried out at both levels — mainly roads, sewers and planning — there is not so much a duplication of activities as a division of labour. For instance, the RMOC is responsible for major arterial roads, while the roads of the area municipalities are intended to serve local traffic. Similarly in planning there are matters of Region-wide significance and matters of purely local significance.

One of the strengths of the two-tier system is that it leaves small local matters — the so-called "parish pump" functions — in the hands of local councils. "Small enough to know you; big enough to serve you." At the same time it offers a scope of jurisdiction at the upper tier which can ensure that issues of Region-wide significance are dealt with in a co-ordinated way. The limited amount of extra juggling necessary, for instance, to ensure co-ordinated snow ploughing schedules for local and Regional roads, seems a small price to pay for the advantage of Regionalization.

Whether the rapid rise in municipal spending in recent years has been effective or wise is of course essentially a political question. Perhaps at this point it is prudent to reconsider the quotation of Jean Lesage at the beginning of this Chapter. Whether the area municipalities and the Region have proceeded too quickly in trying to meet their objectives by the expansion and upgrading of services only the public and their political representatives can judge. Possibly the attainment of some objectives should have been postponed, but it is not for us to say.

The increased spending for large items such as public transit, an improved sewerage system, expanded day care and public housing, all seem to have been preceded by considerable public pressure, and to enjoy public support. Whether the next few years will be a period of moderated demand for public services and a time for taking stock is an open question. To the extent that growth alone generates increased demand for services, Ottawa-Carleton will of course not see a moderation of spending. In our opinion we shall always see a demand for services accompanied by some discontent with the taxation needed to satisfy the demand. This is one of the facts of life which politicians have to learn to live with, and which the public ought to realize.

It follows from what has been said above that we reject the charges of alleged inefficiency and "abnormal expansion in municipal employment and costs" set forth loosely in the Fullerton Report (pp. 75-81). One of the Fullerton "tests of efficiency" is that he found it easier to deal on behalf of the NCC with one municipality, the City of Ottawa, than with the City plus the RMOC! Another charge (by innuendo) is that the rural areas are forced to spend money on services they don't need, e.g., water, sewer; and that it raises the pay for "rural policemen".

On both of these points there is displayed the usual federal lack of knowledge of municipalities. For one thing, water and sewer services are "area rated", and "user charged", i.e., those who do not get the services, don't usually pay for them. As for the wages of "rural policemen", there are no such policemen, except for the OPP which polices, for free, the outer municipalities.

Table 7-10

Area Municipalities, Current Expenditures by Category ($000's), 1969-1975

	General Government			Protection			Transport			Environment			Recreation & Culture			Planning & Development		
	1969	1975	% Increase	1969	1975	% Increase	1969	1975	% Increase	1969	1975	% Increase	1969	1975	% Increase	1969	1975	% Increase
Ottawa	3,585	13,826	286	12,377	26,481	114	8,567	12,528	46	2,866	7,063	146	6,078	14,590	140	1,067	2,406	125
Vanier	214	1,001	372	625	1,690	170	409	669	64	250	674	170	144	507	252	23	744	*
Rockcliffe Park	61	118	93	90	140	56	112	117	5	57	120	111	6	57	850	0	5	*
Cumberland	28	141	404	27	208	670	215	621	189	6	132	*	16	377	*	1	89	*
Gloucester	221	1,820	724	540	2,633	388	510	1,670	227	283	603	113	157	2,151	*	80	485	506
Goulbourn	61	326	434	60	111	85	184	363	97	25	117	368	16	432	*	5	64	*
March	45	171	280	43	167	288	127	252	98	30	77	157	36	415	*	11	43	291
Nepean	340	1,426	319	1,026	3,863	277	583	2,006	244	992	2,352	188	465	4,416	850	39	430	*
Osgoode	35	138	294	13	59	354	198	356	80	2	34	*	24	225	838	4	116	*
Rideau	28	163	482	13	91	600	158	412	161	2	49	*	4	123	*	2	25	*
West Carleton	52	249	379	46	106	130	419	5656	57	8	35	338	8	32	300	8	53	563
Total	$ 4,670	19,389	315	$14,860	35,549	139	$11,482	19,650	71	$ 4,521	11,756	160	$ 6,954	23,325	235	$ 1,240	4,460	260

Source: Municipal Financial Reports, 1960 and 1975.
* More than 1,000%.
Note: The educational and regional levies are omitted as well as several small expenditure categories.

Table 7-11
Area Municipalities-Current Expenditure by Service Category
Aggregate Summary
(Millions of Dollars)

Total Lower Tier	1969	1975	Percent increase
General Government	4.7	19.4	315
Protection Services	14.9	35.5	139
Transportation	11.5	19.7	71
Environmental Services	4.5	11.8	160
Recreation & Culture	7.0	23.3	235
Planning & Development	1.2	4.5	260

Source: Municipal Financial Reports, 1969 and 1975.

Table 7-12
Capital Expenditures in the RMOC, 1969-1975

	1969 $000's	1975 $000's	1969-1975 % Increase
Ottawa	11,718	23,622	111
Vanier	170	2,353	1,284
Rockcliffe Park	12	49	308
Cumberland	457	874	91
Gloucester	766	3,281	328
Goulbourn	94	1,458	1,451
March	48	968	1,916
Nepean	730	14,401	1,873
Osgoode	84	581	592
Rideau	57	1,011	1,674
West Carleton	23	355	1,443
Sub-total (Lower Tier)	(13,619)	(48,953)	(259)
RMOC only	1,262	51,483	3,979
Grand Total	$14,881	$100,436	575%

Source: Municipal Financial Reports, 1969, 1975.
Note: Capital expenditures in several area municipalities were at a low point in 1969, which makes the rate of increase by 1975 appear artificially high.

Table 7-13
Direct Municipal Debt,* RMOC and Area Municipalities, 1969-75

	Total Debt ($000's) 1969	1975	% Increase	Per Capita Debt 1969	1975	% Increase	Debt as % of Taxable Assessment 1969	1975
RMOC only	$31,540	$71,718	127	$ 71	$143	102	0.8	1.2
Ottawa	61,138	59,991	—2	209	199	—4	8.5	6.9
Vanier	3,331	5,416	63	107	269	154	8.4	15.5
Rockcliffe	192	491	156	85	220	158	2.7	7.0
Cumberland	56	620	1007	8	56	646	1.0	6.4
Gloucester	1,987	8,373	321	71	157	121	6.4	14.5
Goulbourn	56	493	780	8	39	384	—	4.7
March	150	539	259	34	78	130	3.4	6.4
Nepean	3,915	14,739	276	69	199	187	6.5	16.7
Osgoode	204	812	298	29	98	237	3.3	10.6
Rideau	33	201	509	9	27	212	—	2.3
West Carleton	34	512	1406	7	66	82	—	0.3
Lower Tier Average	—	—	—	159	182	15		

1975 Total Regional Average: RMOC per capita debt plus lower tier average per capita debt
= $143 + $182 = $325 per capita.

Source: Municipal Financial Reports, 1969, 1975.
* Excludes short term debt and debt of municipal enterprises (OC Transpo, RMOC waterworks, and area hydro commissions, some of which are self-liquidating).

Long term Debt

As indicated in Table 7-13, long term municipal debt has increased greatly at both upper and lower tier levels since 1969. Total per capita debt on the average now stands at $325 with the expected variation amongst area municipalities.[19] Only the City of Ottawa has not shown an increase in debt. This results to a large degree from the fact that when the RMOC was formed it took over the assets and liabilities associated with the new Regional services which in Ottawa included significant debts for arterial roads and sewerage.

That debt should have increased significantly should come as no surprise given the large increase in capital spending shown above except for the special case of Ottawa. (See Table 7-12.) The RMOC and larger municipalities finance most of their debt through public debentures. Other debt is held by senior governments, primarily the Province. For the outlying municipalities with smaller debts, the Province holds a much larger portion of the liabilities.

One of the innovations introduced with the RMOC was the centralization of the debenture issuing function. The RMOC now issues debentures for itself and on behalf of the area municipalities. Not only does this permit more favourable rates of interest to be

---

[19] As a matter of interest the provincial per capita net debt is of the order of $590.

obtained, but it also permits centralization of debt management expertise, in the Finance Department of the RMOC. These are excellent examples of the sorts of benefits that can be obtained through Regional governments.

The school boards, however, still retain their own debt management function separate from the RMOC. For the two reasons mentioned above it would appear to be more efficient to have RMOC handle debenture borrowing on behalf of the school boards as well as the area municipalities. Although most of the school board debentures are issued to the Ontario Education Capital Aid Corporation, therefore the RMOC would handle, in the near future, only a small part of School Board debt.

Summary

Since this Chapter is long and complicated, our findings and recommendations are summarized below.

(1) We endorse the practice that assessment remain a provincial function, (a) on grounds of its efficiency (assessors are likely to be better trained); and (b) for the sake of equity (the whole province will be assessed in the same manner); and (c) it lifts the costs from the municipalities to the Province. Accordingly we dissent from the view sometimes heard that the assessment function should be returned to the municipalities, whether at the Regional or lower tier.

(2) We recommend that all commercial/industrialized assessment in the Region be "pooled", and allocated by the RMOC to the area municipalities on the basis of population.

(3) Further, we recommend that the resource equalization grants (calculated by the Province) be distributed via the RMOC as in (2) immediately above. (At any rate, *some* adjustments in these grants would have to be made if (2) is followed, because "pooling" will affect the deficiencies in assessment on which this grant is made.)

(4) (a) All property tax exemptions should be eliminated, perhaps not all at once, but say over about five years. In certain cases grants should be given to some affected institutions (such as charities) to offset the loss of exempt status. (b) These grants in some cases will be municipal, in other cases provincial. We suggest also that the federal government make full payments-in-lieu of taxes, including the full business tax, on all their properties, and not make any remaining "service deductions", and further that all these payments be pooled in the RMOC, which would allocate them as in (2) above.

(5) On no account should school boards be given the authority to levy and collect their own local taxes. Maintaining the status quo is better than "progressing backwards".

(6) Municipal rates should be collected four times a year, in those municipalities which at present collect them less often. This is in order to improve cash flow, lessen borrowing, and soften the "psychological" impact of paying property taxes.

(7) On no account should municipalities be permitted to levy income or sales taxes; nor should a share of "earmarked" provincial taxes be allocated to them. (In agitating for a share of "earmarked" taxes, municipalities will find themselves with *less* revenue should the Province alter the tax rate that is "earmarked".)

(8) We endorse the provincial proposals for a common business tax, i.e., 50% of full (100%) assessment of commercial/industrial property.

(9) We recommend a simplification of the provincial grant and subsidy arrangements. The details of such a simplification are so involved that we refrain from attempting to specify them. One of the cardinal points however is to make more grants unconditional. (The grants can never be entirely unconditional because of the Province's responsibility to ensure provincial standards — and hence equity — in some services).

CHAPTER 8

Municipal Boundaries
or
Let's not rock the boat, one change in a century is enough

"It is notorious that social institutions respond tardily to the stimuli of technological advances, which do not require consensus among men for adoption. Institutional lag therefore is expected and understood. What cannot be so readily accepted is the continued rationalization of governmental structure and practice in nineteenth century terms. The cry for help comes from an urban-industrial democracy, but the answering voice is that of a wilderness agrarianism of a bygone day."[1]

Introductory

In one way it is a pity that the ambiguous word "region" ever became attached to municipalities. There are "regions" of the whole world spoken of in international relations. Within Canada, we speak often of five "regions" of the country. Within Ontario, there are ten economic "regions." And so it goes. It is almost as bad as the many meanings given that very elastic word "community," of which there are ninety-four definitions in use, and which we should handle with care.[2]

As for the Ottawa-centred "region" — there is within it the National Capital Region (taking in a lot of territory on both sides of the Ottawa River); then there is the Outaouais "Regional" Community (or Municipality) on the Quebec side; and the "Regional" Municipality of Ottawa-Carleton — which is our quarry in this Report. We seem to be stuck with this municipal usage of the word "Regional" unless the provincial government in its wisdom sees fit to substitute for it, say, the word "metropolitan," for every Regional municipality in the Province (or perhaps restore the old word "County," to the "Regional" governments).

The trouble is, of course, that the meaning of "region" varies according to the criteria chosen to define it. For example, some writers define a "functional region" as "an area in which one or more selected phenomena of movement connect the localities within it into a functionally organized whole."[3] Since the boundaries of the "functional region" are delineated on the basis of one common characteristic, fewer planning problems arise. But

---

[1] Roscoe C. Martin, *Grass Roots*, Harper & Row, N.Y., 1965, p. 79.

[2] J. Gould and W.L. Kolb, *A Dictionary of the Social Sciences*, Tavistock Publications, London, 1964, p. 114. (I would never use the wretched word "community", but if I did I would define it as "any human settlement where two or more people live without assaulting one another.")

[3] Brian J. L. Berry and Thomas D. Hankins, *A Bibliographic Guide to the Économic Regions of the United States*, Department of Geography Research Series No. 87, University of Chicago, Chicago, 1963, p. x.

this choice is arbitrary, since there is one obstinate fact: the political boundary which is best for one purpose is not necessarily the best for all purposes. And that is the simple, stark, reason why "Regional" and other municipal boundaries are so hard to draw, and are always a compromise.

Statistics Canada and most university researchers use various transportation and commuting measures as the delimiting criteria for urban-centred regions. The Census of Canada defines Census Metropolitan Areas by outlining the daily commuting field of a continuous built-up area. In 1971, there were 22 CMA's in Canada, containing over 55% of the population.[4] Nine of these CMA's were located in Ontario and contained 66% of the provincial population.

France and the United States have also adopted the concept of daily commuting to work to delineate metropolitan zones. This is very like what the Gloucester Township brief stated: "Generally speaking, the external boundaries of the Region should coincide with the socio-economic area of which the City of Ottawa is the hub and main centre."[5]

As we have noted in Chapter 1, the RMOC is unique in that it adjoins the Province of Quebec. For this reason, the total commuter-shed cannot form the basis of delineation of the boundaries of the RMOC. Hull and its environs must answer to the Province of Quebec while the RMOC must answer to the Province of Ontario. These relationships have their foundation in the BNA Act and cannot easily be changed, despite the large amount of commuting that occurs in both directions between the RMOC and Hull.

One Tier or Two?

With that introduction out of the way, we can now consider the most basic question of all: should the RMOC continue, or should all the municipalities within it be amalgamated into one municipality? The name is secondary, but if such an amalgamation were to take place, it would seem simplest to call it the City of Ottawa.

The Commission has given a good deal of time, discussion and thought to answering this question. In favour of the proposal of one big city, the arguments are as follows:

(1) The total population of the RMOC is only 506,606. There are several cities of that size already in Canada (e.g., Edmonton, Winnipeg), and hundreds throughout the world. Even if it should reach one million by the end of the century, the Region would still not be beyond the population of many cities of the world.

(2) One tier, instead of two, is somewhat easier for citizens to understand. They would have only one council to hold accountable for all municipal functions. They could focus upon it all their complaints when things go wrong, and all their compliments when things go right.

The latter part of the preceding sentence is doubtful, since praise and gratitude for governments at any level are not commonly found in politics. Acquiescence and tacit consent are more common.

Most people may not "lead lives of quiet desperation", as Thoreau thought. But the majority do not, as a rule, have a keen interest in, much less gratitude for, the way their municipalities are run. Moreover, in Rousseau's words, "A people constantly assembled to dispatch public business is impossible to imagine."

---

[4] Canada, Ministry of State for Urban Affairs, *Human Settlement in Canada*, Ottawa, 1976, p. 10.

[5] Gloucester Township, *Submission to the Ottawa-Carleton Review Commission*, March 17, 1976, p. 34.

Municipal rhetoric, however, would lead us to think otherwise, and goes something like this: "we are closest to the people, therefore they are most knowledgeable and interested in what we do." Unfortunately, perhaps, the rhetoric covers a myth. In spite of all kinds of evidence to the contrary — the small voting turnout, seats filled by acclamation, even the difficulty in getting people to run for office — the myth persists. It is especially strong in the small rural municipalities of Ontario, though it flourishes also in the Ottawa-Carleton Region.

"Man is a believing animal," and often does not examine the myths he lives by. That may be why the "true believer" gets angry when someone shows scepticism about his beliefs. In any case, as we have noted at the beginning of Chapter 1, there is very little theory of local government to fall back upon. We must make do with the shreds and patches we have, supplemented with large doses of common sense.

To return now from this slight digression, we have occasionally heard a third argument:

(3) It is not dignified enough for the City of Ottawa to be a municipality within a municipality. The City is the Capital (seat of government) of Canada and is therefore special, not just a municipality like the others, subject as others are to the fatherly supervision (and subsidies) of Queen's Park.

An interesting variation of the above was presented by the Mayor of Ottawa. He proposed that Ottawa should become a "city-state," and that a referendum should be held on the subject, at least within the Greenbelt; and the other areas could also join, again by a referendum. The "city-state," should it be created, would have all the rights of an eleventh Province of Canada.

This proposal is rejected for several reasons:

(a) The method of setting municipal boundaries by referendum has long been abandoned in this Province, in favour of Ontario Municipal Board action, and a good thing too. One has only to see the method of boundary setting by referendum in the U.S.A., to realize in what a fragmented jurisdictional mess the referendum method leaves cities, counties and metropolitan areas in that country. (There is also the point, of course, that a referendum, if held here, might well reject the "city-state" idea, and we should then be back where we are now).

(b) By making Ottawa into a province we should be making its boundaries much more rigid, and leave the city-state-province without any voice or jurisdiction at all in matters (such as planning) outside its boundaries. (It is more difficult to alter the boundaries of a province than those of a municipality.)

(c) Being independent, a city-state-province would have no formal means of co-operating with the municipalities in the Region — one of the very deficiencies which the RMOC was set up to remedy. The idea ignores that the Region is, in many senses, one entity bound together by many ties, and should be governed as an entity. To remove the city-state (albeit a province), from the Region, would be a backward step to pre-1969 when the City (and Vanier) were separate from Carleton County.

(d) The horrendous political and constitutional issues raised by the proposal would make the strongest flinch from the prospect. Another province of some 300,000 in eastern Ontario? One surrounded entirely by a federal Greenbelt? Would the federal government necessarily put (or keep) departments or agencies in the new province as well as in Ontario and Quebec? Would or could the federal government create such a province? Would Ontario agree? Or Quebec? Or the other Provinces? What about amending the BNA Act? What new tangles would be added to the already tangled skein of federal-provincial relations?

No, this kite will not fly, and there is no point in trying to get it off the ground.[6]

Of the 66 briefs heard publicly by this Commission, the only proponent of one-tier government for the Region (as distinct from the city-state-province idea) was the Ottawa Board of Trade. It argued that at present the Region is overgoverned, thus leading to a "costly and unwieldy" system of government. The Board of Trade argued that the duplication in the services provided by the Region and by the individual municipalities has resulted in "a substantial increase in taxes" and "has caused delays in such important areas as planning and welfare". The Board also claimed that two single-tier systems — one urban, one rural — would ensure that services would be available on a uniform basis throughout "all areas of the urban municipality."[7] There was next to no evidence provided to support the charges, or the assertions in favour of a single tier. (Some evidence can be found of course, but it is a matter of judgment what weight to give to it.)[8]

In later newspaper advertisements, in connection with Board of Trade Week, the Board kept to its view of only two municipalities: one urban, i.e., the City of Ottawa expanding to take in all within the Greenbelt; and one rural, outside the City; with no upper tier. These proposals are absurd in calling "rural" everything outside the Greenbelt; and in their lack of any co-ordination for the two suggested municipalities.

In Metropolitan Toronto, the support for one-tier municipal government was much stronger (possibly because Metro Toronto is virtually all urban). Of all the briefs received by the Royal Commission on Metropolitan Toronto, slightly less than one-third were in favour of amalgamating the six lower-tier municipalities into one unit.[9]

We find the arguments for a single tier tempting but not completely convincing, at least for this Region. They would carry more weight perhaps if the Region were totally urban and of smaller area. But the Region is neither of these things.

Again, while a single council is, without doubt, somewhat easier to understand and hold accountable, it is absurd to suggest that the public (or at least the interested part of it) cannot understand a two-tier system. People in all that part of the Region outside Ottawa and Vanier, i.e., the municipalities in the former Carleton County (plus the Township of Cumberland), have been used to a two-tier county system for a century. People in Ottawa and Vanier have lived with the two-tier Regional system now for some seven years. They pay their water bills directly to the RMOC, they ride its buses, they receive its social services, they pop their elderly relatives in the RMOC Homes for the Aged, they see Regional road signs every day, they see the Regional levy on their tax bills.

In the end, then, we recommend the retention of the present two-tier system. It has established itself as part of the municipal scene, and in our judgment has worked well — both

---

[6] Only two federal states in the world (Austria and Nigeria) have their capital city as a city-state. Vienna is the largest "state" in the Austrian federation, as well as the largest city. For several reasons this example is not of much use to Canada. On this I agree with *The Fullerton Report*. See also Donald C. Rowat (ed.), *The Government of Federal Capitals*, University of Toronto Press, 1973.

[7] The Board was more concerned with the "urban" area, and seemed sometimes in favour of a two-tier system for that area, with boroughs of some 40,000 forming a quasi-lower tier. *Brief*, p. 4. They also hinted at two or more "rural" municipalities, *Brief*, p. 9.

[8] It is perhaps a pity that something like the Bureau of Municipal Research (Toronto) does not exist in the RMOC, supported by business, governments and individuals.

[9] The Royal Commission on Metropolitan Toronto, *Update*, June, 1976, p. 3.

in carrying out the functions for which it was set up in the first place, and also those which were later assigned to it.

To say this is not to say that no changes should be made. Indeed, throughout this Report a good many changes are recommended. These changes deal with the division of powers as between the RMOC itself and the area municipalities, with the reduction of ad hoc, or special purpose, bodies; and numerous other matters. (See Chapter 18, Summary of Recommendations, at the end of this Report).

This Chapter therefore deals with questions of the external and internal municipal boundaries of the RMOC, on the assumption that the RMOC will continue. First, the external boundaries.

External Boundaries

(a) *Russell Township, to the southeast*

The daily commuter-shed is an important but not the only criterion which may be used for delimiting Regions. D. Michael Ray's study on the central place functions of urban centres in Eastern Ontario shows that residents of Russell Township travel to Ottawa for medical, legal, dental and optical services.[10] Hospital services are provided to a large extent by hospitals located in the City of Ottawa. The opening of Highway 417, and its links with the Queensway, have increased commuting to the RMOC.

In a meeting with the Russell Township Council, the Commission was told that a majority — up to 90% — of the Russell Township work force have jobs outside the Township, primarily in the RMOC. A study prepared by Statistics Canada shows that 25% to 49.9% of the labour force of Russell Township works in the urban core of Ottawa-Hull. In fact the number of commuters from Russell Township working in the core is higher than the number from some of the areas presently within the Region.[11]

For these reasons, i.e., because there are so many close ties, we recommend that Russell Township (population 4,775 in 1975) should be brought within the RMOC. This would leave the United Counties of Prescott and Russell somewhat smaller than at present, but even so Prescott and Russell would still be more populous (at 42,500, 1975 figures) than several other Ontario counties, e.g., Prince Edward, Dufferin, Lennox and Addington, Victoria; and almost as populous as Lanark.

(b) *West Carleton Township*

In the extreme northwest of the RMOC, we found that the population of a part of the Township of West Carleton is oriented very much towards the Town of Arnprior in the County of Renfrew. At present, substantial co-operation exists between the Township of West Carleton and the Town of Arnprior in the provision of services.

The Township of West Carleton Brief suggests that under The Municipal Act it is possible to accommodate the provision of services to West Carleton from the Town of Arnprior. On the other hand, the Brief also states "there may be boundary adjustments some time in the future in the Arnprior area as a matter of service efficiency."[12]

---

[10] D. Michael Ray, "Urban Growth and the Concept of Functional Region," in N. H. Lithwick and Gilles Paquet, eds., *Urban Studies: A Canadian Perspective*, Toronto, Methuen, 1968, pp. 84-87.

[11] Réal Gagnon, *Study of Commuting in the Ottawa-Hull and Toronto Areas*, Working Paper (Geographical Series) No. 2E, Statistics Canada, December 1975.

[12] Township of West Carleton, *Brief to the Ottawa-Carleton Review Commission*, January 1976, p. 2.

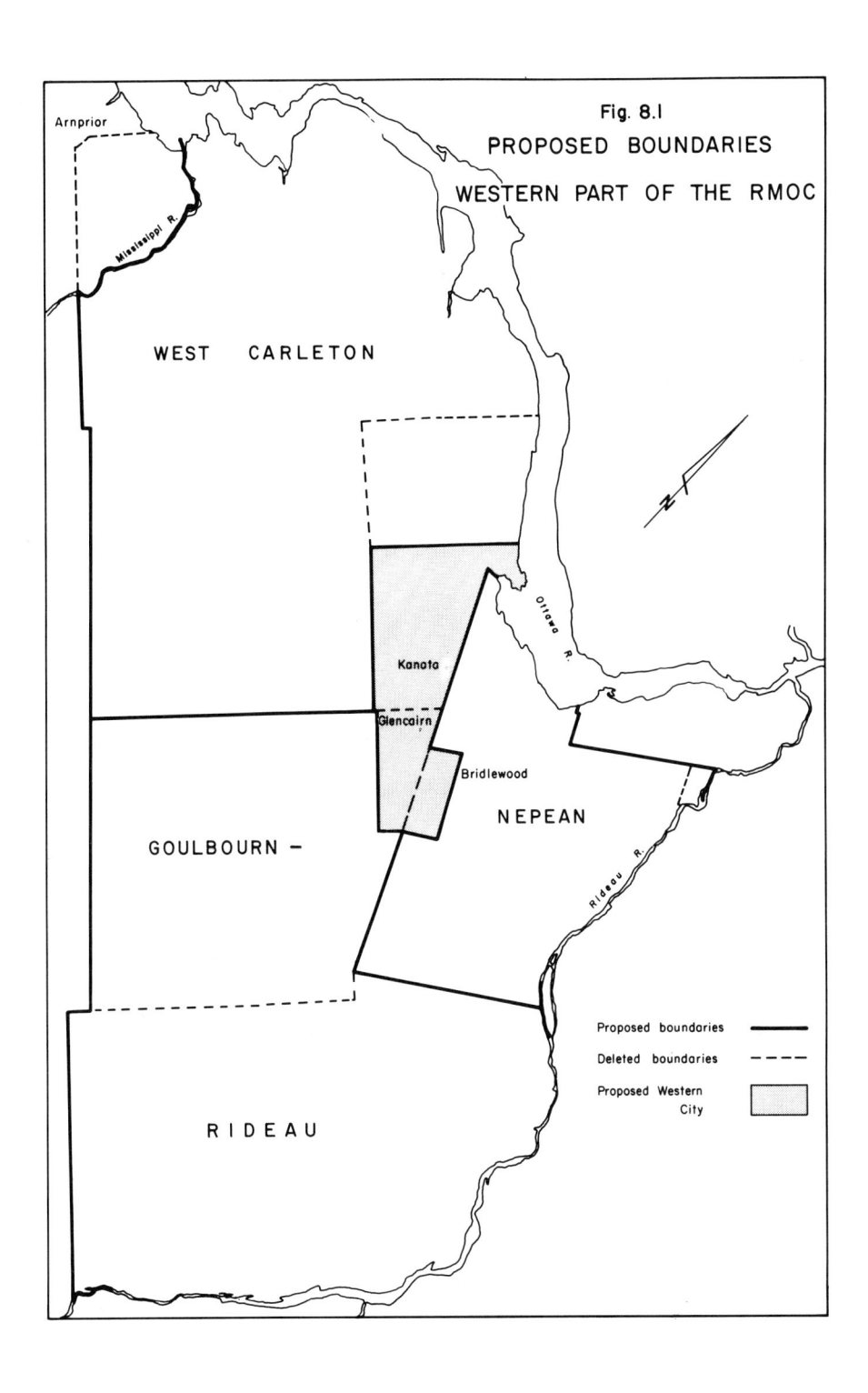

Fig. 8.1
PROPOSED BOUNDARIES
WESTERN PART OF THE RMOC

We believe a minor boundary adjustment is the best solution to the provision of services in the area. A small part of Fitzroy ward, adjacent to Arnprior, should be transferred out of West Carleton. We recommend then that the outer boundary of this part of West Carleton Township should follow the Mississippi River as shown on Figure 8-1. (This boundary does not follow the proposals outlined by either the Renfrew or Lanark County Restructuring Studies, which suggested that all of Fitzroy ward be included in Renfrew or Lanark Counties respectively.)[13]

We have considered at length the proposals of Arnprior presented in their letters and submission. We have attended meetings on the same subject, i.e., that Arnprior should be a "mini-region." We reject these proposals entirely. They are too aggrandizing, too disruptive of Renfrew and Lanark Counties, as well as of West Carleton. On whether Arnprior and the small portion of West Carleton that we have mentioned should go to Lanark or Renfrew County, we make no recommendation.

We conclude that the remainder of the western boundary of the Region (that with Lanark County) and the southern boundary (with Leeds-Grenville Counties) be left unchanged. While there is a certain amount of commuting from the small towns in these counties (Almonte, Carleton Place, Smiths Falls, Kemptville), this does not seem a sufficient reason for boundary adjustments to include them in the Region.

In terms of social characteristics other than employment, these areas appear to have more affinity with their respective counties than with the RMOC. Moreover, the inclusion of the Almonte and Carleton Place areas within the RMOC would seriously weaken the viability of Lanark County. There is a point beyond which commuting alone cannot be used for drawing municipal boundaries without creating unduly large regions. By the commuter-shed criterion, for instance, one might argue that Metro Toronto should include all the area from Burlington to Port Hope, or from Toronto to Barrie.

Internal Boundaries

(a) *Western City (Kanata)*

As discussed in Chapter 4, the Regional Official Plan (1974) calls for the development of three satellite cities in the RMOC. The "Western Urban Community" is being rapidly developed, and is expected to reach 100,000 population by the year 2000. It will include Kanata in March Township, Glen Cairn and North Hazeldean in Goulburn Township and Bridlewood in Nepean Township. It will also include extra land, enough to accommodate the expected 100,000 people. We suggest that this whole new urban development be called "Kanata."

Briefs received from March Township, the March Rural Association, the Kanata-Beaverbrook Community Association and the Goulburn Rural Ratepayers Association state that those parts of March, Goulburn and Nepean Townships to be included in the "western satellite city" (or Kanata) should be joined to form a new urban municipality. We recommend that this step be taken as soon as possible.

This "western satellite city" (Kanata) is to form a self-contained unit. Major centres of employment and commercial activity are expected to reduce, as far as possible, commuting

---

[13] County of Renfrew-City of Pembroke Restructuring Study, *Commissioner's Report*, July 1976, p. 71; Lanark Area Restructuring Study, *Restructuring of Municipal Government in Lanark Area, Final Report and Recommendations*, May 1976, p. V-2.

to downtown Ottawa. The town centre for the new "city" is planned to be in the present Kanata adjacent to the western extension of Highway 417.

There are several problems at present: (1) the planning and responsibility for the new urban area is scattered among three townships; (2) there is friction between the rapidly urbanizing and the rural areas of Goulbourn Township.

These problems would be solved if appropriate alterations were made to municipal boundaries and one new municipality were created, combining the areas at present urbanized, plus enough land for their future planned growth. The presently "rural" (but proposed urban) land portion of the new municipality should not help to pay for the urban services, until these are extended to them. This is a familiar practice now — i.e., differential tax rates to parts of municipalities for special services.

(b) *The remainder of March Township*

That part of March remaining would be left with a very small rural population (about 1,600). Since the number of residents in the area will be too small to form an individual municipality, we recommend that the remaining part of March Township should be added to West Carleton Township. It would slightly more than offset the population of West Carleton which would be lost in the northwest, to Arnprior. West Carleton Township would have a population of over 8,000 in our proposed structure of municipal organization.

(c) *The remainder of Goulbourn Township*

The rural part of Goulbourn Township which would remain should become a part of Rideau Township. The new Township of Rideau would gain approximately 7,000 people from Goulbourn Township, to form a new municipality of 15,000. The Bridlewood area, transferred from Nepean to the new Kanata, is small enough not to affect Nepean seriously. (See Figure 8-1.)

(d) *Ottawa-Nepean Boundary Change*

A natural (straight line) boundary adjustment should be made between the City of Ottawa and Nepean Township in the area south of Baseline Road and immediately west of the Rideau River. The Nepean Township Brief to the Commission requested this change. The Brief said: "This change is not a fundamental one, but one which is more apparent to the general public than the present demarcation line."[14] The areas to be transferred include the neighbourhoods known as Courtland Park, Rideauview, Carleton Square, and part of Carleton Heights. The population given for this area by the 1971 Census of Canada is 5,415. The population in 1976 is considerably higher, because several new large apartment buildings have recently been constructed on Prince of Wales Drive. The new estimated population of Nepean would be nearly 80,000 (1976 figures). We further recommend that Nepean be given City status as soon as possible.

The western portion of the RMOC would, then, consist of the city of Nepean, the town of Kanata (to be raised to city status once it reaches 15,000 population), and the "rural" municipalities of West Carleton and Rideau-Goulbourn. (See Figure 8-1.)

(e) *Orleans and the Gloucester-Cumberland Boundary*

We consider a fairly large change in boundaries necessary in the Orleans area in the east of the RMOC. A medium-sized satellite city is expected in this area. This "Eastern Satellite City" is projected to grow to approximately 35,000-50,000 people. At present, a portion of the "eastern satellite city" lies in Gloucester Township, while a portion is in Cumberland

---

[14] Nepean Township, *Brief to the Commission*, February 18, 1976, p. 8.

Township. We recommend that it all be included in Gloucester Township, and that the Township become a city as soon as possible.

E. M. Stewart, a councillor in Gloucester Township stated in her Brief to this Commission:"'traditionally Gloucester has always lost territory when boundaries changed... I see some argument for reversing the process.''[15]

The Gloucester Township Brief stated that it is "quite content to let the status quo remain" but "in the event that is is felt the area would be better in one jurisdiction the Township would be prepared to assume responsibility". Gloucester Township, being more highly urbanized, should be more capable of planning for a large urban area. At present, some Cumberland residents use the better-equipped recreational facilities in Gloucester Township. For these reasons, we recommend that the boundary between Gloucester and Cumberland Townships be moved to the east as shown on Figure 8-2. The subdivisions of Queenswood Village and Queenswood Heights would then be transferred to the jurisdiction of Gloucester Township.

The new population of Gloucester Township would approach 60,000, on the basis of 1976 figures. By the year 2000, Gloucester Township (City) will contain approximately 170,000, if the Eastern and Southern satellite cities are both completed.

(f) *Cumberland-Russell*

Cumberland Township will have lost the population and assessment of the Orleans area if the foregoing recommendation is adopted. Consequently, we recommend that Russell Township be combined with Cumberland Township to form a new viable municipal unit. The population of this new municipality will be approximately 15,000 (1976 figures) after the amalgamation of the two former eastern townships.

It has sometimes been the harmless practice in Ontario for new names of municipalities to be chosen by a referendum of the population affected by the change. A possible name for the new township could be "Foubert". The Foubert family from France was one of the first to settle in the Cumberland area, and the name would therefore be appropriate, especially since the new township would be largely French-speaking. The name could be voted upon (as mentioned) or conferred by the Province in an amendment to The RMOC Act. At present, we shall refer to the proposed new township by the name "Cumberland-Russell."

Osgoode Township (population 8,286 in 1975) should remain a separate municipal unit, and would have a population comparable to that of West Carleton Township. Osgoode is the only municipality whose boundaries we have not recommended for a change.

(g) *Vanier-Rockcliffe Park, etc.*

The City of Vanier has been losing population in the past few years. In 1961, it stood at 24,555; by 1971, the population had fallen to 22,477 (Census Figures); by 1975, Vanier's assessed population was 20,146. Vanier is hardly likely to grow because its territory is so small, merely one square mile. It has always seemed an anomaly that the City of Vanier should be entirely surrounded by the City of Ottawa.

The Vanier brief to the Commission proposed new boundaries for the City which would increase Vanier's population to 76,000 from 20,146. We agree with the proposal for the enlargement of Vanier, but not with the exact boundaries. We consider that they need not extend as far as those proposed by the Vanier Council.

We recommend the following boundaries for Vanier: the Ottawa River on the north,

---

[15] E. M. Stewart, *Brief to the Commission*, 1976, p. 2.

105

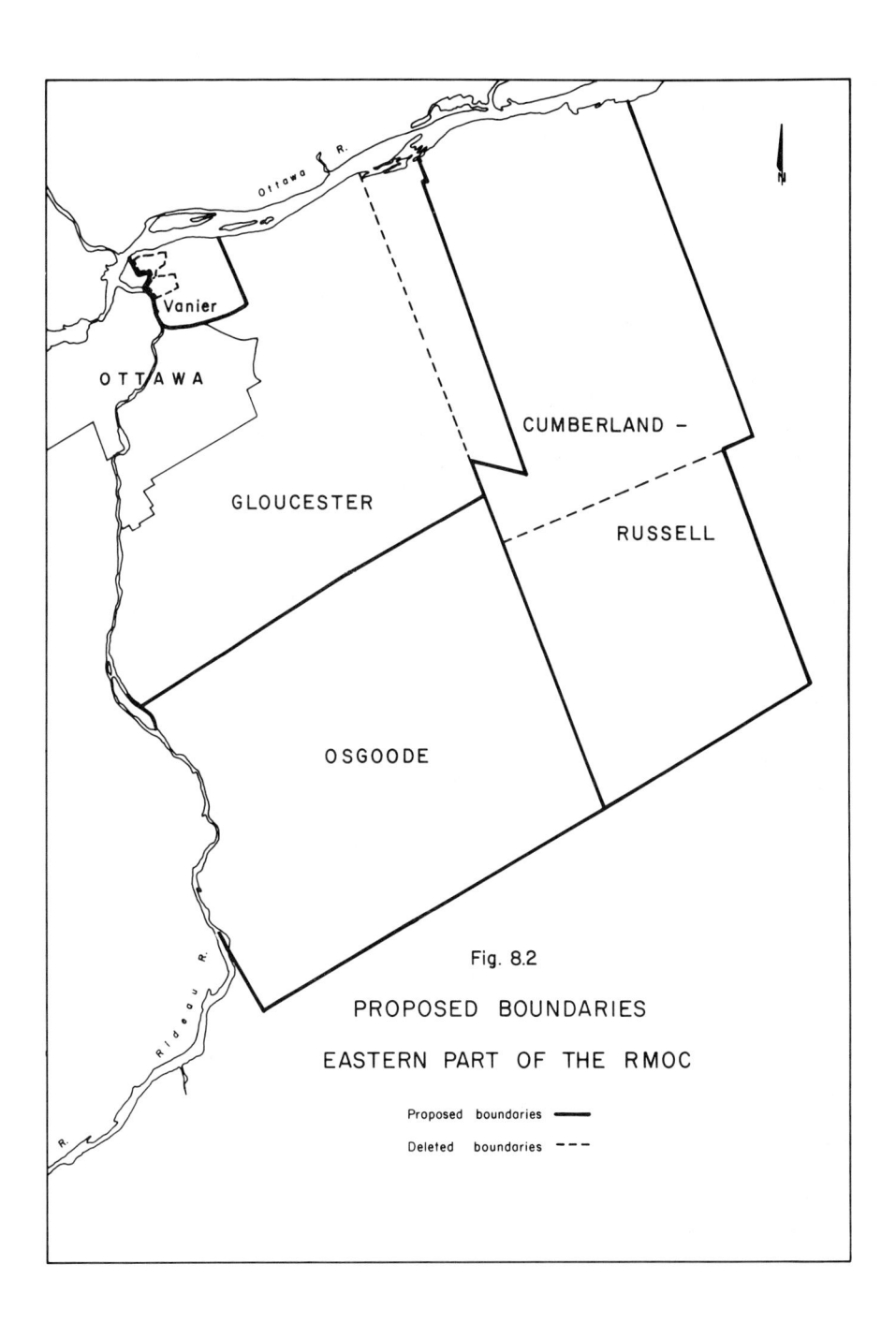

Fig. 8.2

PROPOSED BOUNDARIES

EASTERN PART OF THE RMOC

Proposed boundaries ———
Deleted boundaries - - -

Blair Road on the east, the Queensway to the south and the Rideau River (approximately) on the west. These boundaries encompass the present Village of Rockcliffe Park which would cease to exist as a separate municipality, and be included in Vanier.

The north-west boundary of the new Vanier is not precisely at the Rideau River. This is in order to retain Rideau Hall, the Prime Minister's residence and the City Hall of Ottawa within the City of Ottawa. Therefore, we propose that the boundary in the northwest corner of the new City of Vanier should follow Dufferin Road from the Rideau River to Rideau Terrace, then to proceed along Rideau Terrace to Princess Avenue and along Princess Avenue to the Ottawa River.

Vanier would take over territory from the City of Ottawa in which (according to the 1971 Census) 32,685 people lived, 1,292 people from Gloucester Township and 2,135 people from the Village of Rockcliffe Park, And the City would have room for growth. Its new population would be approximately 56,000. The French-speaking percentage of the enlarged Vanier will be smaller than at present, but we were assured by councillors that they had no objection to this. In any case, we are not deliberately setting up a municipality along linguistic lines, as in the "limited hiving" principle of the Fullerton Report, although Franco-Ontarians may for a long time feel more at home in Vanier than in other municipalities.

In two briefs and several letters to this Commission, Rockliffe Park Village residents strongly supported the retention of the status quo. One Brief states "it is the submission of the Village Council that it (Rockcliffe Park Village) should be permitted to retain its right to deal with local matters."[16] The residents of Rockcliffe Park claim that representation should not be on the basis of population alone. The Council claims that "the local government of the Village has demonstrably succeeded in affording efficient government to the area and has in no way constituted a burden on the Village's immediate neighbours or the Regional Municipality as a whole."[17] We have found that in some instances the Village of Rockcliffe Park does not pay its way. In particular, the contract price of OPP services in the Village does not represent the true cost of policing (see Chapter 15, Police and Fire Services).

The other concern of Rockcliffe Park was for its "identity." Many neighbourhoods in the Region have strong feelings of "identity" without being an incorporated municipality. This is true, for instance, of Manotick, North Gower, Richmond, Carp, Blackburn Hamlet, and so on. Rockcliffe Park will always be a tightly-knit neighbourhood. Rockcliffe Park Village will surely retain its feelings of identity without maintaining the status of a municipality. It has happened before in Forest Hill Village in Metro Toronto. There is also the point that more than 40% of Rockcliffe Park is bilingual, which will help it to feel at home in the City of Vanier.[18]

Many briefs suggested that the Region would benefit if the constituent municipalities were more equal in size. We agree with this general view, and have gone some way to meet

---

[16] The Council of the Village of Rockcliffe Park, *Submission on behalf of Council of the Village of Rockcliffe Park to the Ottawa-Carleton Review Commission*, January 1976, p. 1.

[17] *Ibid.*, p. 5.

[18] Municipal boundary lines are seldom if ever drawn by "nicely calculated gain and loss", as is shown by many decisions of the Ontario Municipal Board. They are drawn by the OMB on what is to the good of the wider area. We are dealing with municipalities — political entities — not with profit and loss statements.

it, although not immediately or by arbitrarily disregarding all present boundaries.

By the year 2000, the Region is expected to have a population of one million. If our proposed municipal structure is adopted, by the year 2000 the populations of the four largest area municipalities will roughly be as follows: City of Ottawa — 300,000, Nepean City — 200,000, Gloucester City — 170,000 and the "Western Urban Community" (Kanata) — 100,000.

The area municipalities will have increased in size unequally. The City of Ottawa's population will have remained similar in size to the present. The population of the City of Nepean will have increased by more than two and a half times. The population of the City of Gloucester will have more than tripled, while the population of the "Western Urban Community" (Kanata) will have increased astronomically. Thus, three countervailing powers will exist, and although Ottawa will still be the largest City, it will not make up three fifths of the Region, as now (unless it becomes a city of skyscrapers).

Table 8-1 shows the proposed municipal losses and gains (of population), with the population adjusted for 1975.

A Few Other Points

1. Some names of municipalities have been suggested, e.g., those of Kanata and Foubert. The Commission is not wedded to these. A rose by any other name, etc. Nor have we juggled the names to yield one city (Ottawa), and several boroughs, as in Metro Toronto.
2. The "umbrella" government suggested in the Fullerton Report is, by implication, rejected. The Report argued that both sides of the Ottawa River should be under one local government, of which only half would be elected. The other half would be appointees from the federal government and the two provinces. (See also Chapter 17.)
3. A few small boundary lines have not been hitherto discussed, but changes in them might well be made. We make no recommendation on them, but they should perhaps be considered by the Province and the municipalities concerned if this Report is acted upon.

    One of these lines concerns the Windsor Park sub-division. In some ways, this is an awkward built-up area. There is something to be said for its being absorbed into Ottawa.

    Again the question of having the Ottawa-Gloucester boundary running zig-zag through the Uplands Airport might well be raised, with all the area (including the Defence Base) put into one municipality, preferably into Ottawa.

    Should these changes be made, the adjusted population figures in Table 8-1 would be slightly different.
4. The Commission also gave thought to a division of the entire RMOC into municipalities of roughly equal size. A number of briefs and meetings did indeed bring forth this suggestion. Some persons suggested units as small as seven or eight thousand, yielding a large number of neighbourhoods or "communities", perhaps linked by some kind of co-ordinating mechanism.

    Others suggested a few large units only, which involved chopping up Ottawa, Nepean and Gloucester, with the final result being twelve or more municipalities of, say, 40,000 people.

    The practical application of these suggestions provoked so many difficulties that we discarded them.

Table 8-1

Adjusted Populations from Proposed Boundary Changes

Cities	1975 Population**	Adjusted Areas		1975 Adjusted Population
1. Ottawa	302,124	To Vanier	−33,000*	263,124
		To Nepean	− 6,000*	
2. Vanier	20,146	From Ottawa	+33,000*	56,775
		From Rockcliffe Park	+ 2,229	
		From Gloucester	+ 1,400*	
Proposed Cities				
3. Gloucester	53,322	From Cumberland	+ 4,000*	55,922
		To Vanier	− 1,400*	
4. Nepean	74,000	From Ottawa	+ 5,000*	78,900
		To Kanata	− 100*	
Proposed Town				
5. Kanata (new western town)	—	From March	+ 5,300*	10,400
		From Goulbourn	+ 5,000	
		From Nepean	+ 100*	
Proposed Townships				
6. Cumberland-Russell	11,458	From Russell	+ 4,775	12,233
		To Gloucester	− 4,000*	
7. Osgoode	8,286	No change		8,286
8. Rideau-Goulbourn	7,860	From Goulbourn	+ 7,500*	15,360
9. West Carleton	7,782	To Lanark or Renfrew	− 500*	8,882
		From March	+ 1,600*	
RMOC Total	506,592	To Lanark or Renfrew	− 500*	510,817
		From Russell	+ 4,775	

* Estimated population of adjusted area
** Source: 1976 Municipal Directory

109

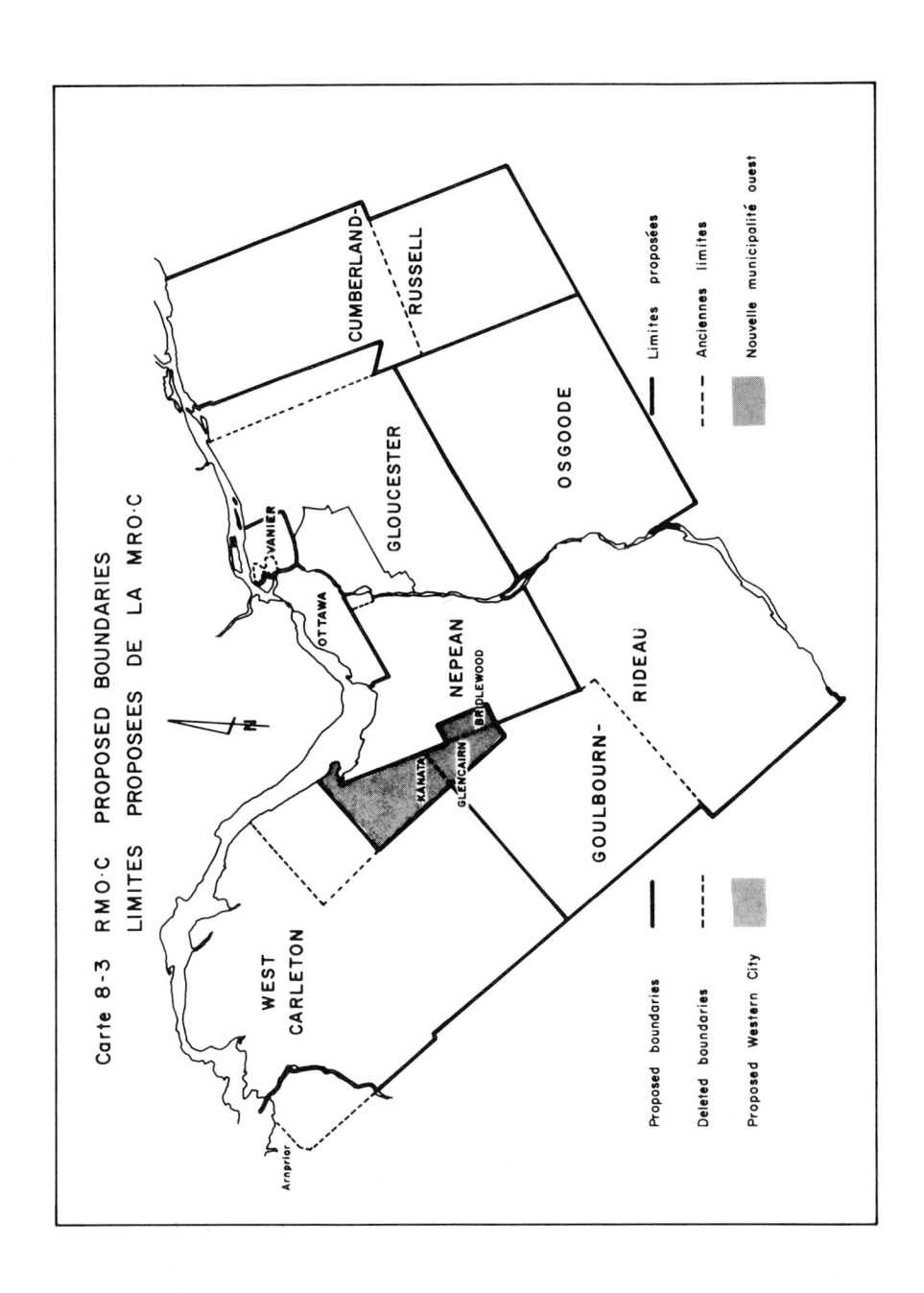

CHAPTER 9

Elections and Sundry Matters
or
Let's all vote — early, but not often

"The election result invests representatives and decisions with legitimacy. In short, the government which is produced — almost as a by-product — and invested with legitimacy is the chief social purpose of the whole electoral process." [1]

Regional Council — (a) Representation

It may be recalled from the preceding Chapter that our recommendations resulted in nine area municipalities, as contrasted with eleven at present. In apportioning the number of members on the Regional Council, two guidelines (one hesitates to call them principles) have been followed:
(1) There should be at least one member on Regional Council from every area municipality.

In practice this means that the smaller units will be over-represented. These are the townships of Cumberland-Russell, Osgoode, and West Carleton. This is slightly anomalous, especially since these townships may be over-represented for a long time, with slow growth being planned for them. We may have to live with these anomalies mainly because of the large acreage involved. (It may be said that even larger areas will be under some of the school boards. True enough, but these are single purpose bodies).

Alternatively, the Province in its wisdom could put the four outer townships into two — on the east, Cumberland-Russell joined to Osgoode; on the west, Rideau-Goulbourn joined with West Carleton. Each would then have about 21,000 and 24,000 people, (adjusted figures).

It is surprising how short a time it takes, after amalgamations and annexations, for residents to forget the old and adjust to the new situation. There have been many instances in recent Ontario history to bear out this statement. There is also no evidence to show that local government reform affects the outcome of provincial general elections. Explanations of election results are always shaky, but they make nice conversation pieces.
(2) Our second guideline was to lean towards the future.

In practice, this means some over-representation in the near future, for rapidly growing areas, a step which time will soon correct. The areas of most rapid growth are Nepean, Gloucester, and the new western town of Kanata.

Taking into account the above, and assuming that the size of the present Regional Council is about right, we then arrive at the following: 4 members for the outer townships (as adjusted), one for the new town of Kanata (as adjusted), making 5. The total number would be 34, three more than at present. (See Table 9-1).
(3) Representation on Regional Council should be reviewed every three or six years, in plenty of time for municipal elections. This needs to be done to ensure that population growth does not result in under-representation of the larger municipalities.

---

[1] H. B. Mayo, *Introduction to Democratic Theory,* Oxford University Press, New York, 1960, p. 73.

Table 9-1
Proposed Representation on Regional Council

Municipality	(000's) Population*	Proposed Number of Representatives	Population per Regional Representative
1. Ottawa City	263.1	15	17,500
2. Vanier City	56.8	4	14,200
3. Gloucester City	55.9	4	14,000
4. Nepean City	78.9	6	13,200
5. Kanata Town	10.4	1	10,400
6. Cumberland/Russell Township	12.2	1	12,200
7. Osgoode Township	8.3	1	8,300
8. Rideau/Goulbourn Township	15.4	1	15,400
9. West Carleton Township	8.9	1	8,900
Totals	510.8	34	Regional Average 15,000

* Adjusted populations, 1975, rounded figures, with the proposed new boundaries of Chapter 8.

Regional Council — (b) Method of Election

Under the present system, Regional Councillors are drawn from the councils of the area municipalities. In the case of Ottawa, all 16 members of City Council (mayor, 4 controllers and 11 aldermen) are members of Regional Council. Other area municipalities are represented by the head of council (mayor or reeve) and other councillors, in some cases deputy reeves, if the population is sufficient. This system, whereby representatives are elected to an area council first and subsequently assigned to Regional Council, is known as "indirect" election to the upper-tier council. All upper-tier municipal councils in Ontario (Counties and Regions) use the indirect method except one, the Regional Municipality of Niagara, where half of the Regional councillors are directly elected. So far as we can find out the direct election works well in Niagara.

We recommend the alternative method of choosing representatives for Regional Council, i.e., "direct" election.[2] That is to say, those who serve on Regional Council should not do so by virtue of being elected to local council on local issues (if any), but rather in elections in which candidates run directly for the office of regional councillor.

To understand the difference between the two methods it is useful to think of the provincial and federal legislatures. Our M.P.'s in the House of Commons do not sit there by virtue of first being elected to provincial legislatures (indirect), but rather are elected directly from their constituencies. One might imagine how radically different our federal government would be if the provincial members were also in the federal Parliament. Direct election has very powerful advantages which are insufficiently recognized. These chiefly revolve around the questions of perspective, or how the regional councillors perceive their role, and of conflicting loyalties.

Firstly, there is a strong tendency for councillors serving at the regional level,

---

[2] Direct election of the upper-tier of Counties has also been recommended by Eric Hardy, *Commissioner's Report, County of Renfrew-City of Pembroke Restructuring Study,* July, 1976, p. 100; and Stewart Fyfe and Ron M. Farrow in *Waterloo Area Local Government Review,* Feb. 1970, p. 179.

representing local councils, to take a parochial "what's-in-it-for-my-municipality" viewpoint with a concomitant failure to view issues regionally. The indirect method produces a United Nations-type atmosphere at regional councils with members acting like ambassadors of nation-states defending "national sovereignty" at the expense of global action. The "indirect" councillors' power base is at the lower tier, hence their chief loyalties lie there also. The result of this is to undermine the authority and effectiveness of regional councils.

Yet there is a clear need for commitment to actions and priorities on a regional basis. That is why the Regional Municipality was established in the first instance, and why it has several important Region-wide responsibilities such as planning, public transport, regional roads, water and sewerage, and social services. The need for a Regional perspective indeed grows stronger yearly, as the entire Region becomes more functionally integrated and its parts more interdependent. A Region-wide approach is also vital for dealing with the difficult and pressing issues raised by the prospect of continuing urban growth. The management of that growth and the provision of the necessary infrastructure of services to support it, will be seriously impaired by parochial tendencies and loyalties.

Secondly, the workload is much too heavy for those persons, especially heads of local councils, who serve also as regional councillors. The neglect of one or other set of duties is almost inevitable. And it is Regional duties which tend to get neglected.[3]

Thirdly, there is the important consideration of accountability to, and access by, the public. These are surely central concerns when establishing our government institutions, as long as we believe in the values of representative democracy. It is extremely difficult for electors to hold councillors accountable for their decisions at the Regional level if they are on the Regional Council by virtue of their positions on the area councils.

One of the main arguments advanced in favour of the indirect system is that close liaison results between upper tier and lower tier councils. This may be so, but there are a number of means of ensuring that liaison occurs with the direct method so this argument does not significantly weaken the case for direct election. Simple procedures such as the mutual exchange of agenda, minutes, reports, between Regional Council and area councils can be adopted. And area councils may, if they wish, designate someone to attend Regional Councils, and vice versa, to report back to their respective councils. Moreover, liaison at the staff level, especially for split functions (e.g., planning, roads, recreation), can be expanded and formalized. We have been unable to find any indications of liaison problems in the two tier system of government in Greater London which uses the direct method of election to the upper tier.

Given direct election there is then a powerful case for Regional representation on a ward basis. Election at-large is too difficult and expensive, and some municipalities might be shut out altogether, depending on the vagaries of the voting. Thus we recommend that Regional Councillors be elected by wards which follow lower tier municipal boundary lines. For smaller area municipalities represented by a single Regional Councillor, this means that the ward is synonymous with the municipality. For area municipalities with several Regional Councillors, i.e., the cities, the wards used for election to city councils (or groupings of lower tier wards) should also be used for Regional Councillors.

---

[3] The Royal Commission on Metro Toronto found that Metro Councillors worked an average of 63 hours a week, of which only 34% was spent on Metro duties. *Update,* June 1976, p. 7. The mayor of York Borough supported direct election to Metro Toronto Council, because of the heavy work load in serving on two councils. *Globe and Mail,* Dec. 11, 1975. Mayors are reported as working an average of 74 hours a week. *Globe and Mail,* April 26, 1976.

It is important that the wards not cross municipal boundaries for regional purposes. Having the city wards identical with regional wards (or groupings of wards), will help serve as a basis for public identification with the Region. Simplicity has great merit, while a multiplicity of boundaries and jurisdictions only adds to public confusion over the already complex nature of modern governments. The overlapping and crosscutting of regional and local boundaries may well have been a contributing factor to the failure of the experiment with Metropolitan government in Winnipeg.

Regional Council — (c) The Chairman

The position of the Chairman of Regional Council is important for the effective operation of the Council. In this respect, the Regional Council has hitherto been fortunate.

At present the Chairman is selected by Council for a two-year term but he is not an elected member of any area council; that is to say, he is not a publicly elected politician, although the RMOC Act provides that he could be if the regional councillors so chose. (In the latter case he must resign his seat on the area council.) He votes only to break a tie. For the first four years upon creation of the Regional Municipality, the Chairman was appointed by the Province, which has also been the practice in other Regions.

We concur with the method of selecting the Regional Chairman by the members of Regional Council at the first meeting of the new Council following the municipal elections. But we recommend that he be required to be an elected member of Council from one of the Regional wards. This is more democratic, particularly since we also suggest that the position of Chairman be strengthened, with a higher profile and a stronger leadership role.

As to the name of the office, the term "Chairman" is a new one for the head of local governments, but is used now to designate the head of every regional municipality in the Province. Perhaps it is not distinctive enough for its importance. Maybe we should return to the venerable name of "Warden" which is used in all the counties, and was used in Carleton County before the RMOC was set up.[4] Alternatively, the term "mayor" has significant public recognition already and could well serve to raise the visibility and dignity of the office. The heads of five of the area municipalities are called "mayor", so no confusion is likely to arise if the head of the RMOC is also called "mayor". (Meanwhile we shall continue to use the title "Chairman" in this Report.)

There is a need for strengthening the Chairman's position so that he can exercise more leadership on matters of policy. The change outlined above, of the Chairman being elected from a ward, should help a little, but the assignment of specific powers is also needed.

First, the Chairman should have a double vote. That is, his first vote is as a Councillor, but he should have a second vote, if necessary, to break a tie, on standing committees, on the Executive, and on the Council itself.

Second, The Chairman should be given the power to select and dismiss the Deputy Chairman, i.e., the person who acts as Chairman in his absence. The Deputy Chairmanship could be rotated, or last for the full term of the Chairman, preferably the latter.

Third, he should have the power to call special meetings of the Executive and of the Council. Once again there could be a safeguard against a domineering Chairman, say by allowing a majority of the Executive without the Chairman, or a majority of Council without him, to call special meetings.

---

[4] This is in accord with our earlier tentative suggestion (not firm recommendation) that the term "Carleton County" be used instead of the "Regional Municipality of Ottawa-Carleton". It does not detract from the City of Ottawa to be in a County any more than in a Regional Municipality.

Regional Council — (d) Committees

The present organization of Regional Council is known as a council-committee system, as opposed to the board of control system which exists in the City of Ottawa, or the council-manager system in use in certain municipalities in Canada and the U.S.A. Under the council-committee system, the members of council are distributed amongst various standing committees with responsibility for defined policy fields. There is also an executive committee composed of the Chairman and eight councillors.

We basically concur with the present council-committee system. However, there are a number of changes which could be made to create a stronger policy role for the executive. As mentioned with respect to the Chairman's position and his policy leadership at the Regional level, this can only be done by creating a strong executive, both of the Chairman and his Executive Committee.

First, the Regional Executive Committee should be chosen as now by Regional Council.

Second, the Regional Executive should be given entire control over the agenda of Regional Council: that is, the power to determine what issues will or will not come before Council and in what order they will be considered.

Third, the members of Regional Executive should be chairmen of the Standing Committees of Council. The Executive should, of course, have the power to appoint and dismiss department heads on their own authority, without approval by Council. Other senior officials within the departments would be chosen by the department heads in conjunction with the Personnel Director, but subject to ratification by the Executive. For expertise, appoint; for representativeness, elect; and expert knowledge and experience are the first consideration for department heads.

Fourth, the Executive will prepare and present the budget, with the advice of the Finance Commissioner with whom Departments will first consult. The Executive will also call for tenders and award contracts.

Fifth, the members of the Executive, as well as the Chairman, will be full-time politicians. In no other way will they be able to carry out their onerous and time-consuming duties.

The standing committees will report to the Executive Committee, as outlined below. (The Chairman will of course be an ex officio voting member of every standing committee). Regional Council will not be downgraded by the existence of a strong Chairman and Executive, since the Council will always be able to vote down an Executive proposal to Council.

The size of the Executive Committee at present is nine. It should be seven to nine (plus the Chairman), corresponding to the number of Standing Committees. The Executive should be chosen in much the same way as provincial or federal cabinets are selected, with due consideration to representation for different parts of the Region, the two official languages, and so on. Every effort should be made to seek out bilingual staff officials, and it is to be hoped that bilingual councillors will also be elected. (Already both official languages may be used at meetings).[5]

The standing committee structure of Regional Council should be altered, to accord with the changes in Regional functions and departments as recommended in other Chapters. The recommended structure is shown in the following Table 9-2.

---

[5] Regional Council meets in the Ottawa City Hall, where there is simultaneous translation. The Executive and other committees meet in RMOC offices on Queen St.

In addition to the standing committees there should also be established a paralled set of citizens' advisory committees. These should be patterned after the successful Social Services Advisory Committee already in existence. The advent of "citizens' participation" in recent years has led to greater recognition of the need for consultation with, and soliciting of advice from, interested groups and the general public alike. This recognition should be formalized with the creation of more committees like the Social Services Advisory Committee.

Table 9-2
Proposed Standing Committee and Department Structure, RMOC

Standing Committees	Departments	Functions
1. Planning	1. Planning	Official Plan, Land division, Sub-division and other controls
	2. Recreation	Conservation, Recreation planning, Regional Forests and Parks
2. Transport	3. Roads	Roads, bridges, Traffic engineering
	4. Public Transit	O.C. Transpo
3. Works	5. Public Works	Water, sewerage, waste management, electricity, buildings (and purchase and expropriations)
4. Health and Social Services	6. Public Health	Present health unit functions
	7. Social Services	General welfare, Day Care, Nursing homes and special care, child welfare (children's aid)
5. Housing	8. Public Housing	Co-ordination, planning and operation of public housing projects, housing programmes, housing information.
	9. Homes for the Aged	Homes for the Aged
6. Watch Committee	10. Police	Regional policing, Emergency measures
7. Administration and Finance	11. Finance	Debt management, helping budget preparation, inter-governmental relations
	12. Legal	Drafting and other legal services
	13. Personnel	Staffing, bilingualism, translations, labour relations

It must be stressed that these Advisory Committees are to be on tap, not on top. As Douglas Fullerton says, they are "almost, if not quite a new level of government."[6] "Not quite," because final authority for decisions on matters of policy must rest with the elected politicians, since only they are accountable to the electorate from which they draw their legitimacy. The make-up of the Advisory Committees should however represent a cross section of interests, including representatives from organized citizens' groups, "experts", "consumers" of the service, and representatives of that rare breed, the interested member of the general public with no axe to grind.

Table 9-3
Proposed Reporting Relationships, RMOC

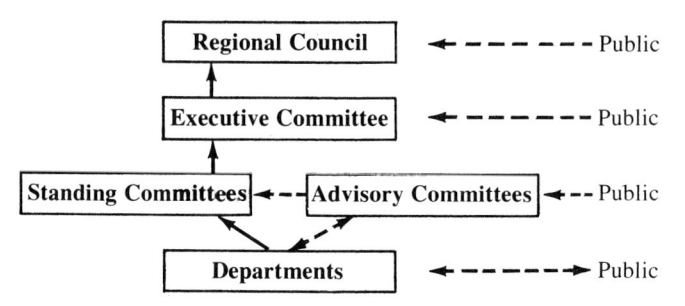

```
        ┌─────────────────┐
        │ Regional Council │ ◄ ─ ─ ─ ─ ─ ─ Public
        └─────────────────┘
                 ▲
        ┌─────────────────┐
        │Executive Committee│ ◄ ─ ─ ─ ─ ─ ─ Public
        └─────────────────┘
                 ▲
┌──────────────────┐    ┌──────────────────┐
│Standing Committees│◄ ─│Advisory Committees│ ◄ ─ ─ Public
└──────────────────┘    └──────────────────┘
           ▲ ▼     ▲
        ┌─────────────────┐
        │   Departments   │ ◄ ─ ─ ─ ─ ─► Public
        └─────────────────┘
```

The public will have access to the system in a number of ways. (a) They will call the Regional Councillor for their ward, as ward residents usually do; (b) they may get in touch with Departments; (c) they may take up matters with the Advisory Committees, on which some of the public will serve; (d) they may take their concerns to Standing Committees; (e) they may send delegations to the Executive and to Council.

Department heads or other officials will usually meet with Advisory Committees, to provide information and receive suggestions and complaints.

Area Municipalities — (a) Representation on Councils

The present system of representation at the lower tier level suffers from two drawbacks. First, several councils are too small. Gloucester has only a five-man council for a population of over 50,000; Nepean has only 7 council members for nearly 80,000 (with adjusted boundaries). Cumberland, March, and Osgoode, though much smaller, also have only five members on their respective councils.

Second, besides the difficulty of representation which a small number presents, there are also the problems of workload and lack of specialization. A municipal councillor's position is a part-time job, but the demands on his/her time are much heavier when there are only a small number of councillors. Moreover, there are insufficient bodies to be able to establish the required committees which can concentrate their efforts and develop expertise and continuity in the various functions of the municipalities.

We recommend that the size of the area councils be increased to a minimum of seven to nine members, with a larger number for those area municipalities with larger populations. Table 9-4 indicates the recommended councils.

---

[6] Douglas H. Fullerton, *The Capital of Canada: How Should It Be Governed?*, Ottawa, 1974, Vol. 1, p. 84.

Table 9-4
Proposed Representation on Area Municipal Councils

Municipality	(000's) Population*	Proposed Council size	Population per Councillor
1. Ottawa City	263.1	15	17,500
2. Vanier City	56.8	12	4,700
3. Gloucester City	55.9	12	4,700
4. Nepean City	78.9	12	6,600
5. Kanata Town	10.4	9	1,200
6. Cumberland/Russell Township	12.2	9	1,400
7. Osgoode Township	8.3	7	1,200
8. Rideau/Goulbourn Township	15.4	9	1,700
9. West Carleton Township	8.9	7	1,300
Totals	510.8	92	5,600 Average

* Adjusted populations, 1975 rounded figures, with the proposed new boundaries of Chapter 8.

It may be that Ottawa would wish to have two aldermen per ward (as formerly), but there should still be only one Regional Councillor per ward. Alternatively, the number of single aldermen wards could be doubled to thirty, with two wards being grouped together to elect a Regional Councillor. We recommend leaving this to the City to decide, provided that Ottawa has a total of only 15 Regional Councillors.

Third, a further weakness is the fact that several area municipalities (Cumberland, Gloucester, March, Nepean, and Osgoode) presently elect all their councillors at large rather than by ward. This of course always leaves open the possibility that certain geographic areas of the municipality will go unrepresented, and it makes compaigning for office more demanding and expensive. There is great virtue in structuring the membership of legislative bodies on the basis of geographic units, as attested to by the longstanding success of the legislatures of the two senior levels of government. Every councillor must then balance his/her consideration for his/her ward against that for the whole municipality. These are the classic roles played by every M.P. or M.P.P.[7]

We recommend therefore that all area municipalities elect their councillors on a ward basis. This is particularly important for those municipalities whose boundaries are being altered by the addition or subtraction of territory. This approach was used in fact during the amalgamations that took place in 1973. The delineation of appropriate ward boundaries should best be left to each council to determine, using as a firm guide that wards should be of approximately equal populations. Apart from Ottawa, the local wards should be grouped together, for election of Regional councillors.

---

[7] The party system at the provincial and federal levels makes the reconciliation of the two roles easier. There is no valid objection to parties at local and regional levels (whatever names they are called). Municipal councils are political not just administrative, no matter how much the rhetoric to the contrary. Parties might even stimulate interest in municipal elections, which is usually very low.

Area Municipalities — (b) Heads of Councils

A final consideration with respect to representation is the position of head of council. In the first instance we recommend that the terminology for this office be standardized throughout the Region. At present the heads of some area councils are "mayors", while in other (and sometimes larger) municipalities they are called "reeves". This can only add to public confusion and the situation should be rectified. We recommend that all heads of councils be called "mayors". (This title also translates into French a bit better than "reeve").

All heads of council are presently elected at large, even in those municipalities where the other members of council are elected by ward. This system has a number of disadvantages and we recommend that the heads of area councils be selected in the same manner as the Regional Chairman, that is by their peers on council.

The drawbacks to an at-large system are both practical and theoretical. First, there is the question of expense and, as a result, limiting the candidates for office. Particularly in a large municipality such as the City of Ottawa, the costs of running an effective campaign to reach all areas of the City are very high. This has the effect of tending to restrict the candidates to those of substantial means, or to those with wealthy special-interest backers such as land developers. Both levels of senior government have recognized the problems in running for public office posed by high election costs, and have recently passed legislation to limit election spending by candidates, as well as to compel disclosure of the sources of campaign contributions.[8] We recommend that municipalities be required to regulate election campaign funds along the lines of the present Provincial legislation.

Second, the at-large election method, though common in Ontario, is essentially American in concept and based upon the separation of powers principle, i.e., the separate election of executive and legislature. As such it tends to set the mayor in conflict with his council. Under the parliamentary approach, where the head of council is selected from amongst the ranks of council, the head of council is rendered more responsible and responsive to his/her elected colleagues. We recommend therefore an end to the at-large method, and that all mayors be selected by their peers on all area councils. We are aware that this breaks with the Ontario tradition, but many things in this Report do the same, and should do so if in our judgment reforms are better than the tradition.

Since area councils will no longer send representatives to sit on Regional Council, the position of Deputy-Reeve, which still exists in certain townships, should be abolished. We recommend this. We also recommend that a mayor should be able to designate a deputy-mayor to act for him in his absence.

Area Municipalities — (c) Committees

The committee structure of the area municipalities currently varies a great deal, reflecting the different sizes of councils and their respective diversity of functions. The question of the number and structure of standing committees can be left to each area council to decide.

However, there should be in all cases an Executive Committee chosen by Council and composed of the mayor, and two to four councillors, depending on the size of each council. As we argued for Regional Council, there is a need for a strengthened executive role. Thus the Executive Committee should have control over the agenda and the power to appoint

---

[8] Once again we note the advantage of a party system: it could help to finance a poor person running for office.

departmental heads, and where possible Executive members should chair Standing Committees. The reporting relationship from departments to committees to council should be similar to that outlined for Regional Council (See Table 9-3).

In one area municipality, the City of Ottawa, the executive role is performed by a Board of Control. This system, once fairly widespread for medium-sized cities in Ontario, is dying out and is now used in only three cities, Hamilton, London and Ottawa; plus some boroughs in Metro Toronto. Indeed, it is a system unique in the world. The distinguishing feature of the Board of Control is that its members are elected at large (as is the Mayor), whereas the aldermen are elected by ward. The Board is given certain statutory powers. Its recommendations to Council may only be rejected by a ²/₃ majority of Council. Two distinct groups are thus elected to Council. The Mayor and the Board of Control can claim a special mandate from the electorate by virtue of their at-large election.

As numerous commentators have observed, the existence of two different groups on Council, elected differently, has tended to create unnecessary conflict and rivalry between the two.[9] There would seem to be very little reason to continue this complicated and divisive system and we recommend the abolition of Board of Control, and further that the ²/₃ majority necessary to turn down the Executive's proposals be altered to a simple majority (as for Regional Council).

Elections — (a) Term of Office

Almost all briefs received by this Commission which commented on the term of office, urged the extension of the present two-year term to three years. This was a blessed relief from the conflict of views on nearly everything else. We recommend a three-year term. There are several disadvantages to a short (2 years) term of office. When one takes into account the period at the beginning of the term when a new council is settling in and learning the job, and the even longer period toward the end of the term when the looming election date interferes with council's operations, a two-year term hardly becomes more than an effective one-year term. Moreover, the scale and complexity of municipal government today requires a longer period between elections so that a council can have time to devise and carry out new or improved programmes. The three-year term is also recommended for Regional Council, and for the Chairman; and for all mayors of local councils.

We recommend also that municipal elections occur on a set date as at present, rather than at the discretion of councils. One hopes that the simultaneous occurrence of elections in all municipalities helps to stimulate election interest (something which is surely needed when one sees the dismal voter turnout figures that are so common). As to the most appropriate date for municipal elections, this has been a matter of considerable debate in municipal cirlces.[10] One must form a balanced judgment on this, weighing the disadvantages of a "lame duck" council resulting from an earlier election date. On balance, we recommend an earlier date, say the second Monday in November, to avoid the uncertain December weather with which Ontario is cursed. We also recommend that the new councils take office on the first of December, but that the calendar financial year be retained.

---

[9] See, for instance, the comprehensive *Decision-Making Processes in Ontario's Local Governments*, Paul Hickey, TEIGA, 1974, p. 153.

[10] Michael Smither, "The Great Date Debate", *Municipal World*, January 1975, p. 11.

Elections — (b) Procedures

The process of enumeration, in order to compose the lists of municipal voters, is handled by the Province through its regional assessment offices. This is a sensible arrangement as several useful types of information are collected at the same time. It should be maintained. A separate municipally-run enumeration would be an unnecessary duplication of effort and expense.

Provisions still exist in *The Municipal Act* for the holding of referenda on certain issues. There is also a procedure for notifying the public of intended capital borrowing for works projects in order to dispense with a vote of the electors. This practice should be abolished (the OMB is sufficient as a financial watchdog); and the issues for which a referendum can be held should be very severely limited. Referenda should be restricted (if kept at all) to such harmless matters as the selection of a new name for amalgamated municipalities (for example, in the case of Rideau-Goulbourn or Cumberland-Russell).

There is a fundamentally different assumption behind the idea of referenda on matters of policy, and that of representative democracy.

Two quite different theories are in conflict. One is that of direct democracy (as in ancient Athens in the fifth century B.C.), the other that of representative democracy. The two cannot be reconciled, either in their assumptions or in the consequences which flow from them. Further discussion of this interesting point of democratic theory may be superflous. We do not live in ancient Athens or any direct democracy, for which we ought to give thanks.

Instead, representatives are elected and govern under the scrutiny of continuing public examination, and the Damocles' sword of the next election. To submit issues directly to the public is to usurp and circumvent the role of the elected representatives, and is an abdication of political leadership.

There are also serious problems associated with the presentation of referendum issues, their selection, wording and alternatives. We have only to look at the experience with referenda in metropolitan areas in the United States to see the disastrous effects of the widespread use of this mechanism of public decision-making. Badly needed structural reforms such as annexations, amalgamations, and forms of government have been frustrated because referenda were required to approve the changes, to say nothing of the long or "jungle" ballots which face voters in many states.

Elections — Parties (political not for cocktails)

Candidates for elections in Ottawa-Carleton, as in most Canadian municipalities, run for office as individuals and are not organized on a political party basis. Although some candidates are known to have a party affiliation with federal or provincial parties, they do not run on that basis locally. Neither are there "civic" or strictly municipal parties in the RMOC. This is perhaps surprising, given the increase in party activity at the municipal level in Canada in several other major centres in recent years.[11]

There are those who maintain, of course, that it is fortunate that there are not municipal parties, that "politics" should be kept out of municipal government. This view is fundamentally wrong, based as it is on an erroneous notion of the nature of government, which is always political and cannot be reduced to "management". If anyone doubts this, let him look at the construction of a budget, or listen to delegations to municipal councils.

---

[11] J. K. Masson and J. D. Anderson, *Emerging Party Politics in Urban Canada,* McClelland and Stewart, Toronto, 1972.

Parties are in fact a useful mechanism for rendering representative democracy more publicly accountable. Without them, voters are faced with difficult choices from a list of individuals, with little basis for distinguishing between them, or for judging their performance when the next election rolls around. If candidates are grouped into parties (or alliances) which have some sort of distinguishing policies, it is easier for voters to make their decisions, and later to hold a party in power to account for its collective actions.

Although the existence or formation of parties cannot be legislated, a number of useful steps can be taken to encourage them. Some of the changes suggested above, i.e., the direct election of Regional Councillors and the selection of the Chairman and of mayors by the councils may help to create party-groupings. Other steps might include: legislation on municipal elections' expenses which would help subsidize election costs incurred by parties or groupings (similar to federal and provincial legislation), and provision for showing "party" affiliation beside candidates' names on ballots.

Sundry Matters

(a) An issue of topical concern is the question of the workload of municipal politicians. For the most part, the job of an ordinary councillor is a part-time one, but increasingly the demands on the heads of council in the larger municipalities are making the position a full-time job. At the moment the Mayor of Ottawa, the Reeves of Nepean and March, and the Regional Chairman are all full-time politicians. However, the heads of two large area municipalities, Vanier and Gloucester, are only part-time. We recommend that these positions become full-time if our other recommendations are adopted, and so too for executive committee members in the large municipalities. The mayors and reeves of the smaller municipalities are at present part-time, and may continue thus for some years.

It is probably on balance a good thing for heads of council to be full-time. Municipal affairs are more complicated and diverse today, particularly for municipalities undergoing rapid growth. When the political head and the executive (if any) are only part-time, the permanent staff tend to assume a greater role in decision-making, a tendency which should be resisted since municipalities, like provinces or countries, are governed not managed. And the politicians, not the appointed officials, get the praise or blame from the electorate.

(b) Rates of remuneration should of course reflect full-time status and be sufficiently attractive to interest capable people to enter politics. The pay for municipal politicians is generally, in our view, too low. Such a situation has the effect of tending to limit the field to those of independent means, or to the flexible professions such as law where jobs do not have to be forfeited in order to serve on council.

We are not saying that there is some undiscovered pool of superior talent not presently drawn upon. By and large our politicians, at all levels, are much better than the public, in its ambivalence towards politicians, seems to think. Politics, like all professions — law, medicine, education, etc. — has some charlatans, but these are exceptions. The case for good pay for politicians rests largely upon the justice of rewarding public servants for their indispensable and difficult work. It would also be a good thing if the politicians' pay could rise automatically by linking it to a suitable index, instead of having large raises every few years, which invariably stirs up a storm of misguided public agitation. We therefore recommend that councillors review their pay scales in the near future, and (while inflation lasts) provide for annual increments.

(c) A third issue of concern is the subject of conflict of interest. Simply defined, this occurs when a politician's personal or private interests conflict with that of the public interest when deciding matters of public policy or expenditure. The procedures for dealing with this issue are established in *The Municipal Conflicts of Interest Act* (1972). In general terms, the Act provides that when a matter comes before council (or one of its subsidiary boards) in which a member has a direct or indirect pecuniary interest, disclosure of interest must be made, and he/she must refrain from discussion or voting on the matter.

These provisions are the mildest form of dealing with actual or potential conflicts. In other jurisdictions more stringent requirements are in force, including disqualification from office for a term of years, placing assets in blind trusts, and even divestment of holdings. The existing procedure is rendered even weaker by the sanctions which are set out in the Act. If a council member fails to disclose his interests and takes part in the voting or discussion on the matter, the only penalty provided is removal from office. Moreover, the proceedings must be initiated by private citizens, who must apply to a county court judge.

These characteristics of the present law mean that in fact very little is done to monitor or prevent conflicts of interest. The weakest aspects of the present law on conflict of interest are the enforcement and sanction provisions. The penalties should be more severe (including fines and jail sentences), and responsibility for seeing that the laws are adhered to should not rest only with private citizens.

The Province, in one of its Ministries (say TEIGA), should be the public's protector against conflicts of interest by initiating investigations. We recommend therefore to the Province that conflict of interest legislation (for municipalities, school boards, etc.) be strengthened, with heavier sanctions, and Provincial inquiries and enforcement. In this age of public cynicism about government, it is important that the standards of conduct of politicians and staff be of the highest calibre, and be strongly enforced. The public expectations are higher today than in the so-called good old days when a distinction was made between "dishonest graft" (bad) and "honest graft" (good).

Inter-governmental Relations

One cannot understand municipal government today without knowing of the continuous and multi-faceted dealings that municipalities have with the provincial government, and to a lesser but increasing extent, with the federal government. Of course, for municipalities in Ottawa-Carleton intergovernmental relations have a unique complexion because of the presence of the elephantine federal government, the neighbouring city of Hull, and the Outaouais Region. However, since the municipalities are legally subordinate to the Province their procedures, programmes and expenditures operate within the context of a multitude of provincial statutes and regulations, and hence most of the inter-governmental relations are with Queen's Park.

This inter-governmental maze (or jungle) can be simplified in a number of ways (for instance with the grant structure, as discussed in Chapter 7). Another reform would be to establish the RMOC as the co-ordinator of all municipal dealings with the provincial government, and for certain matters with the federal government. This was suggested with respect to housing, for example, in Chapter 6, but we recommend that the principle be expanded to other functions as well.

To that end we recommend also that an inter-governmental relations office be set up in the Finance Department of the RMOC but working closely with other Regional departments, to deal with both federal and provincial governments.

Labour Relations

Very little has been written on municipal labour relations except for the now outdated

Frankel and Pratt Study.[12] (There is a rich field here to be ploughed by research workers). A short study was done by a member of our Staff, and a few points from it may be worth mentioning.

For one thing, there is not much legislation governing municipality-union relations in the Province, although police and firemen are covered, and there is the more general Ontario Labour Relations Act. For another, there are some obvious differences (into which we will not go), in employer-employee relations in the public and private sectors. For a third thing, municipal politicians can rarely, if ever, match the experience and knowledge of collective bargaining which union negotiators possess. Further, municipalities sometimes avoid confrontations with unions by contracting out services (e.g., garbage collection).

We recommend that labour relations for the RMOC be entrusted to the Personnel Department, and its expertise be developed. Its professionalism should be made available to the smaller municipalities. The larger lower tier units will presumably develop their own professional negotiating skills.

---

[12] S. J. Frankel and R. C. Pratt, *Municipal Labour Relations in Canada,* Montreal, 1954. Other relevant works are S. J. Frankel, *Staff Relations in the Civil Service,* Montreal, 1973; and D. Kwavnick, *Organized Labour and Pressure Politics,* Montreal, 1972.

CHAPTER 10

Education in Ottawa-Carleton
or
"The child is father of the man, but not for quite a while"

"Education is the right of every child, and each child in the Region should have equal opportunities, regardless of creed, language or area of residence . . ."

(Brief of Mrs. Louise McIntosh, trustee of the Carleton Board of Education)

Introductory

It is quite impossible to study the Regional Municipality of Ottawa-Carleton without paying special attention to the school system. It would be like "Hamlet" without the Prince. The importance of the schools stems from a number of factors: the cost of the system, its organization, its effects (on both parents and children), as well as the demand for equal services for the whole population. Moreover education takes on a unique importance in this Region because it plays, and must play, a primary role in the politics of The Official Languages Act (federal) in the national capital itself and in the whole Region in which it is situated. Apart from anything else, too, we must give it special notice because of the controversies that surround it.

The School Board levies on all area municipalities are larger than the amounts spent by the area municipalities on any other category of expenditure. (See Chapter 7, Municipal Finance.)[1] This important aspect of municipal government is further complicated by the fact that the local school tax accounts for less than half of the total revenues of all the components of the school system. (There is one exception to this — the elementary schools of the Ottawa Board of Education.) In other words, the school system is supported more by provincial grants than by the local education levy, again except for the elementary schools of the OBE. The provincial subsidies in 1975 ranged from 22% (elementary, OBE) to more than 85% in the case of the Carleton Roman Catholic Separate School Board.

Another striking phenomenon of the Region is this: the population of the City of Ottawa is growing very slowly, but some of the suburban townships are rapidly becoming urbanised, especially Nepean and Gloucester. The consequence is that student enrolment is declining in the Ottawa School Boards, and rising in the Carleton Boards. Enrolment with the Catholic Separate School Board of Ottawa, for instance, dropped from 31,569 students in 1968 to 22,188 students in 1975.[2] The Carleton Catholic Separate School Board on the other hand

---

[1] See also *Ottawa-Carleton in Review: A Basic Information Booklet,* August 1975, p. 53.

[2] Appendix "A" of the Board's *Brief*, Feb. 16, 1976. (This includes Grades IX and X francophones.)

Table 10-1

Net Expenditure and Revenue, all School Boards ($000's)
(1974 and 1975)

	Ottawa Board of Education 1974 Elem-tary	1974 Secon-dary	1975 Elem-tary	1975 Secon-dary	Carleton Board of Education 1974 Elem-tary	1974 Secon-dary	1975 Elem-tary	1975 Secon-dary	Carleton Roman Catholic Separate School Board 1974	1975	Ottawa Roman Catholic Separate School Board 1974	1975
Net Expenditure	25,386	44,027	30,741	47,025	23,538	25,057	25,746	30,861	14,831	18,356	24,094	29,671
Revenue												
Government of Ontario	6,121	23,498	8,675	24,361	15,639	17,550	19,744	21,447	12,769	16,256	19,215	23,651
Local Taxation	19,701	19,985	22,325	23,242	8,123	7,790	10,095	9,247	1,949	2,257	4,674	6,016
Over Requisition (previous year)	582	1,021	1,024	485								
Total	26,405	44,504	32,023	48,088	23,762	25,340	29,839	30,694	14,718	18,513	23,990	29,667
Over Requisition (under requisition)	1,019	476	1,282	1,063	225	282	93	(168)	(113)	156	(205)	(5)

Source: School Board Financial Statements, 1974 and 1975.

increased its enrolment by 50% between 1969 and 1975, from 9,961 to 15,472 students.[3]

The Existing School Boards

The four school Boards in the Region were set up in 1969, at the same time as the Regional Municipality itself.

(1) The Ottawa Board of Education (the OBE) provides public education at the elementary and secondary levels for the populations of Ottawa, Vanier, and Rockcliffe Park. The Board is composed of seventeen members. Four trustees are elected at large by separate school supporters in Ottawa and Rockcliffe Park, and one by those in Vanier. The twelve other members are elected by public school ratepayers, six for each of the east and west zones, divided approximately by Bank Street.

(2) The Carleton Board of Education (CBE) is in charge of public education for the eight townships that form the rest of the Region. The Board consists of twenty trustees, of whom four are elected at large by separate school supporters. Of the sixteen others, seven come from Nepean, three from Gloucester, and one from each of the townships of Cumberland, Goulbourn, Osgoode, Rideau, March and West Carleton.

(3) The Ottawa Roman Catholic Separate School Board provides education for Catholic children in Ottawa, Vanier and Rockcliffe Park up to the tenth grade for English speaking and to the eighth grade for French speaking. The Board consists of sixteen members of whom fourteen are elected at large by separate school ratepayers of Ottawa and Rockcliffe Park and two by Vanier.[4]

(4) The Carleton Roman Catholic Separate School Board is responsible for the education of children to grade ten within eight townships of the Region. (The same eight townships that are covered by the CBE). The Board has fourteen members, five representing Gloucester, five Nepean, one each from the townships of Cumberland and March, one for the two townships of West Carleton and Goulbourn, and one for the two townships of Rideau and Osgoode.

All school trustees serve a two-year term, with the chairman of each Board being elected from among its members each year, at the first meeting in January.

School Financing

The policy of the Ontario government has traditionally been that public financial support is not given for Catholic secondary schools. Such support (whether from local taxes or provincial grants) is given only up to the tenth grade. This policy — for the most part — dates from the early years of Confederation. Catholic secondary schools — when they manage to survive at all — are maintained by a system of private subscriptions combined with fees borne by the parents themselves.

The government of Ontario had defended its past policy by reference to Section 93 of the British North America Act, 1867, which guarantees religious minorities in Quebec and

---

[3] Carleton Roman Catholic School Board, *Brief,* March 29, 1976.

[4] The Public Boards are called "Boards of Education", while the Separate Boards are called "School Boards". The former provide school education from Kindergarten to grade XIII, the latter to Grade X.

Ontario those legal (educational) rights and privileges already enjoyed at the time of union.[5]

The provincial policy is a correct but narrow legal interpretation of this part of the Canadian constitution. The BNA Act does not say that tax support for Catholic schools *must* cease at the tenth grade, indeed it went in the early days only to grade eight. A poor province like Newfoundland has always given full support to denominational schools of all kinds, and the guarantee of this system was written into the "Terms of Union", 1949. The tradition in England is similar, i.e., of tax support for other than state schools, (though not for certain independent schools for the children of the wealthy, which the English illogically call "public schools").

Local tax revenues in the RMOC, as we have noted, are never more than 50% of the total school costs. (See Table 10-1). It should also be observed that the commercial and industrial assessment and the taxes resulting therefrom are directed almost exclusively towards the public boards. The justification for this situation is as follows. One argument is that it rests upon historical and traditional attitudes. But there is no good reason why this justification should not be abandoned. The other justification is a practical one: how can the assessment and taxes on commercial and industrial property be fairly assigned as between public and separate school support? Shall it be in proportion to shareholders? On student numbers? On total population? These methods, or any other like them, are no doubt difficult to administer.[6]

For that reason, it seems best to us to cut through the Gordian knot altogether. Hence we have recommended, in Chapter 7, that all commercial and industrial assessment be "pooled" at the Regional level, and then distributed to the area municipalities.[7] The school board levies upon the municipalities would thus allow every board, of what ever kind, to receive a share of revenue from these properties.

In the same way the payments in lieu of taxes, federal and other, are almost all directed toward a few municipalities and thence toward the public school system. Nearly half the population of the RMOC is Catholic (47.5%). The same logic which leads to a pooling of commercial and industrial assessment should apply also to all "exempt" assessment for which payments in lieu are made. The suburban population and municipalities should receive their quota of the payments in lieu, since they bear a large part of school costs.

So with respect to educational financing, we make several wide-ranging recommendations. In so doing we are aware that they break with the Ontario tradition, but if a thing is right it should be done, and the tradition should be broken (when "prudential" judgment allows, as St. Thomas Aquinas might say).

---

[5] S. 93. In and for each Province, the Legislature may make Laws in relation to Education, subject and according to the following Provisions:
1. Nothing in any such law shall prejudicially affect any Right or Privilege with respect to denominational Schools which any Class of Persons have by Law in the province at the Union:
2. All the Powers, Privileges and Duties at the Union by Law conferred and imposed in Upper Canada on the Separate Schools and School Trustees of the Queen's Roman Catholic Subjects shall be and the same are hereby extended to the Dissentient Schools of the Queen's Protestant and Roman Catholic Subjects in Quebec.

[6] As the ill-considered legislation of the Hepburn government in the 1930's plainly testifies.

[7] It may be noted that in the Reform of Property Taxation in Ontario, Budget Paper E, 1976, there is a proposal for pooling assessment on *provincial* property, and assigning it to public and separate elementary schools in the same proportion as taxable residential assessment is assigned. In a sense therefore, the door is already ajar, and our recommendation merely pushes it open.

(1) Provincial aid in the form of grants and subsidies should be available to Separate School Boards for secondary schools up to Grade XIII. In other words, the separate schools should be treated the same as the public schools, to the last grade at the secondary school level. This seems to us merely a matter of elementary justice.

(2) A Regional fund or "pool" should be set up, combining all commercial and industrial assessments in the Region. The Pool should then be allocated by the RMOC to the area municipalities in proportion to their population.

(3) A similar "pool" of exempt assessment on which payments in lieu are made, should be held by the Region, and distributed in the same way as commercial and industrial assessment.

(4) We also make a recommendation which goes even further: that *all* schools be treated in the same way, that is, any other denominational schools of whatever kind; "alternative" schools; those based on the Montessori method, or on the Rudolph Steiner method, etc.[8] Insofar as the other schools accommodate and teach children, they relieve the public school system. The total cost to the local and provincial populations would therefore not be noticeably higher than at present.

    The only exception we make to this is for those "independent" schools for children of the rich who pay large fees in order that their children may go to private, independent schools. (The situation is parallel to that in Britain). There is little enough re-distribution of income under the present taxation system, and tax aid for the poor separate, other denominational and "alternative" schools will help.

(5) Those denominational and other schools mentioned in (4) above, which are at present privately maintained (often at great sacrifice by the parents), should be subject to inspection to ensure that they do in fact educate at least up to Ministry standards.

In view of the fact that our recommendations above depart so much from the Ontario tradition, some further justification may be offered. In summary form, then, our justification for the above recommendations are:

a) Parental rights (on behalf of their children) will be fully recognized. The only exception to this, is that of compulsory education — parents have no right to withhold education from their children. There is no point in arguing further for compulsory education, since it is so widely agreed that child education is necessary in the modern world. There could be debates over the school-leaving age, or the abandonment of Grade XIII, but since these do not affect our recommendations, we can (with some relief) refrain from entering these murky waters.

b) Whatever other schools are set up, thereby relieve the public schools, and should be supported by local taxes and provincial grants, and all payments in lieu of taxes. Our recommended method of doing the latter is to form Regional "pools" of assessment, and have the RMOC allocate the assessment for commercial and industrial, and for "exempt" property on which payments in lieu are made, to the various municipalities upon which the school boards levy. Local school taxes will be collected, as now, by the municipalities. (See Chapter 7, Municipal Finance).

c) By supporting all schools "equally", there is a chance for more experiment and diversity in teaching and learning. We can see no reason why the schools must all be homogeneous

---

[8] It follows that we favour the integration of the Hebrew schools in Metro Toronto into the Boards of Education with full public support, regardless of the compulsory religious studies. If parents do not want the religious instruction for their children they can send them to another school.

and, like the American little red school house, have as their chief function that of the "melting pot". In these days of so much discontent with the public school system, experiment and diversity are positive blessings. Indeed, such discontent and a willingness to try new methods largely explain why parents have banded together and set up "alternate" schools; and why some well-to-do parents (including socialists) send their children to private schools.

There will unquestionably be much opposition to some or all of these recommendations, and a job of bringing the public and governments around to support them will not be easy.

First, there will be argument based on the American doctrine of a "wall of separation between church and state"; an argument that is partly rejected in Ontario already, by the support for separate schools to Grade 10. The doctrine has never been so firmly rooted in Canada as in the U.S. of A. In the U.S., for instance, it was not possible to elect a Catholic as President until the time of John F. Kennedy in 1960. Canada however does not seem to worry about the religion of its prime ministers nor of its provincial premiers.

Second, there will be an argument that religion divides us. But if religious rights are important (and they are), then parents should have the right of ensuring that their children receive religious instruction. Parents also have the right to ensure that their children have no religious instruction, and this too must be respected. Our recommendations do not *force* religious instruction upon anyone, but instead they leave parents with a wider range of educational choices for their children.

All those in the work of education must act on the assumption that education makes a difference to children (for the better). It seems a reasonable axiom from which to start, although it may be hard to prove. However, those non-religious parents and others, who fear the effects of denominational schools, may perhaps take some comfort from an old saying; that religious instruction often turns children against religion. This may sound a trifle cynical, but it is entirely consistent with the drift (or stampede) to secularism in the western world. It is hardly possible to turn around without meeting ex-priests who have given up celibacy for other vows — those of wedlock.

Third, we are assuming that the public and government of Ontario are more enlightened than in the days when mighty political battles took place over religious schools. Think, for instance, of the Titanic struggles over the "Manitoba schools question".[9] It is possible that the enlightenment assumption is wrong, that the old prejudices over schools are still running high. But this is hard to believe in our tolerant and permissive age where almost "anything goes" (especially in the school system).

There are some signs that the Ontario Government and public are in fact not hostile to more aid for separate schools. Among these signs are (a) the easy acceptance by the Ontario legislature of the Foundation Plan of 1964, which extended the tax base of both public and separate schools; (b) the welcome by all parties (except for some initial hedging by the Liberals) of the Hall-Dennis Report of 1968 which, by strong implication, favoured further separate school aid; (c) the Ecumenical Study Commission on Religion in Education, 1969-70, which stressed aid to separate schools, and "plurality" in the school system; (d)

---

[9] On this, and other aspects of public and separate schools, see André Siegfried, *The Race Question in Canada,* ed. by Frank H. Underhill, McClelland and Stewart, Toronto, 1966. Siegfried's book was originally published in Paris in 1906, but is a classic work on Canadian politics, comparable to de Tocqueville's *Democracy in America* (1835 and 1840).

surveys taken independently in 1971, by school trustees and by the Conservative and Liberal parties, which showed that the Ontario electorate was not particularly averse to secondary separate school aid from taxes.[10]

Fourth, we say — with some confidence — that our recommendations will not hand the schools over to the churches, and that the legitimate right (and duty) of the state to provide and/or oversee education is fully maintained. The Ministry of Education is not threatened by our proposals, and the Ontario Institute for Studies in Education and the teacher training colleges (or faculties) will have fresh woods and pastures new opened to them.

No School Boards at all?

We come now to the mechanisms by which our recommendations may be carried out. The most basic question is: should there be school boards at all?

In *Ottawa-Carleton in Review: A Basic Information Booklet,* August, 1975, p. 58, we put that very question, in this form: "Should school boards be elected at all, or should schools instead be run by committees of municipal councils?" Designed to provoke, the question did so.

Yet it was more than a provocation; it was a perfectly serious question. For one thing, it would be quite consistent with the outlook of this Report that school boards, being a special purpose body, should be eliminated and that, say, an education committee of the RMOC should be responsible for all schools.

For another thing, the "experiment" has worked successfully with the County Councils of Alberta since the early 1950's. And none of the fears of the teachers, whose Association mounted a monstrous pressure campaign against it, were realized. The same sort of system prevails in Britain, and both public and separate schools seem reasonably satisfied with it.

So there is really nothing outrageous about our question.[11] Nevertheless, and with great reluctance, we refrain from a recommedation that all school boards be abolished.

Almost all the briefs that we have received, including those of all four school boards (naturally enough), have been against such a recommendation. They have argued that education is so extremely specialized, the problems of its administration are so many and so complex, that it would be unwise to burden the committee system of any municipal council with such an assortment of problems.

They have also argued that parent-trustee relations are different from those of municipal ratepayers to their elected councils. This is perhaps true. At any rate, and taking into account these and many other considerations, we have come down on the side of retaining elected school boards. The question then is, should the existing boards be reorganized?

A Regional School Board

One of the guiding principles of the Ontario Ministry of Education is that of "equal opportunity" for all. Unfortunately as the years have passed, differences in resources and environment have created disparities in the Ottawa-Carleton school system. As school

---

[10] See also Donald C. MacDonald, (ed.), *Government and Politics in Ontario,* Macmillan, Toronto, 1975, Chapter 2. For a lengthier account stressing school financing, see David M. Cameron, *Schools for Ontario,* University of Toronto Press, 1972.

[11] As a private person I favour this kind of educational system, but in a public rôle I must, alas, conclude that it is a "non-starter" at present. But given time . . . .

trustee Louise McIntosh and three trustees from Gloucester on the Carleton Board of Education have pointed out, the Ottawa Boards serve a "dense urban population but are faced with the problems of decreasing student enrolment".

Such social changes do not help the stability of the boards, nor the morale of trustees who are faced with major day-to-day problems such as the scarcity of staff promotions and the possibility of staff dismissals. The financial problems of the Ottawa Separate School Board, which must sell some of its buildings and lay off more than a hundred teachers, are a case in point. As for the Carleton Boards, both separate and public, the number of students is increasing at a rapid rate, involving enormous capital expense and high transportation costs. (It seems to be almost a law of nature that there is higher fecundity in the suburbs than in the inner city.) Added to this is the problem of the more limited tax base, mentioned previously.

A problem brought up many times at public hearings of the Commission was the total lack of any co-ordinating mechanism and of collaboration between members of the four school boards in the Region. Any discussion or collaboration is strictly "ad hoc" and there is no plenary or liaison committee which would permit a continuing dialogue or exchange of ideas. Trustee Lucien Bradet, for example, illustrated this point, by noting that one of the defects in the present system lies in the absence of any attempt to co-ordinate even the transportation of students on a Regional basis.[12]

The creation of a Regional school board (it might be called the Ottawa-Carleton Regional School Board) would seem to be one of the first essentials of a reformed education system in the Region. Its existence would at least ensure some formal basis of co-ordination between the school boards, and it should have powers similar to (but not necessarily identical with) those of the Metro Toronto School Board.

Among the powers of terms of reference of the Regional Board would be:
(1) Long range planning for, and locating of, all new schools.

This would eliminate the difficulties of the so-called "co-operative collaboration", since decisions would be made with the interests of the whole Region in mind.
(2) Transportation of students

Transportation of students at present is by school buses of the different boards, and by O.C. Transpo. A Regional Board would eliminate duplication of bus routes, and would permit one body to negotiate with the RMOC Transport Department, already recommended in Chapter 5.
(3) Negotiation of Salaries

With a Regional Board to negotiate salaries and other terms of employment, useless competition between school boards for teachers would be prevented. (In time a single payroll office could be set up.) Once the contracts are agreed upon, for both teachers and support staff, the local boards would administer the contracts. One single negotiating body would be better able to build up expertise in labour relations, to match the professionalism of the union negotiators.
(4) Financial control

The Regional Board would approve the capital and current budgets of all school boards, as in Metro Toronto. The purpose of this is to ensure (a) that new schools are not built while others are only partly occupied; (b) that there is the utmost co-operation between boards and

---

[12] Mr. L. Bradet's remarks were made at the presentation of the Ottawa Board of Education, *Brief,* Feb. 3rd, 1976.

schools in their use of equipment and facilities; and (c) that there should be co-ordination of programmes where necessary.

As for that part of school board borrowing on the open market, we recommend that this be undertaken and managed by the RMOC Finance Department, which has unrivalled expertise in this matter. (School boards sell their debentures for much of their borrowing, at lower interest rates, to the Ontario Education Capital Aid Corporation, which uses funds generated by the federal pension plan. This is beneficial to the school boards, but probably not to the pensioners).

In addition the capital spending of all boards should be subject to approval of the RMOC — via the Regional School Board — again as in Metro Toronto.

(5) Programmes and services in "Special Education"

The Regional Board would operate these programmes, if it found it necessary, and at the very least would co-ordinate them. Among them are: schools or classes for retarded but "educable" children; schools and services for deaf or hard-of-hearing children; the teaching of the handicapped and children in need of special care, by psychiatrists, social workers, therapists and others. These specialized services are usually beyond the financial capacity of local boards, and in any case the students come from more than one board.

(6) Other miscellaneous services

These would be provided to the other boards by the Regional Board. Among them are: insurances of several kinds including fire, car and bus liability; standardized forms and methods for accounting and other records; centralized purchasing and centralized computer services, refereeing the transfer of students from one school board to another.

A Board on Linguistic lines

During the last ten years, Franco-Ontarian spokesmen of this Region have been advocating one school system for the French-speaking population. The main reason for their requests lies in the anomaly of the present situation — that is to say, in the right of French schools to exist but in the lack of French-speaking trustees for these schools. In fact, school boards are comprised mainly of the English-speaking, and recommendations by the French population are studied by an English-speaking majority. The only exception to this is in the present composition of the Ottawa Catholic Separate School Board, where the French-language members are about equal in number to English-speaking members. But nothing actually guarantees such representation; the results of the latest election were pure chance.

The first group to make known its views to us on the possibility of creating a French-speaking Board (with its own schools) was the Union of Carleton French-speaking Parents and Ratepayers. In a well-prepared brief Mr. André Ladouceur and Dr. André Lafrance stated that "we shall see the disappearance of Franco-Ontarians if the dispersal of children in sixty different schools controlled by four school boards keeps on".[13] Any co-ordinating of French language teaching, or collaboration between French-speaking school trustees appears to be non-existent, according to trustee Father G. Faucher of the Ottawa School Board and trustee Florian Carrière of the Ottawa Catholic Separate School Board.

---

[13] The Co-ordinating Committee of the Union of Carleton Francophone Parents and Ratepayers, *On the Necessity of a French School Board in Ottawa-Carleton, Brief,* February 9, 1976, p. 2.

The chief reason which leads us to think of a French-speaking school board in the RMOC lies in the survival of the French minority in Ottawa-Carleton. In our opinion, this minority represents a cultural and social body of great value to the Ontario part of the National Capital Region. They are not Québécois, but Franco-Ontarians. Moreover, with the decline of the parishes, the schools are now becoming the centre of cultural life for the French-speaking.

The provincial government no doubt believed when it created the French Language Advisory Committees (FLAC) that it would succeed in giving them a voice in decision-making on the school boards. These committees were set up in good faith, and the people who worked on them did so in the hope of having some influence on decisions. Nevertheless, this expectation has turned out to be fruitless. As one English language trustee told us, the Advisory Committees have had little influence on decisions, and "we are of the opinion that something more should be done".[14]

The idea of a French language school board has not been altogether welcome by some on the Separate School Boards. They have gone so far as to say that the creation of such a board would be "selling their birthright for a mess of pottage". Let us put this debate in its proper perspective. The advocates of a French-speaking board are not fanatics, nor French revolutionaries in Phrygian caps seeking the entertainment of the guillotine, nor are they necessarily unbelievers. They are not out to downgrade the separate schools, as some may have feared. No one is talking of abolishing Catholic schools; in fact, we have recommended their extension. (See above). We do not advocate the "de-schooling of society" à la Ivan Illich.

There was also the curious action of declining to circulate a questionnaire on parents' opinions on the creation of a French language school board (*Le Droit,* May 26, 1976). In a letter to the readers of *Le Droit,* Michelle de Courville Nichol gives an opinion with which we agree:

> "The elected representatives of OBE and FLAC of Ottawa are hiding their fear of learning the opinions of parents behind pretexts and lame excuses. Is it so alarming to find out the opinion of one's electors? One can often take polls on political matters, for instance, without going so far as to throw oil on the fire!" (*Le Droit,* June 11, 1976)

In order to examine the implications of the creation of such a Board, the Commission took two steps.

The first was to organize a meeting of all the French language trustees and Advisory Committees in the Region (April 9, 1976). The main object of this meeting was to examine important aspects of the daily life of Franco-Ontarians in the RMOC. The results were excellent, although only two trustees from the Ottawa Separate School Board were present.

It seemed to us that the French-speaking trustees and Advisors were more than sympathetic to the idea of a Board of their own, believing that the present situation gives the Franco-Ontarians very little opportunity to administer their schools. The adverse reaction of some trustees on the Ottawa Separate School Board appears to be a hasty judgment that the mere discussion of a reform desired by a good part of the French-speaking minority in Ottawa-Carleton was not within the Board's jurisdiction. A very odd view.

Our second step was to seek to determine the opinion of parents on the possibility of setting up a French school system. We were given the help and support of the two Boards of Carleton — the Separate School Board and the Board of Education — and also the

---

[14] *Brief* of Mrs. Louise McIntosh to the Commission, March 17, 1976.

collaboration of Dr. André Lafrance of the Union of Carleton Francophone Parents and Ratepayers. Although the questionnaire was not sent through the two Ottawa Boards the sample obtained from the Carleton Boards does show that the parents have no opposition to the creation of a French Board. In fact, nine parents out of ten (of those who answered) say that they are not opposed to the recommendation and the majority were in favour.

Table 10-2

Results of the questionnaire distributed by the Commission to certain Francophone homes in the Region

	Garneau Secondary School*	Carleton Roman Catholic School Board	Carleton Board of Education
Questionnaires distributed	1,200	5,300	700
Questionnaires returned	14	1,975	105
In %	1.0	37.3	14.7
In favour	9	1,178	64
%	64.3	59.6	61.0
Against	1	110	10
%	7.1	5.6	9.5
Not interested in the question	0	27	0
%	—	1.4	—
Want more information	4	638	17
%	28.6	32.3	16.2
No reply or questionnaire spoiled	0	22	14
%	—	1.1	13.3

* The questionnaire was distributed too late in the year to this school for returns to come in.

It appears to us that the problems of the French-speaking population are grave. Almost eight hundred students from the Carleton Board of Education attend secondary schools in Ottawa. This arrangement, although at least a sign of co-operation, is hardly satisfactory to the parents concerned. They are represented by trustees of a system which they cannot control.

A small example of the difficulties encountered by the French-speaking ratepayers could perhaps be illustrated by the reply given by a secretary of the Carleton Board of Education to our request, written in French, for permission to distribute the questionnaire on the possibility of setting up a Francophone system. The reaction was like this: "The majority of our members speak English, would you have a translation for us?" One can easily understand the frustration of a French-speaking ratepayer with a reply of that kind. A later explanation from the Board Chairman, accompanied by a Copy of the Board's rules concerning replies written in the language of the recipient, did little to alter the initial impression.

We therefore recommend that a French language School Board for the Region as a whole (in charge of classes from Kindergarten to Grade XIII) should be formed as soon as possible. A pilot project of this kind could serve as a model for other parts of Ontario where the French-speaking population exceeds a certain proportion of the total number of students in the area, for example in the Windsor area.

In the first instance, this Board would be Catholic and would, of course, preserve the religious rights of Catholics. However, a decision to have a non-confessional sector could be taken in the future, by the elected representatives, after consultation with parents.

Continuity in the education sectors could thus be maintained. French-speaking students are at present part of a separate school system in the elementary grades, and of a public system in high school. Two systems, two kinds of programmes. With our recommendations, if adopted, continuity of comparable education would be achieved in both the public and separate sectors for both French speaking and English speaking.

It is a mistake to believe that only the Protestants of Ontario wished to discourage the use and teaching of French in the schools. The Irish Catholics did their share too in trying to suppress French. For instance, Bishop Fallon of London wanted (in 1910) to "wipe out every vestige of bilingual teaching" in his Diocese.[15] Steadily, however, the teaching of French to Franco-Ontarians grew in the schools, informally and by custom — especially after World War II — in both public and separate schools.

The deliberate legal reforms in making French the language of instruction may be said to have started in 1959, when Leslie M. Frost was Premier, and continued under John Robarts and William Davis throughout the 1960's. By 1963, French as a language of instruction reached Grade X, and later to the end of public secondary school grades in several subjects.

The training of French-language teachers, especially in the Faculty of Education at the University of Ottawa; the increasing consultations between provincial Departments of Education in Ontario and in Quebec in the 1960's; the Ministerial Committee on French-language Secondary Schools; the addition of French-speaking officials in the Ministry of Education; several pieces of legislation; exchange programmes and other steps, all marked the Ontario progress in recognizing and catering for the Franco-Ontarians. In July 1968, a Resolution was introduced in the Ontario Legislature, and passed with the endorsement of all parties, "That, henceforth, every member of this House may, as a matter of right in this House, address the House in either of the two official languages of Canada."[16]

In its brief to the Commission, the Ottawa Catholic Separate School Board proposed that a study be made of the boundaries between the ORCSSB and the Carleton Roman Catholic School Board. We have already pointed out the problems of enrolment of these two Boards. The best way to deal with these problems, as with others, would seem to be to create a single Separate Board for English-speaking ratepayers.[17] We so recommend.

---

[15] F. A. Walker, *Catholic Education and Politics in Ontario*, Don Mills: Nelson, 1964, p. 243.

[16] For a fuller account of the trend to encourage French, see T. H. B. Symons in R. M. Burns (ed.), *One Country or Two?* McGill-Queen's University Press, 1971, pp. 169-204.

[17] There are already some signs that the Ottawa and Carleton Separate Boards are considering amalgamation.

The Public School Boards

It is the rearrangement of the public school boards in the Ottawa-Carleton Region that presents the most difficulties. We agree with the Carleton Board, that the creation of a "huge monster" for the entire Region should be avoided.

According to the data we have gathered, the two Boards we have already recommended — one English-speaking separate, one French-speaking separate — would have, in the first instance, between 20,000 and 25,000 students each. There would remain about 75,000 students in the public school sector.

By creating two public boards, each with some 30,000 or so there would be four boards, each with almost the same number of students. This would help to equalize and simplify the finances of the four boards. There need be no costly new structures, but rather a re-ordering of existing structures. We recommend two public school boards.

A difficulty arises in defining the boundaries of these two public boards. We cannot accept the simplistic concept of creating an urban Board, a suburban Board and a rural Board. The two proposed separate Boards already cut across the three categories of urban, suburban and rural. The boundaries could be one of the following: either (a) one public school Board for Ottawa and the new Vanier, and one for the outside cities and townships. If this is followed, the names could stay the same, i.e., the Ottawa Board of Education and the Carleton Board of Education. Further, there would be the advantage of Board boundaries not crossing municipal boundaries; or (b) one public Board for the western part of the Region and one for the eastern part, with a defined dividing line. The disadvantage of this choice is that part of Ottawa would be in one Board, and part in another. This, however, is how the east and west zones are now, for the Ottawa Board of Education, so it would not be difficult.

We recommend that the boundary separating the two pubic boards be at Baseline and Fisher, thence north on Island Park Drive to the Ottawa River.

We also recommend that denominational schools — other than the Catholic Separate — "alternate" schools, etc., should come under the jurisdiction of the public Boards. These Boards would have committees to deal with these other schools.

Term of Office

In Chapter 9, we have recommended a three-year term of office for municipal councillors. We recommend a three-year term also for elected school board members. The existing two-year period is clearly insufficient and pushes some members into preparing for re-election after only ten or twelve months in office, to the neglect of their duties.

We recommend that all school board elections take place at the same time as municipal elections. That is, on the second Monday in November, and that the new school board assume office on the first of December, while still retaining the same calendar financial year. (See also Chapter 9)

Composition of Boards

(1) We recommend for the French school Board some ten members. These would come as follows: four members (for four wards) to the City of Ottawa, two to Gloucester (two wards), two to Vanier (two wards), one for the whole population of Cumberland-Russell, and lastly one to the entire French population of Nepean, Osgoode, Rideau-Goulbourn, West Carleton and the new western municipality (Kanata). (These re-allocations apply to the new municipal boundaries that were proposed in Chapter 8.)

(2) We recommend also for the English language separate Board, some ten members as follows: four members (for four wards) to Ottawa, one to each of the municipalities of Nepean, Gloucester, Vanier and the new western municipality, one member for Cumberland-Russell and Osgoode; one for Rideau-Goulbourn and West Carleton. (Again, our references are to the proposed boundaries in Chapter 8).

(3) We recommend ten members for each of the public school boards as follows: four for the Western Board (four Ottawa wards), four for Nepean (four wards), one for Kanata and West Carleton, one for Rideau-Goulbourn; and for the Eastern Board, four for Ottawa (four wards), three for Gloucester (three wards), one for Vanier, one from Cumberland-Russell, one from Osgoode.

(4) The composition of the Regional School Board required much thought. Should we propose an ex-officio representation, i.e., with the members of the Regional Board as delegates from the four school boards, rather like the present RMOC, or should there be direct election by the voters?

The ex-officio method would permit a close relationship between the Regional Board and the other boards, but it would hardly contribute to the over-riding importance and duties we have given to the Regional Board. Members serving on two boards would, in our opinion, have too much work.

As for the method of direct election, the chief objection is that it may not permit enough contact between the different boards. Its chief virtues lie in the direct election, i.e., members can be held accountable by the public, and their interests would be Region-wide, not tied to the special interests of any particular board. In the end, direct election is the method we recommend, with one member, ex-officio, from each of the local boards (chosen by these boards) to ensure liaison.

We envisage a Regional Board of some 12 elected members, three from each of the four electorates which elects the local boards, plus four ex-officio — one from each local board — in order to further liaison among the Regional Board and the local boards, and to some extent among the local boards themselves.

The election of a chairman (chairwoman) for the Regional Board, and for each of the local boards, presents no difficulty. Each board should choose its own chairman, at the first meeting of each board. We think he (she) should serve a three year term. It is best, we think, that the chairman of the Regional Board should be one of the directly elected, not one of the ex-officio members.

These, then, are our recommendations on school boards. Doubtless there are many details which could vary and would have to be worked out: let the Ministry of Education in negotiating with local authorities; and the Ontario Municipal Board see to them. Among these are the drawing of ward lines (where required) for elections to cross as few municipal boundaries as possible; the re-distribution of assets and liabilities, including the most important of them — the school buildings; the re-assignment of teachers and other staff; and perhaps an alteration in the size of the boards we have recommended.

As to the voters lists, these would be compiled as now by the regular municipal enumeration, from the regional assessment office of the Province, in Ottawa. So, too, the assessment office would provide the information as to which school board the tenant or homeowner wished his property taxes to go. Finally, it should be made easy for parents to transfer their children from one school board to another, and on this the Regional Board could render great assistance.

Teaching material and Training of Teachers

The training of teaching staff takes on special importance in the Region, with the new school system we have proposed. Three aspects are particularly important: the preparation of teaching materials, programmes for educational television, and the religious training of teaching staff in the separate (and other denominational) schools.

In French Canada, it is often said that many books and teaching materials are produced in France and are not relevant to the Canadian scene. The teaching material used for English-speaking students has also often been criticized in recent years. We are on something of a nationalist jag. One hopes the fever will soon decline. English-speaking Canada is disturbed by the Americanization of school and other books, and of the media, especially of television. Educational TV has not escaped these criticisms.

Government subsidies to encourage the preparation of more (and better) Canadian educational material is certainly needed. The French-speaking minority in Ontario has hitherto received little consideration on this point. One speaks, as the Ontario government has often done, about the cultural values that the French-speaking Canadians bring to the life of the Province; and it follows that these values should be preserved and extended. It follows next that the finances necessary should be forthcoming, to ensure a supply of educational material that gives a true image of, and supports, the French-speaking of Ontario. Research grants to existing teaching personnel, scholarships and summer research, plus funds in aid of publication — these are examples of what might be done.

It is perhaps mainly the field of educational TV that touches on our concept of the RMOC as something unique on the educational scene. In practice, the basic aim of young Francophones in the Ontario part of the Capital Region (as the Ottawa Separate School Board pointed out in its Brief) is to maintain their fluency in their mother tongue while at the same time maintaining their loyalty to the milieu where they live; an environment of an Anglophone majority. Directors of educational TV should be encouraged and helped to produce local programmes with a definite "local flavour". Here the co-operation of teachers, who are themselves living the kind of daily life that could be shown and studied, is indispensable.

Young people, of both languages, who wish to teach in separate schools should receive special religious instructions, or else the teaching will be defective. In relation to the long-term programmes of the school boards that we have proposed we recommend:
1) That Ontario increase its financial aid to ensure the preparation of teaching material relevant to the French-language minority in Ontario;
2) That Ontario educational TV be more sensitive to the needs of Franco-Ontarians and that it make grants for the production of typically Franco-Ontarian programmes;
3) That a special programme in religious instruction for teaching personnel be set up in Ontario, to provide adequate staff for the separate schools; and that this programme be inaugurated in Ottawa if at all possible. As to exactly where this instruction should be given, it seems most appropriate that it be given in the Education Faculty of the University of Ottawa.

Instruction in a Second Language

The RMOC, as we have mentioned earlier, is a unique region of Canada, and of the Province. The fact that many people would like to see this Region reflect the official bilingual nature of the country adds another feature to this uniqueness.

It is worth noting that the Bilingual Districts Advisory Board (Chairman, Professor Paul Fox) pointed out in its Report that it not deem it necessary to recommend that the Ontario part of the National Capital Region should become a federal bilingual district. The reason is, that by Section 9(1) of the federal Official Languages Act the federal government as well as all its agencies are already obligated to give their services in both English and French.[18] The creation of a bilingual district would thus add nothing so far as the federal government is concerned.

The problem is more complex than this, since education is a provincial matter. Therefore it falls upon the Province of Ontario to help improve bilingualism in the RMOC, through the schools.

The latest annual report of Keith Spicer, the Commissioner of Official Languages, made a strong recommendation that it is better to "bilingualize" the school-children instead of "Teaching Old Dogs the New Trick of Obfuscation in Two Languages."[19] Spicer's words seem to apply more to this Region than to anywhere else since many people at home in the two official languages will take up positions in the federal, provincial or municipal spheres:

"The additional federal outlay needed for the provinces to launch us seriously toward this goal [of bilingual public servants] by expanding three well-proven programmes, as outlined below, might require little, if any, increase in costs over what is now being spent on public servants; and it could prove an investment — not, in great part, as it is now, an endless subsidization of the temporary."[20]

It is quite possible that Ontario could establish with the federal government a "new federal-provincial strategy which would make radical progress in such teaching the over-riding goal of Canada's language efforts for the next generation."[21]

French Immersion, or "why can't the English teach their Children how to speak" — French, that is?

All studies available to us seem to be in agreement: French immersion courses for English-speaking children are the quickest and best way of teaching French. As one example, F. Genesee is of the opinion that intellectual quotient, conditions of work and geographical situation all have very little influence on the success of French immersion courses and that children have the advantage in such programmes.[22]

Another study for the Ontario Institute for Studies in Education shows that children learn just as quickly in their own language even if they are being taught another language and that they are in fact well in advance in the second language.[23] A further, somewhat

---

[18] Bilingual Districts Advisory Board, *Report*, Information Canada, Ottawa, 1975, par. 759.

[19] Commissioner of Official Languages, *fifth annual report,* Information Canada, Ottawa 1976, p. 3.

[20] *Ibid.*, p. 26.

[21] *Ibid.*, p. 25.

[22] F. Genesee, "The Suitability of Immersion Programmes For All Children," paper presented at the *Research Conference on Immersion Education for the Majority Child,* Montreal, November 1975, p. 45.

[23] Henri C. Barik and Merrill Swain, *Three Year Evaluation of a Large Scale Early Grade French Immersion Programme: The Ottawa Study,* Ontario Institute for Studies in Education, Toronto, Jan. 1976, p. 27.

specialized and difficult study by Smythe, Stennett and Gardner cites the findings of Jakobovits and Stern who show that the learning of a second language at the youngest possible age is the best means of acquiring the "capacity for communication" in that language.[24]

It seems ridiculous that some people, on the pretext of budget restrictions, want to "phase out the experience" of immersion programmes, thus discouraging communication between French and English speaking citizens in the Region. Learning the language of the Franco-Ontarian minority is one step towards a better understanding of the problems of this minority, and school boards should enlarge rather than contract their immersion programmes in French, whether these are full immersion or "half and half". It may even be possible, and should be facilitated, for some English-speaking children who become fluent in French, to transfer to the French school systems.

Exchange of Teachers, and Monitors

Why is there little attempt to create understanding between Ontario and Quebec by teacher exchanges? Does the salary question constitute a barrier? Of course there are difficulties, but they are not insurmountable. On the two sides of the Ottawa river there should be a system of exchanges for French language teachers in the RMOC and for English language teachers on the Quebec side. The differences in salaries can be worked out if the two provinces exert themselves.

We agree with one of the resolutions of a colloquim of the Alliance for Bilingualism on "The governments and official languages in the National Capital Region", Ottawa, November 26, 1975, which went as follows:

> "The Ministries of Education of Quebec and Ontario, as well as the universities of the two provinces, should establish a method of certifying teachers, which would facilitate their mobility from one province to the other, in order to make up the deficiencies in some places, particularly for the teaching of French and English, as a second language and as a mother tongue."

A good example of inter-provincial cooperation is the established programmes for monitors in the second language: university students helping teachers. This programme should be enlarged and made more flexible. Students from one province, for instance, should be allowed to work in their own province, unlike the present situation whereby student-monitors must come from another province. This would be of great importance to the Ontario part of the National Capital Region, where there are two universities each with the majority of the students having a different language. These monitors would play an important role if all schools gave obligatory instruction in the second language from kindergarten to the thirteenth grade, at least for one hour a day. Half of this time could be with the student-monitors in charge.

Cynics may say we have passed the point of no return, in prescribing a core curriculum in Ontario schools, and the smorgasbord system is here to stay. To that we say, pfui! Confederation is worth saving, and so is a good education system.

---

[24] Smythe, Stennet and Gardner, "The Best Age for Foreign Language Training: Issues, Options and Facts", in the *Canadian Modern Language Review*, vol. 32, no. 1, October 1975, p. 20. (The little evidence against this view is not convincing).

It will be observed that we are not prescribing immersion courses in the English language for Franco-Ontarians. The reason is obvious: students from this minority are plunged every day into the reality of an Anglophone world. We estimate that the existence of a second language course for French students (one hour a day from an early Grade to Grade XIII) is ample to complement with a good knowledge of grammar their grasp of the language learned in the outside world. It is their French language, rather than their English, that is of concern.

Concluding Remarks

In addition to the good-will of the English language majority, some official supervisory body for bilingualism in the RMOC is needed. It goes almost without saying that the Regional School Board will be officially bilingual, and that each local board will be able to offer services in both languages. To do this is not a matter of "bilingualizing" all personnel. It is sufficient that one or two persons within the structure (who are already bilingual) be charged with supervising and helping to initiate services wherever there is some demand for both languages.

Finally, we believe that each local school board be required, like the Regional Board, to submit all complaints about board services, as well as the teaching of the second language, to a Council for Bilingualism in the Region. This Council, which is described more fully in the following Chapter, would help by its enquiries and publicity, to create a greater awareness of the necessity for bilingualism within the Region.

With regard to the teaching of the second language then, we believe that the following measures should be taken without delay in order to ensure a better system of education for a Region that is officially bilingual federally, and which should be so at the provincial level. We recommend:

1) That each school board in the Region provide obligatory instruction in the second language (French for English-language pupils, English for the French-language pupils) from at least Grade V (and earlier at the discretion of the boards) to the end of high school, for at least one hour a day;
2) That French immersion courses be established on a *permanent* basis open to all English-speaking students who desire them and can benefit from them, with the financial support of the Ministry of Education of Ontario;
3) That a permanent federal-provincial committee be established (made up of representatives of the federal Secretary of State, of the Ontario Ministry of Education, and of delegates from each school board in the Region) to set up joint programmes to ensure that all high school graduates from Regional boards are bilingual;
4) That a programme for monitors of the second language (to help the regular teachers) be initiated by Ontario, allowing university students in the province to give younger students of "the other language" some daily practice and a knowledge of "the other culture";
5) That Ontario negotiate with Quebec to try to arrange annual exchange programmes for teachers, allowing English language teachers from Ontario to teach English in the Outaouais part of Quebec, and French language teachers from Quebec to do the same thing in the RMOC;
6) That school boards be required to submit all complaints about teaching of the second language to the Council for Bilingualism in the Region, (as proposed in the following Chapter).

A few points may be emphasized before concluding the discussion of the education system in the Region.

The creation of the Regional School Board which is recommended would in no way take away responsibility for academic programmes from the four local boards. Much the same principles involved in the creation of a regional municipality have been applied to the creation of a Regional School Board. In addition, the Regional Board, in discharging its obligations, would have a closer contact with the finance department of the RMOC. The participation of school trustees in the overall planning and urbanization of the Region will also be improved.

The Commission believes that its recommendations for the educational system of Ottawa-Carleton will help to remedy actual ills and will give rise to more collaboration among all parts of the school system. Who can boast that they know *"the"* solution? It may be better to raise the right questions than to give answers for all problems.[25]

---

[25] It may be noted that our recommendations for a French school board differ somewhat from those suggested in "French-Language Public Secondary Schools in Ontario," Cultural and Educational Subcommittee, *The Confederation Challenge*, Queens' Printer, Toronto, 1970, Vol. 2, pp. 256-272. The Subcommittee preferred French-Language in the ordinary *Public* Schools.

CHAPTER 11

Language of Services
or
Shall we dwell in two solitudes?

"I have no accord with the desire expressed in some quarters that by any mode whatever there should be an attempt made to oppress the one language or to render it inferior to the other; I believe that would be impossible if it were tried, and it would be foolish and wicked if it were possible."

Sir John A. Macdonald,
H. of C. Debates,
February 17, 1890

Introductory

The question of "bilingualism" is one of the great public issues in Canada today. The RMOC, which contains the national capital, is naturally at the full centre of all the storm of controversy surrounding the Official Languages policy.

Part of the policy is that the federal government will supply its services, whether these are in regular departments or in Crown agencies, in both of the two official languages, English and French.

A certain number of misunderstandings surround the policy, and it may be useful to mention two of them.

a) It is not a policy to make everyone in the country bilingual. There are parts of the country which speak only French, and parts which speak only English, and no doubt this will continue for a long, long time.

b) It follows that there are parts of the country where the federal government will need to supply services in only one of the official languages. There will be no demand, on the part of the local public, for the other language.

In this Region, however, as in many other areas where both languages are spoken, the federal services will be available in either language, at the option of the person requiring it. If he (she) writes or talks to the federal department concerned in his (her) own language, the answer will be given, or the business transacted, in that language.

The Ontario part of the National Capital Region (with boundaries roughly similar to those of the RMOC) was designated federally as a "district" in which services will be given in both languages (1969). This was six years before the final report of the Bilingual Districts Advisory Board (Chairman, Prof. Paul Fox) had been received.

The question for us is not therefore one of the federal government services, but rather one of language services in the Region provided by provincial agencies (of which there are many), and more particularly of services by the municipalities in both languages. The RMOC, the City of Ottawa and other area municipalities have thus a special responsibility, one that comes up every day in dealings with the public.

Table 11-1
Statistics on the French Language in the RMOC and in the Province

	Ethnic Group*		Official Language				Mother Tongue			Language Spoken at Home**	
	British Isles	French	English[1]	French[2]	Both		English	French		English	French
Ontario											
1951	3,081,919	477,677	4,115,548	78,974	359,965		3,755,442	341,502		n.a.	n.a.
As %	67.0	5.6	89.5	1.7	7.8		81.6	7.4			
1961	3,711,536	647,541	5,548,766	95,236	493,270		4,834,623	425,302		n.a.	n.a.
As %	59.5	9.6	89.0	1.5	7.9		77.5	6.8			
1971	4,576,010	737,360	6,724,100	92,845	716,065		5,971,570	482,045		6,550,060	352,465
As %	59.4	10.4	87.3	1.2	9.3		77.5	6.3		85.1	4.6
Ottawa-Carleton											
1951	147,599	73,372	163,498	12,148	65,879		172,000	65,000		n.a.	n.a.
As %	59.9	29.8	67.5	5.0	27.2		69.8	26.4			
1961	195,736	97,869	244,497	15,003	89,440		246,332	83,838		n.a.	n.a.
As %	54.6	27.3	69.3	4.3	25.3		68.7	23.4			
1971	264,955	117,460	323,080	18,395	126,140		317,415	96,900		348,610	82,115
As %	56.1	24.9	68.4	3.9	26.7		70.0	21.4		78.5	17.4

Source: Statistics Canada, Catalogues 95-715 (CT-15A) and 95-745 (CT-15B), and others.
n.a.: Not available.
1 English only.
2 French only.
* Ethnicity is traced through the father.
** New category, first used in 1971.

Present Trends

Some of the population language statistics give food for thought. (See Chapter 2). In terms of ethnicity, some 25% of Ottawa-Carleton are of French descent, but for mother tongue (first language learned and understood) only about 21%. This difference is perhaps understandable; after all, ethnicity and mother tongue are not the same.

A comparison of mother tongue with language spoken at home yields a more significant figure: only 17.4% speak French at home. The difference between this and the percentage for mother tongue is a reasonable measure of "slippage" or assimilation of the French-speaking minority. Statistics Canada, in its five-year (shortened) Census of 1 June 1976, did not ask these questions about mother tongue or language spoken at home.

Table 11-1 is designed to show the French language situation in Ontario and in Ottawa-Carleton.

The assimilation of the French minority was emphasized by the Alliance for Bilingualism:

> "Many demographers will acknowledge that assimilation takes place when it is to the economic advantage of the minority to learn the language of the majority and when the struggle for certain cultural goals is won. Indeed there is assimilation in the Ontario part of the National Capital Region today. Of the 116,000 Franco-Ontarians in this Area, the 1971 census figures show that only 70% speak French at home. Of the 122,000 French Quebecois in the Quebec part of the NCR, 99% speak French at home."[1]

This increasing "Anglicisation" among French-Ontarians has been studied by Professor Charles Castonguay of the University of Ottawa. He used the figures of the latest federal census by age group, and shows that young adult Franco-Ontarians are "more inclined than their elders to adopt English as the principal language of the family".[2]

In an illuminating Table on this subject, the same author gives an assessment of Anglicisation in two "regions" by age group, using nine census divisions. It is primarily the first "region" of Ontario that interests us, since it includes Eastern Ontario: Glengarry, Ottawa-Carleton, Prescott, Russell and Stormont. The Northern part takes in Cochrane, Nipissing, Sudbury and Timiskaming. The results, in Table 11-2, show the extremely high rate for the 20-24 age group and the 24-34 age group. When 20% of the young people no longer speak French at home this gives cause for dismay about the future of the language; the figure represents a society in which the French minority is likely to disappear.

Table 11-2
Degree of "Anglicisation" by Age Group in Two Ontario "Regions"

	20-24	25-35	35-44	45-64	65 and over
Eastern Ontario	19%	22%	22%	18%	13%
Northern Ontario	24%	24%	23%	22%	14%

Source: Professor Charles Castonguay, University of Ottawa, from 1971 Census.

---

[1] The Alliance for Bilingualism, *Brief,* 31 March 1976.

[2] Charles Castonguay, *The Growth of Anglicisation among Young Franco-Ontarians,* n.d. (By kind permission of the author).

In a remarkable book, Richard Joy states that if a linguistic and cultural minority does not enjoy legal protection, backed up in practice, "two languages of unequal strenght cannot co-exist in intimate contact and the weaker of the two must inevitably disappear."[3] By the same logic one could perhaps argue that English will inevitably disappear in Quebec. Despite the guarantee in the BNA Act, English is seldom spoken in the Quebec legislature.

Using much the same arguments, la Société Nationale des Québécois de l'Outaouais affirmed in a brief prepared for the federal study on the question of the federal capital (The Fullerton Report) that the formation of a federal district "could very well be a mortal blow to the French language not only in the federal capital region but in the whole of Ontario".[4] So if only for the protection of the French minority in Ontario, proposals for a federal district as the capital of Canada should not be given much attention. One may also add that spokesmen for the two provinces of Quebec and Ontario are on record as opposed to a federal district capital.

While living in Ontario, the Franco-Ontarian desires to live both as French-speaking and as an Ontarian.[5] The Franco-Ontarian is not a Quebecois.

Within traditionally French institutions such as the University of Ottawa (which was given a "bilingual mission"), it seems that assimilation of students is strong for Francophones living on the Ontario side. A study done by Alain Massot bears out this quite well.[6]

The annual statistics of the Registrar of the University of Ottawa show that five years after the 1971 census, the number of French language students — in proportion to the number of students enrolled — is on the decline. (See Table 11-3)

Table 11-3
Mother Tongue of Students and Language of Instruction at the University of Ottawa

	Mother Tongue French (1)	(2)	English (1)	(2)	Language of Instruction French (1)	(2)	English (1)	(2)
1970-71	60.6	42.0	33.2	39.8	48.1	37.6	51.9	62.4
1971-72	62.0	40.5	31.2	39.5	49.9	37.9	50.1	62.1
1972-3	60.2	38.4	31.9	42.3	49.3	32.9	50.7	67.1
1973-4	57.9	33.5	34.3	45.5	48.2	29.4	51.8	70.6
1974-5	54.0	31.3	38.6	48.0	47.5	28.7	52.5	71.3
1975-6	50.0	29.0	41.7	50.0	42.6	25.0	57.4	75.0

Source: University of Ottawa, Registrar's Office, *Statistics on Students. Undergraduate: 1975-76*, pp. 59-60.
(1) Undergraduates
(2) Graduate Students.
Note: The mother tongue, *for these statistics*, was defined as the language spoken and written at home. The language of instruction refers to the language used in the greater part of the courses taken by students.

---

[3] Richard Joy, *Languages in Conflict*, McClelland and Stewart, Toronto, 1972, p. 135.

[4] Brief of the S.N.Q. de l'Outaouais, *La francophonie a reculé dans l'Outaouais*, presented to Douglas Fullerton, printed in *Le Devoir*, September 29, 1973, p. 5.

[5] J.-R. Gauthier, M.P. for Vanier, also expressed this opinion at the most recent conference of the Alliance for Bilingualism.

[6] M.A. thesis, Department of Sociology, University of Ottawa, 1973.

There is evidence of the same kind from the Faculty of Medicine of the University of Ottawa. It comes from a brief presented on January 10, 1976, to the Action Committee on Public Health Services in the French Language in Ontario, at a public hearing held in Cornwall.

In it Dr. André Lafrance recalled that the "Regulation on bilingualism at the University of Ottawa, November 1974" provided no exception to Section 4(c) of the University of Ottawa Act, 1965, that all faculties and schools are bound by the said Section "to further the development of bilingualism and biculturalism and to preserve and develop French culture in Ontario."[7] At present, as Dr. Lafrance went on to explain, courses in the faculty of medicine are all given in English. In other words, no French language student can become a doctor by training at university in his own language. This results in a two-flavoured French medical vocabulary in Ontario — a mixture of English and French. How can it be otherwise, when the French-speaking doctor "has not learned medicine in French?"[8]

We are dealing here with the decline of the French language in Ontario. If other professionals and university graduates are obliged, like the doctors, to use English so often in their work, it is not surprising that the population in general, should live from day to day in English. When for instance French-speaking parents decide to send their children to an English-speaking school closer to their home, what are we to conclude? Of two explanations, one is that Franco-Ontarians have lost hope; the other, that they have become pragmatists and realize that their children must live "en anglais".

We cannot bring ourselves to accept the first possibility. The existence of l'Association canadienne-française de l'Ontario (ACFO) and of movements such as "C'est l'temps", which preach the merits of the French minority, convince us of the vitality of these "unshakeables" who persist in preserving French culture. (It may be noted too that Francophones have been among the most assiduous audiences of this Commission).

So there remains only the second possibility. The French-speaking population does not delude itself; their world is English and their children must take their place in it. As we have often been told by French-speaking citizens: "We hold on to our language, but we fully realize that to claim and obtain something for ourselves we have to do so in English. Our message is more important than the principle of always speaking French . . ." A minority to save its own language, must cry out in another language.

Who is Responsible?

We do not absolve the French minority entirely. It is the French-speaking citizens who must first of all lay claim to services in their own language. Certain organizations, however, "cannot be convinced of the necessity of furnishing services in French, because they have not had much demand for it."[9] We cannot but encourage the French-language population to

---

[7] *Brief* of Dr. W. A. Lafrance to the Action Committee, Jan. 10, 1976, p. 1.

[8] *Ibid.*, p. 5. The Dean of the Faculty of Medicine is a Franco-Ontarian. The collective agreement, with faculty members, is in both languages. Internes and family medicine doctors work in French (with French-speaking patients in the General Hospital and in Hull); and Montfort Hospital is French. There is an internal commission in the Medical Faculty working on the mechanics of making the faculty bilingual. The process can only be evolutionary, because of the high standards of recruits for teaching which must be maintained to keep the medical school accreditation.

[9] Memo of Henry F. Davis, Chairman of the Committee on Biculturalism, Social Planning Council of Ottawa-Carleton, June 9, 1976, p. 3.

demand respect for their rights.

However, we could well be in a vicious circle. Already weary of asking without receiving satisfactory replies, the French minority cannot take this situation seriously if the different levels of government and social organizations seem to turn a deaf ear. Nevertheless, in a democracy it is the minority which must define what it wants. Majorities are often merely indifferent, unless things are brought to their attention, sometimes dramatically, always frequently.

The policy of Ontario was enunciated, as a declaration of principle, in the legislature on May 3, 1971, by Premier Davis:
"Ontario policy accordingly will be to respond and continue to respond to the legitimate aspirations of the French population of Ontario", adding that government policy was "now to give more expansion to our bilingual services . . . ."[10]

Five years later, almost to the day, the Mayor of Hull, Gilles Rocheleau, was the twenty second person to go to jail (the first twenty one people being Franco-Ontarians) in protest against an Ontario court summons issued in English only. If the result of the above declaration of principle is to spend days in jail, then we are nonplussed. At the beginning of August 1976, almost nine months after the Ontario Solicitor-General's promise and almost three months after provincial court forms in Ontario were made available in Canada's two official languages, the O.P.P. of Eastern Ontario had still not received bilingual forms and some policemen in Ottawa were still handing out tickets in one language.[11]

The situation is more depressing when we consider that this Region is part of the National Capital Region of Canada and should set an example. We note with regret that a French language citizen cannot even legally be born (or die) in French in Ontario. As Mr. Gerard Levesque explained to us, "Provincial forms for the registration of the newborn are unilingual — in English."[12] He added that liquor control permits are in one language, as are drivers' licences.

Where Ontario seems to move slowly is within the programme of the federal Secretary of State, which can grant subsidies of up to $100,000 a year to each province, for translating provincial laws and regulations. Ontario has lost some half a million dollars by not taking advantage of this grant, from 1970-1975.[13] The provincial action was said to be justified by the assertion that "Whatever is granted to Ottawa should also be given to North Bay or Sudbury; concessions made to Francophones will create a precedent for the Italians or the Portuguese in Toronto."[14] The Alliance added, "the Province has not really recognized the fact that the status of the Capital of Canada places Ottawa in a special category". Moreover, the French-speaking minority is a special minority, as the federal government, i.e., national policy, recognizes with the Official Languages Act.[15]

The difference between Quebec and the French-speaking people of the diaspora must be

---

[10] It is too bad this statement was not translated sooner.

[11] *Le Droit,* Ottawa, 10 August, 1976.

[12] Mr. Gerard Levesque, *Brief,* Feb. 9, 1976, p. 1.

[13] Information from the office of the Secretary of State.

[14] Alliance for Bilingualism, *Brief,* March 31, 1976, p. 2.

[15] For 1975-76 the Province did apply for and receive $75,000 from the Secretary of State (i.e., less than the entitlement) for approved translation purposes. One should add that if the provincial laws, etc., are translated into French they will be available throughout the Province, and not just in Ottawa-Carleton.

understood if we are to understand the claims and sentiments of the Franco-Ontarians, especialy within this Region.

With modernization of the economy and political and social institutions, the Quebecois could make the political state (province) co-terminous with the "nation" — conceived as identified with language. They are "masters in their own house". Assimilation into the English-speaking, and a pan-Canadian nationalism — unhyphenated as Mr. Diefenbaker conceived it — has been successfully and confidently resisted.

> "For the French minorities outside Quebec, the assimilationist pull from the civil and industrial society was counteracted by the norms of kinship and religion. The solution to the dilemma created by the contradictory pull of these opposing norms was and is perfect bilingualism."[16]

In this way the rights of the individual and of the French-speaking collectivity are reconciled. But it cannot be done unless the Franco-Ontarian feels secure in his language. And the way to confident security is, at a minimum, that the French-speaking are served in their own langauge. Viewed in this light, the creation of a French-speaking School Board, recommended in the preceding Chapter, is also a *sine qua non*.

Provincial services in French are steadily expanding. No doubt the pace is slow, and the Franco-Ontarians are often frustrated by irritants here and there when they come up against prejudice or, what is worse, a bland indifference and complacency. But the tide runs in their favour, often silently and unnoticed. If the winds of change are blowing through the Church, they are also blowing through the Province's language policy.

A few of the indications are: the statement of Provincial policy (cited earlier); the increasing number of books, reports, documents now coming out of Queen's Park in both languages (one has only to note the lists of government publications to see this); assessment notices in the Region in the two languages; the growing translation services in the Provincial Ministries; the expansion of linguistic capacity in the Ottawa-Carleton offices of the provincial government (nearly every ministry has a local office); the French-language secondary school established in Sturgeon Falls as a result of the Symons' Report; the reprimand of a provincial court judge for his offensive remarks about French spoken in his court; the notices in French that are mailed with parking tickets; the policy of hospitals in the Region to have a bilingual admissions person on duty at all times; and so it goes. Sir John A. Macdonald's remark in the Commons, cited at the start of this Chapter, is being transferred into practice.

We come now to the Municipalities, and their use of French. The Regional Municipality in 1973 adopted by-law No. 78 which recognized English and French as its two official languages. The Cultural and Social Institute of Vanier gave us some information, incomplete, and to be handled with care.[17]

Using the RMOC telephone directory for 1975, the authors of the study classified the names of employees of the RMOC. In considering the French-sounding names (first and last

---

[16] Hubert Guindon, in *Contemporary Canada,* ed. by Richard H. Leach, Duke University Press, 1967, pp. 55-56.

[17] The Cultural and Social Institute of Vanier, *The RMOC and the Francophone Community,* by Professor Caroline Andrew and Jacques Servant, of the Department of Political Science, University of Ottawa, Feb. 1976, p. 7.

names), and leaving out maintenance personnel, they found 42 names out of a total of 387 or 11%. The method used is rudimentary, but probably a useful indicator. After all, it is easier to find people with French names who do not know any French (one often meets English-speaking Villeneuves, Trudeaus or Theriaults) than it is to find Smiths or Robinsons who do not know English.

The questionnaires asked members of the Institute if they were satisfied with the services offered to Francophones. Only one out of four was reasonably satisfied. As to which government was the most favourable to the French minority, the study found that the RMOC placed last, far behind the federal government and the city of Ottawa. The government of Ontario, incidentally, received no vote. Finally, all the replies stated that the RMOC "should improve its level of bilingualism".[18]

The RMOC does in fact try to find French-speaking officials for the higher positions. From the beginning, a resolution of Regional Council adopted the two languages as official for its meetings, etc. Telephone calls are either answered by bilingual people, or one is put in touch with a French speaker. A bilingual capacity is found in most departments, although not necessarily at the highest levels. Correspondence is answered in the language of the enquirer, bills are sent to customers (i.e., water bills) in the two languages. Regional road signs are generally also in the two languages. Bilingual meetings were held on the draft Official Plan. The Chairman is bilingual, (but no other top official).

Three area municipalities have a high proportion of French-speaking people, and two of them have a bilingual policy. Vanier of course is the most bilingual, but Ottawa also has a bilingual policy. In Ottawa, where one person responsible for bilingualism has been appointed, the greatest progress has been made. At a meeting with this official, Mrs. E. Cooper, we were told that she sometimes meets resistance from department heads who feel she is going too fast.

The Mayor of Ottawa in his Brief expressed a concern for bilingualism and the difficulty of applying it within a Province such as Ontario.

> "The problems of the courts and court documents, of applications for drivers' licences and vehicle permits, continue to be unresolved and increasingly one is left with the impression that the Government of Ontario is prepared to give to the French language nothing more than an ethnic status and has failed to realize the significance of bilingualism in the development of Canadian unity . . ."[19]

In the case of Vanier, it can be said that the problem is not to speak English, but rather to try to respect French. The new enlarged municipality (see Chapter 8) must insist that all its people should feel at ease in their own language. At the public hearing in Vanier, the only urban municipality in the RMOC with a Francophone majority, we were surprised to find that English was so predominant. This recalls our previous point: the Francophones believe it is more important to get their message across in English.

Gloucester, with a large French speaking minority shows a strong desire to "bilingualise" its services, including its correspondence. All the same, because its officials are mostly unilingual, curious oversights occur. For instance, a notice on recreational services, distributed in French schools for French parents, was completely in English. And

---

[18] Ibid., p. 14.

[19] The Mayor of Ottawa, Mr. Lorry Greenberg, *Personal Brief,* March 26, 1976, p. 16.

the director of recreation is French-speaking!

All French-speaking citizens should feel at home in dealing with local governments in the Region. That is, the RMOC as well as the area municipalities should serve the Francophones, as ratepayers, by providing information and service in French. Technical reports for the RMOC, such as the Paterson Reports are generally in English only and translation should be provided. No doubt this would be costly, but it is a price that should be paid. And it is quite possible the federal government will help financially, either directly or via the Province.

The other municipalities (except Cumberland), are doing little about bilingualism, claiming quite naturally that there is not much demand for it. Here again we have our vicious circle. Francophones are less likely to settle in Nepean or other municipalities that are overwhelmingly English speaking unless they are assured of services in their own language.

Some remedies

The Committee on Biculturalism of the Social Planning Council of Ottawa-Carleton wondered what incentive the Ontario government, the RMOC and private organizations "could and should offer to Francophones to recruit them to their ranks?"[20] The basic incentive, according to the Committee, should be the opportunity to work in the mother tongue, so as to ensure "services of the same quality for the Francophone population as for the Anglophones of Ottawa-Carleton".[21] We subscribe to this proposition. It is undeniable that a French-language citizen who has difficulty with English does not receive the same service as his Anglophone counterpart if no one explains to him, in his own language, the reasons for particular measures or rulings.

In order to recruit qualified bilingual persons, perhaps a premium should be paid to bilingual personnel, rather like that being negotiated for the federal civil service. This would be an incentive for people to become bilingual.

The Alliance for Bilingualism said much the same thing when it stated that, "Provincial and federal governments, Regional and Municipal Administrations should consider bilingualism as a merit factor in hiring personnel who will be in direct and regular contact with the public."[22] And perhaps by having bilingual personnel in all the municipalities, French-language citizens will be attracted to settle in the new western municipality (Kanata) and in Nepean, as much as in Gloucester where Francophones are making progress.

We return to the question of attitudes. As the Commissioner of Official Languages, Keith Spicer, explained in the summer of 1976, one of the difficulties of implementing bilingualism "is that it runs into prejudice, the fears of Anglophones who feel threatened because the federal government has explained its programme badly . . . ."[23] To overcome these fears, we recommend that the RMOC and the area municipalities should have one person responsible for bilingualism within their administration. The City of Ottawa already has one. Such an official (bilingual) could also oversee the translation of documents going to

---

[20] *Brief*, Feb. 18, 1976, p. 4.

[21] *Ibid.*, p. 4.

[22] The Conference on Governments and Official Languages in the NCR, Ottawa, *Resolution*, November 26, 1975, p. 10.

[23] Keith Spicer, on the programme "Question Period", CTV, July 4, 1976.

the public, and receive complaints. (If the complainant is not satisfied with the reply, he could go further — to the Council on Bilingualism. See later.)

The same should be done in the many private organizations dealing with the public. The Social Planning Council of Ottawa-Carleton for instance has undertaken a study to analyse the langauge needs of its 87 affiliated organizations. Its recommendations could be made use of by all private organizations. These should be known by the end of 1976.

Consider this editorial, headed *La vie des agonisants,* (The Life of the Dying), in which Pierre Tremblay repeats the proposals of Mrs. Gertrude Laing, a former member of the Commission on Bilingualism and Biculturalism and ends with his own cri de coeur:

> "The only sure way to resolve these questions is for Canadians to want to do it, and one can write all the research papers, one can appoint all the Commissions one wishes, this will not change anything if, deep down, Canadians do not want to live together . . . and Louis Riel became a hero after his death. Must we wait until minorities have disappeared before we mourn them?"[24]

Dr. Sam Johnson said something similar when he wrote long ago, "I am always sorry when any language is lost, because languages are the pedigree of nations."

We agree with the Biculturalism Committee of the Social Planning Council of Ottawa-Carleton when it noted the shortcomings in the administration of health, recreational and social services (a conclusion confirmed by the Action Committee on the language of health services headed by Dr. Jacques Dubois)[25] and went on to recommend that Ontario "place more emphasis on university training in French in the Ottawa-Carleton Region, so that all Francophones seeking specialist positions in the fields of health, recreational and social services can be trained in their own language . . ."[26]

In asking for a programme of bilingualism with clear aims, Franco-Ontarians must turn the page and forget the bitterness of the past. They must begin discussions on equal terms within the organizations where their language and culture is to be recognized. And in this they need above all the understanding and sympathy of their unilingual English compatriots. "To live together", writes Gilbert Brunet "takes more than bilingual documents . . . we must have mutual understanding and respect . . ."[27] This is a challenge for the Anglophone majority. The theory of democracy supports this view, since majority rule is always coupled with the phrase "minority rights".

A Council for Bilingualism

One hesitates to suggest the setting up of new structures at the local or Regional level, especially when they are special purpose bodies. In this case, however, and in this Region, the French fact is so important, the problems of the French-speaking minority so acute, that a special structure is required.

We recommend that a Council for Bilingualism should be created within the Region.

---

[24] *Le Droit,* December 1, 1975, p. 6.

[25] *The Ottawa Citizen,* "Task Force Confirms French Health Services Lacking", November 17, 1975, p. 3. "We realize there is a serious lack of bilingual personnel in Ontario and that service for francophones in Ottawa is not equal to the requirements of the population . . ."

[26] Committee for Biculturalism, *Brief,* op. cit., p. 6.

[27] *Le Droit,* July 10, 1976.

This Council would have certain powers with respect to the area municipalities and private organizations and the RMOC itself. Its sanction would be publicity in the media. (A comparison might be made with the Ontario Press Council or better still, with the Ontario Ombudsman.)

This Council should be composed along the following lines: a member chosen by RMOC, one by each municipality, one by the Regional School Board, one by Citizens' Associations (say by the Social Planning Council), and one member chosen by the Province. In acknowledgement of the federal interest, a member chosen by a federal department could also be added. If a larger Council should be decided upon, then two members could be chosen by some of the participating sponsors.

The Council's finances should come equally from (a) the Regional Municipality, (b) the Ontario government and (c) from the federal government (possibly through the NCC). It should have a small permanent staff who would conduct studies and inquiries into the language of services within the Region; should attend to complaints received from citizens as to rulings, decisions and even ordinary practices which "are unjust or discriminate against one of the two main linguistic groups in the Region."[28]

With the periodical publication of its findings, as well as an annual report on bilingual services and the position of Francophones, and special reports to the Provincial Ministries, it would aim, by the reforms it proposed, at improving the situation.

It is hard to give any firm estimate of the cost of such a Council (and it would probably cost more than we think). A reasonable estimate for an annual budget would be about $225,000 ($75,000 from each of the three governments).

An Executive Committee (chosen by the Council) could meet, say twice a month, to direct the Council's activities. And the full Council, once or twice a month, depending on the size, under a Chairman chosen by the Council itself, say for a three-year term.

Such then is our recommendation for a Council on Bilingualism in this unique Region.

CONCLUSION

Desperate ills need desperate remedies. An unfortunate situation has to be corrected because this Region is a very special case. It is so because it is the Capital Region of a country that is officially bilingual, and because the future of the country may be at stake.

We are aware that the world cannot be changed overnight. There are no instant Utopias. Nonetheless, it is important to improve the present situation, and that its progress should be seen by all. We feel strongly that Ontario, and the RMOC, cannot write off the dream of saving the French-speaking minority. Nor is the advantage only to that of the minority. Our proposals will also enrich the majority.

---

[28] Alliance for Bilingualism, *Brief* to the Special Joint Committee of Parliament on the National Capital Region, Feb., 1976.

CHAPTER 12

Recreation, Parks and Libraries
or
All work and no play is the recipe for ulcers

"In the past, recreational land could be taken for granted. Today, it has to be planned just as streets are planned with reference to intensities of use, volumes of traffic, and rates of development of neighbouring urban areas".[1]

Ours is an affluent society. We have more leisure time and rising disposable income, both of which have combined to create a vast demand for a variety of recreational pursuits. All sectors of the public and private economy have responded in various ways to this demand, including municipal governments.

Recreation is sometimes defined broadly as any activity which is undertaken in leisure time. We could perhaps find a narrower definition, but it would be a waste of time to seek one. We can say that some recreational activities are "active" as in organized athletics, and some are "passive", such as reading or listening to music. In any case, the recreation programmes of municipalities are both physical and cultural. So we have to say that recreation is whatever the financial statements say is recreation.

Table 12-1 shows the recreation expenditures of the eleven municipalities in Ottawa-Carleton in 1975 as well as in 1969, the first year of the RMOC. The increase is very high, from just under $6 million in 1969 to over $20 million in 1975, or some 254%. This is particularly impressive given that recreation is one of the least provincially-subsidized municipal functions. Provincial assistance will increase somewhat with the advent of the Wintario lottery, and a special grants programme to assist with replacing unsafe arenas.

The provincial *Report of the Special Program Review* in 1975 (The Maxwell Henderson Report) identified a strong increase in recreation spending by lower-tier municipalities, after the establishment of regional governments, as one of the main factors contributing to the overall cost increase of municipal restructuring. That is to say, with several expensive functions transferred to the Regional level (e.g., social services, sewerage system, arterial roads), the lower-tier municipalities were able and willing to spend more on their remaining functions such as parks and recreation. The evidence in Ottawa-Carleton deserves at least one bang of "Maxwell's silver hammer".

The main support of local recreation is for arenas, parks, and playgrounds. All municipalities in the Region except tiny Rockcliffe Park Village and the Township of West Carleton have at least one major indoor arena. The City of Ottawa and Nepean Township are the leaders in providing a wide range of indoor and outdoor recreational facilities, with Gloucester Township following next.

---

[1] Ralph Krueger et al., (eds) *Regional and Resource Planning in Canada*, Holt, Rinehart and Winston, Toronto, 1970, p. 224.

Table 12-1
Area Municipalities, Current Expenditures, Parks and Recreation, 1969-1975

Municipality	1969 $000's	% of T.R.E.	1975 $000's	% of T.R.E.	1969/1975 Percentage Increase	Expenditure Per Capita 1975 ($)
Ottawa	5,023	88.0	11,572	57.2	128%	38.30
Vanier	125	2.2	429	2.1	243	21.29
Rockcliffe Park	6	0.1	37	0.2	516	16.60
Cumberland	15	0.3	376	1.9	2406	32.82
Gloucester	136	2.4	1,912	9.4	1305	35.86
Goulbourn	16	0.3	448	2.2	2700	35.87
March	26	0.4	354	1.7	1361	51.23
Nepean	335	5.9	4,780	23.6	1326	64.60
Osgoode	21	0.4	205	1.0	876	24.74
Rideau	1	0.0	99	0.5	98	12.60
West Carleton	7	0.1	28	0.1	300	3.60
Total	$5,711	100.0%	$20,240	100.0%	254%	39.95

Source: Municipal Financial Reports.

The major municipal parks and facilities in the Region include Lansdowne Park and Civic Centre, Mooney's Bay, Brewer's, Carlington and Britannia Parks in the City of Ottawa. Nepean Township has the magnificent Sportsplex with a variety of facilities, and is in the process of developing a riverfront park at Graham's Bay on the Ottawa River, as well as a significant conservation-recreation project along the Jock River. Throughout the Region are smaller, local parks, playing fields, skating rinks, arenas and "community centres". Recreation programmes cover a wide range of activities from organized sports to individual pastimes and entertainment.

The administrative organization of the recreation function differs considerably among the eleven area municipalities. In most cases overall responsibility rests with an appropriate committee of council, although in certain cases (e.g., Nepean) the recreation committees also have non-council members sitting on them. The small size of some councils militates against having very many council members on these committees. Some area municipalities delegate a great deal of administrative responsibility for recreation programmes to citizen groups or recreation associations. Gloucester Township is notable in this regard.[2]

There are as well a number of formally constituted special purpose recreation bodies. Gloucester, Osgoode and Rideau Townships, for example, have "community centre" or arena boards managing certain of their facilities. In Ottawa, the main annual fair is run by the Central Canada Exhibition Association (the CCEA) which operates independently of the City administration, and of Lansdowne Park where it is held. The degree of autonomy of this body has been the subject of some dispute, as when the CCEA recently opposed the right of City Council to review its annual budget.[3] Such lack of accountability can only be deplored. Citizen participation is a very good thing, but it should not be permitted to usurp the

---

[2] Gloucester Township, *Submission to the Ottawa-Carleton Review Commission*, March, 1976. p. 42.

[3] Ottawa Citizen, April 26, 1976.

policy-making role of elected representatives. The functions of the CCEA should be carried out directly by municipal staff, answerable to the appropriate committee of council. However, as argued below, there may be a case of putting the entire Lansdowne Park complex under the jurisdiction of the RMOC.

The question of the appropriate or "optimum" amount of public parkland and open space which cities should have, has been discussed by "experts" and laymen alike for a long, long time. For many years the standard of 10 acres per 1,000 population has been widely accepted in North American cities as an appropriate parkland supply. No one knows who discovered this magic ratio, although one suspects geographer-planners. This standard, even if accepted, does not of course answer more complex questions such as the best distribution of parkland throughout an urban area, nor how parks should be developed or used. The Ontario Ministry of Culture and Recreation — a delicate name which, like Plato, puts things of the mind first — now recommends that 20 acres per 1,000 population be adopted as the standard for open space in urban areas, though open space includes more than parks.

It has been a subject of concern in Ottawa that the City falls considerably short of this standard. A recent open space inventory compiled by the City reveals that there are only 2.74 acres of municipal parkland per 1,000 population (830 acres for 302,000 people). With federal parkland (733 acres) and school-board park properties (616 acres) added, the ratio improves considerably to 7.2 acres per 1,000.[4] Nonetheless this is still short of the "proper" standard.

A second report by Ottawa explored ways of making better use of existing open spaces which are not at present being used for recreation, including church lands and cemeteries, hospital grounds, open land next to federal office buildings, hydro rights-of-way, abandoned railway lines and even rooftops![5]

As to the distribution of parkland, a recent academic thesis concludes that in the central areas of the City where the need is greatest, public parks are in the shortest supply. That is, where average incomes are lower, car and cottage ownership lower, population densities higher and apartments more numerous, the supply of parkland is as low as 2.5 acres per 1,000.[6] This makes a strong case for the City not to permit build-up on all land which comes vacant through demolition, etc.

To ensure that municipalities set aside more public parkland the provincial government has required, through The Planning Act, that 5% of the land area of subdivisions be dedicated for public parks (or in certain cases cash-in-lieu of land can be accepted by the municipality from the developer). This appears to be a reasonable requirement for low density developments such as single family subdivisions, but even so this requirement by itself would not provide sufficient land to meet the 10 acres per 1,000 standard. An average of 16 to 20 people per acre produces only approximately 2½ acres per 1,000. It is more obviously inadequate in the case of high density apartment developments. To help meet this deficiency The Planning Act was amended in 1973 to allow an alternative park dedication of one acre

---

[4] *Inventory of Open Space Lands*, City of Ottawa, Planning Branch, May, 1975, p. 33.

[5] *Open Space Study: Analysis and Policy Recommendations*, City of Ottawa, Planning Branch, March, 1976, p. 45.

[6] *A Need-Oriented Approach to Urban Recreation Space Allocation*, by Harro-Volker Trempenau, M.A. Thesis, Department of Geography, Carleton University, 1975, p. 103.

per 120 dwelling units. This Act is now being reviewed by a provincial committee and the parkland provisions may possibly be altered in the near future.

Federal Recreation Activities

As in several other respects in this Region there is a strong federal presence in parks and recreation, particularly through the NCC. Other relevant federal agencies include Parks Canada (Department of Indian and Northern Affairs) which is responsible for the Rideau Canal system; Department of Agriculture which operates the Central Experimental Farm and arboretum; and the Department of National Defence which has the large Connaught Rifle Range on the Ottawa River, as well as the Uplands and Rockcliffe air bases.

The NCC is, however, the major federal landowner in the RMOC (the Greenbelt alone contains approximately 42,000 acres) and, as documented in the Fullerton Report, has become increasingly active in the recreation field. Since 1969 the NCC has shifted its development emphasis partly away from roads and other hard infrastructures, and more towards "people oriented" projects.[7] There are at present several large-scale recreational projects either directly run by the NCC, or undertaken in some form of joint arrangement with other government bodies.

The single largest recreational asset in the National Capital Region is the vast Gatineau Park (130 square miles) in the Quebec portion of the N.C.R. While this Park is not in Ottawa-Carleton, it is used extensively by residents of the RMOC for a variety of recreational purposes.

Perhaps the most dramatic recreational undertaking of the NCC in the RMOC is its maintenance of 5 miles of ice on the Rideau Canal from Dow's Lake to the National Arts Centre, as a splendid outdoor skating rink during winter. This popular and successful project, was used last winter by some 750,000 skaters. Also close to the central urban area of the Region, the NCC owns and operates the large Vincent Massey/Hogs Back Park on the Rideau River. Close by, the NCC owns Mooney's Bay Park, containing the only public beach in the Region allowed to remain open by public health authorities this year. It is leased to and operated by the City of Ottawa. As well, the NCC maintains Rockcliffe Park, leased from the City of Ottawa. This park is situated on the Ottawa River, partly in the City and partly in Rockcliffe Park Village. A further NCC project has been to provide several miles of bicycle paths.

Several areas in the NCC's extensive Greenbelt holdings have been developed for outdoor recreation. These include the Stoney Swamp Conservation Area and Pinhey Forest in the west end, Pine Grove, Mer Bleue, and Green's Creek in the east. Recreational activities include trails for skiing and snowshoeing in winter, hiking and nature study in summer, interpretation centres, picnic grounds and so forth. The NCC also owns two golf courses, one run by Gloucester Township, and the other operated by the NCC itself. As well the NCC leases a number of sites in the Greenbelt to private clubs or associations, such as the Boy Scouts. A similar programme leases allotment gardens to individuals.

The NCC provides Greenbelt land for two other recreation projects in the west end, the Ottawa/Nepean Campsite Authority and the National Capital Equestrian Park which is a joint Nepean-March undertaking.

The Equestrian Park, perhaps one of the most controversial recreation projects in Ottawa-Carleton, is a good example of a facility with regional significance. Greenbelt land is

---

[7] The Fullerton Report, *op. cit.,* Vol. 1, p. 39.

leased from the NCC. Nepean and March Townships jointly financed the construction of the buildings and facilities. (It has also been designated for a Wintario grant for further construction). The City of Ottawa, which had given preliminary indications that it would participate in the project, in the end did not. As a large, specialized facility, however the Equestrian Park receives considerable usage from residents of the City of Ottawa, as well as other parts of the Region. But Nepean and March were the only municipalities which contributed to its construction.

The NCC has three more parks of Regional significance in the early planning stages. Besides the Green's Creek Park mentioned above, the NCC is planning two major riverfront parks, one at Shirley's Bay on the Ottawa River and the other at Black Rapids on the Rideau River. Development plans for these parks are at the moment tentative. The Shirley's Bay Park may include facilities for non-motorized boating and swimming, as well as further trail development, potentially linking up with the Equestrian Park on the southern edge of the Shirley's Bay Park. The Park at Black Rapids may include boating and overnight camping facilities to serve the growing number of Rideau Canal users.

Other Actors in the Recreation Field

There are other government agencies involved in recreation in Ottawa-Carleton besides the local municipalities and the federal government. These include the provincial government, Conservation Authorities, Boards of Education and the RMOC itself.

The Provincial government is directly involved through its ownership and management of two provincial parks — the Rideau River Provincial Park at the Region's southern extreme near Kemptville, and Fitzroy Provincial Park close to the western extreme of the Region near Arnprior. These parks come under the jurisdiction of the Ministry of Natural Resources. This Ministry also manages certain of the NCC conservation areas as well as the regional forest owned by the RMOC in the western part of Rideau Township. The other main provincial ministry involved is, of course, the Ministry of Culture and Recreation which administers the municipal recreation grant programmes and is responsible for developing policy guidelines as well as providing advice to municipal recreation departments.

Two of the three Conservation Authorities which operate in the Region have some involvement in the recreation field, although their primary responsibilities are not recreational but watershed management. The Mississippi Valley Conservation Authority has acquired the Pinhey Conservation Area, an 80 acre site on the Ottawa River in March Township. The development of the site, including the restoration of historic stone buildings, is being handled by March Township.

The Rideau Valley Conservation Authority has purchased the Baxter Conservation Area in Rideau Township. This 160 acre site, presently under development, will include a beach, picnic facilities, interpretive centre and nature trails. The Authority has also recently acquired a smaller site on the Rideau River in Osgoode Township which may be developed.

However, the Conservation Authorities in Ottawa-Carleton have played a relatively minor part in the recreation field compared to the large role played by the Metro Toronto and Region Conservation Authority in the Toronto region. The MTRCA has been the major supplier of parkland there. Within Metro boundaries a large amount of land owned by

MTRCA has been turned over to the Metro Parks Department, and in some cases leased to area municipalities.[8]

The Boards of Education possess considerable recreational resources including playground facilities and indoor gymnasia. There has been a growing trend in recent years to make school facilities available for public use after normal school hours and during summer holidays. This trend includes wider use also of school libraries, classrooms, and auditoria. The Carleton Board of Education particularly has shown initiative in this kind of use of schools. In most cases, the arrangements involve leasing school facilities to private groups or associations. In a few cases, however, more formal agreements exist between the school boards and municipalities, e.g., between Nepean Township and the Carleton Board of Education. More of these joint agreements would be worthwhile to help avoid duplication or under-utilization of facilities.

The RMOC has hitherto played only a minor role in recreation. When the RMOC began in 1969 it inherited the Marlborough Forest from its predecessor, Carleton County. Since then, the RMOC has purchased considerable acreage to add to this Regional Forest, which is managed for it by the Ministry of Natural Resources. The Forest has modest recreational potential, limited mainly to nature study and trails of various kinds. At present snowmobiles use it a lot during the winter, but one may doubt whether such usage is compatible either with civilization or with nature in the raw.

In 1975 an amendment to the Regional Act formalized the Region's power to acquire land for recreational purposes. It reads as follows:

> The Regional Council may pass by-laws for acquiring land for, and establishing, laying out, and improving and maintaining public parks, forests, zoological gardens, recreation areas, squares, avenues, boulevards and drives in the Regional Area and for exercising all or any of the powers that are conferred on Boards of Park Management by *The Public Parks Act*.

Since the RMOC began it has made a small annual budget allocation for acquisition of recreational land. The total amount for the RMOC's seven years of operation is less than $1 million, most of which has been spent on additions to the Regional Forest. For 1976, the RMOC land acquisition budget is a mere $100,000 which allows very little purchases, especially in urban areas. It might buy two or three lots.

Regional planning staff have undertaken a number of useful planning studies, particularly oriented to conservation areas beyond the Greenbelt as well as the two river corridors. Nine of these conservation/recreation areas have been carefully assessed from an ecological viewpoint.[9] Some are ecologically sensitive and can withstand only limited development pressures, whereas others have more recreational potential. The former would be appropriate for wildlife and nature study activities, e.g., birdwatching; the latter could provide hiking or skiing trails, picnicking, or hunting. Since most of these lands are in private ownership it will require the zoning co-operation of the area municipalities to ensure their protection, unless they are purchased by the RMOC.

---

[8] *Royal Commission on Metropolitan Toronto: Background Report — Social Policy in Metropolitan Toronto*, June 1975, p. 190.

[9] Robert Reed, *An Ecological Study of Conservation-Recreation Areas in the RMOC*, University of Ottawa, 1975.

The pertinent question at this point is what is the appropriate role of the Regional Municipality in the recreation field? To answer this question, the characteristics of a regional recreation facility should be defined. A possible list of such characteristics, or criteria, is as follows:
- (a) involves costs which would place an undue burden on a single area municipality
- (b) appeals to a specialized interest group whose numbers assume significant proportions only on a wide-area basis
- (c) requires very large areas in natural or semi-natural state
- (d) displays a "scope of usage" which involves a region-wide base

The most important item in this list, corollary to all the items, is the question of "scope of usage" — the area from which the users of the facility are drawn. The primary effect of placing regionally used facilities under the jurisdiction of the Regional level of government would be that the financing and accountability for them would also be Regional. Thus the costs and benefits would be more equitably shared; the scope of usage and control more closely matched.

Certain of the largest facilities of the area municipalities fit these criteria reasonably well. These include Lansdowne Park, and the associated Central Canada Exhibition (it may be noted that Metro Toronto took over the C.N.E. from the City of Toronto in 1965);[10] the Nepean Sportsplex, the National Capital Equestrian Park, and possibly other large urban parks such as Britannia or Mooney's Bay. There is certainly a prima facie case for believing such facilities draw users from all the Region (and even beyond it). Surveys could be conducted to determine the exact geographic patterns of usage of these and other recreation areas.

Clearly the National Capital Commission is already fulfilling a recreational role that might otherwise be the responsibility of the RMOC. The large-scale projects that are undertaken as joint ventures with local municipalities (the NCC usually supplying the land, the municipality providing the structures, site development, or programme staff) might more appropriately be joint ventures between the NCC and RMOC. Examples could include the Pineview Golf Course (now NCC/Gloucester-Ottawa), Equestrian Park (now NCC/Nepean-March), Mooney's Bay (now NCC/Ottawa), Campsite Authority (now NCC/Ottawa-Nepean), Stoney Swamp (now NCC/Nepean).

The assumption by the RMOC of any of the recreation projects listed above does not necessarily imply that the Region would actually operate the facilities or that staff be transferred from area municipalities to the Region. It would be possible for the Region to be responsible for the overall policies and financing involved, while the administration could be contracted back to the area municipality in which the facility is located (*not* to a special purpose body).

Neither does it imply any net increase in costs resulting from the transfer. Costs would simply be moved from one level to another and hence more equitably distributed in relation to usage. Inflation, improved facilities, or new programmes, are separate issues from the question of regionalizing.

A recreational concern which is Region-wide in nature and discussed at some length in the Regional Official Plan is the question of public waterfront access and facilities. Most of the usable recreational shoreline of the Ottawa and Rideau Rivers is already developed with

---

[10] *Royal Commission on Metropolitan Toronto: Background Report — Social Policy in Metropolitan Toronto*, Ch. 4, Recreation, June 1975, p. 198.

private cottages and housing. There is a distinct shortage of public access and parkland on these two valuable recreational resources. (The NCC's plans will help in this regard). A recent provincial recreation survey (TORPS) revealed that water-related activities are the most preferred type of recreation.[11] Yet the extremely high cost of water-front property, and the pressures exerted on local municipalities for private development are so strong, that the lower tier (especially if the municipality is small) is the least able to satisfy demand for public waterfront uses. A partial solution to this problem would be for the local municipalities to allow use of some of the approximately 40 unopened road allowances which have access to the two rivers.

A further function that could appropriately be performed at the Regional level is recreation planning. A strengthened planning role for the RMOC could involve the setting of park standards, guiding the location and distribution of parklands and recreational facilities throughout the Region, and above all the co-ordination of planning required to link parks and open spaces together into an integrated system or network. This concept is hinted at in the NCC's plan *Tomorrow's Capital*. To establish successfully such a comprehensive system involving the urban centre, the Greenbelt and the areas beyond the Greenbelt, would require a co-ordinated effort between the NCC and RMOC.

There are a few specialized projects which meet the Regional criteria set forth above, which do not yet exist in Ottawa-Carleton but which perhaps could be undertaken by the RMOC if there were sufficient public demand. These could include a zoo, aquarium, planetarium, and botanical gardens. (Alternatively the last could easily be formed federally by an expansion of the arboretum at the Central Experimental Farm). By way of comparison we may note that on the Quebec side of the Ottawa river a provincial agency, the Outaouais Development Corporation, is undertaking such large-scale, specialized facilities including a marina complex on the Ottawa river at Aylmer and a zoo near Meach Lake.

The Central Experimental Farm of some 1,200 acres is one of the "sacred cows" in Ottawa. Part of the Farm, say 200 acres near the Rideau Canal, is or could be open to the public, as mentioned above. Field crops are grown on the remainder, and there is no public access. When anyone suggests an alternative use for this acreage, the reaction from authorities and public alike is one of horror. For instance, a suggestion was made two years ago that the acreage should be given over to housing. The outrage could not have been worse had one suggested the legalizing of incest.

Nevertheless, there is something to be said for a more public use of this large urban field. It need not be for housing, but it could perhaps be a park of some kind, or a site for one of the museums (say Science and Technology). There is also the point that an even larger federal farm (some 4,000 acres) already exists a few miles further west, so there is plenty of federal farm land in the Region.

However, we make no recommendation on the Central Experimental Farm, but merely bring the question of its future use to the attention of the appropriate (federal) authorities.

Libraries

Public libraries in Ottawa-Carleton are the responsibility of the lower tier or area municipalities. Table 12-2 illustrates the expenditures and revenues on public libraries in the Region for 1969 and 1975. Average spending stands at just under $10 per capita and has

---

[11] *Ontario Recreation Survey*, by Tourism and Outdoor Recreation Planning Study Committee, Queen's Park, Toronto, September 1974.

increased considerably since 1969, by some 223% to a regional total of $4.9 million in 1975. Only Cumberland Township does not operate a library, although they are preparing to open one soon.

On the revenue side, the total municipal contribution outweighs provincial grants by more than 4 to 1, although four of the small municipalities get more from the province than they contribute locally. The provincial grant at present is $1.70 per capita, and is paid directly to the library boards. Public libraries have expanded considerably in the last few years, several new libraries were built, and library services diversified into "non-book" services (records, exhibitions, etc.), which form an increasingly large part of the services offered.

The RMOC is not itself involved in public libraries, but there is a "regional" body which performs certain services for the local libraries — the Eastern Ontario Library System (EOLS). EOLS covers several counties in Eastern Ontario as well as the RMOC. Its services to local libraries include: inter-library loan privileges; purchasing reference books; rotating collections; and technical and specialist assistance. It is completely funded by the Province, which has been very active in promoting libraries.[12]

Local library boards are responsible for the management of the municipal libraries and are of two types. For municipalities of more than 10,000 population, the boards have 9 members: the head of council, 3 members appointed by municipal council (non-councillors), 3 members appointed by the appropriate public school board, and two by the separate school board. For small municipalities (under 10,000) the library board has 5 members, the head of municipal council, plus 4 members appointed by council.

These boards function with considerable independence of their municipal councils: they determine operating policies, appoint senior staff, and prepare the budget which is submitted to council for overall approval. Councils can only control the amount of municipal grants given (as mentioned, the provincial grants are paid directly to the library boards, not to the municipal treasury). They have little influence over the programmes and services provided by these funds.

In keeping with our general outlook on special purpose bodies, we recommend that the control of municipal libraries be vested in a standing committee of council rather than in appointed boards. In the case of the smaller councils, a minority of the public could be co-opted as members of the Library Committee. Advisory Committees should also be formed.

As we have argued elsewhere, public policy and priorities, especially concerning the spending power, should be firmly in the hands of those elected to municipal office. To remove functions from "politics" is to remove them from public accountability.

As to whether the RMOC should play a role in public library services we are inclined to think not. While libraries are an upper tier function in several counties in Ontario, and are a two-tier responsibility in Metro Toronto, circumstances in Ottawa-Carleton do not seem to show a need for a Regional role. The main function of the Metro library board in Toronto is to

---

[12] The Ottawa Publice Library was started in 1906, as part of the Carnegie benefactions for libraries in many parts of the Province (and elsewhere in the world). Not until 1961 was another library started in the Region (at Osgoode). The rest of the libraries were founded in the 1960's and 1970's. Next to that of Ottawa, the Nepean library is by far the best.

Table 12-2
Public Library Boards, Expenditures and Revenues, 1969, 1975

Municipality	Total Expenditures $000's 1969	Total Expenditures $000's 1975	Per Cent Increase	1975 Per Capita Expenditure	1975 Revenues $000's Municipal	1975 Revenues Provincial Grants
Ottawa	1,256	3,598	186	11.91	2,861	504
Vanier	22	92	318	4.55	45	38
Rockcliffe Park	—	5	—	2.29	1	4
Cumberland	—	2	—	0.13	2	—
Gloucester	35	263	651	4.93	148	82
Goulbourn	—	64	—	5.15	46	18
March	18	56	207	8.16	42	11
Nepean	176	744	322	10.05	689	122
Osgoode	n.a.	21	—	2.53	3	14
Rideau	3	22	630	2.79	13	15
West Carleton	—	20	—	2.60	4	13
Total	1,511	4,886	223	9.64	3,853	821

Source: Public Library Statistics, 1969; Municipal Financial Reports, 1975.
Notes: (1) Cumberland does not have a library of its own, but makes a grant to Gloucester Township for use of its libraries.
(2) Libraries have small amounts of "other revenue", but the percentage is very small, except for Vanier at 10%.

operate a large central reference library.[13] Other functions include a single metro-wide borrowers' card, central bibliographic services and audio-visual materials.

In Ottawa-Carleton the federal presence looms large in the library field, as in many other respects. It would make little sense for the RMOC to establish a central reference library when the largest collection in Canada, the National Library, is already in this Region.

As to other co-ordinating or centralized specialist functions, these seem to be quite manageable under the EOLS arrangement. Therefore, we cannot concur with a recent provincial study (the Bowron Report) that public libraries should be an upper-tier municipal function.[14] This may suit other regions, but is not necessary in Ottawa-Carleton. Although, as the Bowron Report argues, the need for a co-ordinated approach to the developing issue of library automation and central processing is strong, and deserves to be given serious attention by EOLS.

There may be room for a greater inter-changeability of library cards in the Region, something which we are content to leave to negotiation by the area councils.

We do recommend, however, that the holdings of books and other materials in French be greatly increased, and more bilingual staff be added in certain libraries. (The Ottawa Public Library has a good record on these points). We endorse the Bowron Report's recommendation (p. 179), that an additional provincial grant be given to improve Francophone library services in this area.

---

[13] Royal Commission on Metropolitan Toronto, *Background Report: Social Policy in Metropolitan Toronto*, 1975, p. 221.

[14] Albert Bowron, *The Ontario Public Library: Review and Reorganization*, 1975, p. 160.

CHAPTER 13

Social Services
or
Justice for all, and compassion for some.

"To some degree there will always be conflict between economic and social objectives . . . Those who stress social objectives emphasize the need to redirect income generated by productive enterprises to social investments, and to redistribute income among citizens. This age-old debate is arbitrated by elected governments which continually must define the relative emphasis to be placed on social and economic goals." [1]

Introductory

Social services within the Region are a network of programmes, cost-sharing, and administering agencies. These include the federal and provincial governments, voluntary organizations, and both the RMOC and the area municipalities. The whole system is so complex as almost to defy description. Truly, we live in a "welfare" or "service" state in Ontario.[2]

The *first* point to note is that the municipal administration of social services is almost wholly by the RMOC, not by the area municipalities. This transfer of functions was one of the wisest steps taken when the RMOC was set up. To have the social services under one management promotes "conscious planning, co-ordination and evaluation . . . centralization of effort and resources . . . in order to achieve equality of opportunity, uniform policy and standardize programmes." It removes disparities and ad hoc development.[3]

In 1975, the RMOC spent almost $25 million on social services, which came to 30% of its total current spending.[4] The area municipalities generally spend little, and that little is paid to the Region in order to provide particular services to their residents. (See Table 13-1.) The most striking increase since 1969 has been on Day Nurseries.

The *second* point is that a few programmes, however, are administered directly by the province through its offices in the Region. (Something more is said on these below.)

The *third* point is that there is an agglomeration of voluntary services, under boards of directors of the many private organizations. These usually have intimate financial and other connections with the various services provided by governments.

---

[1] Report of the Ontario Joint Committee on Economic Policy, *Directions for Economic and Social Policy in Ontario*, August 1974, p. 23.

[2] Vernon Lang, *The Service State Emerges in Ontario*, Ontario Economic Council, January 1974. For the classic work in this field see Leonard Marsh, *Report on social security for Canada*, University of Toronto Press, 1975. This book first published in 1943, has a new introduction by the author.

[3] S.R. Godfrey, *Brief to Ottawa-Carleton Review Commission*, April 1976, p. 3.

[4] *RMOC Financial Statements*, 1975.

Table 13-1
Regional Social Services, Current Expenditures, 1969, 1975

	1969 ($000's)	1975 ($000's)	% Change
General Assistance	8,018	15,538	94
Assistance to Aged Persons	1,610	4,896	204
Assistance to Children	815	1,539	89
Day Nurseries	228	2,982	1,208
Total	10,698*	24,956	133

Source: RMOC Financial Statements, 1969, 1975.

* Includes $27,000 unclassified expenditures.

Fourth, there are direct federal expenditures on such things as pensions, family allowances and unemployment benefits.[5]

All three levels of government are involved in funding the work of the Social Services Department of the RMOC, perhaps more so than in any other Regional function.

The costs of the RMOC Social Services are shared in various ways. In general, the larger proportion is borne by senior governments: well over 40% of the costs are borne by the federal government, slightly over 40% by the Province, leaving about 14% by the RMOC, and a small 2% or so by the area municipalities. (This does not count the direct federal payments.) The RMOC, even so, makes a larger contribution to its social services than do most other municipalities in the Province. This is because the RMOC has taken advantage of optional programmes which receive less provincial funding, and not because of more poverty in the Region. The Department is both innovative and imaginative within the limits set by law and regulations.

The Social Services functions are helped by the citizens themselves. They play a formal role in advising and assisting the RMOC Department through the Social Services Advisory Committee which deserves much credit. The Committe (which includes some "clients") advises the Standing Committee of Council, which in turn examines Department proposals before they go to the Executive Committee of Council.

When the RMOC Department was set up, there were transfers from the City of Ottawa of social services personnel who had more experience and were more up-to-date in their attitudes than those in many of the area municipalities. With Regional administration there are fewer complaints about humiliation from clients receiving the service. The effect is most noticeable in Vanier, Gloucester and Nepean where the new organization delivers service in a more professional way to clients.[6]

(1) General Welfare Assistance (RMOC)

The chief work of the RMOC Social Services Department is to administer the provisions of the provincial General Welfare Assistance Act and Regulations.

---

[5] If social welfare policy is conceived more widely, one would have to count legislation to protect health and safety of workers; and also income tax exemptions, etc. These occupational and fiscal policies are omitted here.

[6] Social Planning Council, *Brief to the Ottawa-Carleton Review Commission*, December 12, 1975, p.1.

The Assistance programme offers short-term financial help in the form of a monthly budgeted living allowance and other benefits, to those who find themselves temporarily without means of support. In this group are those persons unable to work because of physical or mental illness ("unemployables"), female heads of families, unemployed persons, and children who require short-term foster care. Funding for the programme comes from all three levels of government (federal 50%, provincial 30%, and municipal 20%) through the help of the Canada Assistance Plan (CAP). The CAP helps to fund many, if not most, of the social services, and is said to be under revision.

There are many myths, cherished by those who are well-off, about Welfare Assistance.[7] It is almost impossible for facts and figures to damage these myths, which invariably concentrate upon a few exceptions to the general rule. In the RMOC, "unemployed-employables" account for only 12% of the case-load, and in Ottawa-Carleton only 1.2% of the population were on general welfare.[8] (The Ontario average was 1.5%).

Other minor programmes administered by the RMOC are: back-to-school allowances and Christmas supplements for welfare families, and free dental services for children of marginal income families.

(2) Family Benefits (Provincial Direct Assistance)

For persons in need over a longer period, the provincial government through its local (regional) office provides long-term assistance under The Family Benefits Act (1966). Those receiving benefits are not expected to be able to support themselves, for instance the elderly, the disabled, and some female heads of families.

The Province, through CAP, recovers half of its expenditures from the federal government. Complaints have been made about the separation between this programme and the RMOC Welfare Assistance programme. Families and persons in need cannot always know how long they will require assistance; having to apply for assistance to two different offices, to prove one's need over again, is a discouraging and confusing process for the applicant, and involves a duplication of effort and office staffing, to say nothing of confusing the public.[9] It is also said that the Provincial office is not flexible enough in its procedures, or in the time it takes to make decisions.

For these reasons, suggestions were made to us that these direct provincial benefits should be administered through the RMOC Department, and so too should those contracted out on a fee-for-service to voluntary agencies.[10]

---

[7] It is often forgotten too that under the Act a municipality is *obliged* to help persons in need. In other words, the needy have a legal right to assistance.

[8] Ministry of Community and Social Services (Ontario) Quarterly Statistical Bulletin, April-June, 1975.

[9] S.R. Godfrey, *op. cit.*, p. 37. Some progress has been made in working towards identical Forms. One of the obstacles towards having all the social assistance administered from one office is that the provincial (local) offices serve people in other counties, outside the Ottawa-Carleton Region.

[10] Report of the Special Senate on Poverty, *Poverty in Canada*, Information Canada, 1971, also criticized strongly the lack of co-ordination of welfare programmes, not only in Ontario but in nearly all the country.

(3) **Supplementary Aid and Special Assistance**

In addition, several aid programmes of a more specialized nature are handled by the RMOC. Supplementary Aid is for "extraordinary needs", for example, of those living on pensions and provincial allowances which do not meet their full expenses. Special Assistance makes funds available for such things as prescribed drugs, funeral costs, dental and optical services, prosthetic appliances, vocational training, and emergency travel.

To qualify for this programme, a person may or may not be in receipt of social assistance. Eligible persons include those living on a marginal income from full, or part-time, employment. A person is not necessarily disqualified from this programme by living in public subsidized housing. Special Assistance is both for purposes of rehabilitation, and to relieve hardship.[11]

These two forms of aid under (3) above are permissive and not mandatory. "Special Assistance" is funded by the federal government (via the province), and 50% by the RMOC. "Supplementary Aid" is mostly paid for by the province (80% shared with the federal government), while the RMOC pays for a 20% share.

(4) **Low Income Supplement Experiment (L.I.S.E.)**

A new project, the Low Income Supplement Experiment (L.I.S.E.) was begun in October, 1975 in RMOC. The Province is conducting the same experiment in Toronto and Peterborough. The provincial government picks up 50% of the cost through CAP while the Region contributes the other 50%.

Under the present welfare/wage system it is possible for families on welfare to be better off than if the wage earner is working. The reason is simple. Welfare takes account of family *needs*, and also provides fringe benefits (day care, free dental care for children), while wages are set by the market (or collective bargaining) and take no account of family size or needs.[12] There is a floor under wages of course, the minimum wage, but this wage is often not enough to support a family, especially a large one, with only one wage earner.

The aim of L.I.S.E. therefore is to help low-income workers stay in the labour force and avoid welfare, or to get off welfare. Working persons already getting assistance from some other programme (day care, rent-to-income housing, visiting home-makers) are not able to qualify. Qualified persons can receive up to $100 a month, in addition to their net earned income. The question is whether this extra $100 is sufficient incentive to keep people at work.

To the end of August 1976, some 400 applications were received, and some 200 persons were helped, and about $50,000 spent. The others were turned down because, among other

---

[11] The welfare schemes of the Region, the province and the country are a patchwork (or chaos) partly because they have "just grown"; partly also because they have built into them quite conflicting goals: (a) hold costs down, (b) relieve distress, (c) try to get people off welfare by "rehabilitation" and counselling. It is doubtful whether any of the so-called counselling is worth the effort, or has ever succeeded in getting welfare cases out of their poverty. The poor don't want to be talked at, they want money or work. If the premises of policies are not clear, the conclusions are bound to be confused. It is a wonder that welfare workers, or recipients, can possibly endure their conditions. The Senate Report on Poverty, *op. cit.*, is a much neglected document on the whole welfare question.

[12] This question, and others related to it, are discussed more fully in *Background Paper on Income Support and Supplementation*, The Federal-Provincial Conference of Ministers of Welfare, Information Canada, February, 1975. See especially p. 99, "The Incentive to Become Employed."

things, their income was too high.[13] (Application Forms are in both French and English. The general policy for Social Services is that where Forms can be Regional, they are in both languages; but where they are prescribed by the Province, they are still unilingual, although the provincial Ministry is "looking at" the question of bilingual Forms).

The formula for calculating the L.I.S.E. aid is as follows: "needs" plus up to $100, minus net earned income. Obviously if the "needs" are high, and the net income very low, the $100 incentive is not enough. In other cases the incentive *is* enough, i.e., if the assessed "needs" are lower, and the net earned income higher. Hence L.I.S.E. helps some wage earners (on welfare or not), but not others. By and large, the experiment must be judged a success. It could be more successful if a few changes were made, as suggested by those in charge of the programme: for example, if the maximum award were raised, and less of the applicant's earned income were deducted.

This is such an important experiment, and its principles so widely approved, that we recommend its continuation and improvement by raising the award and lowering the deductions.

A possible criticism of the scheme, by the historically minded, is that it is like the notorious Speenhamland system in Britain in the early nineteenth century, where large-scale farmers kept wages down, knowing the "poor rate" would subsidize them to pay the working farm labourers. The difference between L.I.S.E. and the Speenhamland system is that the minimum wage provides a floor income for the worker. Moreover, there has been no sign that employers are looking upon the L.I.S.E. scheme as a way of holding wages down.

The Social Planning Council of Ottawa-Carleton submitted (and we agree with them) that to correct the situation where families on welfare are better off than the working poor

". . . is a major national issue. It results not from too-generous welfare allowances, but from low wages and inadequate earning power . . . The RMOC, through the limited introduction of an income supplementation programme is taking a gentle but sensible step in the right direction."

It is barely possible that L.I.S.E. and similar programmes may help pave the way to a national guaranteed annual income plan.

Other Services: (a) Day Care

Unlike services under the General Welfare Act, which are mandatory, there are some services which the RMOC delivers only upon the request of the area municipalities.

These are services under The Day Nurseries Act, and under The Homemakers and Nurses Services Act. Ottawa-Carleton is anomalous in this respect. Other regional governments in Ontario may take the initiative under these Acts, and not wait for local requests.

Day care for young children is one of the newer social services, and is financed mainly by senior levels of government. There are signs, at budget times, that governments are especially alarmed at the almost explosive demand for, and costs of, such day care centres.

When the RMOC provides day care, upon request, it charges the local operating cost (20%) back to the area municipality, on the basis of the number of children from that locality. In 1975, the RMOC spent almost $3 million on day care, approximately a twelve-fold increase from the 1969 level.

---

[13] Source: Director of the Programme.

The Day Care Services Branch of the RMOC Department owns and operates 14 centres providing for some 440 children. The centres have a full range of care: 11 full-day centres for children aged 2½ to 5; one nursery school (half-day for 3 and 4 year olds); and two school-age centres for before school and "after-four" activities, and full-day programmes on holidays and during the summer months.

In addition, the Branch purchases services from some 26 private "corporations", and nursery school half-day services from some 20 centres. "Family Day Care" operated out of three "purchase-of-service" organizations. There are about 100 day care centres altogether in the Region.

Day care has been made available so far almost exclusively to the English-speaking. Although many centres include French activities in their programmes, there are only two among the "full-day care" centres with a full French milieu. There are as well about half a dozen bilingual centres. We therefore recommend that day care, as it develops, serve the French speaking much more.

Where purchase-of-service agreements are in force, they are negotiated by the RMOC with each centre. The Day Care Branch processes the budgets submitted by the centres, and these ultimately reach Regional Council for approval. With the recent formation of a special joint committee between the Branch and the Ottawa-Carleton Day Care Association (a private organization) there will be more "input" from the day care centres themselves.

The lengthy procedure for paying out approved funds has put hardship on centres which, in most cases, are already hard-pressed. Budgets submitted in early November 1974, for the calendar year 1975, were not approved until August, 1975. Retroactive money was not received until October. To make innovations in day care, too, is often a long process.[14]

Day care services are expensive. For one family with two children, of 2 and 4 years of age, the cost of full-time day care is said to be $6,672 per year.[15] A means test is administered to those who apply for a subsidy, because the family is required to pay as much of the fee as possible. Parents receiving the subsidized service were 60% of the 1,450 full-time day care placements in the Region, in September, 1974.[16] The Day Care Association believes there should be a "subsidy appeal committee".

The province strictly regulates all aspects of a centre's spending. Given the level of training required (two years community college after high school), persons who work in purchase-of-service Centres still earn little more than the minimum wage, which is much below that of workers in the municipally-run centres.[17] There seems to be a high staff turn over.

The Family Day Care approach is somewhat different. It refers to the supervised care of children up to 10 years of age, in a home other than their own, but nearby. This approach began as a federally-supported three-year demonstration project.[18] At present, under the Regional purchase-of-service, two such Family Centres are operating in the City of Ottawa,

---

[14] Ottawa-Carleton Day Care Association, *Brief*, March 11, 1976.

[15] Community News Service, No. 34, January 14, 1976, City of Ottawa Day-Care Advisory Committee.

[16] Philip Hepworth: *Day Care, Kindergarten and Other Similar Programmes*, Canadian Council on Social Development, Ottawa, October, 1974, p. 86.

[17] Ottawa-Carleton Day Care Association, *Brief*, March 11, 1976.

[18] Andrew Fleck Child Care Centre, *Family Day Care Demonstration Project, A Team Approach*, Ottawa, 1972.

and one in Gloucester Township.

The demonstration project showed that, because of the greater adult to child ratio, Family Day Care does not cost less than group care.[19] The best model for day care (they concluded) was one by which the child received a combination of family and group day care.[20]

In 1974, when day care expansion was at a peak, the Region sought an amendment to the day care legislation. We recommend that the RMOC Act be amended in line with other Regional Municipality Acts, so that the RMOC may be responsible for (although not necessarily operating) all day care centres and day nurseries; and we go further and recommend that the area municipalities not be permitted to "opt-out". This proposal would make for easier Regional planning of the service and (possibly) lower fees. It is taken for granted that there will be participation, through Advisory Committees at both the Regional and local levels.

Other Services: (b) Homemakers and Nurses' Services

These services are provided by the RMOC to families during the temporary illness or absence of the parent, and to the needy elderly and disabled. As with Day Care, the area municipalities must request that such services be provided to their residents, and must bear the local municipal costs. The programme is financed by the Province (80%) of which 50% is recovered from the federal government.

The RMOC Department purchases the actual homemaking services from the Visiting Homemakers of Ottawa (V.H.A.), and nursing services from the Victorian Order of Nurses (V.O.N.). In 1975, $998,000 was spent on Homemakers Services in the Region of which the City of Ottawa paid 89% of the local share.[21] For Nurses' services, expenditures in the same year totalled $140,000, of which 92% was contributed by the City of Ottawa.[22] Not all area municipalities request these services.

After considering the immediate benefits which home care and support services can realize, and the lower long-term health costs that they make possible (as pointed out by the Social Planning Council's Home Support Services Study), we recommend:
1. That the RMOC develop a co-ordinated Region-wide system of home support services. This would involve changing the RMOC Act, S. 86, so that the RMOC would assume full responsibility for nurses' and homemakers' services from the area municipalities,[23] with no "charging back".
2. That a "homehelp" service, less costly than the V.H.A., be set up by the RMOC. This service could be purchased for one or more hours at a time, unlike the V.H.A., which is

---

[19] Andrew Fleck Child Centre, *op. cit.*, p. 43.

[20] *Ibid.*, p. 42. Some people have spoken of the excessive and detailed provincial regulations as an obstacle to making many more small day centres available. There is something to this point of view. How far shall we go down this road? The government, having removed itself from the bedrooms of the nation, is now acting *in loco parentis* in the nurseries.

[21] RMOC Department of Social Services, July, 1976.

[22] *Ibid.*

[23] The RMOC has already (1974) requested a similar amendment to the RMOC Act.

only available for a minimum of four hours; and would require less qualified personnel.[24] The rationale for this recommendation is not only because the services cost much less than the alternatives — hospital or nursing home care — but also because the persons receiving the services prefer to be helped at home rather than put into an institution.

Other Services: (c) Children's Aid Society

The Children's Aid Society of Ottawa-Carleton (CAS) is a quasi-independent, non-profit, incorporated agency operating under the terms of The Child Welfare Act and offering assistance to families and children in distress. It has a membership of about 500, which elects annually a Board of Directors of 24. The RMOC appoints four persons (councillors) to the nine-member Executive Committee, with the other five being appointed by and from the larger Board of the Society.[25] The duties of the society and standards of service are laid down by the Act and Regulations.

The Board prepares the annual budget which goes to the RMOC, and then to the Ministry of Community and Social Services for approval. Should disagreements occur at either of these stages, a Child Welfare Review Board may adjudicate, but in the last analysis the Minister's decision is final. The local CAS is linked with some 50 others in the Ontario Association of Children's Aid Societies.

Since 1975, the Society has been financed mostly by an 80/20 cost-sharing arrangement between the Province and the RMOC. The Ontario government's recent budget restrictions have forced the Society to accept less than its approved 1975 expenditures, and to meet the restraint, a reduction in the number of staff employed, and in services, is foreseen.[26]

Table 13-2 gives a good idea of the kind of work the Society performs. Table 13-3 shows the revenues, by source, of the CAS.

Many of the CAS activities are well known. Among them are the advisory services to children and families in their own homes, foster care, and adoptions. Almost everyone has seen the newspaper advertisements for "Today's Child".

Other services are less familiar, including the *Headstart Nursery* (an enrichment programme for a few children and their mothers); *Infant Stimulation* (for children under three needing special help); *Family Groups*; joint work with the multi-service community centres; and the *Child Abuse Team* (108 cases handled last year).

The most important point for us to consider is whether the CAS should be virtually independent as now, or whether it should be brought within the fold of the RMOC Social Services Department.[27]

The arguments for the independence of the CAS are:
(a) It has always been independent since 1893.
(b) It has more flexibility than a Regional Social Services Department.

---

[24] Social Planning Council of Ottawa-Carleton, *Report, Home Support Services Study*, December 1975, p. 15.

[25] *The Child Welfare Act*, R.S.O. 1970, c. 64.

[26] Children's Aid Society of Ottawa, *83rd. Annual Report*, p. 7.

[27] There is one school of thought, represented by the Director of the Ontario Association, that believes the CAS should take over *all* child welfare and family services. Speech of H.H. Dymond to ACRO Conference, Cornwall, Ontario, October 21, 1975. This is an absurd position to take on behalf of a private agency, almost wholly financed by government. The CAS has no monopoly on compassion.

Table 13-2
Services Delivered, Children's Aid Society, 1974, 1975

	1975	1974
1. Children helped in their own home	4,054	4,367
2. Children admitted to care	702	685
3. Children returned to their home	408	421
4. Children in care during the year	1,852	1,893
5. Children in care at the end of the year	1,139	1,148
6. Children placed in adoptive homes	170	207
7. Children in foster homes	728	721
8. Children in C.A.S. institutions	110	97
9. Children in an Ontario hospital	21	15
10. Children in an outside institution	79	65
11. Children in the home of (a) parent(s)	57	94
12. Families served in their own home	1,957	1,828
13. Unmarried Parents New Cases	318	363
14. Foster Homes	499	459
15. Group Homes	5	9
16. Treatment Homes	12	7
17. Assessment Units	5	4
18. Assessment Centre	—	1
19. Staff	316	268
20. Volunteers	224	172

Source: Children's Aid Society of Ottawa, *83rd Annual Report* 1975, p. 7.

Table 13-3
Children's Aid Society, Expenditure and Revenue 1969, 1975

	1969 ($000's)		1975 ($000's)	
Expenditure	3,278		7,526	
Revenue Sources:		%		%
Province	2,369	72	5,748	76
RMOC	729	22	1,499	20
Other	180	6	304	4
	$3,278	100%	$7,551	100%

Sources: Children's Aid Society, 83rd Annual Report, 1975. Statistical Supplement, *Annual Report of the Ministry of Community and Social Services*, 1969.

(c) The provincial standards and controls ensure that government money is not squandered.
(d) It can more easily draw on the dedicated work of volunteer workers.
(e) Being semi-independent it can advocate the rights of children from a stronger position than a Department can.

The arguments against are to some extent mirror images of the arguments for:

(a) Many social services (perhaps all) started in the private (and sometimes religious) sectors, but this argument from origins, has little or nothing to do with present day affairs. (To argue from origins is to commit the "genetic fallacy".)

(b) The RMOC has now the expertise that permits it to extend to all aspects of the CAS work; and in any case, presumably CAS workers would join the RMOC. Further, the RMOC has developed a capacity for bringing the public and volunteers into its work.

(c) There would be closer co-ordination of the present CAS work with that of the RMOC, so that social services in the Region could be planned more as a unity. (They can never be a complete unity as long as the provincial direct services exist separately). The adversary system does not necessarily get more money for CAS.

(d) There is very little more flexibility in a large organization like the CAS, than in the RMOC.

(e) Where a local service is so largely financed by government it should be subject to control by elected governments. The CAS is no longer privately financed, as it was in the beginning.

On balance we judge that the special and semi-independent status of the CAS and its Board be abolished and that all its functions be transferred to the RMOC Social Services Department and administered by a new branch, the Child Welfare Branch.

In making this recommendation we freely acknowledge the debt which society owes to the pioneering work of the CAS. But there will always be new fields for dedicated volunteers to pioneer, to show public and governments what new needs should be met, either inside or outside of the many agencies of the "United Way."

Other Services: (d) "Senior Citizens" (i.e., the elderly)

In Canada, 8.1% of the population is 65 years old or over. It is estimated that in Ottawa-Carleton the number is between 40,000 and 45,000 persons. Services for the elderly are scattered among separate agencies: homes for the aged, nursing homes, retirement homes and senior citizens apartments, and support services.

The most immediate need seems to be for co-ordination between institutions and professionals dealing with the elderly as suggested by the Council on Aging.[28]

High rise apartment buildings have become a prevalent form of supplying "rent-to-income" housing for elderly people. In 1972 there were 7 such buildings in Ottawa while today there are nearly 20. The evidence on whether this is the best way to house the elderly is inconclusive.[29] (By and large we are against such housing, unless the elderly desire

---

[28] *First Annual Report*, 1976, p. 17. (We should not forget the various financial aids to the elderly, such as the Ontario Tax Credit for property tax relief).

[29] See, e.g., Ottawa-Carleton Regional Health Unit: *An Investigation Into Health Care Needs of the Elderly in Senior Citizen Apartments*, August, 1975; and D. Flett, *Health Status of Elderly People in Public Housing*, May, 1976.

it, after seeing alternatives. See also Chapter 6, Housing.)

Simply providing new shelter for the elderly is not enough. In the subsidized buildings, three-quarters of the tenants live alone, while for 70 per cent the federal old-age security, with provincial supplement, is the sole source of income. Problems such as loneliness, alcoholism and mental illness exist. The Health Unit found that there is a need for an informal network through which help can be obtained quickly.[30]

Among the help are such things as more health care and preventive medicine, perhaps through Public Health Nurses in the buildings themselves.[31] The Council on Aging criticizes the "institutional" and "drug-therapy" approaches which are too often followed, and recommends more study of geriatrics and preventive medicine for the elderly. We endorse this recommendation.

Again more home help services could be provided, especially with heavy cleaning and chores thus leaving the elderly able to do other necessary jobs for themselves. While 97 per cent of tenants are independent in their self-care activities (bathing, dressing, etc.) only 64 per cent are independent in their domestic activities (shopping, laundry, financial affairs, etc.). The great majority need help in only one or two activities.[32] The first consideration is, of course, help for those in need, But the forms of help just mentioned also provide outlets for volunteer work; and save government expenditures on expensive hospital and other institutional care.

In the private nursing homes, complaints about service and treatment of patients are said to meet an unsympathetic response from staff. Upon inspection by provincial authorities, at least one such private home in the Region was found to be below the standards required by its license to remain open.[33]

Other Services: (e) Homes for the Aged

Homes for the Aged in the Region are the responsibility of the RMOC. At present two homes, Island Lodge with 403 beds and Carleton Lodge with 132 beds, provide for those who, because of age or infirmity, can no longer live alone or in an ordinary functioning home.[34] Other homes for the aged are provided by charitable institutions and by private nursing homes. These operate separately from the RMOC Homes.

The RMOC negotiated with Lanark County to operate jointly a new Home for the Aged, Carlan Lodge at Almonte, to serve the western part of the Region.[35] Capital and operating cost were to be shared, pro rata, with Lanark County. The negotiations have terminated without any joint Lanark-RMOC agreement. Lanark is going ahead with the project alone, and so will decide alone whether to admit any residents from this Region.

The primary source of revenue for the two existing RMOC Homes for the Aged has shifted from the residents to the provincial government. Operating deficits of the Homes for

---

[30] Ottawa-Carleton Regional Health Unit, *op. cit.*, p. 23.

[31] Flett, Last, Lynch and Mousseau: *The Public Health Nurse as Primary Care Provider for Senior Citizens*, Department of Epidemiology and Community Medicine, University of Ottawa, June 1976.

[32] Flett, D.: *Health Status of Elderly People in Public Housing*, May, 1976. See also the Social Planning Council, *Study on Home Support Service*, December 1975.

[33] Ottawa Journal, June 16, 1976, p. 3.

[34] Ottawa-Carleton Municipal Homes for the Aged: *Report* June, 1976, p. 1.

[35] RMOC Executive Committee: Report Number 3/24 to the Council (March 12, 1975) p. 638.

the Aged are shared 70 per cent by the Province and 30 per cent by the RMOC while capital costs are shared on a 50-50 basis.[36]

Sixty per cent of the residents receive benefits under the province's Extended Health Care (Extendicare) Plan. Full-pay residents are charged $20.00 per day, which is adjusted for those who are not able to pay the full amount. All residents, regardless of how much money they have, receive a minimum of $43.00 per month for spending money. Apart from medical and nursing, other services are provided in the Homes by their respective Auxiliaries and by volunteers.

To help alleviate the pressure for accommodation, Homes in the Region and across the province are involved in Outreach Programmes. These strive to keep people in the "community" and, if possible, in their own homes. The programmes include: "Meals on Wheels" (being assessed by the Council on Aging to see if the Ottawa-Carleton service is adequate); "Vacation Care" (admits elderly persons to the Home temporarily while their families are on vacation); Day Care (for persons who are left alone during the day); Satellite Homes (accommodation in suitable private homes).

Other Services: (f) Information Services

(i) The Community Information Centre runs a bilingual programme to inform individuals and groups about "community" resources. The Centre collects and files up-to-date information, and operates a telephone referral service, as well as publishing a very useful Directory of Social Services in Ottawa-Carleton (circulation of more than 2,500).

The agency began as a programme of the Social Planning Council in 1965 and by 1974 became independent. It has a paid staff of three, and is accountable to its 60 members through its twelve-member Board which is elected annually.

Senior levels of government have recognized the need for local information centres (or citizens' advice bureaux). Health and Welfare Canada, under proposed legislation, will share with the Province costs of "the important connecting links of Information and Referral Centres" under The Canada Assistance Plan. The Province announced in 1974 that it would grant these information centres up to one-third of their budgets, providing they could secure municipal or regional support. (Metropolitan Toronto provides 50% of the funds for a similar organization).

The service provided is useful, and might well be expanded. "An important aspect of citizen participation involves the awareness on the part of the citizens themselves of the services and facilities available to them in their own communities and province".[37]

We recommend that the RMOC continue to fund the Centre, and do so on a continuing basis.

(ii) The Federation of Citizens' Associations was formed in 1969 as an alliance of many citizens' groups in the Region. In 1975 a L.I.P. grant, plus a City grant, and the assistance of the National Capital Commission, allowed the Federation to be very active.

To some extent, the Federation does work similar to that of the Community Information Centre, i.e., in acting as a clearing house for information and advice. To a greater extent, however, the Federation does other things: for instance, it compiled "profiles" of other citizens' associations, their structure and interests; and, through the weekly Bulletin

---

[36] Homes for the Aged, *op. cit.*

[37] The Honourable Robert Welch, announcing the Ontario Programme of Assistance to Information Centres, April 1970.

"Community News Service", ran a calendar of events in Ottawa and the Region, together with articles and comments (sometimes very opinionated), and in general encourages "citizen participation".

One of its efforts drew considerable criticism. It monitored the voting at City and Regional Councils, according to its own ideological bent, and disseminated this and other information on civic affairs. The City and Regional Councils declined to continue their support last year.

No one knows how far the Federation (housed in a NCC building) is representative of its sixty or so member organizations. There is no doubt that through its member organizations, and its Bulletin, it could play a useful role in stimulating citizen interest in, and spreading information on, civic affairs.[38] It is a narrow plank to walk however, between citizen participation on one side and confrontation tactics on the other. But if it can be done successfully (which has not always been the case) the Federation could complement, not overlap with, the work of the Information Centre.

(iii) The Citizens' Advisory Committee for the Regional Department of Social Services (C.A.C.) has already been mentioned. The name perhaps does it less than justice. It works with the Social Planning Coucil on the one hand, and the Department on the other. It identifies new social concerns, "educates" its members, brings clients and the Department together, and spreads reliable and factual information to the public. We have found the Committee to be one of the most concerned and informed groups we have met.

(iv) There are other less well-known voluntary agencies providing information to the residents of the Region. The Social Planning Council has brought them together to discuss their roles, in order to avoid duplication. Partial funding for several of them comes from the United Way. Other sources of monies include L.I.P., the City of Ottawa, Gloucester Township and the Province.

A few of these groups are: The Olde Forge (serving residents of the Pinecrest-Queensway area), Information Gloucester, the Ottawa Distress Centre (a 24-hour listening and befriending service), the New Canadian Welcome Centre (referral services and direct assistance to immigrants), Outreach (a telephone referral service for social services working out of South-East Ottawa), the YM-YWCA, Mental Health Ottawa, Information for the Disabled, the Council on Aging, the Ottawa Senior Citizens' Council, the Patient Placement Co-ordination Service (Ministry of Health), and Information Russell Heights.

Other Services: (g) "Multi-Service" Centres

These Centres are much discussed today. They involve a de-centralized approach to the delivery of social and other services, bringing together public health with social services workers from both the public and voluntary sectors.

Two such Centres already exist in the Region, one in Lower Town (Cobourg Street), the other in Dalhousie Ward (Eccles Street). Other are at various stages of planning for Vanier and Overbrook. In South-East Ottawa, the RMOC has recently taken over the Outreach referral programme and put its funding (by grants) on a more solid base. The Director of Centres will report to RMOC Council upon the evaluation of the programme.

---

[38] The Bulletin has recently suspended publication. In reporting the voting at Regional Council the Federation scored the votes as "correct" and "negative" according to whether the votes favoured "the general wishes of Citizen's groups." There was almost no recognition of the legitimacy of the decisions of elected representatives.

Expenditures in the RMOC for the existing Centres have risen sharply in the past two years: in 1974, the RMOC expenditure was $55,000; in 1975, the Ministry of Health added primary health care to the Dalhousie Centre, and expenditures were $92,000.

These are not the only funds going into the operating expenses of the Centres. The RMOC share is ³/₅ of the overhead, but 50% of this is recovered from the Province. The other ²/₅ is picked up by agencies participating in the Centre, notably the Children's Aid Society. The various government departments and agencies pay the salaries of their employees at the Centres. The Ministry of Health goes further and pays all overhead, operating costs, and salaries for the clinic component of the Centres.

The range of services available is similar but not identical at the two Centres: Children's Aid; Family Benefits; Community and Social Services; Teaching Homemaker; Catholic Family Service; Youth Services Bureau; Low Income Supplement Experiment; Public Health Nurse; Nurse Practitioner; and Family Physician.

The Lower Town Centre forms a small part of a larger physical complex which also contains the Patro Association[39] with its own gymnasium, swimming pool and meeting rooms. The Centre and the St. Anne Clinic are on a lower floor, where there is also a municipal full-day care centre, with the City of Ottawa as landlord.

Both Centres and clinics are, so to speak, part of a new health care delivery system which emphasizes preventive health measures. The Province states that it wants to encourage these prototypes, which are designed to "show the way to an alternate delivery system".[40] The initiative was however taken by the Commissioner of Social Services.

The nature of the Service Centres' functions and mode of operations require that residents in the neighbourhood take part in the management. At the Eccles Street Centre a management committee has been operating since November 1975. The Lower Town Centre (Cobourg Street) is in the process of setting up a management committee, while St. Anne Clinic (adjoining the Centre) has had a committee for some time.

Several features distinguish the Centres from each other. The clientele is different culturally and socially. In Lower Town, French is spoken most of the time, while English with some Italian, predominates at Eccles Street. Then again, their organization and history are not the same: Eccles Street is more integrated, in offering both medical and social services.

As the number of Centres increases, the question of co-ordinating them will arise. The Social Planning Council could perhaps take on the role of co-ordinator for the Centres, as some have suggested. We are more inclined however to think that this role be played by RMOC Social Services Department, and we so recommend.

In any case these multi-service Centres seem to us to be a forward-looking way of integrating many services — social and health — under one roof in given neighbourhoods throughout the Region. We recommend their extension, with the co-operation of the provincial ministries concerned.

Other Services: (h) Volunteers

The Central Volunteer Bureau, a member of the Social Planning Council, acts as a

---

[39] A well established French-speaking voluntary organization which receives funding from the United Way to promote recreational and socio-cultural activities.

[40] Department of Community and Social Services, *Background Paper to the Community Service Centres*, May, 1975.

central registry for bringing together volunteers and social service agencies. It is funded by the United Way. A recent study of the Bureau, although somewhat critical, acknowledges the need for volunteer service, a conclusion that is hard to quarrel with.[41]

In the City of Ottawa, 132 organizations are said to use or want volunteers. Of these groups, 86 see a need for a centralized recruitment service which they could call on to provide the hundreds, even thousands, of volunteers required each year. When these agencies were asked what priorities they felt the C.V. Bureau should assign itself, recruitment of volunteers ranked highest.

At the same time high priority was given to the need for a referral and follow-up service, to match the volunteers with appropriate organizations; and to provide the information which would enable the Bureau to determine what volunteers were used and what organizations had acquired the volunteers requested.[42]

The research on the Bureau also discovered that more attention should be given by the various organizations to meeting the needs of the French speaking population (a position we endorse); and that volunteers should be used to help carry out the administrative functions of the Bureau itself.

Among the private agencies which recruit skilled volunteers only a few can be mentioned: the Probation Service, which uses a special kind of volunteer; the Big Brothers Organization, which attracts volunteers with boys from families without a father; the Children's Aid Society, which uses volunteers for a wide variety of tasks, including "case-aid" work.[43]

---

[41] Maser, Karen: *Central Volunteer Bureau Study*, Ottawa, United Way, May, 1976.

[42] Some 42% of the sample of persons from the C.V.B. file were interested in volunteer work but were not doing any when questioned.

[43] We assume these volunteers will still be needed, and will come forward should the CAS be absorbed into the RMOC Social Services Department.

CHAPTER 14

Health Services
or
Mens Sana in Corpore Sano — Tennis Anyone?

"Most persons regard health as the mere absence of pain and disease. Consequently they see health care as the major force leading to improvements in health . . . (But) . . . the health care sector must devote a substantial effort towards health promotion, disease prevention and health maintenance on the part of the individual." [1]

Hospitals

Municipalities now have little involvement with hospitals, which are primarily a provincial responsibility. However, municipalities are often requested to contribute a portion of the capital costs of new hospitals, and often have a representative on hospital boards of directors. In 1974, the RMOC granted $1.5 million to area hospitals for capital purposes and in 1975 a further $1.8 million. These contributions are, however, entirely optional under present legislation.

In Ottawa two hospitals (Civic and Riverside) are still under the ownership of the City, but the Province is responsible for operating budgets. There are in total eleven hospitals in the Ottawa-Carleton Region, including the recently opened Queensway-Carleton near Bells Corners. One of the eleven, the National Defence Medical Centre for war veterans, is federally owned and operated. [2]

Ambulance services, which are ancillary to hospitals, are a provincial responsibility, operated directly by the Ambulance Services Branch of the Ministry of Health. We see no reason to upset this arrangement, although there has been some public debate over rates charged, and unnecessary use by the public for non-urgent calls.

District Health Council

There are nonetheless several important issues concerning the local administration of hospitals which merit comment. The most significant recent development was the formation of the Ottawa-Carleton District Health Council in late 1973, the first in Ontario. (Several more have since been established in the Province.) The formation of district health councils is the start of a large scale reorganization of the health care delivery system in Ontario.

The seventeen members of the District Health Council are appointed by the Province and serve in an advisory capacity to the Ministry of Health. Of the seventeen, seven are health professionals, seven are consumers and three are from the municipalities. The financing is provincial. The Council has a small permanent staff including an executive

---

[1] Health Planning Task Force, *Report*, Ontario, 1974, pp. 1, 2.

[2] For further information on hospitals see *Ottawa-Carleton in Review, A Basic Information Booklet*, Aug., 1975.

director. The chief functions of the Health Council are the identification of health needs and "the planning of integrated health services" within the Region. Hospitals are the largest and most costly element of the system, which also includes components such as the Public Health Unit, nursing homes, the Victorian Order of Nurses, etc.

The main reason for the formation of Health Councils is to ensure that the health care system is being run as economically as possible, while maintaining the quality of treatment. Rising health care costs have been the subject of strong concern by provincial and federal governments, and rightly so. In Ontario, spending on health care far exceeds expenditures in any other category of the provincial budget. In the fiscal year 1975-76, health spending amounted to almost $3 billion or 28.4% of the provincial budget.

Faced with a federal announcement in May of 1975, that the existing cost-sharing arrangements with the provinces will be altered; as well as with the declining proportion of Ontario Health Insurance Plan (OHIP) premiums to total health costs, the Province has had to re-assess its entire health care system. The Province has reacted with a number of measures including the raising of OHIP premiums as well as closing down some hospitals or reducing the number of beds in others.

One of the chief factors contributing to the rapid increase in health care costs in recent years has been the over-use of active treatment hospitals, instead of less expensive alternatives such as chronic and convalescent care facilities, nursing homes, and home care programmes.[3] The single most important cause of this over-emphasis on active treatment hospitals was the introduction of the hospital insurance plan a decade in advance of medicare. Institutional care received in facilities other than hospitals had not previously been insured.[4]

A complicating factor in determining whether there is an over-supply or over-use of hospitals in Ottawa-Carleton is the extent of use by residents of Quebec, estimated at 14% of total admissions. On this, the Health Council has already held inter-provincial meetings for co-operative planning with the Conseil de la Santé et des Services Sociaux de l'Outaouais. Other important issues that the District Health Council must address include the appropriate distribution of doctors, the consolidation of smaller hospitals, the conversion of acute care to cheaper alternative care facilities, centralized services such as common laundry facilities, bulk purchasing, integrated computer services, food service, laboratory services. In some of these the Health Council has already achieved considerable savings.

With regard to the distribution of doctors, the Mustard Report made a suggestion to ensure that too many physicians do not congregate in urban centres and leave rural areas under-served. The suggestion was that the District Health Council have physician manpower-planning powers which would enable it to establish the number and types of doctors required in its area.[5] This number would be registered with the Ontario Health Insurance Plan, but any doctors above this quota would not be able to participate under OHIP. Whether the suggestion can be carried out, no one knows. It is not easy to shift doctors (and their wives) to the far-flung outposts.

Given the important role which will be developed by the District Health Council, it is appropriate to ask whether there should be closer links with municipal government. As hospitals are a provincial responsibility, it would perhaps not be best for the District Health

---

[3] Ontario Economic Council *Health: Issues and Alternatives* 1976, p. 6.

[4] *Ibid*, p. 6.

[5] Health Planning Task Force, *Report*, Ontario 1974, p. 66. The boundaries for the District Health Council are coterminous with those of the RMOC.

Council to be made entirely responsible to the RMOC, at least not yet. However, given the strong role of RMOC in the public health field (see below), we recommend that the three municipal representatives on the District Health Council be appointed by the RMOC, instead of being selected by the Province, as now. This would not upset provincial control of the Health Council in carrying out its functions. The RMOC could also request that the District Health Council report through the RMOC rather than directly to the Ministry of Health. This option has been offered by the Province.[6]

Public Health Unit

The Ottawa-Carleton Regional (Public) Health Unit is a municipal special purpose body responsible for a variety of public health programmes including: control of communicable diseases, public and home care nursing, school nursing, certain dental services, family planning, public health inspections (including septic tank approvals for land severances), the testing of the rivers for germs to see whether the rivers are fit enough to swim in, etc.

The Health Unit is governed by a Board of Health which consists of six appointees from Regional Council and three provincial appointees. The senior staff person is the Medical Officer of Health. Spending by the Health Unit has increased dramatically since its establishment in 1969, when it was formed by amalgamation of the former boards of health for Carleton County and the cities of Ottawa and Vanier. The growth in spending has been from $1.4 million to $4.6 million in 1975, or some 229%.[7] The budget is heavily subsidized by the Province, with provincial grants accounting for approximately 74% of total revenues, and the RMOC making up all but a small fraction of the remainder.

In keeping with our general principle that authority should be exercised by elected officials so that there is one clear focus of political accountability rather than a confusing gaggle of semi-autonomous special purpose bodies, we recommend an end to the special status of the Regional Public Health Unit and its Board of Directors. The staff and programmes of the Health Unit should form a Regional Department of Health directly under a standing committee of Regional Council. The Medical Officer of Health would become Commissioner of Public Health, with the same programmes as now.

In addition to the advantage of clearer political accountability, this move would also facilitate greater co-ordination with the programmes of the Social Services Department. At present several aspects of the functions of the Social Services Department, and those of the Health Unit, parallel each other and deal with much the same clientele.

The Standing Committee of Regional Council to supervise the Public Health Department should, we recommend, be the re-organized Social Services Committee (re-named the Health and Social Services Committee). In a similar vein the Citizens Advisory Committee on Social Services would be enlarged to deal also with public health matters.

Naturally enough the Health Unit and its Board will argue that it is "special" and should have what it called "relative autonomy". It is really remarkable (and amusing) to see how *every single special purpose body that has presented a brief, argues in exactly the same way for its continued separate existence.*

---

[6] W.A. Backley, (ADM), *Speech*, 16th Annual ACRO Conference, October 21, 1975, p. 4.

[7] RMOC Financial Statements, 1975.

In the case of the Board of Health they said:

> "We submit that the intent of the Province in this respect was to obviate the possibility of parochial political considerations interfering with the objective administration of a vitally important health protection service".[8]

Translated, this means public health should be "taken out of politics". But all government functions are political, in their budget, their priorities, and their execution. Government and its functions cannot be reduced to "objective administration". At any moment any issue, no matter how trivial, may appear in the political arena, i.e., become a matter of conflicting opinions and interests. This is as it should be in a democracy. (The lack of accountability by the Public Health Unit came in for hard criticism in the Nepean Township Brief).

We recommend also the District Health Council take into its "over-view" the Regional Public Health Department services. This is not of course, a recommendation that the Council should have an operating function, but only that it have a planning and recommending function in public health, as it already has for other elements of health care.

In the interests of economy by relieving the hospitals, we recommend also that the following less costly services be continued and enlarged: the Home Care Programme (visiting nurses) for convalescents, the Visiting Homemakers Service, and the Victorian Order of Nurses, etc.

We have given some thought to the establishment of "community health centres". These would presumably bring under one roof, in many locations throughout the Region, a kind of all-purpose health clinic. Such centres or clinics would give advice (e.g., on family planning); would foster preventive health measures (through information and testing); do innoculations; provide some medical services, and so on.

It has also been suggested that these "centres" should be managed — or at least advised — by local (neighbourhood) residents.

The idea is an intriguing one, but we have not pursued it in any depth, so we merely draw it to the attention of the District Health Council, the Public Health Unit and others who may find it within their purview. We have, however, already discussed the same topic under the heading of "multi-service centres", which combine health and social services under the same roof. (See Chapter 13.)

---

[8] The Board of Health of the Ottawa-Carleton Regional Health Unit, *Brief*, Feb. 26, 1976, p. 2.

CHAPTER 15

Police and Fire Services
or
From felons and fire, O Lord protect us

". . . the modern police officer must play a variety of roles. . . . a sympathetic and helpful friend. . . . an enforcer of laws who is prepared to engage in physical combat . . . ready to face mass protest, dissent, verbal abuse and physical violence." [1]

Ottawa-Carleton is the only regional municipality in Ontario which does not have a Regional Police Force. Instead there are four local forces: in the cities of Ottawa and Vanier, and the townships of Gloucester and Nepean. Rockcliffe Park Village contracts its policing (four policemen) from the Ontario Provincial Police, and the rest of the Region gets free policing from the Ontario Provincial Police (OPP). The OPP also patrol provincial highways within the Region, while the RCMP are responsible for certain federal properties, such as the Ottawa Airport and the federal (NCC) driveways.

Local Police departments are responsible not directly to municipal councils, but to Boards of Police Commissioners. Public discussion has been going on for years, whether such local Boards should be abolished throughout the Province. The local Boards consist each of three persons: the head of the municipal council, ex officio; plus a judge and one other person appointed by the Lieutenant Governor-in-Council. The Board sets the general policy and over-all budget of its police force. A municipal council which disagrees with the quality of policing or the budget set by the Board may appeal to the Ontario Police Commission (O.P.C.), which is in the Ministry of the Solicitor General.

Service standards for police departments are laid down and enforced by the OPC. *The Report of The Task Force of Policing in Ontario* (1974) — the Hale Commission — recommended that the local Boards of Police Commissioners be expanded to five members, the extra two representatives coming from local councils and citizens (p. 49).

The Hale Commission also recommended that policing in the RMOC be Regionalized. The recommendation was based on the view that wherever possible, only one Force should operate in a given area, and partly on a judgment of the advantages of a Regionalized Force. The Hale Commission's actual words were (p. 43):

> The Task Force believes that to avoid duplication, overlap or fragmented responsibility, only one force should operate within a given municipal jurisdiction, and should be responsible for the entire delivery of police services in that area with the only exception being policing of King's Highways and provincial parks.[2]

---

[1] Brian Grosman, *Police Command*, Macmillan, Toronto, 1975, p. 3.

[2] The argument for one Force only in a given area, led the Hale Commission (p. 63) to recommend one Force for "waterway policing", on duties not carried out by the RCMP under federal statutes. The rivers in this Region make this point of some relevance here.

Some Briefs to this Commission have argued that the deficiencies of the Hale Report are enough to dismiss it. They have said that there is little evidence to support the claim that duplication, overlap, or fragmented responsibility exists between police forces in Ottawa-Carleton, and have offered counter arguments questioning the benefits of a Regional Force.

The argument against amalgamation rests on three main points (which are examined later in this Chapter):
(1) A regional police force will necessarily cost more to the tax payers in those municipalities with lower police costs per capita.
(2) A genuine need for a regional force is not apparent at this time.
(3) A large regional force will be less personalized with less intimate relations between the police and the public.

As may be seen from Table 15-1, there is a slight positive correlation between the police population index and the number of residents per acre (population density), except for Vanier. There is a similar correlation between this index and the per capita cost. Two factors may account for these relationships.

First, consolidated crime reporting bears out the close association between high population densities and high levels of crime. This fact is also borne out by comparing criminal statistics for urban, suburban and "rural" areas. The degree of social stratification in cities is sharper than in non-city areas. Evil doers tend to gravitate to cities. The more impersonal relations between city inhabitants, together with environmental obstacles to police surveillance provide more opportunities for crime. The worst enemy of man, is man, especially when many people live closely together.

Second, (a natural consequence of the first), police strength must necessarily be highest in more densely populated areas in order to provide adequate protection. Since salaries make up the greatest part of police expenditures, a higher police/population index (or ratio) accounts for a higher per capita cost.

The municipalities with the lowest per capita police costs have voiced the strongest opposition to a Regional Force. These are notably the townships of Gloucester and Nepean. Their general feeling is that a Regional Force will necessarily cost more to their taxpayers.

However, the question of whether Regional policing will cost more in municipalities such as Gloucester and Nepean will depend on the cost-sharing plan devised by Regional Council. In discussion with Vanier regarding amalgamation (Vanier has the highest per capita cost), the Council seemed to favour a partial move. Ottawa council is divided on the question judging from the debates at Regional Council.

One fact seem plain. The provincial government, by offering a per capita subsidy increase from $8.00 (as now) to $12.00 for Regional Police Forces deliberately encourages their formation. This $4.00 additional subsidy should be included in any cost projections for a Regional Force. In the RMOC, the cost-sharing plan between municipalities for regional services is generally based on two factors:
(a) The level of regional service received, as with transportation and sewerage; and
(b) The total equalized assessment for the municipality, as in the case for the Regional levy.

Table 15-2 is a recalculation of the per capita police cost for the four municipal police forces, based on their relative proportions of equalized assessment. The net cost in column 9 includes the $4.00 per capita subsidy increase given by the provincial government for Regional Forces. The policing costs are calculated on the basis of 1975 operating expenditures for each of the four police departments.

Costs of Policing

Table 15-1
Municipal Expenditures and Police Strength for the Area Municipalities, 1975

Municipality	Population	Population Per Acre	Police Strength	Police Population Index	Operating Expenditure	Per Capita Cost
Ottawa	302,124	9.9	576	1/514	$11,916,500	39.44
Vanier	20,146	30.5	35	1/586	915,358	45.44
Gloucester	53,322	0.7	53	1/1000	1,286,923	24.13
Nepean	74,000	1.4	94	1/760	2,315,979	31.29
Rockcliffe Park	2,229	6.1	4	1/557	67,600[3]	30.33

Sources: Ontario Police Commission, 1976; Municipal Directory, 1976.

As Table 15-2 indicates, the per capita cost of policing in all four municipalites would have been lower had the forces been amalgamated. The differences between present net per capita costs in column (8) and net per capita costs for a Regional Force in column (9) can be accounted for partly by the $4.00 extra per capita subsidy granted by the Province for Regional policing, and partly by the redistribution of total operating expenditures on the basis of equalized assessment.

The main assumption we have made was to hold the level of service constant in the two cases being compared, that is, we have not assumed a higher level of service or new services offered by a Regional Force.

If the level of service were to be improved or expanded, this would of course change the cost figures. However, if this happens it will not be "regionalization" per se that causes higher costs, but changes in level of service, made by political choice.

Table 15-3 is tabulated in the same manner as Table 15-2, except that the former includes municipalities now policed by the OPP.

The figures in column (4) show the operating costs for 1975 in the four municipalites with their own departments. The costs for all other municipalities in column (4) are based on OPP estimates of the actual costs to police them. For the OPP detachment at Bells Corners, which serves more than one municipality, the operating costs were estimated on the percentages of occurrences in each municipality.

The per capita costs in column (5) show the amount the municipalities would pay if they were obliged to cover OPP costs. Rockcliffe Park Village, for example, is the only municipality charged by OPP for service, but the fee charged covers less than 70% of the OPP outlay for policing the Village.

Presumably if the area municipalities were obliged to cover OPP costs they would be eligible for the $8.00 per capita subsidy granted by the provincial government. The per capita costs in column (8) include this subsidy. Column (9) figures are total operating costs

---

[3] For Rockcliffe Park, this figure is not the actual cost, but the contract price, i.e., the fee charged by the OPP. The fee at most is about 70% of actual cost. The Village provides a police office. Rockcliffe Park is thus getting a bargain with its policing, and is not in fact "paying its way". (The figures were supplied by the OPP, Ministry of the Solicitor General, in *Study on Ontario Provincial Police Assistance to the Regional Municipality of Ottawa-Carleton*, July, 1976.)

Table 15-2
Estimated Costs for a Regional Police Force, 1975

Municipality	(1) Equalized Assessment ($000's)	(2) % of Total	(3) Population	(4) Operating Expenditure ($000's)	(5) Current Per Capita Cost
Ottawa	4,049,055	76.13	302,124	11,917	$39.44
Vanier	173,285	3.26	20,146	916	45.44
Gloucester	390,749	7.34	53,332	1,287	24.13
Nepean	705,746	13.27	74,000	2,316	31.29
Total	5,318,835	100.00		16,435	

Municipality	(6) Contribution to Budget if Redistributed on E.A. (000's)	(7) Per Capita Cost Based on E.A., i.e., for a Regional Force	(8) Net Per Capita Cost, Discounting Provincial Subsidy for Non-Regional Force ($8.00 per capita)	(9) Net Per Capita Cost, Discounting Provincial Subsidy for Regional Force ($12.00 per capita)	(10) Change in Cost Per Capita from Non-Regional to Regional Force
Ottawa	12,512	$41.41	$31.44	$29.41	—$ 2.03
Vanier	536	26.60	37.44	14.60	— 22.84
Gloucester	1,206	22.62	16.13	10.62	— 5.51
Nepean	2,181	29.47	23.29	17.47	— 6.62
Total	16,435				

Source: Municipal Financial Reports, 1975.
Notes: Column (8) — Obtained by subtracting the current provincial subsidy of $8.00 per capita for non-regionalized police forces from the figures in Column (5). Column (9) — Obtained by subtracting the provincial subsidy of $12.00 per capita for Regional Police Force from the figures in Column (7).

redistributed on the basis of equalized assessment. To arrive at these figures we have assumed that the policing of the areas where the OPP presently has jurisdiction will not change significantly if a Regional Force assumed the policing.

Column (10) indicates the change in per capita costs from non-regional to Regional Policing. Here again we are comparing what municipalities would be charged to cover OPP costs, and what they would pay for a Regional Force, which would receive an additional $4.00 per capita subsidy from the Province.[4]

The figures show increases in all OPP-policed areas except one (Cumberland). The four municipalities that maintain their own police forces would still be paying a lower per capita cost, whether the amalgamation included only existing municipal forces or whether it included a Force for the entire Region.

A few changes in external boundaries were recommended for the RMOC in Chapter 8. These were the addition of Russell Township, and the subtraction of a small area from West

---

[4] In a speech to the Provincial-Municipal Liaison Committee, on September 10, 1976, the Treasurer of Ontario announced that the per capita police grants will be increased in 1977 from the present rate of $8 for local forces and $12 for regional forces to $10 and $15 respectively. *Background*, TEIGA, September 17, 1976.

Table 15-3
Police Costs for a Regional Force
Including OPP-Policed Areas, 1975

Municipality	(1) Equalized Assessment (EA) (000's)	(2) % of Total (EA)	(3) Population	(4) Total Cost ($000's)	(5) Per Capita Cost
Ottawa	4,049,055	69.74	302,124	11,917	$39.44
Vanier	173,285	2.98	20,146	915	45.44
Gloucester	390,749	6.73	53,332	1,287	24.13
Nepean	705,746	12.16	74,000	2,316	31.29
Osgoode	66,816	1.15	8,272	100	12.09
Rideau	65,547	1.13	7,860	145	18.48
Goulbourn	85,905	1.48	12,489	180	14.41
West Carleton	74,400	1.28	7,782	173	22.23
March	72,044	1.24	6,910	122	17.66
Cumberland	75,205	1.30	11,458	258	22.52
Rockcliffe Park	46,841	.81	2,229	99	43.52
TOTAL	5,805,593	100	506,592	17,519	

Municipality	(6) Total Cost redistributed on EA ($000's)	(7) Per Capita Cost Based on EA, for a Regional Force	(8) Net Per Capita Cost Discounting Provincial Subsidy for Non-Regional Force ($8.00 Per Capita)	(9) Net Per Capita Cost Discounting Provincial Subsidy for Regional Force ($12.00 Per Capita)	(10) Change in Cost Per Capita from Non-Regional to Regional Force
Ottawa	12,211	$40.42	$31.44	$28.42	− $ 3.02
Vanier	522	26.91	37.44	14.91	− 22.53
Gloucester	1,178	22.09	16.13	10.09	− 6.04
Nepean	2,129	28.77	23.29	16.77	− 6.52
Osgoode	201	24.30	4.09	12.30	+ 8.21
Rideau	198	25.19	10.48	13.19	+ 2.71
Goulbourn	259	20.74	6.41	8.74	+ 2.33
West Carleton	224	28.78	14.23	16.78	+ 2.55
March	217	31.40	9.66	19.40	+ 9.74
Cumberland	228	19.90	14.52	11.90	− 2.62
Rockcliffe Park	142	63.70	35.52	51.70	+ 16.38

Source: Ontario Police Commission, 1976; Municipal Financial Reports, 1975

Carleton (near Arnprior). These areas are so small, that they would not seriously affect the estimates for the cost of Regional Policing.

The usefulness of all these cost estimated depends on what policy the provincial government decides to adopt regarding the municipalities now policed by the OPP. Four options are possible. It is impossible to be certain, but (d) appears most likely to be adopted.
(a) To continue OPP services without charge to these municipalities
(b) To commence charging a fee-for-service contract for OPP services
(c) To withdraw the OPP service and establish local police forces
(d) To withdraw the OPP service and extend the jurisdiction of a Regional Force to all the RMOC

Policing "Needs"

The concept of "needs" (brought up as the second objection to Regional Police) is a tricky one and should be handled with care. The local police departments vary widely both in their degree of specialization and in the number of their support services. For instance only the City of Ottawa has a computer-assisted filing and reporting system. These tasks are performed manually in other departments. Ottawa and Nepean are the only forces that maintain personnel assigned to specialized investigative functions on a full-time basis. These differences stem either from financial constraints or from municipal policy, or both. Table 15-4 lists the functions to which specialized police personnel are assigned in the four municipal departments, 1975.

As Table 15-4 shows, Ottawa and Nepean are the most specialized of the four departments. Ottawa has all the organizational characteristics and functional capacities of a big-city department. On the whole, Nepean's specialization with the limitation of a staff of 90, is substantial. The Township maintains, on a full time basis, specialized investigators in areas where a high incidence of crime has historically been reported, but the bulk of its criminal investigation department consists of general assignment detail.

Senior officers in Vanier and Gloucester, on the other hand, argue that their local policing does not require specialization. Their general policy is to develop police officers who are qualified in many fields. This policy is regarded as inadquate by senior officers in the Ottawa and Nepean departments. Vanier and Gloucester would almost certainly benefit from the criminal investigation unit of a Regional Police Force.

One fact that cannot be documented in precise detail is the degree to which the smaller forces rely on Ottawa's criminal investigation resources. There is little doubt, however, that this reliance amounts to a considerable subsidy to the smaller forces. Savings are also made to some extent at a cost to the OPP and the RCMP.[5] The information gathered by Ottawa's criminal intelligence department is readily made available to outside investigators. In addition, Ottawa has the only municipal department in the RMOC with the Solicitor-General's authority to conduct wire-tap investigations.

Other costs that the Ottawa department assumes arise from (a) the large influx of working population that commutes into Ottawa every day; and (b) the influx to the more exciting night life of Ottawa. The number of offences committed by this transient population adds significantly to the workload of the department. Because of these factors, the comparing of police performance between forces is difficult. (In any case criminal statistics are notoriously unreliable).

---

[5] Even with a Regional Force the OPP would supply, on request, Aircraft Patrol, Identification Services, Canine, Marine and Scuba Services, from the Special Services Division.

Table 15-4
Specialization of Police Functions in the RMOC

Function	Ottawa	Vanier	Nepean	Gloucester
Criminal Intelligence	X			
Youth liaison	X		X	
Court liaison	X	X	X	X
Fraud	X		X	
Theft	X		X	
Collision investigation	X			
Auto theft	X			
Arson	X			
Homicide				
Crime prevention	X		X	
Identification of persons	X		X	
Bombs, hostages	X			
Identification of property	X		X	
Underwater rescue	X			
Narcotics	X		X	
General Criminal — investigation assignment	X		X	
Riot squad	X			
Morality	X			

Source: Interviews by staff with Police chiefs and other officials

The large-scale movement of people between Ottawa and the suburbs requires co-operation and assistance between the different police forces, particularly for criminal investigation. One of the disadvantages of having a number of independent forces operating in a given area is that this co-operation is not guaranteed. Unnecessary duplication of investigative functions is one possible, perhaps even likely, result, although the extent and costs cannot be calculated exactly. This opinion was also expressed by the Task Force on Policing in Ontario, and we see no reason to question it.

Amalgamated Support Services and Cost Benefits

Support services, (i.e., services which are accessory to policing) vary widely between the departments both in quality and in technological sophistication. Two fields in which these differences are most apparent are communications and central records maintenance. These functions are mistakenly thought to entail high conversion costs to amalgamate them. The four municipal departments have recently installed a common radio wave band to be used only on occasions when two or more police forces are engaged in some common effort. Difficulties have been encountered in the past in co-ordinating joint pursuit of criminals and investigations — a problem that the common wave band was intended to solve.[6]

Ottawa has the most sophisticated communications apparatus of the four departments. It has been designed to accommodate the increased volume of calls and transmissions which would be needed by a Regional Force with a centralized communications system. The system is operating now at only 60% capacity. Its radio transmission and reception apparatus is capable of covering the entire RMOC area. The cost of conversion from comunications stations manned separately by each force, to a centralized communications system would involve little if any capital expenditure. In addition, Ottawa's system has other technical features not available to the smaller municipal departments.

The benefits to be derived from a centralized communications system in the RMOC are the following:
(1) Improved co-ordination and monitoring of mobile and foot patrol police.
(2) An increase in effective police strength for field operations, because some staff would be released from the present communications stations.
(3) A reduction in total communication costs through economies of scale in manpower costs and capital equipment usage.

Ottawa's filing and records equipment is presently operating well under capacity. The system eliminates the tedious task of typing and manual filing of occurrence reports. (One of the limitations of manual filing is that cross indexing is possible only if several copies of occurrence reports are made). The statistics processed by the automated system facilitate evaluation on a daily basis of the number and type of infractions, the solution rate, the investigating officer, the locations where infractions have been common. This information is useful in the deployment of personnel; and the cost savings, in terms of man-hours, is considerable. This system could easily be adapted to serve as a central records file for a Regional Force. The change-over merely involves the installation of a computer terminal at each of the satellite or "precinct" stations located throughout the Region.

The benefits to be derived from a central records file may be summarized:
(1) Uniform accessibility to *all* information gathered by police personnel throughout the Region.
(2) More efficient processing of the information upon which the deployment of investigation and surveillance personnel is based.
(3) Reduction in clerical staff involved in records maintenance.
(4) Elimination of records typing and reproduction costs.
(5) Reduction of filing space costs.

A number of other costs would be avoided, at least in part, with a Regional Force. Nepean and Gloucester have large capital expenditure plans in hand. The Nepean force has submitted a proposal of $2.5 million for the construction of a new police station. Gloucester has asked for $750,000, to construct an addition to its present facilities. Under a Regional Force, the present facilities in Nepean, Gloucester and Vanier could serve as satellite stations, with the bulk of the administrative function carried on in Ottawa. Thus, the space requirements in the other three municipalities, and the planned expansions, would be reduced.

The Ottawa department has withheld its building plans until the issue of a Regional Force is settled. In any case, whether or not amalgamation does occur, the Ottawa Force will

---

[6] Interviews of staff with police officials.

need some new facilities to meet its present requirements. Its total capital expenditure, however, will depend to a large degree on whether the facilities will be designed as a central operation for a Regional Force.

Court liaison costs would be reduced under a Regional Force. At present, all municipal forces supply an officer on a daily basis for court purposes, to process infractions charged by the department. Amalgamation could return some of these officers to field service — that is, the entire court operation for the Region could be performed by one or two officers. In addition, all forces are responsible for the transfer of prisoners to and from the Provincial Regional Detention Centre on a daily basis. With this duty being handled by a Regional Force, some savings should be realized in manpower and transportation.

How do the policemen themselves feel about membership in a large Regional Force? We did not think an attitude survey was worthwhile, in terms of the time and money involved. According to Mr. M. Cameron (President of the Ottawa, Ontario and Canadian Police Associations), the overall consensus in the present forces is in favour of regionalization.

Some of the benefits rank and file policemen could expect as members of a Regional Force have been expressed as follows:
(1) In Nepean, Vanier and Gloucester, the head of each Police Association (bargaining unit for police staff) carries out his functions on a part-time basis. Few policemen aspire to the position because the time and effort required are not in keeping with the pay received. A full-time representative of the Association would be financially feasible with a much larger bargaining unit.
(2) Grievances could be settled more easily, since the Association head would be working on a full-time basis.
(3) The upward mobility in a small force is limited. A large force would open up greater opportunities for advancement and promotion.
(4) More prestige is said to be associated with membership in a larger force.

Although senior officers in the Ottawa force are strongly in favour of amalgamation, the attitude in the smaller forces is quite the opposite. The dissent expressed by senior officers in Vanier, Nepean and Gloucester may perhaps stem from uncertainty regarding the rank and responsibility those officers would be assigned in a larger organization. These are the normal difficulties experienced whenever a Regional Force is set up; and indeed whenever any two or more forces are amalgamated, as with annexations by a city. They present no great obstacles, and there are many precedents to follow in order to do justice to the personnel in the amalgamation process. (See, e.g., The Hale Commission, p. 57).

Finally, the argument that smaller forces maintain greater rapport with the public they serve is questionable. The Ottawa Department, which is the largest and serves a mostly urban population, has the highest percentage of its police personnel assigned to public relations functions. These functions include youth liaison, crime prevention and public safety. Ottawa too has the only force where policemen are assigned to foot patrol — a method of policing which promotes greater public-police contact than vehicle patrol.[7]

To summarize the above: amalgamation of municipal forces in the RMOC presents several benefits, both in terms of cost and level of service. The transitional costs, arising

---

[7] We do not wish to disparage the work done by other departments in public relations, with schools, youth groups, citizens' committees and the like. But it is a trifle hard to accept the contention that "Gloucester has the finest and most efficient Police Force in Canada". Letter to Reeve R. W. MacQuarrie, re. the Review Commission Study, by S. J. Evans, Chairman of Gloucester Community-Police Relations Task Force, Nov. 12, 1975, p. 2. (Many cities make this claim).

from a transfer of capital asset and liabilities, may be safely left to the O.M.B. At the same time, the overall per capita costs to the taxpayers now policed by separate forces would be about the same with a Regional Force, and in some cases less.

The cost, however, to the municipalities now being served free by the OPP would, of course, be higher. (Anything is higher than nothing.) But these costs are very likely to be small because of (a) the higher subsidy for a Regional Force; and because (b) the costs would be shared among the RMOC population at large, and the outlying municipalities have relatively small populations to influence the per capita costs; and (c) the computations in Tables 15-2 and 15-3 should not be taken as more than rough indicators, since if assessment (commercial and for grants-in-lieu) is pooled, entirely new cost calculations would replace them; and (d) transition and start-up grants will very likely be available. Taking everything into consideration we recommend the following:

(1) That the municipal forces in the RMOC be amalgamated into a Regional Police Force; and that the Force undertake policing in those municipalities now policed by the OPP.

(2) That the Force be in a police department of the Regional Municipality, under a police chief heading the department.

(3) We have recommended earlier (See Chapter 9), that the Regional Police Department report to the Watch Committee of Regional Council, and that the Committee in turn (like all Standing Committees) have an Advisory Committee attached, drawn from a broad spectrum of the public.[8]

It is by this means that we take sides in the debate over whether there should be Boards of Police Commissioners. We recommend the abolition of such Boards in this Region (and for that matter, in other municipalities, too).

First, because these boards are quasi-independent special purpose bodies, and it is almost impossible for municipal Councils, let alone the public to have any influence upon, or input to, them. More "openness" should prevail, both in the Watch Committee and in the Advisory Committee we have suggested.

Second, because they have judges upon them; and the judiciary should not be closely linked with local police who may appear before them in the courts.

In making the recommendation to abolish Boards of Commissioners of Police, we dissent from the Task Force on Policing in Ontario, 1974 (The Hale Commission, pp. 48-54).

In recommending that judges be kept separate from police, and thus ensuring not even the appearance of a conflict of loyalty between police and judiciary, we are in distinguished company. To mention a few: the Ontario Royal Commission, *Inquiry into Civil Rights*, 1968, (The McRuer Report); the Ontario Law Reform Commission, *Report on Administration of Ontario Courts* (1973); and seven members of the Hale Commission, including Arthur Maloney (now the Ontario Ombudsman).

(4) There have been many instances in recent years of public complaints against police treatment. All too often, these are dealt with in the internal police structure. "Where a citizen feels that the power of the police has been abused he needs a credible avenue through which he can take his complaint."[9]

---

[8] This does not mean we had our "verdict first, trial afterwards" as in the court scene in Alice in Wonderland. In fact, the Chapters on policing and several other functions were written before we could devise the organizational Table 9-2 in Chapter 9.

[9] The Hale Commission, p. 31. (The Commission goes on to recommend an "impartial procedure" that is different from ours.)

Our recommendation is that a person should be able to take his grievance informally and publicly to the Advisory Watch Committee and then to the Watch Committee itself. If he receives a reply that is unsatisfactory, he should be entitled to turn to whatever grievance appeal body the Province may set up. (We do not, and cannot, rule out more formal legal remedies).

We make no recommendation on the internal discipline of a police force, but we note that the military model, on which forces have largely been patterned, is under criticism by nearly all the sources we could find; and better procedures for internal discipline are being devised.[10]

A few other points may be touched upon briefly:

(5) The first concerns the distribution of stations (or "satellites") throughout the Region. These should be no fewer than at present, and preferably more. Such a distribution will go a long way towards meeting the objection that a larger Force is more impersonal than a smaller one.[11] "Police policy and style of enforcement which is appropriate to an urban core may be completely inappropriate if applied to a suburban or residential area".[12]

Some argument was presented to us on the virtues of neighbourhood (or "community") control of police. This is all very well, and some of the so-called evidence may even be true, although it is certainly not conclusive, and there is evidence the other way. In any case, the question is irrelevant for large and growing townships such as Nepean and Gloucester, on the edges of a capital city. These are not small neighbourhoods or "communities".

(6) The second concerns bilingualism in the Force. At present there are too many complaints about unilingual police dealing with persons in the other language. Every effort should be made to recruit bilingual police, and to train further those whose command of the two official languages is weak. The same argument and recommendations apply to the OPP, who may continue to police provincial highways and parks in this Region and throughout Eastern Ontario. On this we fully endorse the Hale Commission (p. 34).

(7) We also endorse the Hale Commission's proposals (p. 35) that more women police officers be recruited, and that they not be discriminated against either in "recruiting or promotional opportunities."

(8) The training of police, in the narrow sense of training for police work; and their broader education, say in post-secondary institutions should be encouraged and financially supported. At the same time it is easier for a larger force to do this, with released time, and accelerated promotions and/or bonuses for the better trained and educated.

The days of simple police patrolling, with poorly educated policemen, are over. Sir Robert Peel did a great thing when he invented the "bobbies", but that was in the 1830's. Today larger proportions of the public are more sophisticated and educated, especially the younger ones. Moreover a higher proportion of police work involves a semi-social-service component, and this requires special training and/or personnel.[13] There are more "cats in trees", and family quarrels, than hard criminal cases.

---

[10] See, for instance, *The Report of the Commission of Inquiry Relating to Public Complaints, Internal Discipline and Grievance Procedure Within the Royal Canadian Mounted Police*, Ottawa, 1976.

[11] In the study done for this Commission by the OPP, Carp and Manotick were suggested as two convenient sites. Another would be needed in the east, since Cumberland is now served by the OPP detachment in Rockland.

[12] Brian A. Grosman, *op. cit.*, p. 57.

[13] Gloucester Township is already looking for a social worker, for police work.

(9) The police chief and the higher ranks have the greatest responsibility.
"In Ontario, before a municipal Police Chief is selected the Ontario Police Commission informally suggests a number of names of those who, in its opinion, would make a suitable Police Chief for the interested municipality, although the municipality is under no obligation to accept anyone from this list."[14]

We recommend that the Ontario Police Commission (O.P.C.) be given the power to veto the appointment of a Chief suggested by a municipality. Still better, the O.P.C. should follow the United Kingdom practice and provide a list of names from which the municipality must choose.

(10) We also recommend that regular police officers, with their important statutory duties, be relieved of some of their "non-police" functions such as ticketing illegally parked cars. This kind of duty merely makes the public annoyed with policemen. Again, some of this is already being done (Green Hornets), but should be extended further, e.g., for the enforcement of some by-laws.

(11) We recommend that the O.P.C. further strengthen both the standards it lays down for recruiting and all aspects of policing, including training and education, and also its supervision of police forces. This will provide for local (Regional) administration, with the necessary provincial controls.[15]

There is very little that keeps a thin veneer of civilization over the barbarian within all of us. The police are our front line of defence, and we cannot praise them too highly or pay them too much.[16]

Fire Services

Some fire departments in the RMOC have all-volunteer fire fighters, others have all full-time personnel. Still other departments maintain a few paid personnel to operate heavy equipment and are assisted by a large number of volunteers. The level of training of the fire department personnel is equally varied. Table 15-4 shows the composition and costs of fire departments in the Region.

Fire inspections are conducted in all area municipalities, although only the City of Ottawa has a substantial staff for this purpose. Co-ordination and assistance for all fire departments are provided under the "Mutual Aid Agreement". This arrangement is headed by a Mutual Aid Co-ordinator who is appointed by Order-in-Council and certified by the Ontario Fire Marshal. The usual policy has been to appoint the chief of the largest fire department (Ottawa) to act as Co-ordinator.

The Fire Marshal of Ontario is responsible for co-ordinating, directing and advising on virtually every aspect of firefighting and fire investigation as prescribed under The Fire Marshal's Act and other provincial statutes.

The Mutual Aid Agreement, established in 1965 and ratified by municipal by-laws, applies to all fire departments in the RMOC. The Agreement fulfills a twofold purpose: *first*

---

[14] Grosman, *op. cit.*, p. 23.

[15] To a great extent the O.P.C. is doing this already, and we mention it merely to strengthen its hand. There are two police colleges, the Canadian Police College (Ottawa), which trains all forces; and the Provincial Police College at Aylmer, Ontario.

[16] The Newfoundland Constabulary, which polices the City of St. John's, is the only unarmed police force in Canada. Moreover, the Chief of Police is determined to resist all efforts to compel the police to carry guns. He and his force surely deserve the highest awards possible for maintaining this civilized practice.

Table 15-5
Fire Departments in the RMOC, 1975

Municipality	Fire Fighters Paid	Fire Fighters Volunteer	Number of Stations	Operating Expenditure ($000's)	Per Capita Cost
Ottawa	468	—	10	$10,113	$33.17
Rockcliffe Park	No fire department		—	72	32.18
Vanier	30	—	1	633	31.40
Cumberland	7	60	4	201	17.50
Gloucester	63	—	3	1,192	22.34
Goulbourn	1	48	2	56	41.52
March	8	19	1	131	19.00
Nepean	73	—	2	1,364	18.42
Osgoode	*	51	2	40	4.78
Rideau	*	45	2	71	9.06
West Carleton	*	90	4	83	10.61

Source: Mutual Aid Co-ordinator; Municipal Financial Reports.
* Part-time chief.

it establishes policy regarding fire stations in close proximity to fires that occur in adjoining municipalities. All departments will answer "border calls", i.e., calls that may be outside a municipality's boundaries but have been identified by the caller as within its boundaries. The general rule observed is that a department will fight the fire in a neighbouring municipality until the arrival of its own department, and will then act as directed by the senior officer in whose municipality the fire occurs. Since the time lag involved in relaying the call to the appropriate fire department is eliminated, response times, so it is argued, are improved. This seems to be a sensible arrangement.

In responding to calls deep inside another municipality, the practice is somewhat different. A neighbouring department will not provide assistance until all other fire stations within the municipality in which the fire occurs have responded.

Secondly, Mutual Aid has a scheme of reimbursement for fire services rendered to another municipality. One fire department is not charged by another, unless the assisting department is providing fire fighting equipment which the other department does not have. This scheme is designed to prevent a department that fails to purchase the necessary equipment from relying upon another department that has a large inventory of equipment. One exception is the City of Vanier, which has a contractual arrangement with the City of Ottawa, whereby Vanier is charged $625 per hour for a pump, and $750 per hour for an aerial ladder when Ottawa responds to any call for assistance (i.e., any call other than a border line call). Rockcliffe Park Village, on the other hand, has no fire department of its own and is charged on a per fire basis for the service of the Ottawa Department. The rates are the same as those charged to Vanier. The total cost to Rockcliffe in 1974 was $96,917 compared with $71,733 in 1975.

Evaluation

The efficiency and fire fighting capabilities of the many departments is difficult to assess. Annual per capita fire loss figures provide little insight, because the figures vary so much from one year to the next. We have not thought it worthwhile to publish these figures. Again, the per capita spending on fire fighting varies, but tells little without knowing the quality of service.

The quality of the *prevention* practices varies among departments. The larger departments — in Ottawa, Vanier, Gloucester and Nepean — maintain separate personnel assigned to fire inspection, whereas the smaller departments either have no inspection staff or inspection duties are carried out by the chief.

Although fire prevention by-laws for buildings are relatively uniform between municipalities, they are not, in all cases, enforced with the same rigour. Some townships only inspect buildings or approve building plans, on request; others, such as March, review all plans with the building inspector; the general policy in the four urban municipalities is to inspect all commercial and industrial buildings annually, and to approve all building plans except those for detached dwellings.

The efficiency of fire prevention by-laws has not been evaluated in the RMOC since comparative data are not available. For these reasons we recommend:

(1) that all commercial and industrial properties not now inspected be inspected at least every two years;
(2) that all rental housing be inspected annually, where this is not now done;
(3) that all fire departments approve all building plans except for detached dwellings;

There is nothing much new in these recommendations. They are designed only to bring the inspection and approvals by the smaller departments up to the standards of the larger departments.

Amalgamation?

The chief reason offered in favour of regional amalgamation of municipal fire services are: (a) that economies of scale will be achieved by such things as bulk purchasing; (b) that duplication of some costly capital assets will be avoided; (c) that overlapping jurisdiction will be eliminated. In order to determine whether these arguments have much validity, one must examine the nature of the fire fighting function.

Adequate fire protection requires stations in close proximity to potential fire occurrences. That is why fire stations must be located within what are called acceptable "response-time distances". For muncicipalities with high population densities, good response times are between two and five minutes, and acceptable times between five and seven minutes.

In the RMOC, 90% of the area is covered by five to seven minutes response times. Each station must, then, have at its disposal fire fighting equipment suitable to the area of its responsibility; that is, one station cannot depend on equipment (with some exceptions, such as aerial ladders) situated at another station in the municipality. Because of the need for dispersal of equipment and manpower throughout a given area in order to ensure rapid response, only two functions are capable of being centralized: administration and communication.

In large departments with paid rather than volunteer fire fighters, salaries constitute the bulk of the fire department budgets; other operating costs are proportionately very low. Depreciation and building maintenance are the only other major expenses besides salaries. Because a fire department performs only one function, little need exists for a large administrative staff. Therefore few, if any, economies of scale could be realized in administrative costs. Since the turnover of machinery and equipment is small, there is limited opportunity for bulk buying and hence little saving by centralized purchasing.

For centralized communication, one proposal has been to install a "911" emergency telephone number, for police, fire and ambulance. According to Bell Canada, such an emergency number does not require amalgamation, and may not decrease *overall* response time.[17] The benefits appear to be slight. No reduction in communication manpower is foreseen unless fire departments convert to a common radio band, and this in turn would be unnecessary without a centralized administration.

The problems which could arise from overlap (e.g., a fire station in one municipality being closer to a potential fire in a neighbouring municipality) appear to be soluble under the Mutual Aid Agreement. In practice, the number of occasions in which the Mutual Aid Agreement has been used is very small. The majority of cases have been border-line calls (i.e., where the caller misidentifies a fire as being in one municipality when it is actually in another). About twelve calls were answered by the Ottawa Fire Department in neighbouring municipalities in 1975, and only three in 1974. (Rockcliffe Park Village is a special case because of its contract).

One of the problems which could arise with a regional fire department is how to share the costs. Almost certainly, those municipalities that already have adequate fire fighting capacity (i.e., up-to-date equipment and enough fire fighters and fire stations) would make the largest contribution to the RMOC fire budget, while only the fire services in the smaller townships would benefit. This argument is strong, but not conclusive.

The cost of fire fighting equipment has quadrupled in recent years, largely because of inflation. The municipalities that have lagged behind in their purchases of new equipment will make the smallest contribution while receiving a substantial improvement in fire protection.

It may also be true that citizens' expectations of the quality of fire services would be greater. To satisfy these, would mean the raising and/or standardization of fire fighting capacity, that is, uniform or interchangeable equipment, improved fire fighting training, physical fitness programmes, public education, "sprinkler" equipped buildings, etc.

For the moment, the sentiment in the smaller municipalities appears to be in favour of maintaining volunteer or composite fire departments with their comparatively low cost. Some of these small departments have very good records.

In Chapter 8 we recommended that the City of Vanier be expanded to include parts of the City of Ottawa and Gloucester Township, as well as all of Rockcliffe Park Village. Hence, it will be necessary for Vanier to enlarge its fire department considerably. This may involve the takeover of a fire station presently owned by Ottawa, located on St. Laurent Boulevard, which will be within the proposed new boundaries for Vanier. This can be done by negotiation, or in the absence of agreement, by the OMB.

In conclusion, we recommend no change in the organization of fire fighting services in the RMOC. We do however draw the attention of some of the departments, to those points above where improvement can be made without "regionalization."[18]

---

[17] London, Ontario, is presently experimenting with the 911 system.

[18] This is not so very different from the findings by the Bureau of Municipal Research, *Fire Protection Services in Metro: Is Unification the Answer?*, Toronto, Nov. 1975.

CHAPTER 16

Environmental Services
or
Let's keep the whole thing clean

> ". . . man's destructive habits are at least three thousand years old, . . . but today the process is accelerating dangerously, keeping pace with our increased industrial skills and technological ability . . . (but) there are encouraging signs on the horizon . . . when a small boy urinates into a stream in Ontario, he is contravening some fourteen federal, provincial, and local laws . . ."[1]

Environmental services, for purposes of this Chapter, comprise the following: sewerage and storm sewers, water and hydro supply, garbage collection and disposal, and pollution control. These services do not make up a large proportion of the total municipal spending, but they are among the more useful services rendered by the RMOC and the area municipalities.

Two of these services are reported separately in financial statements, i.e., that of the Regional Waterworks, and of the area Hydro Commissions. The costs of these services are billed directly to the consumer, and are not paid for out of general revenue.

Expenditures on environmental services have remained stable over the years, *as a proportion*, but in absolute terms have gone up by 124%. Thus, the percentage increase has gone only from 5.6% of total expenditures in 1969, to 5.7% in 1975 (see Table 16-1); but within the municipalities, the percentage ranges from a low of 1.6% in West Carleton to a high of 9.4% in Nepean. The higher rate in Nepean is accounted for by the need to serve the Township's rapidly growing population. One should remember also, in interpreting Table 16-1, that some services such as garbage pick-up, were not provided at all by some municipalities in 1969, and hence some percentage increases by 1975 look very high indeed.

Water Supply

The Regional Council is responsible for all municipal water supplies. Its jurisdiction extends from the initial water collection and treatment, to the distribution to the ultimate consumer. The Council is prohibited by statute from delegating this authority to a public utilities commission.

The Regional Waterworks serve some 90% of the Regional population, mostly in the "urbanized" areas, but excluding nearly all of the outlying townships. The latter rely mainly on private wells for their water.

Of those receiving Regional water, 99% are served by the Central Supply System which draws its water from the Ottawa River through the Britannia and Lemieux Island purification plants. The other 1% of the serviced population, in certain outlying subdivisions, is supplied

---

[1] M. J. Dunbar, *Environment and Good Sense*, McGill-Queen's University Press, 1971, pp. 1, 7.

with water from Regionally-operated well systems.[2]

Two new reservoirs were added in 1974, bringing the total to seven and increasing the storage capacity by more than 50% over the 1969 capacity. These new reservoirs allow for new pressure districts and the extension of the Central Supply System. The number of pumping stations rose from 13 to 17, and fell again to 15 as service was first extended to new areas, and then transferred to the Central Supply System from well systems. The number of well systems fell from 13 to 6 as the Central Supply System expanded.

Table 16-1
Expenditures on Environmental Services,
RMOC and Area Municipalities, 1969-1975

Municipality	1969 ($000's)	% of Total Munic. Expend.	1975 ($000's)	% of Total Munic. Expend.	% increase 1969-1975	Expenditure per capita 1975
RMOC	3,176	12.0	5,480	7.4	73%	$11
Ottawa	2,866	3.3	7,063	4.5	146%	$23
Vanier	250	8.2	674	8.2	176%	$33
Rockcliffe Park	57	7.2	120	8.6	111%	$54
Cumberland	6	0.7	132	4.8	2100%	$12
Gloucester	283	5.8	603	3.5	113%	$11
Goulbourn	25	2.2	117	3.9	368%	$ 9
March	30	3.3	77	3.0	157%	$11
Nepean	992	8.6	2,852	9.4	188%	$39
Osgoode	2	0.2	34	1.8	1600%	$ 4
Rideau	2	0.3	49	2.4	2350%	$ 6
West Carleton	8	0.8	35	1.6	338%	$ 4
Total Region	7,697	5.6	17,236	5.7	124%	$34

Sources: RMOC and Area Municipalities Financial Reports 1969-1975, excluding Waterworks and Hydro Commissions.

Water supply in the Central Supply System undergoes a number of treatments, including filtration, chlorination and fluoridation. The water is sampled daily in 19 different locations to check water quality. The well water system is checked weekly.

Total water consumption in the Region has increased 26% from 1969, amounting in 1975 to an average daily consumption of 86 million gallons. The maximum daily use for the year 1975 was 65% greater than on the average day. If these maximum and average loads continue to increase fast, additional storage facilities and more filtration plant capacity will soon be required.

---

[2] The subdivisions which have Regional well systems are Barrhaven (Nepean), Hillside Gardens (Rideau), Queenswood South (Cumberland), Jiulia (West Carleton), Kings Park and Munster Hamlet (Goulbourn).

Water consumption is metered, the charges being based on 100 cubic feet (65 gallons). The net deficit of the RMOC water supply system in 1974 was converted to a net surplus in 1975 by raising the water rate from 26.5 cents to 40 cents per 100 cubic feet of water (i.e., 64.1 cents per 1000 gallons).[3] The reading of meters has been cut back from three times a year to once a year, in order to save in the order of $80,000 in operating costs.[4] Billing, however, is every four months, with two of the bills being estimates while the third, given after the meter is read, is adjusted to show the actual annual consumption.

Water supply, unlike electricity, is not under a special purpose body. It is a normal department function, under the Works Department of the RMOC. We recommend no change in this arrangement, which has the advantage of closely integrating water supply with over-all Regional planning.

Private developers often bear the cost of water lines to new subdivision, up to and including 12" pipe. The lines are later taken over by the RMOC. The effect of this arrangement is to raise housing prices, and there is something to be said for these costs being municipal, and later being paid for by "local improvement taxes".

A general principle arises here. Developers often have to finance not only water lines, but also roads, sidewalks, etc., before these are taken over by the RMOC or the area municipality. Consequently, this increases housing prices ("front end loading") and tends also to increase downpayments. If the municipality instead bore these costs, the housing price and downpayment would be less, but the monthly payments would be higher because of "local improvement taxes". The effect would also be to increase municipal debt. It is a question therefore of whether to make more housing available by some lowering of the initial price, and to do so at the cost of higher municipal debt. Our inclination is to give a higher preference to making more housing available, especially since most municipalities are not yet anywhere near their allowable debt limits. (See also Chapter 6, Housing.)

Sewerage

Sewerage is one of those functions divided between the RMOC and the area municipalities. The latter are responsible for connecting individual properties to the local mains which in turn connect with certain trunk sewers. The RMOC itself is responsible for trunk lines and sewage treatment plants. This division of powers has existed from the start of the RMOC in 1969.

The RMOC does however, have the option of assuming other sewer lines from the lower tier municipalities, where more than one municipality is involved. These municipalities provide some sanitary sewers, although nearly all of them rely on private septic tanks, especially in outlying areas.

The Regional control of trunk sewers and treatment plants, was seen to be necessary on two grounds: one to spread the enormous costs and avoid competing systems; the other because of the intimate relation between sewers and Regional planning.

The region has extended the trunk sewers greatly since 1969 and sewage treatment has

---

[3] The rates for the Boroughs in Metro Toronto vary from 54.7 to 66 cents for 1000 gallons on metered domestic consumption.

[4] Ottawa Journal, July 22, 1975. (By special arrangement with the Ottawa Hydro Commission, residential water meters are read by Ottawa Hydro within its territory. The more expensive non-residential readings are done by the RMOC).

improved enormously. The capacity of the Green Creek Pollution Centre (serving the east end) has been doubled. The Watts Creek Plant (for the West end) provides primary, secondary and tertiary treatment, and its capacity has been expanded several-fold. In both cases phosphate treatment has been added. The Bilberry Creek Treatment Plant has recently been phased out of production. A sewage "lagoon" has been taken over and managed by the RMOC, in Munster Hamlet. A second lagoon in Richmond built by the Ministry of the Environment, may soon come under the RMOC.

The RMOC sewerage system is financed largely by the sewer area levies on those local municipalities which it services. Certain smaller amounts of revenue are received from recovered costs (e.g., a "fire supply charge" on the area tax bills) and from a special Provincial-Municipal Incentive Programme. A source of revenue for area municipalities with local sewers is the surcharge (or "service charge" as it is sometimes called) which is placed on the RMOC water bills on behalf of the area municipalities. This sewer charge on water bills varies widely, at one time being as high as 100% in Nepean (now reduced), and lower for the City of Ottawa and for Gloucester.

Capital expenditures on sewers are subsidized to a considerable degree by the senior levels of government. Sewage systems are so costly that they are beyond the financial capacity of cities and other municipalities acting on their own. Besides, since most of the provincial and federal income is generated from cities, there is nothing unfair about senior governments helping the cities.

The Province for instance, has a programme which funds 15% of the extra costs involved in building systems intended to accommodate future as well as current needs, or "over-sizing" at it is called. So let us not say that politicians always think only of the short term, and leave posterity to look out for itself. The CMHC provides the Region with loans for treatment facilities and trunk sewers, one-sixth of which is forgiveable. There is also a major programme, involving $42 million during its first phase, the costs of which are shared by the federal government (through the NCC), the province, and the Region, with each assuming one third of the total cost. (Not all aid is on this formula of one-third from each level of government).

Table 16-2 shows the breakdown of the expenditures on sanitary sewerage systems in the Region for the years 1969 and 1975. Although the area municipalities take care of the local sewer collectors, the RMOC must approve the standards, and it also inspects all the sewers in the Region. Further, an area municipality can only extend its local system with the approval of the RMOC.

Regional influence and control over the sewage system is so substantial that it raises the question whether it should be complete. We are inclined to recommend that the Region assume the total sewerage system. It makes sense for the Region to manage both sewerage and water supply, since they are so closely related. The administration and planning of both facilities would be easier, and it would remove the confusion experienced by the customer, who must pay for two systems (maintained by two different levels of government) on the water bill which is paid to the Region.

Hydro (Electricity)

Within the RMOC there are at present four local Hydro Commissions: (1) Ottawa Hydro which serves the cities of Ottawa and Vanier, and the village of Rockcliffe Park; (2) Nepean Hydro which serves Nepean township (since 1964) (3) Gloucester Hydro which operates in Gloucester township (since 1965); and (4) the small Richmond Hydro (1928) which provides

Table 16-2
Sanitary Sewer Expenditures, RMOC and Area Municipalities, 1969-1975

	1969 (000's)	1975 (000's)	% increase 1969-75	Expenditure per Capita 1975
RMOC	3176	5080	60	$10
Ottawa	1168	2336	100	8
Vanier	187	100	47	5
Rockcliffe Park	32	49	53	22
Cumberland	0	74	—	6
Gloucester	239	329	38	6
Goulbourn	4	59	1375	5
March	20	43	115	6
Nepean	758	1398	84	19
Total Region	$5584	9468	70	$19

Source: RMOC and Area Municipalities Financial Reports, 1969, 1975.

service to the unincorporated village of Richmond in Goulbourn township. Other area municipalities within the Region are serviced directly by Ontario Hydro.

The number of customers, the sales and other financial data are given in Table 16-3. Residential customers are by far the majority of total customers of each hydro commission. But in Ottawa and Nepean the "general service" customers account for the lion's share of electricity sales (in kilowatt hours) and pay the largest proportion of revenue received by their commissions.

The residential rates for each hydro commission differ somewhat, being lowest for Ottawa Hydro.[5] Wholesale power costs from Ontario Hydro are the same for each retail hydro commission, therefore the differences in rates reflect the differing operating costs, including that for debt charges, of the commissions. In general the debt of the hydro commissions has declined since 1969. But with the planned expansion of services to the new "southern cities" in Nepean and Gloucester, their capital and debt costs are likely to increase. As one might expect, the Ottawa debt is much the lowest, the original installations having long been paid for. Ottawa Hydro was formed in 1950, by merging two firms which went back to the 1880's, and has a small amount of its own generating capacity.

The provincial Task Force Hydro recommended that: "Municipal utilites be rationalized into upper tier regional utilities where and as new municipal government is

---

[5] For instance, the rates for the first 100 KWH are for Ottawa 4.6 cents, for Nepean, Gloucester and Richmond 6.0 cents. The usual practice is followed of charging less per unit for bulk buyers. With the present energy-saving campaigns, some folk have argued that the charge should *rise* per unit for heavy users of hydro. This would save energy, but it would raise costs for commercial, industrial and other large purchasers — with economic consequences on competitiveness, on price of products and services to consumers, etc.

implemented. The area to be served by the regional utility be the entire area served by the new municipal government."[6] The Hogg Report in 1974 reaffirmed this recommendation stating that "Further throughout any area defined by municipal boundaries there should be one retail authority."[7]

We agree with these statements, and recommend that all hydro, for retail sales, be placed within the RMOC Works Department. The RMOC would assume all the Ottawa, Nepean, Gloucester and Richmond Hydro assets and liabilities as determined by the OMB. There is no need to have hydro under special purpose bodies. They are among the relics of ad hockery with which history is littered. They, and the people on them, have served well in their day but that day is passing.

As for the rural areas presently served at retail by Ontario Hydro: *either* the Region could take over these areas according to the procedures outlined in the Hogg Report; *or* they could continue to be served by Ontario Hydro, as now. We recommend the former. It is in accord with the thinking of Task Force Hydro, which spoke of the "need to rationalize the existing 353 municipal utilities."

Regionalization of hydro service would produce several benefits.

(a) It would help to reduce or eliminate rate disparities.

(b) The high revenue received from the "general service" customers would benefit all of the Region's residential customers.

(c) Regionalization would provide a broader financial base than the present, so that rapid growth would produce less strain on the newer Hydro Commissions through borrowing.

(d) Regionalization would ensure that hydro was more effectively integrated into the planning by Regional government.

(e) Regionalization would also overcome the confusion of customers who cannot identify hydro service boundaries with political boundaries.

(f) The hydro and water bills could be consolidated into one, be less costly to produce, and more convenient for the customers.[8]

To repeat: the present local hydro commissions are special purpose bodies, (under The Public Utilities Act) and we believe that it is preferable to return all such special functions to one all-purpose Council, unless there is an overwhelming case against it.[9] (So far, we have found only one such special case, the "Sacred Cow" of the school boards).

It could be debated perhaps whether the hydro function should be absorbed into their local councils rather than Regional Council. But for purposes of planning, uniformity,

---

[6] Task Force Hydro, *Hydro in Ontario — An Approach to Organization*, Report Number Two, Toronto, December 1972, p. 7.

[7] The Hogg Report, *The Restructuring of Public Utilities*, Toronto, 1974, p. 47.

[8] Papers accompanying the Hogg Report also mention that the broader financial base "should be able to attract a higher degree of technical efficiency."

[9] The Hydro Commissions offer an amusing instance of the defences for the status quo. The Ottawa Hydro Commission is made up of the Mayor and two appointees, one by the city, and one by the Ontario Hydro. They argue this is the best way to constitute a Commission. Nepean and Gloucester Commission are composed of the Reeve with elected Commissioners, four in Nepean and two in Gloucester. The Richmond Commission is a splendid anomaly, with a staff of two; the Commission however, is chosen like that of Nepean and Gloucester. (There is an even smaller hydro in Grey County with only 86 customers).

convenience, financing and equity, we recommend the latter course. It is understood that "the transfer of assets is fair and equitable . . . (and there) will be fair treatment for staff."[10]

Table 16-3
Local Hydro Commissions, 1975

	Ottawa Hydro	Nepean Hydro	Gloucester Hydro	Richmond Hydro
Customers				
Total	103,667	17,112	13,738	859
As a % of total:				
Residential	88	89	91	91
general service	12	11	9	9
Sales				
Total (000,000 KWH)	3,160	547	327	15
as a % of total:				
residential	27%	40%	47%	66%
general service	72	59	52	33
street lighting	1	1	1	1
Revenue				
Total ($000's)	49,789	8,775	5,715	259
as a % of total:				
residential	27	43	52	67
general service	72	56	47	32
street lighting	1	1	1	1
Revenue per KWH ($):				
residential	1.58	1.72	1.94	1.80
general service:				
(under 5,000 KWH)	1.61	1.55	1.67	1.71
(over 5,000 KWH)	1.34	1.09	1.21	
Capital Assets				
Total ($000's)	90,260	14,268	9,337*	563
Long Term Debt				
Total ($000's)	2,040	5,172	2,854*	68

Source: Ontario Hydro, *Statistical Yearbook*, 1975. Municipal Financial Reports, 1975.
* Gloucester figures 1974; because of consolidated reporting, 1975 figures are not available.

Garbage (or, more delicately, "solid waste")

The collection of garbage and other solid waste is a function performed by the area

---

[10] Papers, *op. cit.*, p. 4.

municipalities. There is considerable variation from one municipality to the next in the type and frequency of collection. All of the area municipalities that offer this service (i.e., all except Osgoode and West Carleton) contract with private firms for the collection of garbage, rather than maintaining a staff of their own. This was not always the case in the past. But it has the advantages for area councils of their having no labour relations to handle, and usually the cost is lower. The lower cost is alleged to be at the expense of the workers who are paid less than municipal employees, which is probably true, and if true is something to be deplored.

Expenditures on garbage collection and disposal are shown in Table 16-4. The total expenditures have increased by 80% since 1969 with the greatest increases occurring in Rideau and West Carleton (because they didn't offer the service in 1969). Revenue to pay for garbage collection is usually obtained from the general municipal tax levy, although in some outlying municipalities which do not provide collection service to all households, the revenue is derived from a special charge to the recipients of the service. (There are still about a dozen small garbage dumps, managed and financed by the townships).

Sanitary landfill sites (i.e., dumps) came under the authority of the Regional Municipality on January 1, 1976. It is now a Regional responsibility to manage all garbage disposal, and to operate landfill sites in the Region.

This shift in responsibility will ensure that the urban municipalities will not experience the problem found in Toronto which is trying to find sanitary landfill sites outside its boundaries. (There are more possible sites in the RMOC than in Metro Toronto because Ottawa-Carleton is less built-up).

The RMOC has not yet taken over the management and operation of dumps and landfill sites. The status quo still exists. It takes some time to iron out wrinkles. For instance, controversy has risen over the location of the Region's proposed landfill site in Nepean. Some area councils believe that the location of the site will lead to extra haulage costs for them. They have suggested that a garbage "equalization fund" be created to help overcome these disparities in transport costs. We do not think this is a good idea. Municipalities will benefit by not having to incur the expense of operating their own dumps (the estimated saving in 1974 would have been some $600,000). Moreover, although Nepean will benefit from lower transport costs, it has to bear the cost of some undesirable side effects from the dump within its borders, arising from the increased heavy traffic that is generated.

We see no good reason to upset the division of powers over collection and disposal of garbage, and therefore recommend that the arrangement of January 1, 1976 be retained, and worked out as soon as possible. When, if ever the time should come, and the local municipalities agree to shift the entire function (including collection) to the RMOC, a series of "transfer points" could no doubt be set up, to shorten the haulage distance for some of the municipalities. Modern technology is wonderful.

Pollution Control

Concern over environmental pollution is the "in" thing today. It ranges all the way through air, land, freshwater and ocean, to noise and "people" pollution.[11] One hears less of

---

[11] In case the reader is skeptical about the last-named, we cite Milton M. R. Freeman, *People Pollution*, McGill-Queen's University Press, 1974. (The book is actually about population issues, with special reference to Canada.)

Table 16-4

Expenditures on Garbage Collection and Disposal, Area Municipalities 1969-1975

Municipality	1969 ($000's)	1975 ($000's)	% Increase 1969-1975	Expenditure Per Capita 1975
Ottawa	1,699	2,556	50	$ 8
Vanier	62	94	52	5
Rockcliffe Park	25	52	108	23
Cumberland	6	59	883	5
Gloucester	45	206	358	4
Goulbourn	21	58	176	5
March	10	27	170	4
Nepean	233	647	178	9
Osgoode	2	34	1,600	4
Rideau	2	49	2,350	6
West Carleton	8	31	2,875	4
Total Region	2,113	3,813	80	$ 8

Source: Municipal Financial Reports, 1969-75.

aesthetic, or touch, or word pollution, but no doubt these will be in fashion soon. It is nearly enough to make one stop living at all.

Indeed, some zealots tell us we *shall* stop living unless we mend our ways: if nuclear war doesn't get us, pollution will. Buckminster Fuller, for instance, says "I made a bargain with myself that I'd discover the principles operative in the universe and turn them over to my fellow men". Luckily he did discover "the principles", with the result that we face Utopia or Oblivion.[12] Oblivion, maybe; but too many leaders have promised Utopia, and dragged their followers through rivers of blood into prison houses that were worse than those they dwelt in before. A firm hold on the doctrine of Original Sin is the best inoculation against the disease of Utopianism.

The RMOC Works Department, through its Pollution Control Branch, is responsible for the sewerage system and sewage treatment, and has done much to limit pollution by sewage. (One cannot say as much for the other side of the Ottawa River). Nor can pollution of the Ottawa River by logging operations be laid on the conscience of this Region. Moreover, not being an industrial city, there is not much pollution of air by industry in the Region.

Whence then does pollution of air and water come?

As to water there are several sources: (a) One is the lack of separation of all sanitary and storm sewers. The RMOC Pollution Control Branch has a programme of investigation and abatement of pollution. Except for the older parts of Ottawa, storm and sanitary sewers are separate. The city began such a separate system in the mid 1960's.

Where there is no such separate system of sewers, heavy rains overload the sewers, and some pollution by sewage is the inevitable result. It often happens with the Rideau and Ottawa Rivers.

---

[12] R. Buckminster Fuller, *Utopia or Oblivion: the Prospects for Humanity*, Bantam Books, 1969. The quotation is on p. 1. The blurb says Fuller was *nominated* for a Nobel Prize. Well, well.

Even with separate storm sewers, urban run-off contains many pollutants (including salt); and a very heavy capital investment is needed to cure this state of affairs. The same is true of snow-dumping in the winter. As the snow melts in the Spring, the salt, sand and other wastes are a never ending source of pollution, and a constant challenge to technology to overcome it at a reasonable cost. Presumable the RMOC is the logical body to undertake such a pollution control when, if ever, the public is willing to pay the cost.

Upstream pollution, say on the Rideau, arises from run-off in drainage ditches, from farm land (chemicals and animal wastes), from imperfect tile beds and some small towns. It is certain that the almost unlimited "strip development" of cottages and homes allowed on both sides of the Rideau by laissez faire councils will give rise to pollution, and to some extent does so already. The Province and the outlying municipalities help to a considerable degree with drainage ditches, and tile-drainage of land. (The land owner also helps to pay). It must be remembered that some of the pollutants enter the Rideau from further upstream, i.e., outside the RMOC boundaries.

Hence arises the importance of CORTS (the Canada-Ontario-Rideau-Trent-Severn) agreement which among its purposes includes pollution control of this entire water system of combined rivers and canals.[13] The Federal Government has the easier job (dredging, maintaining the canals). But the municipalities, of which there are scores, have the hardest job. They are under heavy pressure to allow lot severances, and some of the municipalities, as yet, scarcely believe in pollution. Strict land division controls by the municipalities (which are far too lenient at present, especially in rural counties), and even stricter control by the Province, are required to ensure that the waterway is kept pure enough for swimming and fishing. (If one wishes to see what happens without planning controls, one need only look at the critical state of some Ontario lakes).

(b) As to air pollution the chief causes are automobiles and buses. (The Region is fortunate in not having industrial fumes, except those from the paper industry across the Ottawa River.)

Given the projected reliance on buses for public transit, and upon the automobile too, since the Region is widely scattered, there is not much the RMOC can do about this type of pollution, except perhaps to monitor it, and inform the public. Everything depends on technology to reduce car emissions, and the willingness of the public to pay the private and social costs.

On pollution in general, since the public and government became aware of it in the 1960's, more or less traditional methods were used to preserve the environment. These were statutory measures and regulation. In Ontario, for example, there is the recent Environment Assessment Act, with an Environment Assessment Board. (It is this Board which has been involved with the garbage disposal site in the RMOC).

Such methods, with government financial assistance, have some remarkable achievements to their credit. The air in London (England), like water in the river Thames, is purer today than it has been for generations.

Economists, however, are taking a somewhat different approach from identifying polluters and fining them. Their approach is to look at the industries or plants which do in fact pollute (regardless of whether there are complaints against them) and to provide incentives for them to clean up their operations. The incentives could take several forms: one is an

---

[13] CORTS *Agreement*, Feb. 20, 1975, p. 2.

"effluent charge" (over and above any legal limits of "acceptable" pollution).[14]

A similar, though not identical, system has been suggested by another author. Here he condemns the old approach through "property rights", i.e., of the owner to use and treat air and water as common property which he can use at will. Instead he suggests the development of "new forms of property rights . . . to the *use* of air and water.[15]

As in the first suggestion, the government would not measure air and water quality, but would measure the effluent from a plant (or sewage outfall) and would then impose a "pollution charge" (or perhaps give a subsidy for every 5%, say, by which the pollutant is reduced). The "pollution charge" — the preferred method — becomes a "pollution right", for which the polluter must pay, and this gives him an incentive *not* to pollute. These and other ingenious devices to reduce pollution are presumably being studied by the Ministry of the Environment, as well as by the federal government.

As for indoor air pollution by the smoking of cigarettes, etc., we recommend that the Province enact legislation similar to that of the Minnesota Clear Indoor Air Act, 1975.

Conservation Authorities

Within the Region, three Conservation Authorities have jurisdiction. This is because the Region is within three watersheds. These are: in the west, the Mississippi Valley Authority; in the middle, the Rideau Valley Authority; in the east, the South Nation Authority.

These Authorities are provincial bodies, under the Ministry of Natural Resources. They are made up of municipal representatives, and are funded for ordinary operations 50/50 by the province and the participating municipalities while for special projects the Province pays a higher share. There is no way, as far as we can see, that these Conservation Authorities can have boundaries that coincide with political entities. Watersheds are no respecter of municipal boundaries.

The work of the Authorities comprises flood control, building dams and reservoirs, mapping and acquiring flood plain land, checking and improving water quality, wildlife management, etc. They also have recreational and historical sites. In many ways the Conservation Authorities are the unsung heroes of local-provincial relations and their work is too little appreciated by the public.

We see no reason to change the composition or work of the Conservation Authorities. However, in certain aspects of their work, relating especially to recreation, pollution control, and planning, the Authorities and the municipalities could certainly work more closely together.

---

[14] See, e.g., Allen V. Kneese and Charles L. Schultze, *Pollution, Prices and Public Policy*, The Brookings Institution, Washington, D.C. 1975, pp. 105-120.

[15] J. H. Dales, *Pollution, property and prices*, University of Toronto Press, 1968, pp. 75-76. See also, D. A. L. Auld, ed., *Economic thinking and Pollution Problems*, University of Toronto Press, 1972.

CHAPTER 17

The Capital Question
or
Here we go round the Mulberry bush

". . . A country's capital is an essential instrument of national pride. In a federal, bilingual and multicultural country, it must also be an essential instrument of national unity. It must reflect equitably all aspects of that country's character, and each citizen should have a true sense of ownership in the capital of his country regardless of the distance which separates him from the seat of government."[1]

Introductory

When Ottawa was the capital in 1857 there were no complications arising from federal-provincial-municipal jurisdiction. The reason is simple: there was one Province only — the United Province of Canada; and Ottawa was the "seat of government"; and there was no federal government. The position was rather like that of provincial capitals today: each has only one master the provincial government.

With Confederation in 1867, the situation was changed drastically. Ottawa became the capital, but was then a City within the Province of Ontario, and the federal (or national) government was, so to speak, the tenant of a provincial city. Since municipalities are under provincial jurisdiction, the federal government did not (and could not) have a share in the governing of the City of Ottawa. This is the situation today.

Naturally, the Ottawa of 1867 was not of the same size as today. It has been enlarged many times by amalgamation and annexation, most of all in 1950 with the large annexations of territory from the townships of Nepean and Gloucester. The expansions have not, of course, been by federal law, but by municipal request and provincial law.

Some idea of the small size of the original capital may be gained from points such as these: when Lansdowne Park (now containing the Civic Centre, Stadium and Exhibition grounds and buildings) was bought by Ottawa, it was outside the City limits; and so was the Central Experimental Farm of some 1,200 acres, sometimes called "the largest urban farm in the world". Today these two large areas are entirely surrounded by urban growth. We have also seen how mistaken Jacques Greber was in believing that the Greenbelt was far enough out to allow the City of Ottawa to grow indefinitely within its confines. In any case, the Greenbelt was much too narrow a barrier; that around London — *the* London — is from five to ten miles, and even that is not wide enough.

What is the Capital?

A curious point arises in many of the federal publications. It concerns the mixing of the words Capital, National Capital and National Capital Region. That is to say, a distinction is not made between Capital (or National Capital) on the one hand, and National Capital Region on the other.

---

[1] The Special Joint Committee of the Senate and of the House of Commons on the Constitution of Canada, *Final Report*, Ottawa, 1972, p. 41. (The Committee recommended "a movement by stages towards the possible creation of an autonomous Canadian Capital". *Loc. cit.*)

This is done either through carelessness or in some kind of easy assumption that the NCR is already the *de facto* Capital of Canada.

A few examples, from scores:

(a) The Special Joint Committee's advertisement, paragraph one, mentions "reviewing . . . the National Capital Region;"but paragraph two has ". . . hearings . . . and submissions . . . about *the future of Canada's Capital*".[2](Italics added).

(b) From the Fullerton terms of reference, ". . . the co-ordination of those federal activities which bear upon the development of *the Region as a national capital*".[3] (Italics added). Fullerton says, "My mandate is really with the government of the Capital. . ."

(c) An Act respecting the development and improvement of the National Capital Region, C. N-3, is cited in its short title as *the National Capital Act*, 1958, C. 37, S.1.

(d) The NCC in *Canada's New Capital*: "It used to be said that musty old Ottawa was known as the nation's Capital. Technically, it still is. But let's drop the technicalities . . . it's not just Ottawa anymore. It's the National Capital Region".

(e) The NCC's *Annual Report 1973-1974*, p. 1:
> "The Canadian Capital is not a city like other cities, nor a capital like other capitals. . . It is a social and cultural microcosm of Canada itself: *The 640,000 people living in the National Capital Region. . .*" (Italics added)

(f) The NCC's Concept Plan: *Tomorrow's Capital, Invitation to Dialogue, 1974*, is generally careful to distinguish National Capital Region from Capital. But its very title and the Concept Plan itself show that the NCR is meant as the Capital. And in the text, for example, are such remarks as "*the image of Ottawa-Hull as the Nation's Capital.*" (p. 12). (Italics added)

(g) The Senate Report, *Poverty in Canada, op. cit.*, p. 73, speaks of "*The Regional Municipality of Ottawa-Carleton, the capital of Canada. . .*" (Italics added).

Douglas Fullerton was right in saying that "Capital" has not been officially defined: the B.N.A. Act speaks only of "seat of government", which is the City of Ottawa. We must therefore equate Capital and "seat of government" on constitutional grounds. So Ottawa remains the Capital until changed by the government of Canada — which can be done by Order-in-Council. We thus have to live with the constitutional reality that Ottawa is the Capital (seat of government), however much the federal agencies and others speak and act as though a wider area is the Capital.[4]

It may be that the federal Executive, or perhaps Parliament, may one day alter the Capital (seat of government) and define it as the NCR. But should that come about, it could not alter the fact that the municipalities within the NCR would still be under the provincial governments, not under the federal government. The designation of a new Capital, would of itself make very little difference to the municipal status quo. It would not and could not,

---

[2] The Special Joint Committee of the Senate and of the House of Commons, 1975. Joint Chairmen: Senator Jean-Paul Deschatelets, P.C., and Ralph W. Stewart, M.P. The Committee sat first on July 17, 1975, sat again on July 23, and started again on October 20, 1975, and went on intermittently until June 29, 1976, the date of its last public sitting. Since the First Session of the Thirtieth Parliament ended, the Joint Committee is now in limbo, and must presumably be "re-struck" in the Second Session. It could, perhaps, assemble informally and make a Report on its hearings so far.

[3] The Fullerton Report, p. 5.

[4] The NCC, *Report to the Joint Parliamentary Committee*, June, 1975, p. 7, says, ". . . the National Capital Commission sees no useful distinctions to be made between 'the seat of government', the Capital of Canada, the Capital Area, or the National Capital Region."

because to alter the municipal structures is only within provincial jurisdictions. And both provinces have displayed considerable willingness in recent years, to change the municipalities, but none at all to share jurisdiction over them with the federal government. They have displayed even less desire to cede territory.

The strongest objection to a cession of territory has come from Quebec, through the Dorion Report, which said that in the federal capital, the initiatives should be provincial.[5] The Report argued for the "return of territories which are, at present, the property of the NCC." It was equally firm in its stand against yielding jurisdiction to any new form of government in the NCR.

Faced with a stand such as that, the B. and B. Commission argued that "To find a formula that reconciles Quebec's territorial integrity with the need for an integrated federal capital is perhaps the central obstacle to be overcome".[6] It went on to meet the points raised by the Dorion Report, and suggested territory need only be leased, but not in perpetuity; and that the federal interest need only be "suitably represented in the governmental arrangements for the Territory".

The conclusion from all of this is hardly startling, and has been hinted at earlier: the federal government has the authority to designate the "seat of government". No one disputes this, although it is difficult to know what the phrase "seat of government" means, unless it is identical with "capital", which is also undefined. At any rate, unless the federal government does take action, then Ottawa remains the "seat of government" (Capital), and all the other meanings or synonyms for Capital (such as those quoted above) are either loosely used, or meant to convey that the NCR is the *de facto*, although not *de jure*, the Capital (seat of government).

The Fullerton Report (a) general

In 1973 Douglas Fullerton resigned as Chairman of the National Capital Commission (NCC). He was then asked by the Prime Minister,

"to undertake a study of the most effective arrangements for the future administration of matters directly affecting the National Capital and its development, including the role of the National Capital Commission and its relation to other bodies concerned with the governing of the Capital Region and the co-ordination of those federal activities which bear upon the development of the Region as a national capital".

The Report, in two volumes, was released in 1974.[7] Volume One contains the description, analysis and recommendations. It was given a distribution much larger than is common for government documents, being printed in full (with additional pictures) as a special supplement to the *Ottawa Citizen*. Volume Two of the Report contains the appendices, made up of supporting documents of several kinds.

This informative Report is valuable reading for all those interested in the National Capital Region, in the presence and impact of the federal government; in the City of Ottawa

---

[5] *Rapport de la Commission d'étude sur l'intégrité du territoire du Québec*, Québec, 1968, especially p. 65 ff.

[6] Report of the Royal Commission on Bilingualism and Biculturalism, *The Federal Capital*, Book V, Appendix III, Ottawa, 1970.

[7] Douglas Fullerton, *The Capital of Canada: How Should It Be Governed*? Information Canada, 1974. (The question in the very title of the Report shows that Fullerton wanted a different Capital. There is no mystery about how *Ottawa* is governed.)

and the other municipalities on both sides of the Ottawa River. One should therefore be grateful for it, in the same way as one is grateful for other task force reports which have not been adopted and are not likely to be. It is an historic document of reference, not quite a monument, and will no doubt be read often by students of local government in this part of Canada.

Upon first (and indeed second) reading of it, the reader gets several strong impressions from the Report.

The *first*, naturally, is that it is totally and relentlessly pro-federal government in its point of view. Fullerton lays about him, usually with a broad sword, sometimes with a rapier, and his opponents litter the verbal battleground. The opponents are, of course, the municipalities on both sides of the Ottawa River, and the two provinces of Ontario and Quebec. They don't and won't admit that the federal government knows what is best for them; instead they perversely adhere to the consititution and their provincial and municipal loyalties.

The *second* is how divided the federal departments are. This will not surprise professional students of government, who are quite aware both of the forked tongues of governments and of their hydra-headed nature. (With governments, as with life, logic is not everything). The department overlappings, rivalries, and even conflicts of policy can thus be taken for granted. Perhaps this is a good thing if, as Thomas Hobbes thought, liberty lies in the interstices of the law.

The Fullerton Report documents the federal lack of co-ordination with some vivid examples, the chief perhaps drawn from the conflicts between the Department of Public Works (DPW) and the NCC, over property acquisition and land management, and over the maintenance of federal buildings and grounds. As to buildings:

> "In brief, the DPW is responsible for such maintenance inside the building skin, the NCC outside it. For example, the flowers inside the Governor General's greenhouse are managed by the DPW, those outside it by the NCC; every spring the NCC takes formal custody of the greenhouse goldfish when they are shifted to the outside pool, and returns them to DPW's custody in the fall!"[8]

Besides the NCC, other federal departments or agencies with large land holdings, are the Department of Agriculture, the Department of National Defence, the Ministry of Transport, and CMHC. For the most part these are not co-ordinated with the NCC.

It is not our purpose here to detail the actual or potential conflicts within the federal government. But it is our legitimate concern to know who speaks for the federal government, and whether it should be with one voice, when dealing with the municipalites of the Region.

The *third* impression one receives is how little the federal government seems to understand or "have a feel" for municipalities. It is as though federal bureaucrats (or technocrats) were wrapped in a cloak of infallibility, and had nothing but scorn for municipal politicians. This impression comes through strongly as the Report details some of the federal relations with the municipalities. The "feds" are always right — on building heights, on grants-in-lieu of taxes, on public transit, on bridges.[9] And yet, the National Defence Building (federal) is perhaps one of the worst examples of siting in Ottawa, blocking as it does the view from Colonel By Drive, of the Chateau Laurier and the Parliament buildings.

---

[8] The Fullerton Report, Vol. 1, p. 46. A more serious instance of too many federal fingers in the pie occurs when so many of the Ottawa bridges seem to be out of action at the same time.

[9] One can hardly deny that the "feds" are sometimes right — they are bound to be, since they do so much and spend so much.

Fullerton himself seems to share something of this anti-municipal bias. It comes through often between the lines, but now and then is put plainly, as when for instance, he speaks of the "problem . . . of attracting good people into local politics", (p. 101); and says "Until very recently there was very little local planning done except by the NCC and its predecessors . . ." (p. 54); and "the local government process has not been working very effectively . . ." (p. 85). There are many such remarks.

Although the City of Ottawa, and Carleton County, and other municipalities were here long before the NCC and its predecessors, their record is brusquely swept aside. Unless one is alert, one almost believes that the NCC or Mackenzie King built the Rideau Canal, and perhaps invented the Parliament buildings for good measure.[10]

The same slightly arrogant federal outlook was noted by Humphrey Carver, as being prevalent at CMHC as late as 1962, when he wrote "of a view traditionally held by federal officials, that local governments, like women before 'women's lib', were by nature inferior and incompetent".[11]

With this kind of attitude in federal agencies, it is no wonder that they — especially the NCC — have come in for so much municipal criticism. The wonder is that federal-municipal relations in this Region are not constantly in a state of feverish hostility. Indeed, the situation is such that the City of Ottawa has appointed an intergovernmental affairs officer, and we have recommended the same for the RMOC. (See Chapter 9.)[12]

The Fullerton Report (b) Form of Government

Fullerton's diagnosis of governments in the NCR was roughly this: (1) there are too many governments in the area, especially too many municipalities on both sides of the Ottawa River; (2) although the City of Ottawa is technically the Capital, in effect the whole NCR is the Capital; but if it isn't, it ought to be; (3) the federal government should have "a seat at the table" — probably the biggest one.

---

[10] King is mentioned because of his strong interest in beautifying the Capital and the area around it. The first federal interest in Ottawa, the Ottawa Improvement Commission of 1899 set up by the Laurier government, was the outcome of several influences, one of them the City's petition of 1897, asking for a grant because of the expenses to which the City was put in providing civic services for federal buildings. The annual grant to the O.I.C. for "improving" Ottawa was $60,000 minus the $15,000 being paid to the city before, for water supply. Very generous, no? The Secretary of the O.I.C. did his work in his spare time. In 1927 the O.I.C. was replaced by the F.D.C. (Federal District Commission), largely owing to Mackenzie King's interest. The "District" was an area "surrounding the City of Ottawa to be known as the National Capital District", later extended over both sides of the Ottawa River, and later still enlarged and called the National Capital Region, 1958, with the setting up of the NCC.

[11] *Op. cit.*, p. 145.

[12] Although the Fullerton Report dislikes "consultation" (pp. 99-103), this is in sharp contrast with the more diplomatic and realistic remarks of Edgar Gallant cited on pp. 99-100. The National Capital Commission (NCC) has 20 members, appointed by Order-in-Council for a four-year term. The members are drawn from every province, plus two from Ottawa and one from Hull, (residents, not municipal councillors). The Executive Committee has five members and meets monthly. The Commission has several committees, a permanent staff of 600, a Chairman appointed by the federal government, and a General Manager. The NCC owns about 10% of the land in the NCR, and about 30% of the built-up area. The Commission itself is non-partisan, in the sense that it has been supported by both Liberal and Conservative governments.

His preferred proposals, after dismissing a modified status quo and a Federal Territory as the Capital, were:

A single "umbrella" government should be set up to govern the Ottawa-Hull area, i.e., the new capital, the National Capital Region.[13] This "Supra-regional Council" would be composed as follows:

federal appointees	25%
Ontario provincial appointees	12½%
Quebec provincial appointees	12½%
elected municipal representatives[14]	50%
Total	100%

In addition, "recognition" and "participation" of community groups should somehow be provided for in governing the new capital, the NCR.

The "Supra-regional Council" would number less than 25. It would have taxing and other financial powers; and other powers now exercised by (a) the existing regional governments on both sides of the River, and by (b) the local municipalities in Ontario and Quebec; plus powers (c) delegated by two provinces, and (d) others delegated by the federal government.

The most difficult question was what to do with the existing municipal structures, which were to be subordinate to the "Supra-regional Council". Several options were offered:

(1) two cities only, Ottawa and Hull, both greatly enlarged, and no regional governments;[15]
(2) the two regional governments, stripped of much power, would stay on both sides of the Ottawa River, and the territory they cover would be divided into smaller "boroughs", both urban and rural; no City of Ottawa, no City of Hull — both would be "carved up";
(3) the two regional governments would disappear, and only strong "boroughs" would remain, under the "Supra-regional Council".
(4) three cities on the Ontario side, one to three on the Quebec side, plus some rural townships on both sides.

Any of these options could be determined by "local residents, their elected representatives, and the two provinces". The important thing is the strong "Supra-regional Council".

There does not seem much point in going further with this analysis, into, for instance, the dubious contrast of urban and rural. The signs do not point in favour of the Fullerton scheme. It is possible to call for many things, but whether they will come to pass is a different

---

[13] The recommendation was that Parliament should amend S.16 of the BNA Act and declare "the Seat of government of Canada shall be the National Capital Region". (p. 213).

[14] This point gave Fullerton a lot of trouble (see his Report pp. 199-200), because of the question whether an equal or unequal number of elected councillors should come from the Ontario and Quebec parts of the NCR.

[15] This is very like one of the options set forth in W. Eggleston, *op. cit.*, p. 279. Mackenzie King at times inclined towards a Federal District. Eggleston, p. 175. A full discussion of the pros and cons of a Federal District is in Donald C. Rowat, "The Proposal For a Federal Capital Territory for Canada's Capital", *The Confederation Challenge*, Ontario, Queen's Printer, Vol. 1, 1967, pp. 215-279.

matter. Shakespeare's Owen Glendower boasted "I can call spirits from the vasty deep". But the realistic Hotspur replied:
> "Why, so can I, or so can any man;
> But will they come when you do call for them?"

Both provinces are against the major proposals, nor is there any evidence that the federal government wants to get mixed up with them. At a conference held on the Fullerton Report in December, 1975, only one person supported the "Supra-regional Council" idea.

One of the Fullerton proposals however, has been adopted, namely that for a joint committee of the Senate and the House of Commons, on the National Capital Region (to which we have referred earlier). What will come from the Special Joint Committee we do not know, nor if anything does come from it, whether the government(s) will act upon its recommendations. (There a few signs that it will recommend the NCC should be more accountable to Parliament.)

The Committee heard many witnesses, from all levels of government, and from numerous groups and individuals. The NCC came in for sharp and sustained criticisms from many sides, but especially from the municipalities, and especially from Regional government spokesmen. Two examples may suffice.

(a) Denis M. Coolican, Chairman of the RMOC, recommended
> "That the Government of Canada recognize the overall planning authority and jurisdiction of Regional and local communities in the National Capital area and that Federal programs be in accord with the objectives and policies of municipal governments in the National Capital area."

And "That the National Capital Act be amended to limit the powers of the National Capital Commission."[16]

(b) Addressing the Fullerton proposals on forms of government directly, the Outaouais Regional Community said
> ". . . the key elements of the structure he recommends are unacceptable . . . we are amazed that Mr. Fullerton can recommend such a centralized structure . . ."[17]

Without provincial and municipal support, the "umbrella" government of the Fullerton Report may thus be ruled out of court.

Who speaks for the federal government?

First, let us clear a bit of ground. So far as the Ottawa-Carleton Region is concerned, there is a freely acknowledged recognition that the federal government has a stake in the Capital and the area around it. The same sentiments are held by the public, to judge by the submissions to the Special Joint Committee. (But what this means is not agreed upon.)

Second, there is general agreement that the NCC and its predecessors have done a great deal for Ottawa and the area. What has been done, for which thanks are given, is concerned with what may be called "embellishments" or "improvements" of an aesthetic kind.

---

[16] *Submission to the Special Joint Committee of the Senate and of the House of Commons on the National Capital Region*, March 2, 1976.

[17] *Brief to the Special Joint Committee*, etc., by the Outaouais Regional Community, February 1976, pp. 46, 47.

Starting with the old O.I.C., the banks of the Rideau Canal were cleared of their clutter, driveways have been put in, landscaping done, parks established, recreational facilities promoted (including skating on the Rideau Canal), "heritage" buildings preserved, etc.

It is often difficult to separate the cosmetic from the utilitarian, as with driveways, Airport Parkway, and the like, because they serve two purposes: appearances are improved, and traffic flow assisted.

Third, the influence of the federal government generally, and of the NCC too, in promoting bilingualism in the Region is for the most part welcome. On the Quebec side the welcome given to federal expansion, say by moving Departments there, is tempered somewhat. On the one hand, the economic development is acknowledged. On the other, there is a fear that such an "invasion" of English speaking Departments may threaten the French-speaking character of West Quebec. There is of course something to this fear, and the federal government could have recognized it, and instead say of locating Environment Canada in Hull, could have substituted the Department of the Secretary of State which is more French speaking.(The fear of assimilation was strongly expressed to the Joint Committee of Parliament, and was in one instance called "cultural genocide.")

Fourth, one may say that the re-organized municipalities on both sides of the Ottawa river, and the growth of their planning capability, have had two results, and altered somewhat their relations with the NCC.

For one thing, there exists no longer the large number of municipal jurisdictions which the Fullerton Report pointed to. Regional governments have been set up in both provinces. On the Ontario side there are only eleven area municipalities, and there will be only nine if our recommendations are followed. On the Quebec side, the ORC (created in 1969) is roughly equivalent to the Ontario RMOC; and in 1974 the number of ORC municipalities was reduced from thirty-two to eight.[18]

As to planning, the Regional governments, and some of the area municipalities, have had for some years planning expertise to match that of the NCC. The City of Ottawa had the expertise even before municipal re-organization. Consequently, it is no longer true that only the NCC plans and cares for the National Capital area.

That being said, we come now to our question: who speaks for the federal government? The answer is manifold: it is the NCC, the CMHC, the Treasury Board, and many other federal voices. If the federal government wants only one spokesman, they should designate one. On this we are inclined to agree — partly at least — with the Fullerton Report (p. 217), which recommended a single spokesman. (The same kind of problem emerges in provincial-municipal relations. The municipalities, especially the smaller townships, are often dispirited in dealing with a multitude of provincial authorities.[19] It is a pity in many ways that a provincial ministry of municipal affairs is not the chief or only channel to the municipalities).

---

[18] Outaouais Regional Community, *Brief, op. cit.*, p. 29. (A diagram of the municipalities is given on p. 30 of the *Brief*.)

[19] The Township of Lanark, *Brief to the Cabinet*, Ottawa, December 11, 1974, cited (sorrowfully) the small but annoying troubles encountered in dealing with a large bureaucracy at Queen's Park: one ministry saying go ahead with certain public works, another saying stop; notices being sent to a township clerk who had been dead for eight months; and other notices sent to the wrong address, and keeping on to that address even after being notified by the Township; and ended with "those who qualify for civil service positions should at least be competent enough to copy an address from a letter to an envelope."

The problem of "living with an elephant" (the federal government), or rather with a whole zoo, is one which the RMOC and area municipalities will have to learn to endure. (This strengthens our earlier recommendation for inter-governmental expertise at the RMOC level). As far ahead as we can see, there will continue to be all kinds of relationships between the RMOC, some of the area municipalities, and the federal government — mostly at the staff level, some at the political level. It would in our judgment be a mistake for heads of municipalities to take the view that they should speak *only* to federal politicians (preferably cabinet ministers), and not to federal civil servants.

The question of conflicting Plans for the Region is perhaps the most important, if not the most pressing, of the operations that involve the RMOC and the NCC. We have mentioned this elsewhere (see Chapter 4), but the mains points of conflict may be recalled. The NCC "Concept Plan" calls for growth in the Region to the south east, and on the Quebec side roughly to the north west, all on a transportation axis crossing the centre of the built-up area of Ottawa and Hull. The land in the southeast (Carlsbad Springs area) is largely held by governments already; it is not much good for farming, but it may be more costly to build on because of the leda clay soil. There is very little technical documentation in the "Concept Plan", which is a kind of preliminary planning step.

The RMOC Official Plan, drawn up and adopted earlier, is for growth to the west (Kanata), to the south in Nepean and Gloucester, and to the east. This Plan is detailed, has had massive public input, has been approved by the RMOC, and is actually going ahead. It will probably be more economical to go with this Plan, and certainly faster, but some good agricultural land will be built on.

Is there a mechanism for resolving the conflict of Plans? There is not. A few key points may be stressed:

(1) The federal government, including NCC and CMHC, can do what it likes with land it owns. It is not subject to provincial or municipal controls.

(ii) Conversely, the NCC cannot interfere with municipal plans, that is, in any legal sense. It may advise and protest, as with its Design Committee; it can expropriate or purchase privately held land; it may refuse to allow utility lines to cross its land,[20] and doubtless in other ways it (and the CMHC) could put pressure on municipalities.

It is clear that the only possible mechanism available to settle conflicts and to undertake joint development, is some form of consultation, before and during the drawing up of Plans. Whether this is done or not done (usually the latter), the NCC takes the lofty view that it is the only planning body which can interpret the national interest in the Region and therefore should prevail over parochial municipal plans.

Quite naturally, this infuriates the municipal bodies, on both sides of the Ottawa River, who have their own plans and interests. A body like the RMOC is not speaking merely for one municipality, but for the Region as a whole in Ontario, while the ORC does the same in Quebec.

We share the view that "where there is a requirement for consultation and co-ordination on substantive policy issues, such as location of employment policy, or cost-sharing arrangements, that such discussion take place at the senior political level among the three

---

[20] Something very close indeed to this threat has been posed by an NCC spokesman. See Denis M. Coolican, *Submission to the Special Joint Committee, op. cit.*, p. 26. *The Submission* questions the NCC responsibility for *urban* planning, (p. 24). The Fullerton Report (p. 217) wants a club over the head of municipalities — no federal leasing unless the buildings are approved by the NCC.

levels of government."[21] It is obvious that the location or relocation of a federal Department sets up many repercussions; for public transit, roads, bridges, planning and so forth. For this and many similar reasons there is a need for "melding" the federal decisions with the municipal.

When planning and similar decisions are involved, the federal representative would presumably be the minister to whom the NCC reports. There is no case, we think, that the NCC should report directly to the Prime Minister. The Minister (we suggest Urban Affairs) would presumably be advised by the NCC and other agencies, and somehow would have to fight off other federal departments who at present have a finger in the pie. Otherwise the municipal political representatives would be overwhelmed by a battery of federal ministers. There is also the valid point that federal ministers have other things on their plate besides the NCR: they have a country to look after.

As the 1956 Joint Senate-Commons Committee, which recommended the change from F.D.C. to National Capital Commission (NCC) said, "We think that the realization of the National Capital Plan must imply the co-operation of Federal, Provincial and Municipal authorities."

Apart from this top level consultation, there will be much need for staff level consultation. Some of these mechanisms are already in place, the chief being the Joint Committee on Planning and Transportation. And as we have said earlier, once the main frictions are smoothed out, there is no reason (except perhaps vanity) why municipalities could not talk to federal officials (staff).

Who speaks for the municipalities?

So far as Ottawa-Carleton is concerned, we have, at various places in this Report, recommended a strengthening of the RMOC. As to Ottawa itself, our recommendations would temporarily make the Capital City slightly less populous. But there is every prospect that Ottawa will, before long, grow to its former population of about 300,000. It will also, if the forecasts are at all reliable, be surrounded by larger municipalities than at present, especially the cities of Nepean, Gloucester, Vanier and (in time) Kanata. Ottawa will thus be *relatively* smaller, so that its representatives on the RMOC will no longer be half of Regional Council. The consequences of this are not alarming, nor need it be regarded as "down-grading" the City of Ottawa.

We ask, then, who, at the municipal level, should talk to and negotiate with the federal government?

The *first* point to take up is that with respect to finance, i.e., federal grants-in-lieu of taxes. On this, the federal government has little alternative to putting the negotiations into the hands of the Department of Finance. It would be almost ridiculous to delegate this power to the NCC. The Department of Finance has to bear in mind that what is given in this Region has consequences for the whole country. The NCC, by contrast, is limited only to the NCR. It follows from our earlier recommendations of "pooling" these grants, that the RMOC is the appropriate body to negotiate with the Department of Finance. The City of Ottawa may feel, because of its status as the Capital, that it is not dignified enough, to approach the federal government through the intermediary of the RMOC, especially since Ottawa receives (and will receive, after "pooling") the largest share of grants-in-lieu. If feelings run high on these

---

[21] Denis M. Coolican, *op. cit.*, p. 28.

matters, Ottawa may join the RMOC to negotiate with the federal government, whenever Ottawa alone is directly affected.

A corollary of this is the negotiation with the provincial government on grants-in-lieu. Here we think the RMOC alone is the appropriate body. The Capital question does not arise, since Ottawa is not the capital of Ontario.[22]

The *second* point concerns the many other functions — among them housing, major roads, bridges, public transit — which affect both the Regional Council and the area municipalities. On this we see no alternative to concentrating most of the negotiations into an RMOC-federal-provincial (i.e., tri-partite) negotiating body or bodies, some as Standing Committees, some *ad hoc*. These functions relate to planning matters, on which, since the RMOC is responsible for overall planning of the Region, we have already recommended it as the appropriate body to negotiate with the federal government.

It is not a valid argument to say that because of the area municipalities are affected, they also should each negotiate when any given municipality is mainly affected. The RMOC exists to look after the Region, *and that includes every municipality within it*. (The comparison is with, say, the Provincial legislature whose members have the double duty of caring for the whole Province and for each riding within it. But the Province does not negotiate with each riding.)

We come now to the relations of Ottawa-Carleton and the municipalities on the Quebec shore. The situation has been greatly simplified since the setting up of the RMOC and the ORC. The number of area municipalities in the Ontario Region is now eleven, with the RMOC over them all to look after common or Region-wide matters. If our recommendations are followed, there will be a further reduction to nine. (See Chapter 8).

On the Quebec side there has been an even greater reduction. Instead of 32 municipalities, when the ORC was set up in December 1969, there are now eight. In addition, there is the Outaouais Development Corporation (OCD), for economic development; and the Outaouais Regional Community Transit Commission (ORCTC), for public transit.

The RMOC is thus not like the ORC in every respect. The latter has fewer functions, but it has a few that the RMOC does not have, viz., assessment, the billing and sending of tax accounts, and construction standards. It also has permissive powers, e.g., to co-ordinate police and fire protection. Nevertheless, the two Regional governments are sufficiently alike so that we can say, on matters of concern to both, it is the upper tier, the RMOC and the ORC, that should be the chief bodies to talk and negotiate with each other. This has already been done for one function — public transit — so that there is "an integrated public transit system connecting the suburbs to the downtown areas of Hull and Ottawa."

Further detail on this matter is perhaps unnecessary, and can be left to the RMOC and the ORC to work out together. Although Ottawa-Hull may be an "entity" in some respects (for instance, in commuting and federal employment), in other important ways the two sides of the NCR are different. As the ORC pointed out,

---

[22] At the municipal level there is already a mechanism in place for Ontario, the Municipal Liaison Committee (MLC). When this body sits with the provincial Treasurer (and other ministers) it is known as the Provincial-Municipal Liaison Committee (PMLC). Both seem to be very useful instrumentalities. The municipalities may not always get their way (and perhaps should not), but at least they can present their views, obtain the provincial response, and find out what the provincial ministries propose.

". . . the Quebec and Ontario sectors of the Ottawa-Hull area have very different basic characteristics. We consider these characteristics as basic because they deal with the most intimate aspects of individual and social life: property, the matrimonial system, family life, health and security, language, culture and education, local and political life, religious institutions and community associations."[23]

The Capital as Microcosm and/or Symbol

(a) There has been much loose talk, not to say nonsense, on the subject of the capital (or, sometimes, the NCR) being a microcosm, or small scale replica of Canada as a whole. The NCC and voluntary organizations have both indulged in rhetoric on this point, but there has been little analysis of the basic concept.

In what way is the Capital (or NCR) a "microcosm"? Maybe it reflects the ethnic composition of Canada? Not so. The Canadian population is roughly 45% of British Isles descent, 29% French and 27% "other". Ottawa-Carleton is about 56%, 25%, and 19% respectively. If the Quebec side is taken into account (i.e., taking the NCR), the proportions are about 45%, 40% and 15%. Whatever figures we take, the non-British, not-French parts of the Canadian population are much under-represented.

Well, then, perhaps the composition of the "Capital" reflects the five "regions" of Canada — Atlantic, Quebec, Ontario, Prairies, B.C.? But this is too absurd. The population of the Capital is not made up in this way.

These two measures, ethnic and regional composition, have been the chief reasons for saying the Capital is a "microcosm" of the Canadian mosaic. Since these collapse at the first touch of analysis, it is not worth time or effort to pursue any of the lesser will-o-the-wisps. (One could perhaps say the Capital area reflects the ratio of the two sexes in Canada. But this would be equally true of any city — though not of the Yukon or Northwest Territories.)

What then remains? One thing only, and that a very important one namely, that the RMOC (or the NCR) reflects (or should reflect) the two official languages, English and French. Put another way: both English and French-speaking should feel at home in a milieu which serves them both in their own language, and which is increasingly bilingual. This is federal policy, and we endorse it so far as the RMOC is concerned. That is why we have gone to some lengths in Chapter 10 (Education) and Chapter 11 (Languages) to make many recommendations on the use of French and English.

(b) The argument that the Capital should be a symbol for all Canadians is one of a quite different order from that of "microcosm".

Here the arguments are rather like this: Canada is very provincial or regional in outlook, it is a wide and difficult country to govern and, to overcome the centrifugal forces, symbols of nationhood should be found to bind the country together. Well, maybe. This makes sense if it means the federal purse in helping to make the Capital and the NCR good-looking places; in helping the Quebec and Ontario parts of the NCR to forge closer links; and in helping to further the use of the two official languages.

As to the other new symbols, we are dubious. There are a great many nasty little nation-states in the world today, whose nastiness is limited only by their lack of power. It is a

---

[23] *Brief to the Special Joint Committee, op. cit.*, p. 13. The ORC also says (*op. cit.*, pp. 26-27) that when the FDC was created in 1927, it was largely because of the efforts of Father Arthur Guertin, Oblate and curé of Notre-Dame (Hull) from 1910 to 1916, that "the idea of a federal district was discarded."

great mistake to believe that only great powers are bad, and only little states good. To believe that small or medium size states are somehow more virtuous is rather like Marx's idealization of the proletariat, because they were poor and "oppressed". The "workers" are no better or worse than other people. They want the same things, especially money and material comforts and luxuries.

Canada should not, we feel, get very excited by national symbols — especially if they have to be deliberately invented, like the Pearson flag. All this concern for symbolic unity, for pan-Canadian nationalism, for national identity, etc., seems to us an unhealthy state of affairs. The Americans do it all the time, as they seek national purposes, goals, etc. It is all very like a hypochondriac worrying about his health. Normal people do not go around examining themselves for symptoms of disease, and buying all the nostrums in the drugstores.

In the same way, everybody knows that Parliament, the Peace Tower, the two languages, etc., are in the Capital. We are bound together by a unique system of Parliamentary and federal government. Symbols of the federal government are in every town in the country — the post office, the flag — and so are direct benefits such as family allowances and old age pensions and federally-aided plans such as medicare.

Federal-provincial relations have been going on since 1867, and though somewhat abstract to the ordinary citizen on the street, they are — like disputes about "bringing home the Constitution" — about the most binding and typical of all Canadian ties. So are such ties as Air Canada, the railways, the CBC, the Canada Council, the Grey Cup, the Dionne Quintuplets, and perhaps former Mayors Charlotte Whitton and Camilien Houde.

It is a great relief to live in a country where patriotism is low key, where we haven't even a common version of a national anthem.[24]

The Regional Municipality

The Fullerton Report (pp. 186-7) made a good deal of a public opinion survey which it commissioned and which purported to find that the people thought the area was over-governed," favoured a federal role in governing "the Capital", regarded the profile of the Ontario government as low, etc. In short, it concluded, the people were ahead of the local politicians (especially on the Quebec side).

Well, all this may be so. It may even be true that the Regional governments, being new, do not as yet stand out constantly in the public mind as much as the local municipalities. The same is said of the Regional or Metropolitan governments in Quebec:

> "When we look at the existing metropolitan governments, we find that they have not, so far, been very highly regarded either by the public in general or by the local municipalities concerned. And they have not succeeded in generating strong feelings of loyalty to our three main metropolitan areas.
>
> *On the one hand*, the public sees in them an extra level of bureaucracy, more remote than the lower tier municipalities, and over

---

[24] There is something more to be said for the federal desire to make Ottawa, and perhaps the NCR, "models" of urbanity for the country. The only trouble with this is, that one can hardly envisage other cities or metropolitan areas in the country having so much money lavished on them, as the federal government spends in this Region.

which they have no direct control. These metropolitan councils are composed of representatives from the local councils, and as such as not directly elected by the citizens.

On the other hand, the local municipalities within the metropolitan boundaries are of varying sizes, and the suburban ones, being dominated by the central cities, are naturally on the defensive and more concerned with their own affairs than with the destiny of the whole metropolitan area. This obviously gives rise to considerable friction between the lower and upper tiers . . ."[25]

All this is true of the RMOC, yet it is becoming increasingly untrue as people get used to the RMOC and see and understand the services which it performs. We must remember that the level of interest in, and knowledge about, politics and government is not high in the population at large. And it is lowest of all with respect to the municipal level. We should not blame anyone for this state of affairs. Almost nothing can change the fact that there are lots more interesting things in life than politics, especially local politics.

The Regional Municipality of Ottawa-Carleton and the area municipalities too are, so to speak, in bed with the federal elephant. The federal pressure is visible or tangible everywhere: in Parliament, in the buildings of the many Departments, in employment, in the works of the NCC, and much, much more. It is no wonder that local residents think of the federal presence as "governing" them. But they are mistaken in this belief.

This Region, like others in the Province, is governed by two municipalities — the local and the Regional, with the usual division of powers between them. Apart from that, the Region is like, say, Sudbury or Niagara: the people in the Region are all subject to Queen's Park and the federal Parliament, but so is everyone else in Ontario. The only difference is the planning function of the NCC. But the NCC does not govern, in any normal usage of the word "govern".

The Canadian citizens who live in Ontario and in this Region are an ingenious people, and readily adapt to technological change. It is hard to believe that they and their political leaders cannot adapt also to the recent reforms in municipal government. After all, our problems are those of affluence, not those of poverty as in the 1930's. Surely we can bear prosperity and its changes, better than we bore the hard times of adversity.

Finally, we end with the words of the poet George Johnston:

"Ottawattawattawa
Mother of our country's law, . . .
The ship of state is navigated here:
Canada is afloat as I am afloat
On her capital city's waters,
And where is she going? She is going round and round
Like the United States, but further north."[26]

---

[25] *Rapport du groupe de travail sur l'urbanisation au Québec*, présidé par M. Claude Castonguay, Editeur officiel du Québec, 1976, p. 141. (Free translation).

[26] From the poem "Bicultural" in *Happy Enough*, Oxford University Press, Toronto, 1972, pp. 62-63. Quoted with kind permission of the author and of Oxford University Press, Toronto.

CHAPTER 18

Summary of Recommendations and Suggestions

Chapter 4.   Planning

We recommend:
1. That the development approval process be simplified and shortened, and that more aspects of development approval be delegated from the Province to the RMOC.
2. That the RMOC be given the power to engage in land-banking for various purposes, especially housing; that a certain proportion of building lots be sold at market value, and a portion retained in Regional ownership for rental purposes; that profits from the sale of market-value lots be used to finance further purchases to replenish the land bank; that the land bank scheme be administered by the Regional Housing Department.
3. That a citizen's advisory committee on Regional Planning be established to assist the Planning Committee of Regional Council and the Regional Planning Department in developing planning policies.
4. We suggest that the NCC reconsider Greenbelt policies; we suggest that the land take the form of wedges or corridors instead of a "belt". (By selling some of the existing Greenbelt holdings the NCC could finance the purchase of extensions to the corridors or wedges.)

Chapter 5.   Roads and Transport

1. We endorse the policy of the Regional Plan which calls for decentralization of jobs from the core area to "employment centres", in densities sufficient to make public transit more financially feasible, and to relieve downtown traffic congestion.
We recommend:
2. That control of transport policy be centralized in the RMOC, to plan and co-ordinate the inter-related elements of the Regional tranport system — roads, traffic, public transit, parking.
3. That an Advisory Committee to the Regional Standing Committee for Transport be established.
4. That transport policy continue to emphasize public transit. To the federal government we suggest that staggered working hours be continued and expanded, and that free downtown parking for federal civil servants be phased out. To the Region we recommend that the express bus-lane policy be further emphasized, and that a system of separate rights-of-way for buses be actively pursued.
5. That OC Transpo be eliminated as a special purpose body; that staff and functions be transferred to the RegionalTransport Department, headed by theTransport Commissioner, answerable to the Transport Standing Committee of Regional Council.
6. That responsibility for licencing taxis be given to the RMOC, and that the Region assist in establishing a central dispatching system for the entire area; and furthermore, that regulations permit taxis to "cruise" and be flagged down by pedestrians.

7. That the RMOC endeavour to set up an inter-urban transport committee with representatives from the RMOC, federal government and private industry, in order to plan with these bodies any future extensions of inter-urban transport facilities that affect the RMOC traffic flow.

Chapter 6.   Housing

We recommend:
1. That a Regional Housing Department be established, headed by a commissioner responsible to Regional Coucil, and assisted by a citizens' advisory committee and a standing committee.
2. That the Regional Housing Department take over responsibility for all public housing projects in the Region, i.e., those which are now handled by the Ottawa Housing Authority and by the City of Ottawa Housing Company Ltd., and by the Ontario Housing Corporation in other area municipalities. (We disagree with the Paterson recommendation that these duties be handled by an "independent" Regional Housing Authority. That is, we agree that public housing should be a Regional function, but not with the argument that it be administered by a special purpose body. Municipalities are governed, not managed. Public housing decisions are essentially political, not technical, and politics in a democracy should be out in the open, not driven underground for *apparatchiki* to deal with.)
3. That where a local board of directors is set up by the Housing Department to administer a particular public housing project, at least two members of the board be tenants; and tenants or prospective tenants take part in the planning stages of such projects.
4. That the Regional Housing Department administer the assisted housing programmes of senior governments, such as rent supplement schemes (where the landlord is a private person, or a company).
5. That the Housing Department maintain an information office to which all area municipalities, co-operative groups, and individuals may obtain information on all housing programmes.
6. That for all triune housing programmes — federal-provincial-municipal — the RMOC be the negotiating and administering level of municipal government rather than the area municipalities; that the same apply to such programmes as the Ontario Housing Action Programme (O.H.A.P.), and other provincial programmes.
7. That Regional Council be vested with powers to determine
    (a) the location, distribution and standards of public housing;
    (b) the location, distribution and standards of mobile home parks;
    (c) the housing density and "mix" in all subdivisions. (We are not saying that all subdivisions should have exactly the same "mix".)
    (d) that no area municipality be permitted to veto (a), (b), (c), whether by zoning or other means.
8. That in order to reduce the initial cost of housing, municipal lot charges be abolished and developers be required to provide fewer services; that the municipality recover its developments costs by local improvement taxes. (This is a recommendation to the area municipalities; and to the RMOC for lots sold from a "land bank".)

9. That the Regional Official Plan shift its goal from the present proportion of detached and semi-detached dwellings towards a larger proportion of multiple-family structures — row houses and apartments — including those for rental; and that lower construction standards be required.
10. That the Regional Council promote a much larger public housing supply with rent-to-income, low-income supplement, and other forms.
11. That the RMOC actively promote more co-operative housing projects, and non-profit housing.
12. That the Rent Scale for public housing tenants (rent-to-income) be revised by the Ministry of Housing, made more flexible (to enable tenants to save and buy homes), and that rent not exceed 25% of income whether for working families or those on welfare.
13. That the provincial Home Ownership Made Easy (H.O.M.E.) plan be revised, so that free, quick capital gains for the lucky owners of building lots be avoided.
14. That the RMOC exercise the power to control, and even forbid, conversion of rental housing to condominiums.
15. That housing for the elderly not be in high-rise buildings, but in low and medium rise buildings; conveniently located to shopping and other facilities; and be spread more throughout the suburbs, and the hamlets of the outer municipalities.
16. That a separate residence (public housing) be provided for elderly alcoholics; and in general both municipal and voluntary social services to the elderly be expanded (e.g., Meals on Wheels).

Chapter 7.   Municipal Finance

We recommend:
1. That all commercial/industrial assessment be "pooled" in the RMOC, and then apportioned to the area municipalities on the basis of population.
2. We strongly suggest that all assessments of federal properties be also "pooled" in the RMOC, and allocated to the area municipalities on the basis of population.
3. That provincial payments-in-lieu go to the RMOC, and thence to the area municipalities, in proportion to population. We strongly suggest that the federal government and its agencies follow the same practice. (The advantages are that both senior levels of government would then deal with payments-in-lieu through only one municipality, the RMOC, instead of with many). Further, none of the provincial payments-in-lieu should be "earmarked" (as some are now, e.g., for school boards and Regional Government).
4. That resource equalization grants then be re-calculated by the Province, allocated to the RMOC and used by the RMOC to reduce the Regional levy upon appropriate area municipalities.
5. That school boards not be given the authority to levy taxes and issue their own tax bills, but that the present system be retained by which municipalities collect school taxes and pay the revenue collected to the school boards. (It is rumoured that municipalities may, in the near future, be permitted to send out two tax notices, one for municipal and one for school purposes. We do not endorse such a scheme.)

6. That all municipalities use at least quarterly tax billings (most do so now), in order to avoid temporary borrowing and cash flow problems.
7. (a) That all (repeat all) property tax exemptions be gradually abolished (say over five years) whether for private or public property; whether these properties are provincial, municipal, school board, special purpose bodies, charities, churches, cemeteries, etc.
(b) That *classes* of presently exempt properties be shown separately on municipal finance statements.
(c) That in some cases the municipalities or Province make countervailing grants equal to the property tax on behalf of certain properties.
8. We strongly suggest that the federal government make full payments-in-lieu of taxes (without "service deductions") on all its properties and on those of its numerous agencies; and that full business tax also be paid on all buildings. (The province proposes to pay business tax on all its administrative facilities, a proposal which we endorse).
9. That no new tax source be given to municipalities (especially not sales tax and income tax), and that the Province not allocate any "ear-marked" provincial tax revenues to municipalities.
10. That the Province try to simplify its conditional grant system (now so complicated), and that wherever possible (i.e., where provincial standards and equity are not involved) more of the grants be made unconditional.
11. That assessment remain at the Provincial level and not be returned to the municipalities.
12. That a uniform business tax be levied, as proposed by the Province, to replace the present variable rates.
13. That for several of the above recommendations, the Provincial-Municipal Liaison Committee be used as a forum for discussion, insofar as the recommendations have general application beyond the confines of this Region.

Chapter 8. Municipal Boundaries

We recommend:
1. That the temptation of a simple one-tier system for the whole Region be resisted, and that the two-tier system be retained, with some change in boundaries.
2. That the external RMOC boundaries be altered as follows:
    (a) to include Russell Township to the south-east (from the United Counties of Prescott and Russell).
    (b) by the severing from the Region of a small portion of Fitzroy Ward from West Carleton Township, at the Mississippi River; and that the severed portion be included in either Lanark or Renfrew County.
3. That the internal boundaries be changed as follows:
    (a) the proposed "western city", now in parts of March, Goulbourn and Nepean Townships, be separated from these townships as soon as possible; that it become a town, and in the near future a city, with boundaries as suggested in the text and in Figure 8-1, under the name Kanata.
    (b) that the small remainder of March Township be absorbed into West Carleton.
    (c) that the remainder of Goulbourn Township be amalgamated with Rideau, to make a new township of Rideau-Goulbourn, perhaps under a new name or simply that of Rideau.

(d) that the boundary between Ottawa and Nepean be straightened, so that it runs along Baseline Road to the Rideau Canal, thus transferring to Nepean that area (roughly) known as Carleton Heights.

(e) that Nepean Township be at once raised to City status.

(f) that the Gloucester-Cumberland boundary be altered, to put the area of the proposed "eastern satellite city" (now containing the sub-divisions of Queenswood Village and Queenswood Heights) entirely within Gloucester Township, as shown in Figure 8-2.

(g) that the Township of Gloucester be at once raised to City status.

(h) that the remainder of Cumberland Township be amalgamated with Russell Township to form a new township, to be known as Cumberland-Russell (or perhaps as Foubert).

(i) that the City of Vanier be extended to Blair Road on the east, to the Queensway on the south and the Rideau River (approximately) on the west; that Vanier include the present Village of Rockcliffe Park; that the north-west boundary of Vanier follow Dufferin Road from the Rideau River, to Rideau Terrace, to Princess Avenue, thence to the Ottawa River. Rideau Hall, the Prime Minister's residence and the Ottawa City Hall would remain in the City of Ottawa. (See Figure 8-2.)

(j) that (perhaps) the Windsor Park sub-division be absorbed into Ottawa, and also (perhaps) that the boundary between Ottawa and Gloucester be changed so that all of the Uplands Airport be included in the City of Ottawa.

Notes: (i) We reject the following suggestions: *one*, that the whole Region be sub-divided into equal small units of about 8,000 people, or into larger equal units of 40,000 or so; and *two*, the Fullerton Report proposals for an "umbrella" government over the whole National Capital Region.

(ii) The area municipalities will thus be reduced in number from eleven to nine.

Chapter 9.   Elections and Sundry Matters

We recommend:
1. That from every area municipality there should be at least one member on Regional Council.
2. That representation on Regional Council be reviewed every three or six years, to adjust population to representation.
3. That, in the first instance, Regional Council consist of about 34 members, as outlined in Table 9-1.
4. That Regional Councillors be directly elected, to replace the present system of indirect election.
5. That election be on a ward basis (or groupings of two or more wards if necessary) following lower tier boundary lines; and that wards not cross municipal boundary lines.
6. That the Chairman of the RMOC be elected from and by Regional Council, at the first meeting of the new Council after the municipal elections.
7. That the Chairman have a double vote, one as Councillor, one to break a tie.
8. That the Chairman should have the power to select and dismiss the Deputy Chairman; the Deputy Chairman to have the same term of office as the Chairman, unless he is dismissed.
9. That the Executive Committee (seven to nine members) be chosen by Council, as now.

10. That the Chairman have the power to call special meetings of the Executive and the Council; that a majority of the Executive (without the Chairman), and a majority of Council (without the Chairman) have the same power.
11. That the Executive Committee control the agenda and order of business of Regional Council.
12. That Executive members act as chairmen of Standing Committees. (See Table 9-2.)
13. That the Executive have the power to appoint and dismiss Department heads; that other senior officials be appointed by Department heads (in conjunction with the Personnel Director), subject to ratification by the Executive.
14. That the Executive prepare and present the budget, with the Finance Commissioner; and call for tenders and award contracts.
15. That the Chairman and Executive be full-time, at salaries ratified by Council, and that councillors' salaries be set by Council.
16. That the Standing Committee for each Department report to the Executive and thence to the Council.
17. That every effort be made to recruit bilingual officials, including Department heads (Commissioners), and to train existing officials in the other official language.
18. That for every Standing Committee and Department there be an Advisory Committee, patterned after the Social Services Advisory Committee representing a cross-section of interests, "experts", consumers, and the public; that Department heads (or their nominees) meet periodically with Advisory Committees.
19. That the smaller area municipalities have Councils with no fewer than seven to nine councillors; that within this lower limit the municipality set the size of its own Council.
20. That all councillors be elected on a ward basis; that all "at large" elections be eliminated (except where a comparatively small municipality elects only one Regional Councillor); and that the delineation of wards be left to each area Council, subject to roughly equal population in each ward.
21. That the head (Mayor) of every area council be elected by the members of council, instead of being elected at large.
22. That the municipalities (Regional and other) be required to regulate campaign funds, along the lines of the present provincial and federal legislation, with some public subsidy, spending limits and disclosure of donations and donors.
23. That the position of deputy reeve (where it exists) be abolished, and that the Mayor designate the Deputy-Mayor.
24. That the committee structure of area councils follow, as much as feasible (depending on function and size),the system outlined for Regional Council, but in all cases there should be
(a) an Executive Committee of from two to five councillors plus the Mayor (the number depending on the size of Council and the number of departments, if any).
(b) Standing committees and citizen advisory committees, the number depending on Council's functions.
25. That the Ottawa Board of Control be eliminated, and its place taken by the proposed Executive Committee; and the requirement of a $2/3$ majority to overturn Board of Control (Executive) recommendations be abolished, and replaced by a simple majority.
26. That the term of office for all Councillors, including the Regional Chairman and mayors, be three years.

27. That all municipal elections take place on the same date; that this date be moved backward, say, to the second Monday in November; and that the new Council take office on the first of December, but that the calendar financial year be retained.
28. That requests for separate enumeration by municipalities be rejected, and that enumeration be done as now by the provincial assessment offices.
29. That the requirements for holding of a referendum on money by-laws be struck from the legislation; and hence too the requirement to advertise for permission to dispense with a vote of the electors; but nevertheless that public notification be retained as it is for zoning by-laws, OMB hearings, etc.
30. That the position of Mayor of at least the larger area Councils — Ottawa, Vanier, Nepean, Gloucester — be full-time, and paid accordingly. (Some of these Mayors are already full-time.) That the Executive members also be full-time, if the councils so decide.
31. That remuneration of heads of Councils and Councillors be reviewed and set anew; and that provision be made for annual increments, while inflation lasts.
32. That conflict of interest legislation for Councillors, School trustees, et al., be strengthened by
    (a) registration and disclosure of interests and holdings with the clerk of council;
    (b) investigation of alleged cases of conflict of interest by TEIGA upon its own initiative, or upon request of any Councillor, or upon the petition of, say, 200 eligible voters from the appropriate ward;
    (c) penalties for proven cases be fines and/or jail sentences, plus removal from office and disqualification for a minimum of three terms.
33. That the RMOC appoint a senior inter-governmental relations official, say in the Department of Finance.
34. That the RMOC Personnel Office develop expertise in labour relations, and that it be put to use for the RMOC and for area councils which may request it.

Chapter 10.   Education

We recommend:
1. That provincial aid, in the form of grants and subsidies, be available for separate secondary schools to the end of high school.
2. That the "pools" of assessment for, (a) commercial/industrial assessment, and for, (b) exempt assessment on which payments-in-lieu are made, be held by the RMOC and distributed to the area municipalities according to their population.
3. That area municipalities levy upon the re-allocated assessment, for schools as well as municipal purposes.
4. That the federal and other payments-in-lieu be distributed by the RMOC to the area municipalities on the basis of population, and used for school as well as municipal purposes.
5. That all schools, whether separate, other denominational, French-language, or "alternate", be treated (financially) the same as the public schools, with the exception of "independent" schools which are fully supported by fees, etc.
6. That the other denominational and "alternate" schools be subject to inspection by inspectors from the public school system; and for other purposes also, these schools come under the public school boards.

7. That a Regional school board be established with powers similar to, but not identical with, those of the Metropolitan Toronto School Board. Among its powers should be:
   (i) Long range planning, and siting of all schools.
   (ii) Transportation of students, i.e., co-ordination of school bus routes and negotiation with O.C. Transpo.
   (iii) Salary negotiations for all school board employees (and, in time, setting up a single payroll office).
   (iv) Approval of all school board budgets, both capital and current; and co-ordination of programmes where necessary.
   (v) Where borrowing on the open market is done, the RMOC should approve the Regional board capital budget, and take on the actual borrowing and debt management.
   (vi) The Regional school board to operate, and in some cases co-ordinate, special programmes such as those for the retarded, the deaf, the handicapped, etc.
   (vii) Provide special services to other boards, such as insurances, standardized forms and accounting methods, centralized purchasing and computer services.
8. That a school board for the French-speaking be set up, for the whole Region, taking children from kindergarten to the end of high school; in the first instance, the board to be denominational; but later at the Board's discretion a public sector be set up.
9. That an English-speaking separate school board be established for the whole Region.
10. That there be two public school boards in the Region, one for the west, one for the east; that the boundary follow the Rideau River and Canal north to Baseline and Fisher Avenue, thence along Fisher and north on Island Park Drive to the Ottawa River; thus giving about the same number of students for each public school board.
11. That all the lower boards have about ten members, with wards and other electoral units as outlined in Chapter 10; and that board members be elected.
12. That the Regional Board members (some 12 in number) also be directly elected, together with one member ex officio, designated by each of the lower tier boards for liaison purposes.
13. That the chairman of every board be chosen from the board, at the first meeting of the new board following the elections; and that the term of office of all members (and the chairman) be for three years (the same as recommended for municipal councillors in Chapter 9).
14. That elections and the assumption of office be at the same time as for municipal councillors, and the calendar financial year be retained.
15. That more teaching material, including TV programmes, be produced in French for the French language schools.
16. That a special programme for training in religious instruction, for teachers, be set up, probably at the University of Ottawa.
17. That the immersion programmes (of various kinds) in French be continued and made permanent in the English speaking schools; and that all schools give at least one hour a day in the second official language.
18. That the Regional Board be officially bilingual, and that other boards offer services in both languages; and — with the Province — take advantage of all federal aid for second language teaching.
19. That Ontario and Quebec pursue actively such programmes as annual teacher exchanges between the two provinces; that the "monitor" programme in the schools be extended and made more flexible.
20. That school boards be required to submit all complaints about second language teaching

and services to the Council on Bilingualism (outlined in Chapter 11).
21. That a permanent federal-provincial committee be set up (with school board representation) with the aim of making all high school graduates in the Region bilingual.

Chapter 11.   Language of Services

We recommend:
1. That the RMOC should have a senior official responsible for bilingualism policy and translation, say in the Personnel Office, and to receive complaints about language services.
2. That each of the area municipalities have a staff person responsible for bilingual services, able to deal with the public in the two official languages.
3. That the local offices of the Province have a bilingual capacity.
4. That private organizations dealing with the English-speaking and French-speaking public offer services in both official languages.
5. That a Council for Bilingualism be established in the Region,
    (a) composed, say, of a member from each of the following: one from the RMOC, one from each of the area municipalities, one from citizens' associations (say, the Social Planning Council), one from the Province;
    (b) financed equally by the RMOC, the Government of Ontario, and the federal government;
    (c) receiving complaints about language services, investigating them and publishing the results;
    (d) issuing an annual report;
    (e) having a small staff to conduct studies and inquiries into the language services offered in the Region by provincial departments and agencies, municipalities, and voluntary organizations, and publishing reports thereon.

Chapter 12.   Parks, Recreation and Libraries

We recommend:
1. That the Central Canada Exhibition Association be eliminated as a special purpose body and that its functions be transferred to a municipal department, either of the City or of the Region (see #4 below).
2. That, as land becomes vacant in central areas of Ottawa, a certain amount not be built on but be retained as open space for playgrounds and urban parks.
3. That the school boards and municipalities enter into more joint agreements for mutual use of recreational facilities.
4. That an evaluation be made by the RMOC of the extent to which major parks and recreational facilities are used on a region-wide basis. On the basis of this evaluation, (a) appropriate parks and facilities (present and future) be designated Regional and transferred from the area municipalities to the jurisdiction of the RMOC; (b) where such projects are now joint ventures between the NCC and an area municipality, they become joint ventures between NCC and the RMOC.
5. That the RMOC rôle in recreation planning be expanded, to involve: the setting of park

standards; guiding the location of park lands and recreational facilities throughout the Region — especially for waterfront park land along the two rivers; co-operating with the NCC in the planning of open space networks (corridors, wedges, etc.).
6. That the RMOC open up the municipal road allowances to the Ottawa and Rideau Rivers.
7. That libraries remain as a lower-tier function; that library boards be eliminated and their functions be taken over by the appropriate standing committees of the area councils; that the public be brought in by establishing library advisory committees.
8. That the smaller libraries particularly increase their French-language collections.

Chapter 13.   Social Services

We recommend:
1. That, where possible, the assistance programmes of the RMOC, the Province and private organizations in this Region be co-ordinated to avoid duplication of forms and effort, and to render more convenient services; and that the RMOC Social Services Department take the lead in trying to achieve such co-ordination.
2. That the Low Income Supplement Experiment (L.I.S.E.) be continued and improved, say, by raising the maximum awards and lowering the deductions.
3. That Day Care (including Family Day Care) become an RMOC responsibility, and area municipalities not be allowed to "opt out", (we are not saying that all Day Care Centres be Regionally-run); and that Day Care services be expanded for the French-speaking population.
4. That the RMOC develop a Region-wide system of home support services (including nurses' and homemakers' services), with no "charging back".
5. That the RMOC set up "home help" services, less expensive than the V.H.A. and V.O.N.
6. That the Children's Aid Society be abolished and its functions and staff be transferred to the Child Welfare Branch of the RMOC Social Services Department.
7. That in housing for the elderly, there be provided more "home help". We endorse the call of Council on Aging for more study of geriatrics and preventive medicine for the elderly.
8. That the sundry home services involved in the Outreach programmes be continued and expanded.
9. That the RMOC continue to fund, on a permanent basis, the Community Information Centre and its bilingual services.
10. That the "Multi-Service" Centres be further encouraged by the RMOC, the Ministry of Health and others, to increase in number and in the range of services offered as an "alternate delivery system" for health care and social services; that they be co-ordinated by the RMOC Social Services Department; and that they expand their bilingual capacity. (This recommendation should be read in conjunction with No. 1 above.)
11. That the Central Volunteer Bureau (bringing volunteers and social agencies together) be partially funded by the RMOC; and extend its work more to the French-speaking.

Chapter 14. Health Services

1. That the municipal representatives on the District Health Council be appointed by the RMOC, instead of by the Province.
2. That after further experience, say a year or two, the District Health Council report through the RMOC rather than directly to the Ministry of Health; and later become an RMOC responsibility, as in the Regional Municipality of Waterloo.
3. That the Public Health Unit become a Department of Health in the RMOC, headed by a Commissioner of Public Health; answerable to a Standing Committee on Health and Social Services, with an Advisory Committee; the functions of the Department and its personnel be those of the present Public Health Unit.
4. That the Public Health Department be taken within the purview of the District Health Council, i.e., that the Council Plan for the co-ordination of the Health Unit with other elements of the Health Care Delivery system.
5. That the District Health Council promote the less costly health programmes such as Home Care, visiting nurses, Visiting Homemakers, VON, etc.; and the "multi-service centres", as mentioned in Chapter 13.

Chapter 15. Police and Fire Services

Police

We recommend:
1. That the municipal forces in the RMOC be amalgamated into a Regional Police Force which would also extend its jurisdiction to those outer municipalities now policed free by the Ontario Provincial Police (OPP).
2. That the Regional Force be a department of the RMOC under a police chief, answerable to a standing committee of Regional Council (the Watch Committee) with an advisory citizens' committee; and that there be no Board of Police Commissioners.
3. That grievances by the public against police treatment should not be handled internally by the police, but by the Advisory Committee, thence to the Watch Committee, and to any appeal tribunal the Province may set up.
4. That greater efforts be made to recruit and train bilingual policemen (policewomen).
5. That more women be recruited into the Police Force.
6. That post-secondary training for police be encouraged and financially supported.
7. That *either*, (a) the Ontario Police Commission (OPC) have the power to approve the appointment of a police chief suggested by the Municipality, *or* (b) that the OPC provide a list of approved candidates from which the Municipality can select a chief.
8. That the police be relieved of more of their "non-police" duties involving by-law enforcement (e.g., Green Hornets for parking tickets).
9. That the supervisory rôle of the OPC over the standards and duties of municipal police forces be strengthened.

Fire Protection

We recommend:
1. That greater emphasis be placed on fire protection, by (a) inspecting at least every two years all commercial and industrial properties not now inspected; (b) inspecting annually all rental housing where this is not now done; (c) having the fire department approve all building plans (except for detached dwellings).
2. That fire services remain the responsibility of the area municipalities.

Chapter 16. Environmental Services

We recommend:
1. That the initial purchase price of housing be reduced by transferring development costs such as utility lines to the municipality to be paid for by local improvement taxes.
2. That the RMOC take over all remaining local sewerage functions to complete its control over the entire sewerage system.
3. We endorse Task Force Hydro and the Hogg Report and recommend that there be one retail electricity utility for the entire Region, merging the four existing utilities in Ottawa, Nepean, Gloucester and Richmond, and taking over responsibility for the outlying areas now served directly by Ontario Hydro.
4. That the electrical utility be part of the RMOC Works Department (and not a separate hydro commission), accountable to Regional Council through the Works Committee.
5. That there not be a garbage "equalization fund" to redistribute garbage hauling costs among area municipalities.
6. That the present division of responsibility for garbage continue, i.e., Regional disposal and management, local collection.
7. That provincial clean indoor air legislation be enacted, similar to that in Minnesota.

Chapter 17. The Capital Question

We recommend:
1. That the "umbrella" or "Supra-regional Council" of the Fullerton Report be rejected out of hand by the Province of Ontario, so far as the Ontario side of the National Capital Region is concerned.
2. That the RMOC be the recognized municipal body to negotiate with the federal government on finance, including payments-in-lieu of taxes (especially if our "pooling" recommendations of Chapter 7 are followed); that the City of Ottawa or other area municipality may join with the RMOC, when the City or other municipality is particularly affected.
3. That the RMOC be the normal channel through which the area municipalities negotiate with the Province on grants-in-lieu of taxes.
4. That where co-ordination of the policies of the three levels of government is required in the Region, there be a tri-level political committee, standing or *ad hoc*; that there also be a joint committee, standing or *ad hoc*, of mixed staff and politicos, on particular matters, possibly by a strengthening of the Joint Committee on Planning and Transportation with a wider mandate.
5. That the RMOC be the body to negotiate with the ORC.
6. That the search for a capital of Canada that is a microcosm and /or symbol cease, but that the RMOC join with other governments to make the Region a place where people can feel at home in both the two official languages.

APPENDIX A

List of Briefs heard at public meetings by the Ottawa-Carleton Review Commission

1. MUNICIPALITIES

Official Municipal Briefs
Cumberland Township
Gloucester Township
March Townwhip
Nepean Township
Osgoode Township
Rideau Township
Village of Rockcliffe Park
City of Vanier

Other Municipal
Brian Bourns	Alderman, City of Ottawa
Grant Carman	Councillor, Nepean Township
R. P. Cunningham	Councillor, Goulbourn Township
Lorry Greenberg	Mayor, City of Ottawa
Rolf Hasenack	Alderman, City of Ottawa
Don Kay	Alderman, City of Ottawa
Trip Kennedy	Alderman, City of Ottawa
Don Lockhart	Alderman, City of Ottawa
Ihor Nakonecznyj	Councillor, Goulbourn Township
Patricia Nicol	Alderman, City of Ottawa

2. SCHOOL BOARDS AND OTHER EDUCATIONAL
Carleton Board of Education
Carleton Roman Catholic Separate School Board
Ottawa Board of Education
Ottawa Roman Catholic Separate School Board
Comité de Langue française, Conseil d'Education de Carleton
Louise McIntosh, Trustee Carleton Board of Education

3. SPECIAL PURPOSE BODIES
Board of Health, Ottawa-Carleton Regional Area Health Unit
Children's Aid Society of Ottawa
Gloucester Hydro Commission
Nepean Hydro Commission
Ottawa Hydro Commission
Joint Libraries (Mr. C. Aubrey, Director of Ottawa Public Library, on behalf of 10 Library Boards in the Region.)

4. ORGANIZATIONS
Action Sandy Hill
Alliance for Bilingualism
Beacon Hill North Community Association
Blackburn Community Association
Centretown Citizens' Community Association
Citizen's Advisory Committee for Regional Department of Social Services
Community Information Centre
Concerned Ratepayers of West Carleton
Federation of Citizens' Associations
Goulbourn Rural Ratepayers' Association
Institut culturel de Vanier
Kanata-Beaverbrook Community Association
March Rural Association
Nepean Review Committee
Non-Smokers' Association
Ottawa Archdioceson Council of Catholic Parent-Teacher Associations
Ottawa Board of Trade
Ottawa Tenants Council for Public Housing
Ottawa-Carleton Day Care Association
Pinecrest-Queensway Citizen's Committee
Queensboro Citizens' Group
Rockcliffe Park Conservation Authority
Social Planning Council Biculturalism Committee
Social Planning Council of Ottawa-Carleton
Union de Parents et de Contribuables francophones de Carleton
Vanier Community Group
Windsor Park Village Community Association

5. PERSONAL
David Bryden
Michael Cassidy, MPP
Evelyn Gigantes, MPP
Gérard Lévesque (re. Ottawa Board of Education)
Peter Martin
Robert Stevenson (Goulbourn Township)
Geoffrey Wasteneys
Marianne Wilkinson (March Township)

APPENDIX B

Partial list of other meetings held and/or attended by the Ottawa-Carleton Review Commission

Arnprior, public meeting on County Restructuring
Douglas Cameron, Regional Solicitor, RMOC
Charles Bens, Executive Director, Bureau of Municipal Research
Denis Coolican, Chairman, RMOC
Council on Aging
Yvon Dugas, Social Planning Council

Carleton Place meeting to discuss the Western boundary with
    Reeve S. Brunton — Township of Beckwith
    Reeve W. J. Buffam — Township of Montague
    Mayor W. G. Gomme — Town of Almonte
    Mayor Eldon E. Henderson — Town of Carleton Place
    Mayor C. M. Johnson — Town of Arnprior
    Reeve W. R. Monette — Township of Ramsay
    Mayor R. A. Stewart — Township of Pakenham
Francophone Trustees and French Language Advisory Committees of the
    Carleton Board of Education
    Carleton Roman Catholic Separate School Board
    Ottawa Board of Education
    Ottawa Roman Catholic Separate School Board

Conservation Authorities
    Mississippi Valley
    Rideau Valley
    South Nation River

Liaison Advisory Committee (several meetings)
Edgar Gallant, Chairman, National Capital Commission
Mayor L. Greenberg, City of Ottawa
Jock River Ratepayers' Association
Bruce Keith, Social Planning Council
William Koops, former councillor, Nepean Township
Alfred Lécuyer
Ottawa-Carleton Regional District Health Council
Ontario Planning Act Review Committee (Toronto)
Port Hope, on reviews and restructuring
John Rook-Greene, General Manager, Commercial and Industrial Development
                        Corporation of Ottawa-Carleton
Russell Township Council
Tom Shoebridge, President, Committee on Alternate Schools

Betty Stewart, Councillor, Gloucester Township
Tom Williams, OC Transpo
R. G. Wilson, Commissioner, Personnel Services, City of Ottawa
Mrs. E. Cooper, Bilingual Advisor, City of Ottawa

APPENDIX C

Some private briefs, letters, etc., presented to the Ottawa-Carleton Review Commission

1. OFFICIALS (PERSONAL)
   Denis Coolican, Chairman, RMOC
   Stuart R. Godfrey, Commissioner, Social Services Department, RMOC
   David T. Gowing, Executive Director, Children's Hospital of Eastern Ontario
   Danielle Lafrance, Le Mouvement C'Est L' Temps
   D. B. Rattray, re. Pollution Probe
   Jean Trudeau, Chairman, Ottawa Housing Authority
   M. W. Zimmerman, Execututve Director, Social Planning Council of Ottawa-Carleton

2. CITIZENS' GROUPS
   "A Capital for Canadians"
   Alta Vista Drive Residents' Association
   Country Place Community Association
   Crestview Community Association
   Crystal Beach Community Association
   Jock River Ratepayers' Association
   Tanglewood Community Association
   Lloyd Stanford, President, Rothwell Heights Property Owners' Association

3. PERSONAL
   David M. Baird
   John I. Butler
   J. M. Cape
   Grant Carman
   Leonard Amable Foubert
   Peter J. Green
   J. G. M. Hooper
   John D. Hylton
   George Kidd
   Anne-Marie Lamarche
   Alfred Lécuyer
   Gérard Lévesque
   Guy F. Lorriman
   T. J. Mousseau
   K. W. Noble
   F. R. Park
   Fern G. Payne
   Yves Potvin
   Patrick M. Ryan
   Ralph Spratt
   C. I. Taggart
   Rev. George Theckedath
   L. G. Thériault